BORN TO KILL → PIGEONING → FANZINE →

ISSUE # 93

BUSHWICK WE OUT HERE

"LE DRAME INCESSANT"

COMMONISM ISSUE
BROOKLYN ROOF REPORT
HAWK DEFENSE!
AND HAM RADIO!
RECIPES! FLIGHTS!

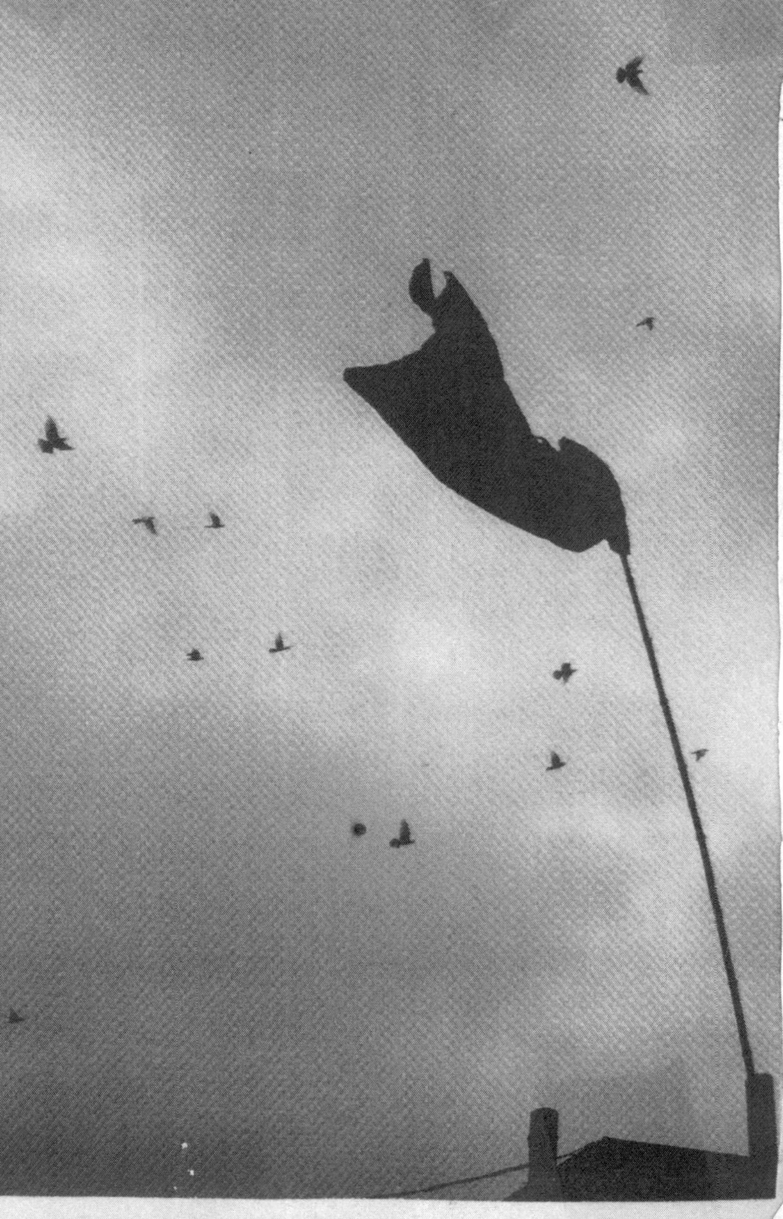
STARE AND STARE

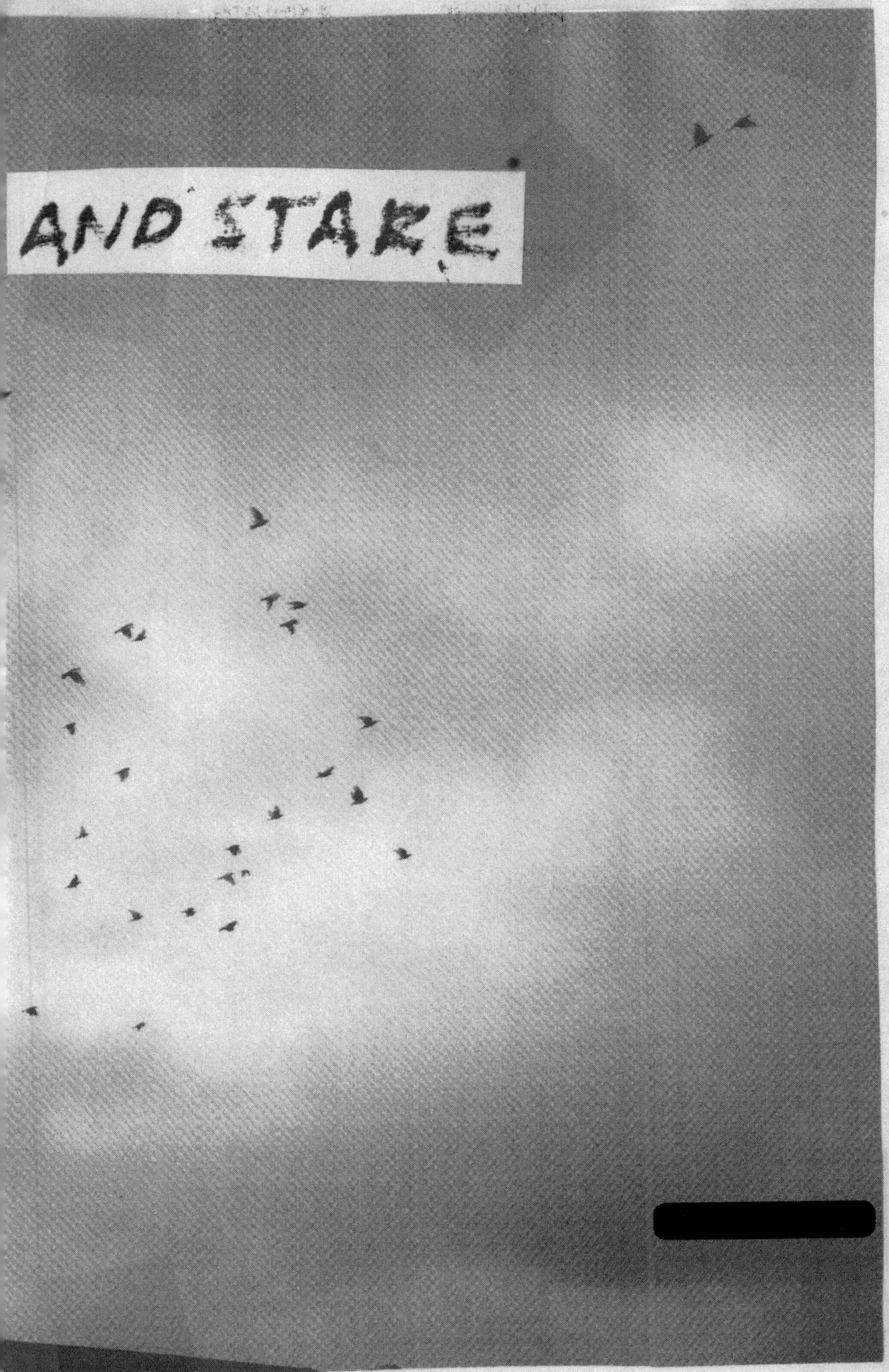

AND STARE

I study the complexities of this city by way of ~~study of imagining a farm~~ raising ~~the~~ birds.
Many hundred birds if not yet a thousand.
Pigeons. ~~xxxxxxx~~ Which thru history have
been humanity's ~~xx~~ winged sidekick. ~~x~~ In all the
worlds corners, pigeon live with us, not around us.
~~xx~~ They occupy all the alleyways and avenues, ~~xx~~
every port, every park, every rooftop.

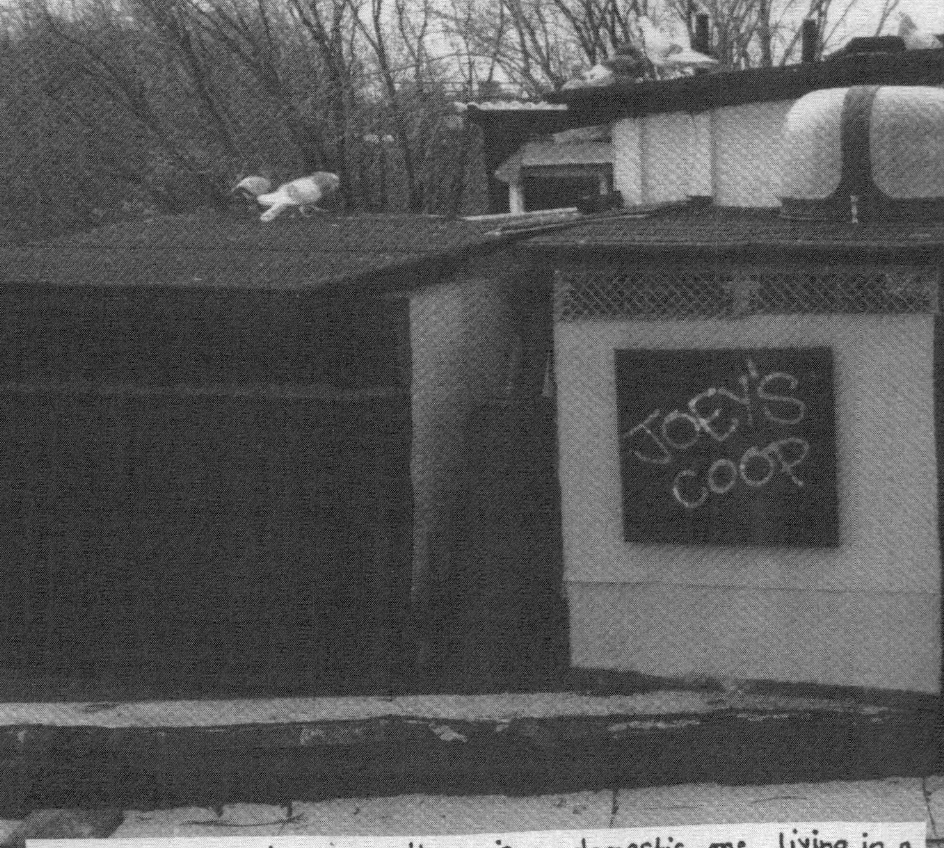

For every feral pigeon there is a domestic one, living in a
coop on a rooftop or farm or~~a~~ driveway, ~~xxxxxx~~ under
the care of a shepard. There~~ are certain cities,
~~xxxxxx~~ scattered across the globe that have
vast communities of these shepards. The most storied
of these Mecca's are Antwerp, Cairo, and Brooklyn.
This is Brooklyn. ~~xxxxxxxxxxxxx~~

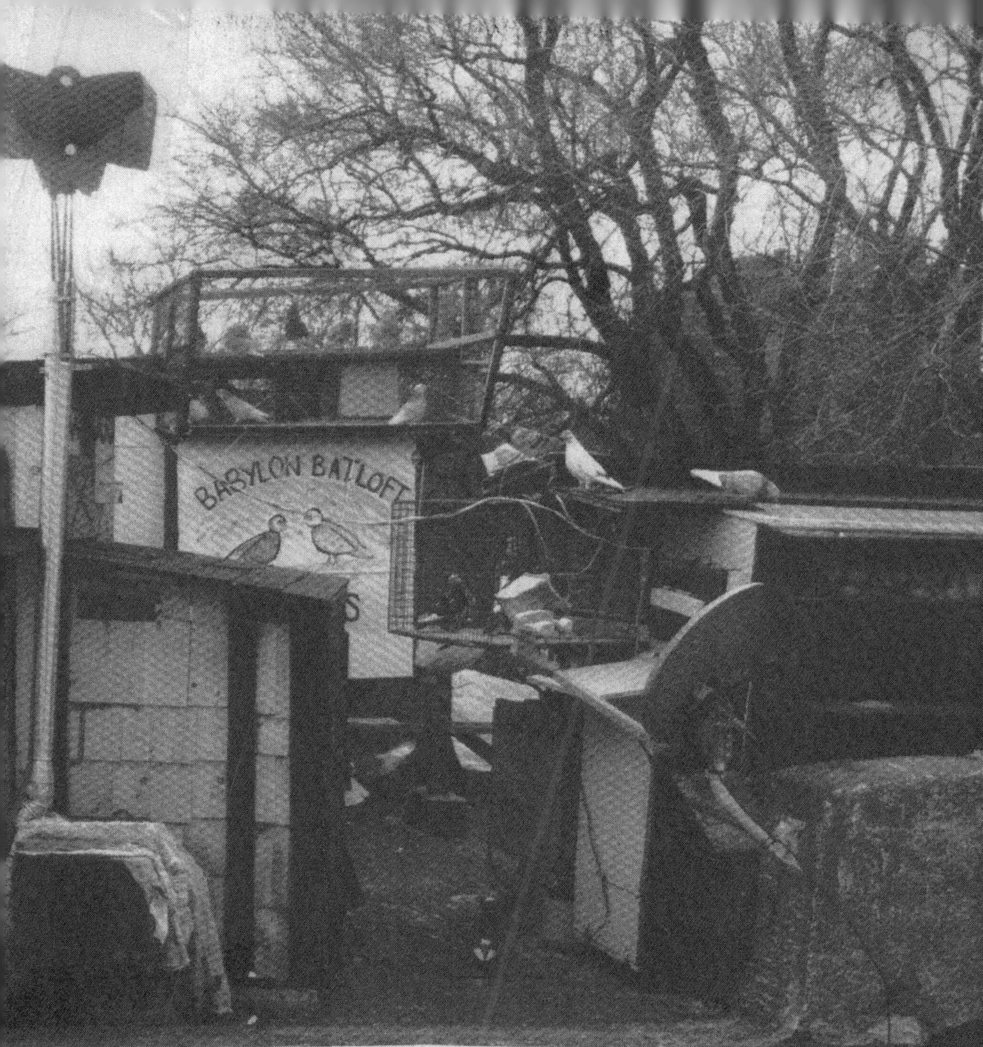

Home of the largest pigeon flocks in the modern USA. Daily they fly in bundled formations, high above the dense wall of rowhouses, captivating the sky. Us pigeon keepers, alone on our rooftops below, do what we humbly can, wave our flags and blow our whistles encouraging the birds to really dance... To fly powerfully and happily, in harmony with 100 comrades, or 500. Our pigeon flocks are capable of sycronized acrobatics, which are simply unparrelled to any other bird. Its stunning. This is Bushwick, pigeon coop ground zero, like clockwork (for generations) the afternoon skies are lit up with pigeons. To each flock a roof, each roof a town to itself, a sweeping drama.

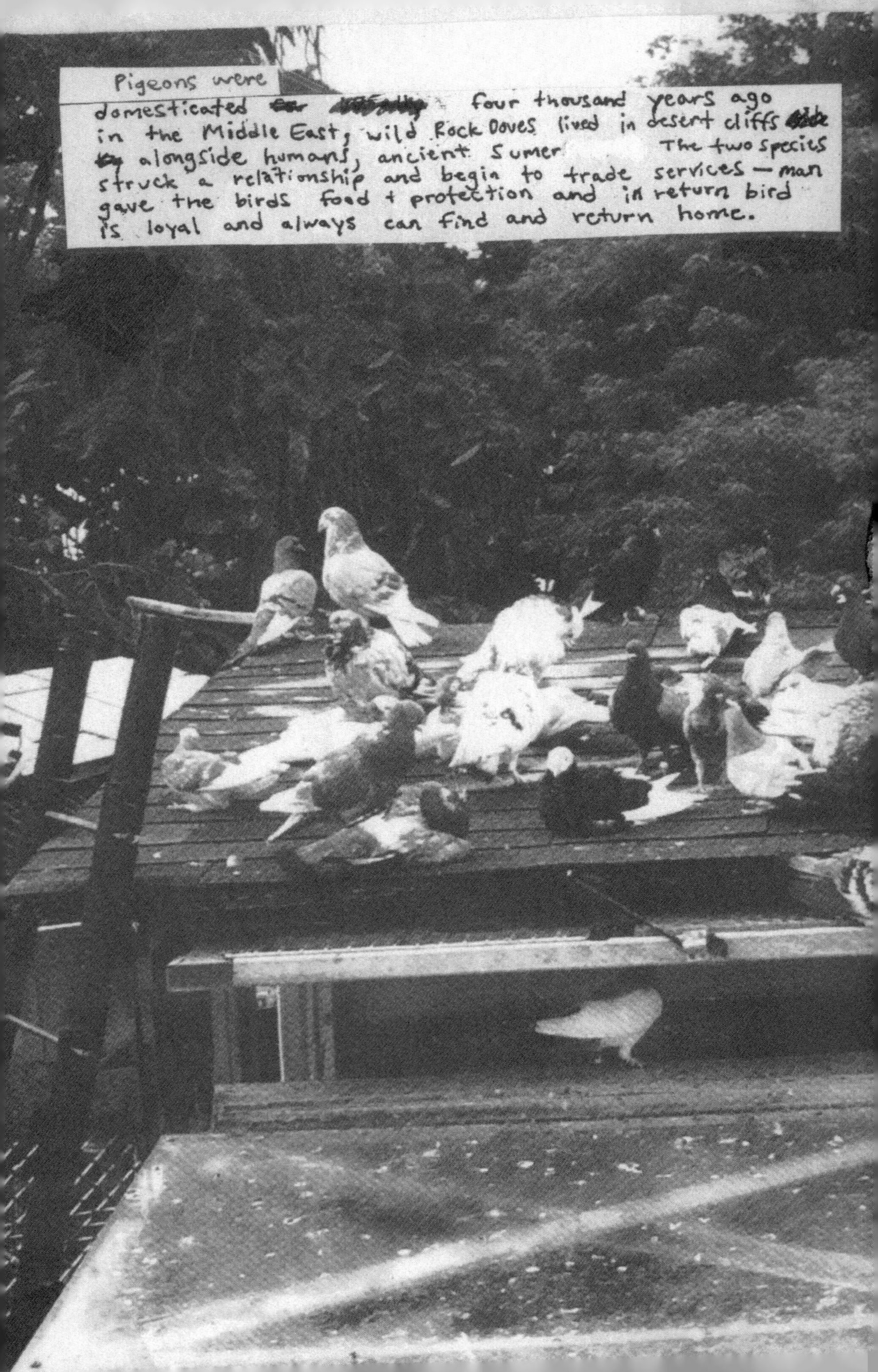
Pigeons were domesticated ~~for~~ ~~roughly~~ four thousand years ago in the Middle East, wild Rock Doves lived in desert cliffs ~~side~~ ~~by~~ alongside humans, ancient Sumer   The two species struck a relationship and begin to trade services — man gave the birds food + protection and in return bird is loyal and always can find and return home.

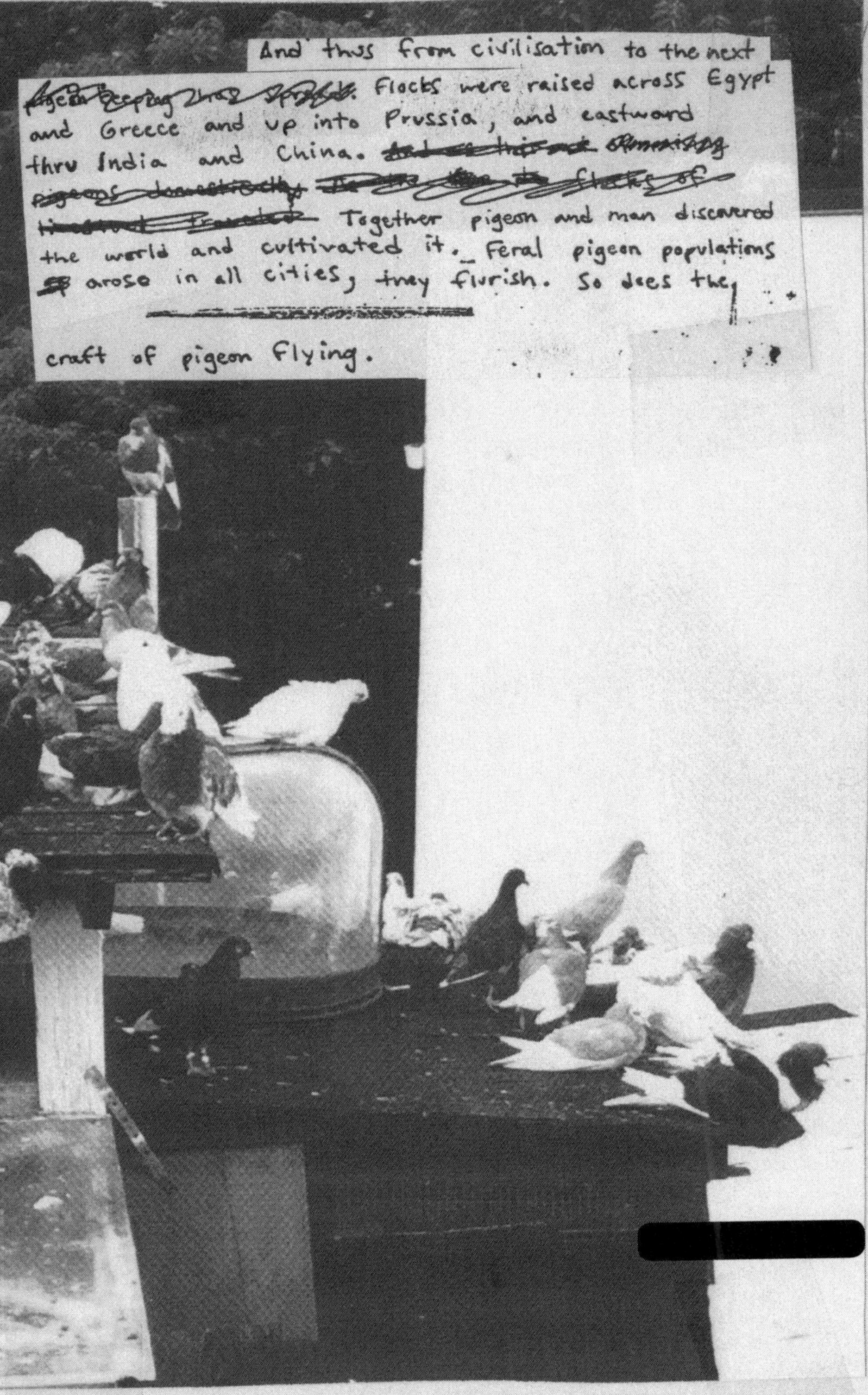
And thus from civilisation to the next
Flocks were raised across Egypt
and Greece and up into Prussia, and eastward
thru India and China.
Together pigeon and man discovered
the world and cultivated it. _ Feral pigeon populations
arose in all cities, they flurish. So does the
craft of pigeon flying.

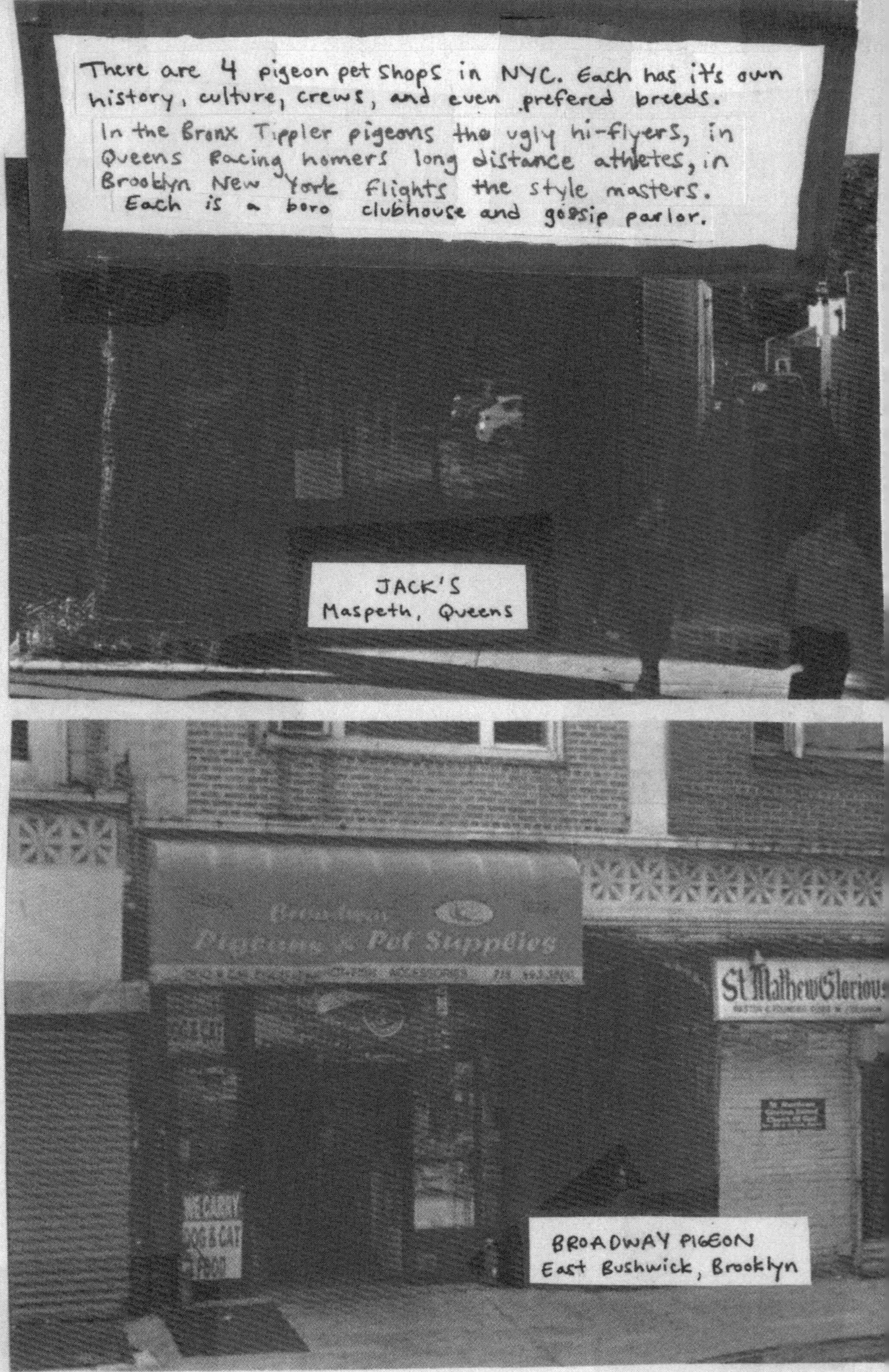
There are 4 pigeon pet shops in NYC. Each has it's own history, culture, crews, and even prefered breeds.
In the Bronx Tippler pigeons the ugly hi-flyers, in Queens Racing homers long distance athletes, in Brooklyn New York flights the style masters.
Each is a boro clubhouse and gossip parlor.
JACK'S
Maspeth, Queens
Pigeons & Pet Supplies
St Mathew Glorious
BROADWAY PIGEON
East Bushwick, Brooklyn

PIGEON PET SHOPS

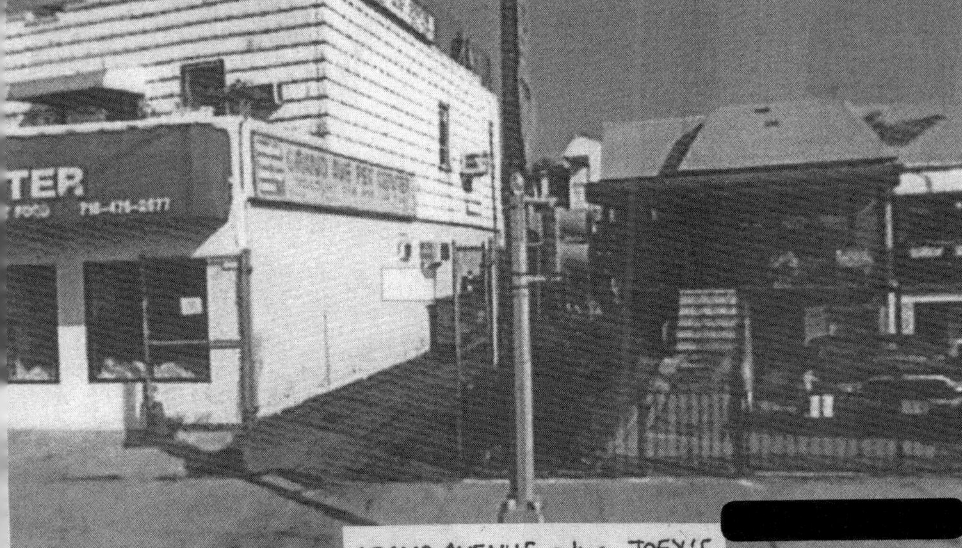

COOPS OF THE WORLD

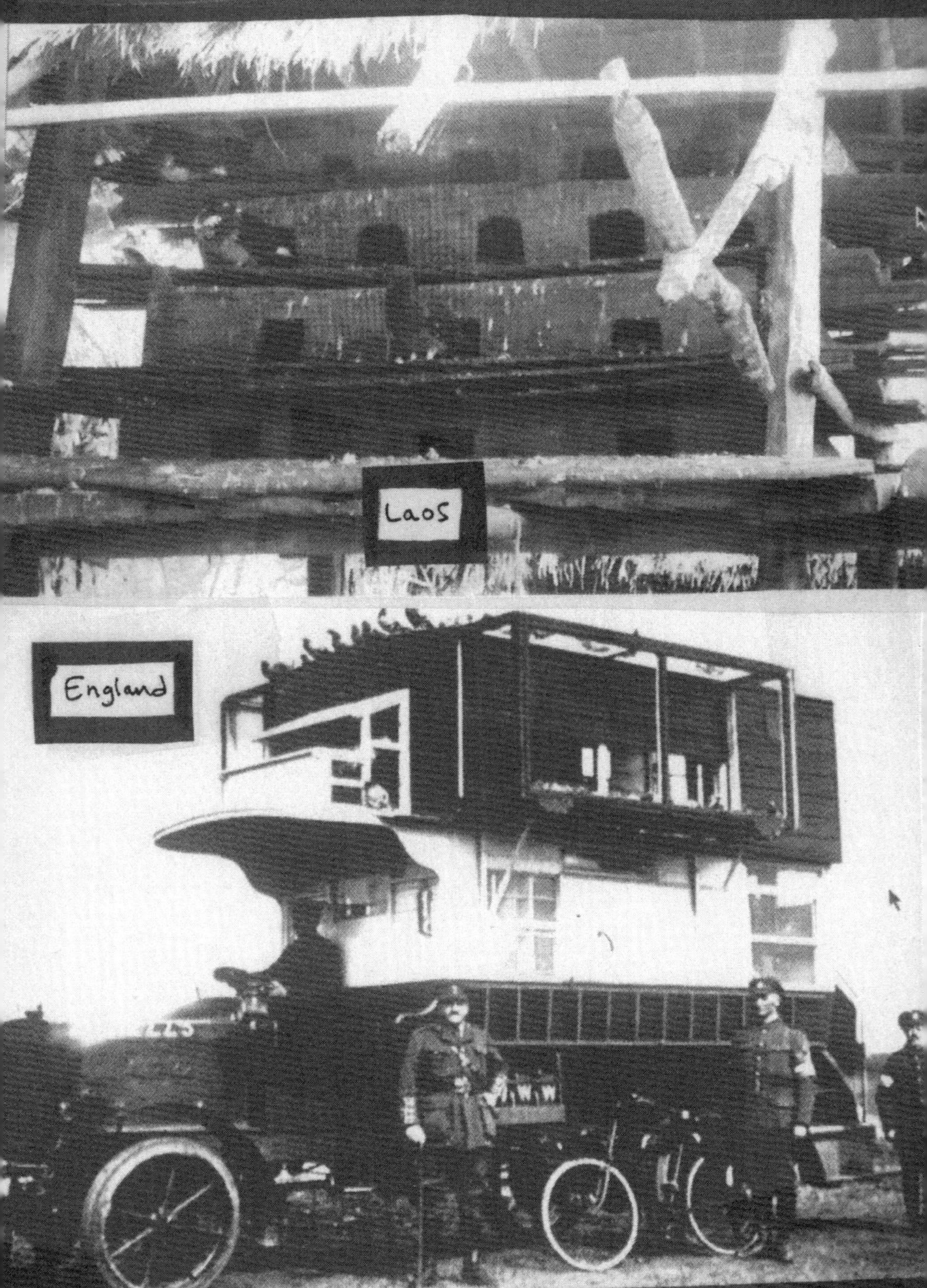

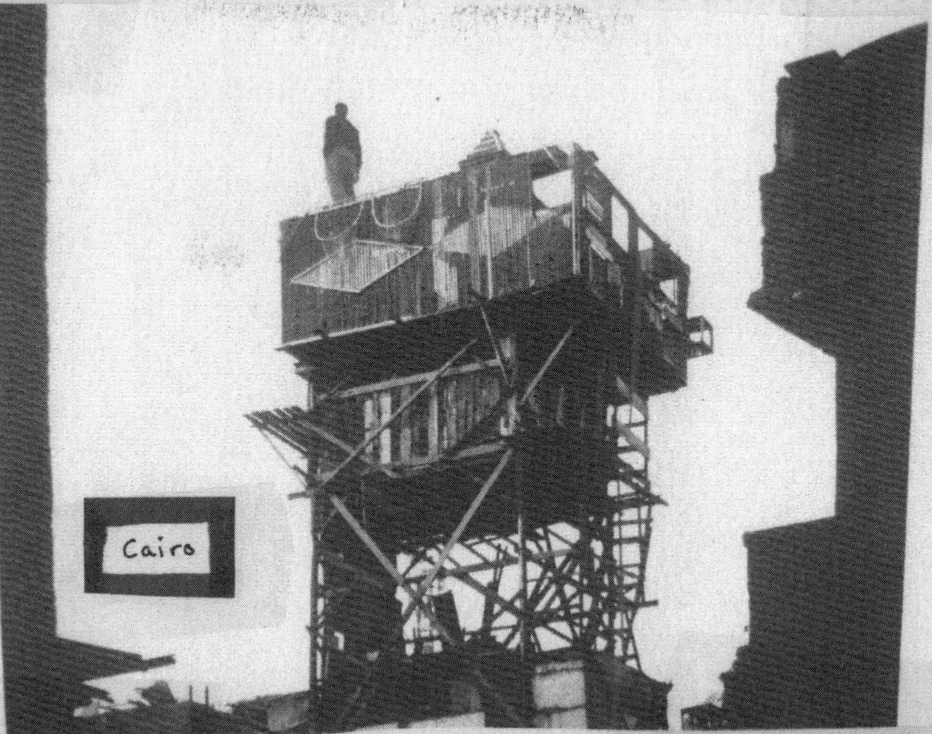

Cairo
Cuba 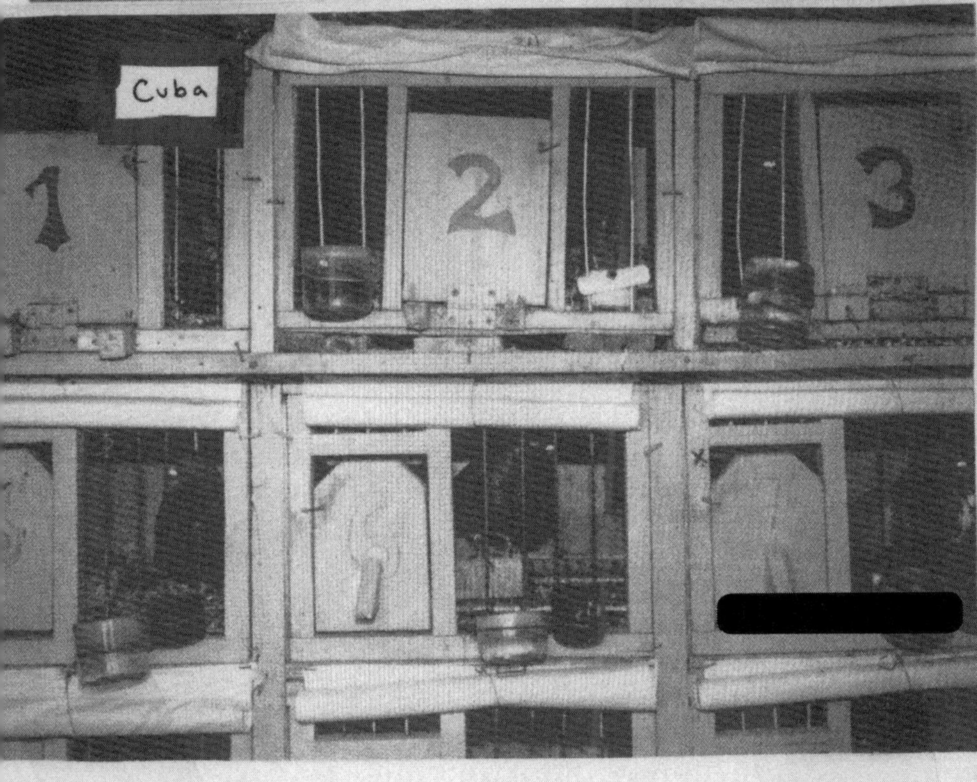
1
2
3

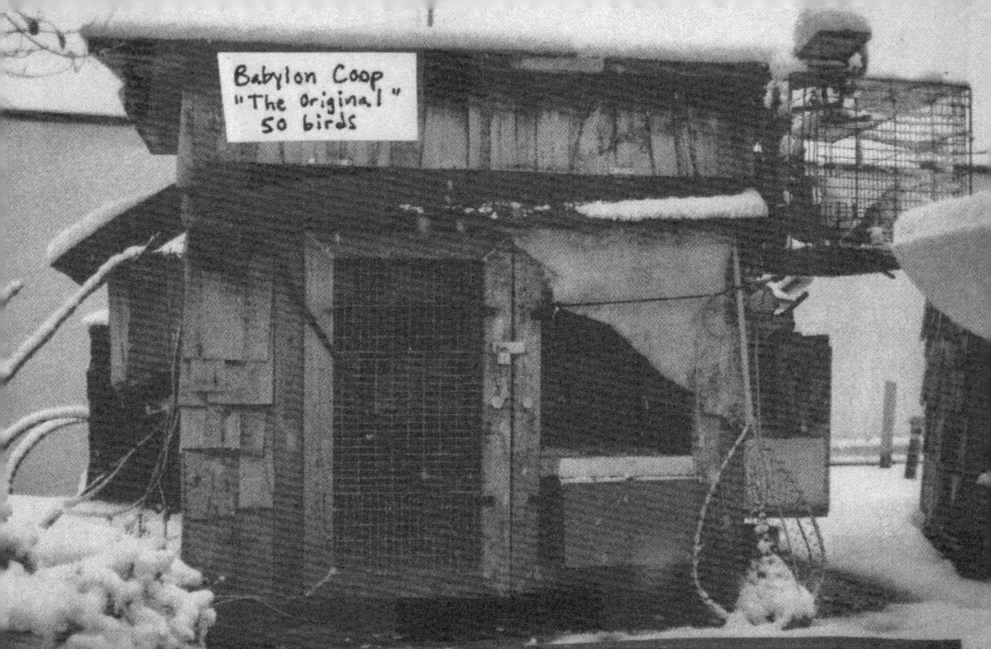

Babylon Coop
"The Original"
50 birds
BABYLON ROOF
BABYLON BATLOFT
ROLLERS
Batloft
"Best Rollers in Bushwick"
100 birds

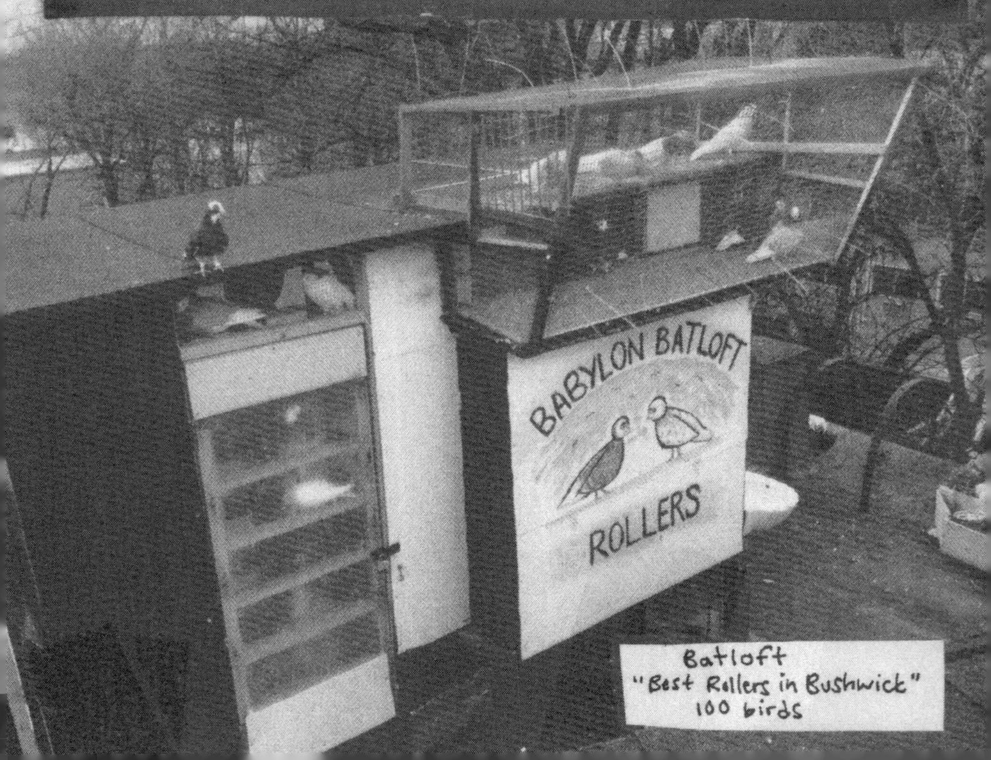

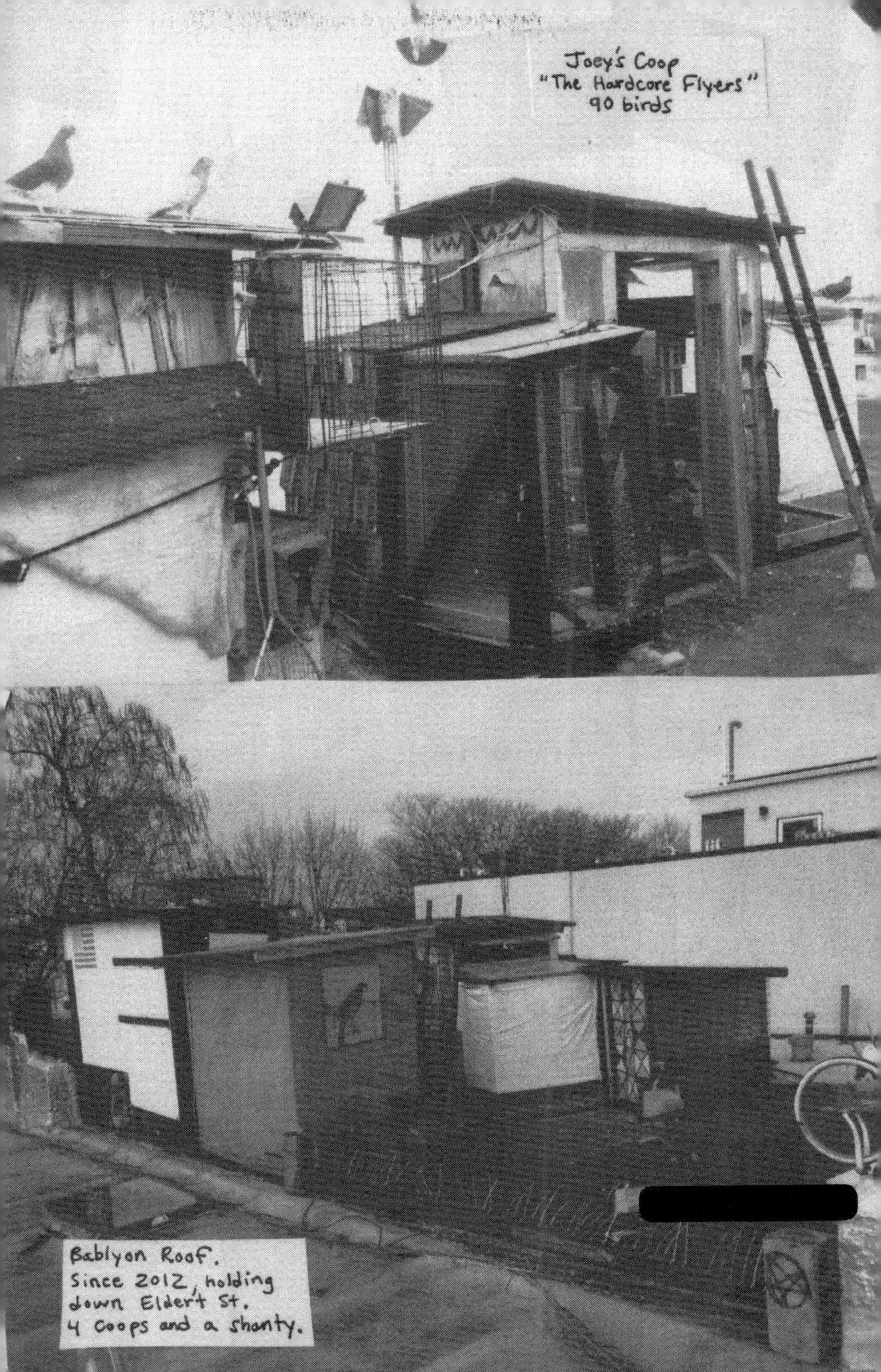
Joey's Coop
"The Hardcore Flyers"
90 birds
Bablyon Roof.
Since 2012, holding
down Eldert St.
4 coops and a shanty.

BELGIAN FEED

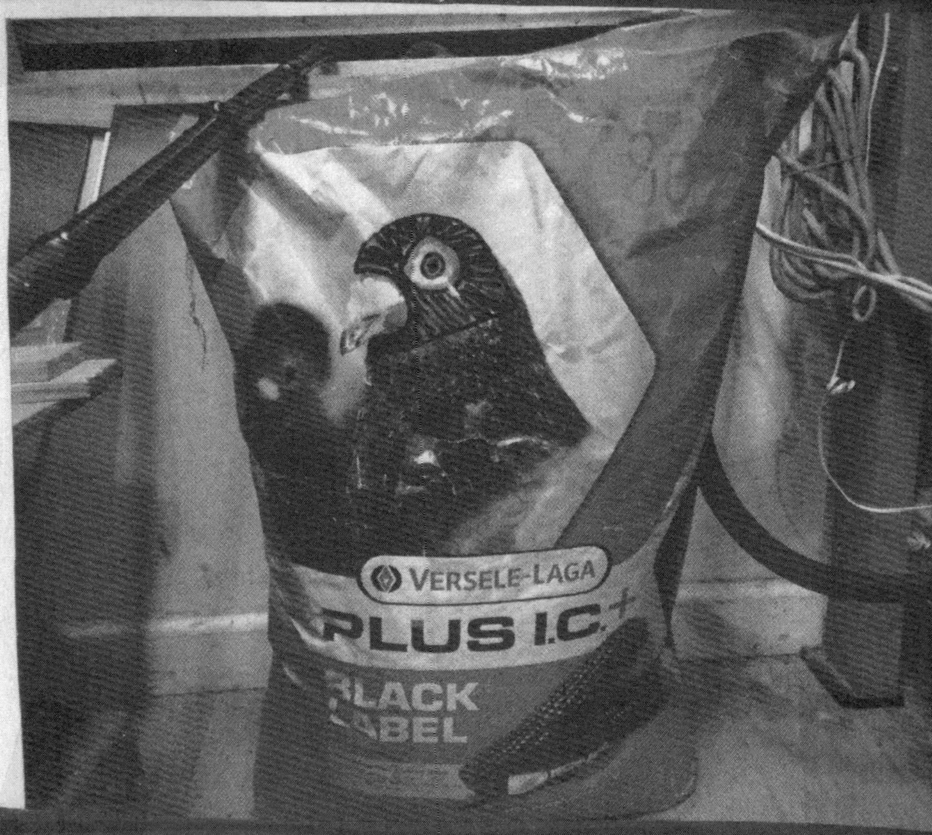

. Versele-Laga, kings feed in Europe. ▬ This chapellerie formed in 1937 in Deinze Belgium. ▬ For centuries its been believed the soils of Belgium breed ▬ a miraculous corn, a corn said to be the fountain of youth for pigeons. A corn that fuels the fastest pigeons ever known. Versele-Laga put their mark on this legend by creating the original "Black Corn" pigeon feed. The black maize contains a unique dose of antioxidants which cleans the blood and muscles of a bird mid-flight. 15% protein. 9% fat. 7% fibre. Black maize, Bordeaux maize, red maize, french cribs maize, soy beans, maple peas, tares, mung beans, red darry, safflower, oats, hemp, canary seed, linseed, rapeseed, coleseed, german thistle seed. Wowzers. ▬ With a whoollop of a price. £35 for 20kg.

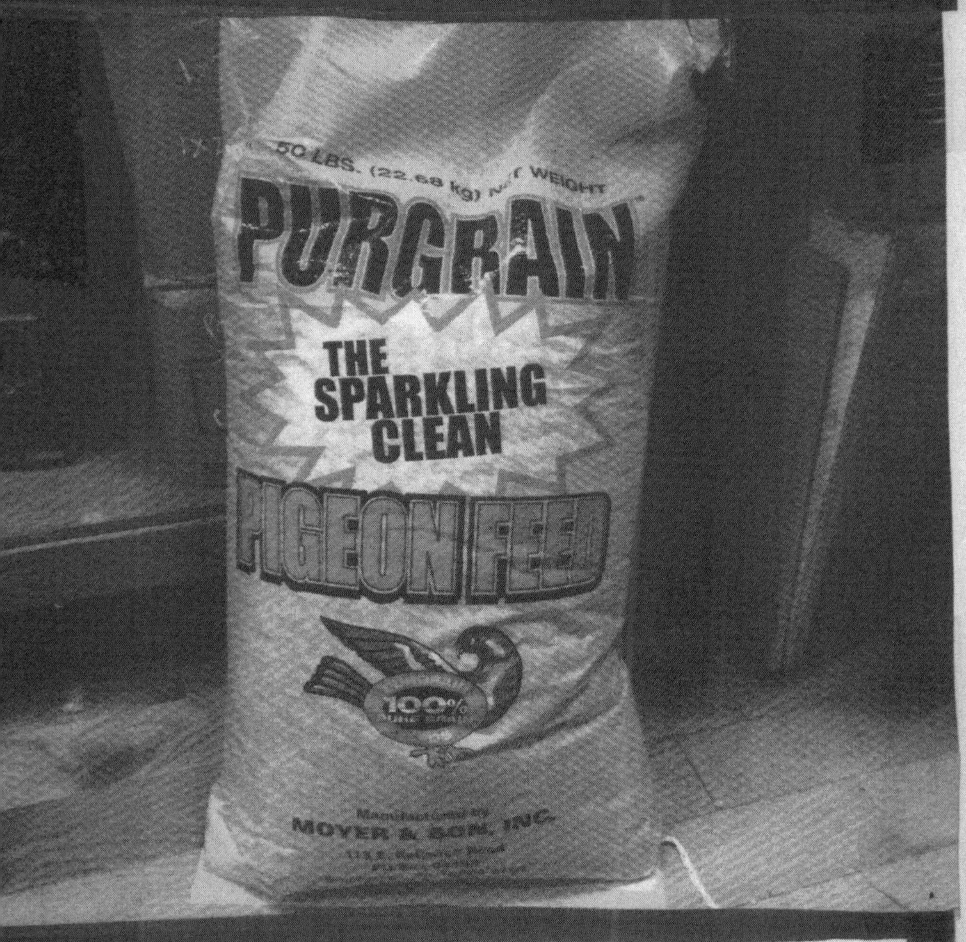

Purgain. Our ~~father~~ founding father's feed. "The feed that flew America". ~~Purgain~~ The company formed in America's first capital, Philadelphia in 1869 and to the day is family-owned. ~~Purgain~~ Purgrain makes over a dozen different seed mixtures, around this town the mix called "Vinny's" is the benchmark with which all the other feeds are rated. ~~~~~~~~ Its heavy, hearty, high carbohydrate diet that only pays off if the pigeons are flying hard. 14% crude protein. 7.36% crude fat, 11.90% crude fibre. Small yellow corn, maple peas, ▮▮▮▮, red milo, white milo, whole wheat, Austrian peas, and whole rice. Solid. Average price ฿23 for 23 kg.

BABY JOE JR. SAVED BY RICKY!

As tragic as the blackest plague, a baby bird hatched in Alamo Joe's nestbowl the day he flew the coop. I'm sure the mother, sweet Angie, was at quite the loss. Without Big Joe to share the parenting, Baby Joe #9 would surely not see even 2 weeks. Though, reader, cruel fate is not straight as an arrow. Miraculously within a week Ricky Badlands usurped Alamo Joe's empty throne and, with Angie's permission (!), began nesting on and feeding the mouse-sized bird. By amazing stroke of coincedence, Ricky had been nursing his own eggs with his other woman (eggs I ultimately threw away) and thus expecting already to be a dad, had been developing for weeks the neccessary milky crème to feed a newborn.

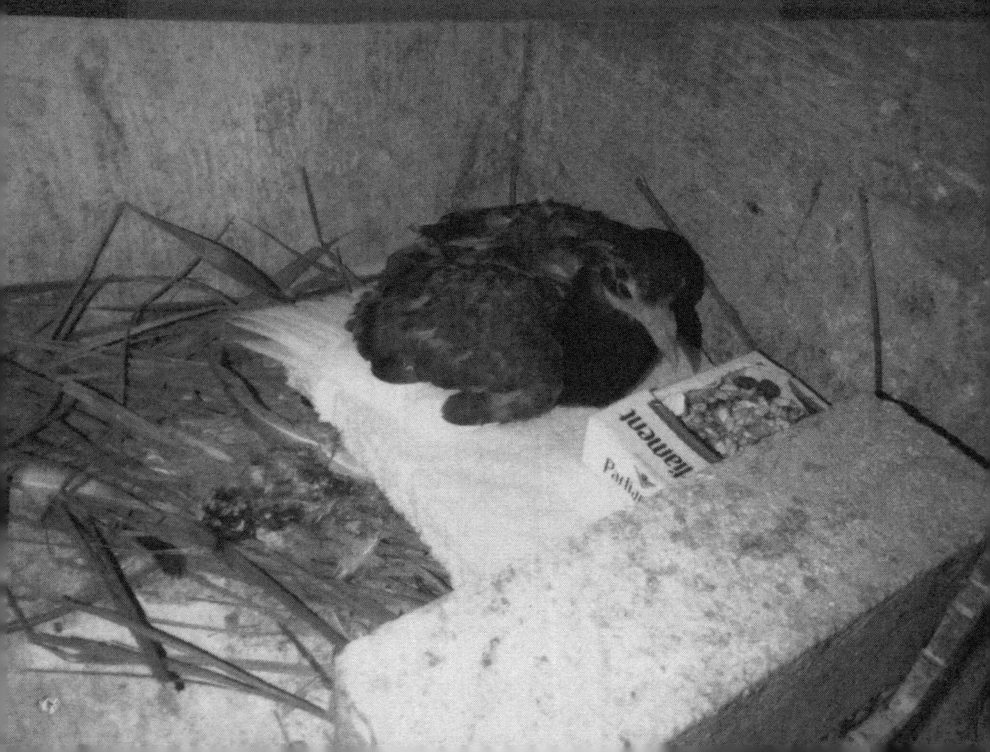

BABY JOE JR. CRIPPLED BY RICKY!

As is tradgically oft the case in the complex modern world, the weight of a stepfather overwhelmed a young boy. A child whom had to grow never knowing in the flesh his heroic true father, the famed Joey, Champion of the stock. No the baby bird only heard these tales, from ~~underneath~~ underneath the stoic homing pigeon Ricky. Now Homers are a great deal heavier than Rollers and little Baby Joe at some point lost his grip. Literally. All baby birds need a nest — twigs, hay, whathaveyou — because they need a soft tight bed to cling their little feets to. Otherwise mom and dad would flatten him. Well fat fucker Ricky flattened him. His legs grew straight outwards and his poor chest pressed against the bowl. Legs like this are known as "splayed". If uncorrected it is fatal. A splint was made from soft foam. ~~maybe~~ God Bless this bird; may he maintain through his sufferings some spirit to survive. And a prayer to Alamo, that in his wanderings he should find safety in the nite

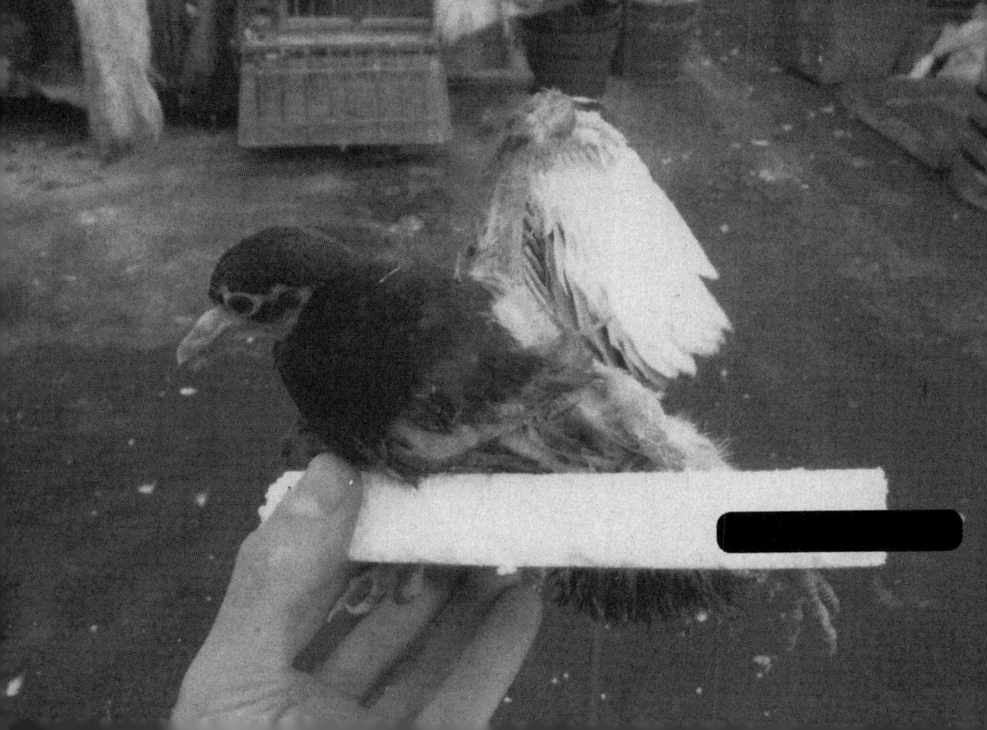

El Capitan + Two Teardrops
Since 2013. Royalty.
BIRDS
BI
Justine, a
satinette with
a cap and an
attitude

Dribble, a spastic bald head roller, born to Fastrunner.

The Boss, a huge Egyptian swift nurses her baby boy.

About 5 minutes into
a racing homer hatching.

White bar Homer
called Sensation
watchs her baby hatch.

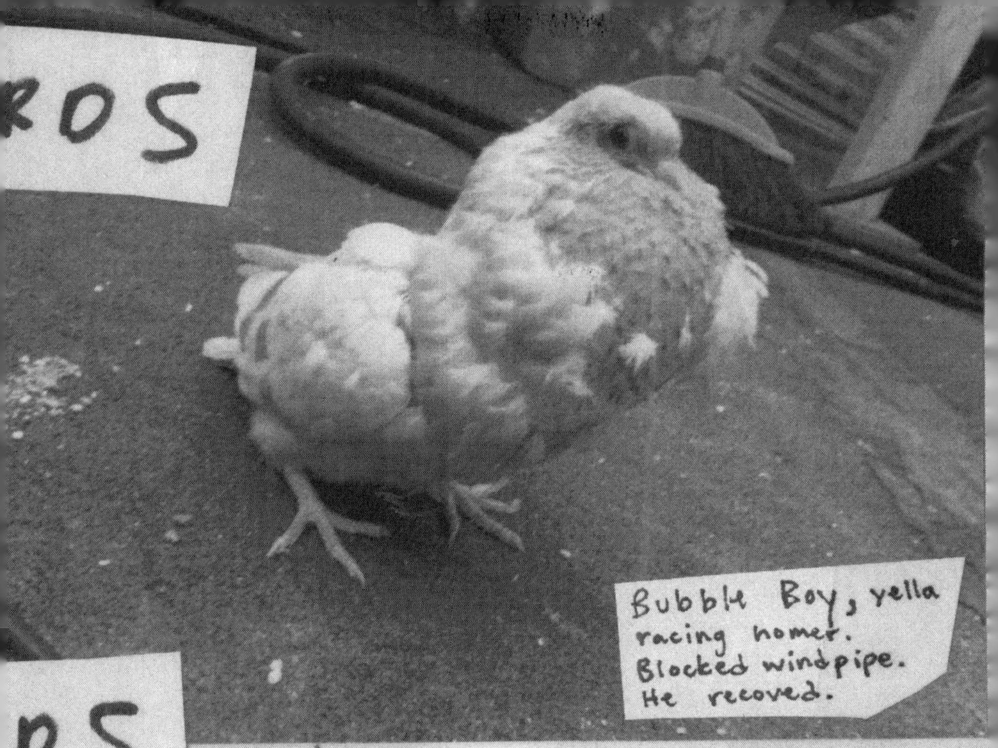

Bubble Boy, yella
racing homer.
Blocked windpipe.
He recoved.

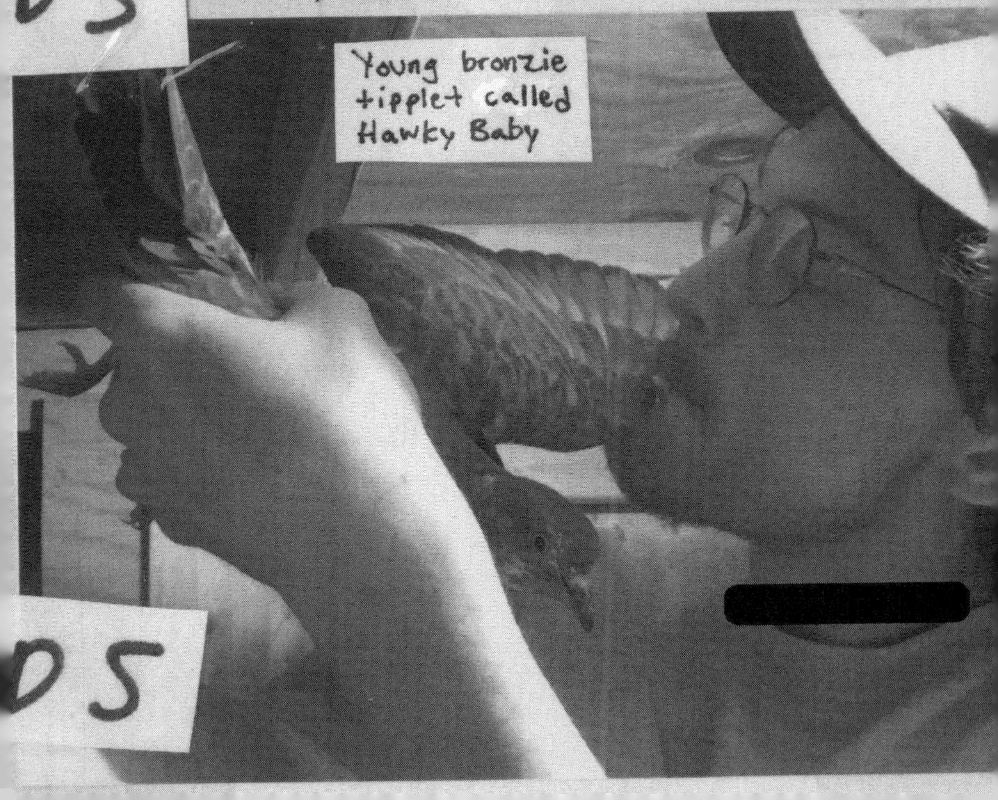

Young bronzie
tipplet called
Hawky Baby

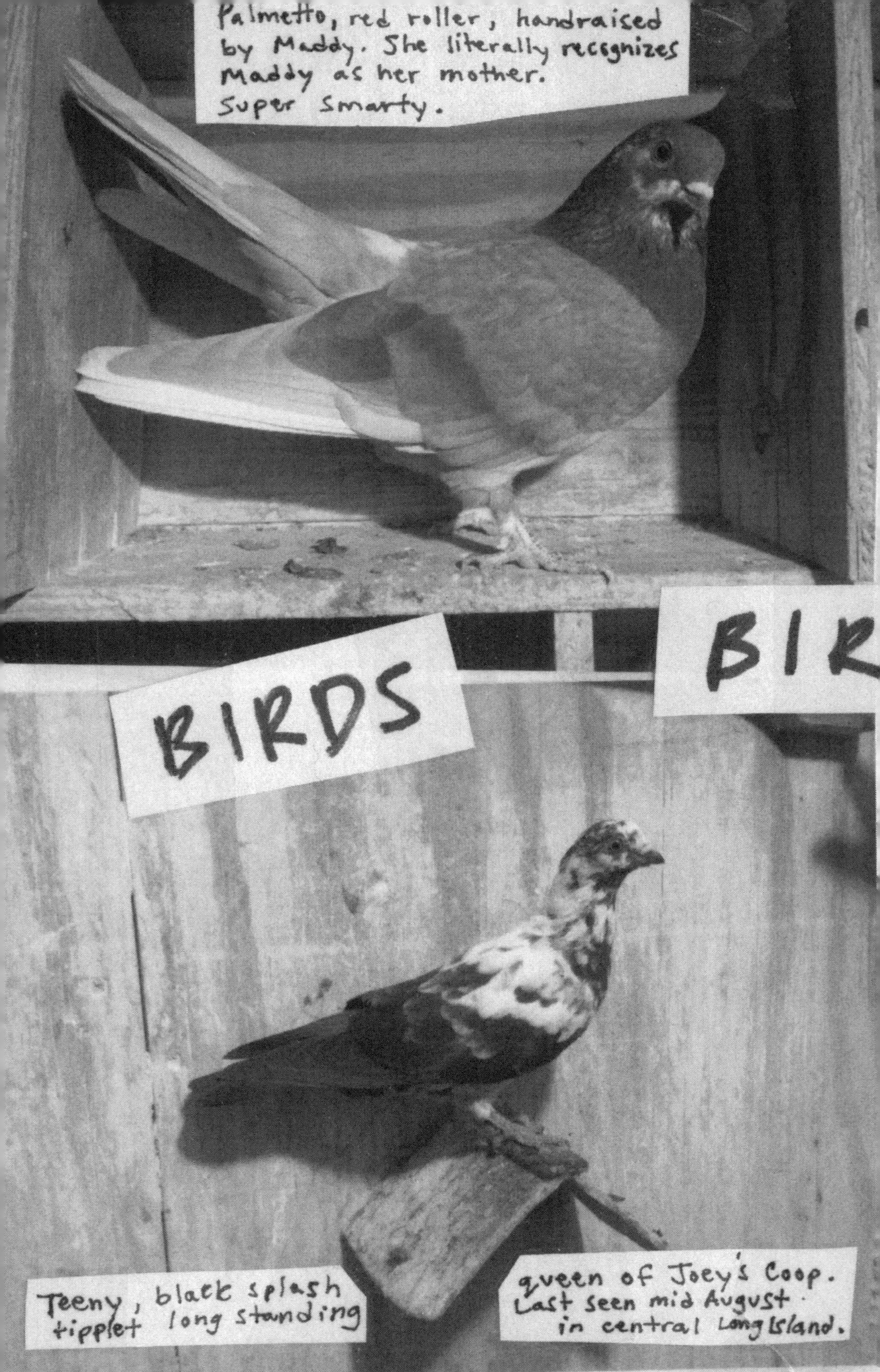

Palmetto, red roller, handraised by Maddy. She literally recognizes Maddy as her mother. Super smarty.
BIRDS
BIR
Teeny, black splash tipplet long standing
queen of Joey's Coop. Last seen mid August in central Long Island.

Skylar, bronzie tipplet, crazy colors like that of a hawk..
DS
BIRDS
L.D. here, a mottle tipplet does donuts round the sun!

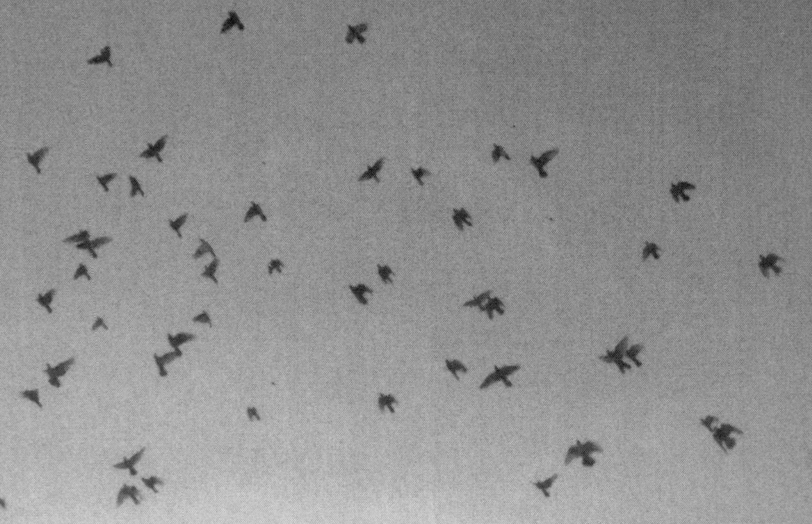
SOME FLIGHTS

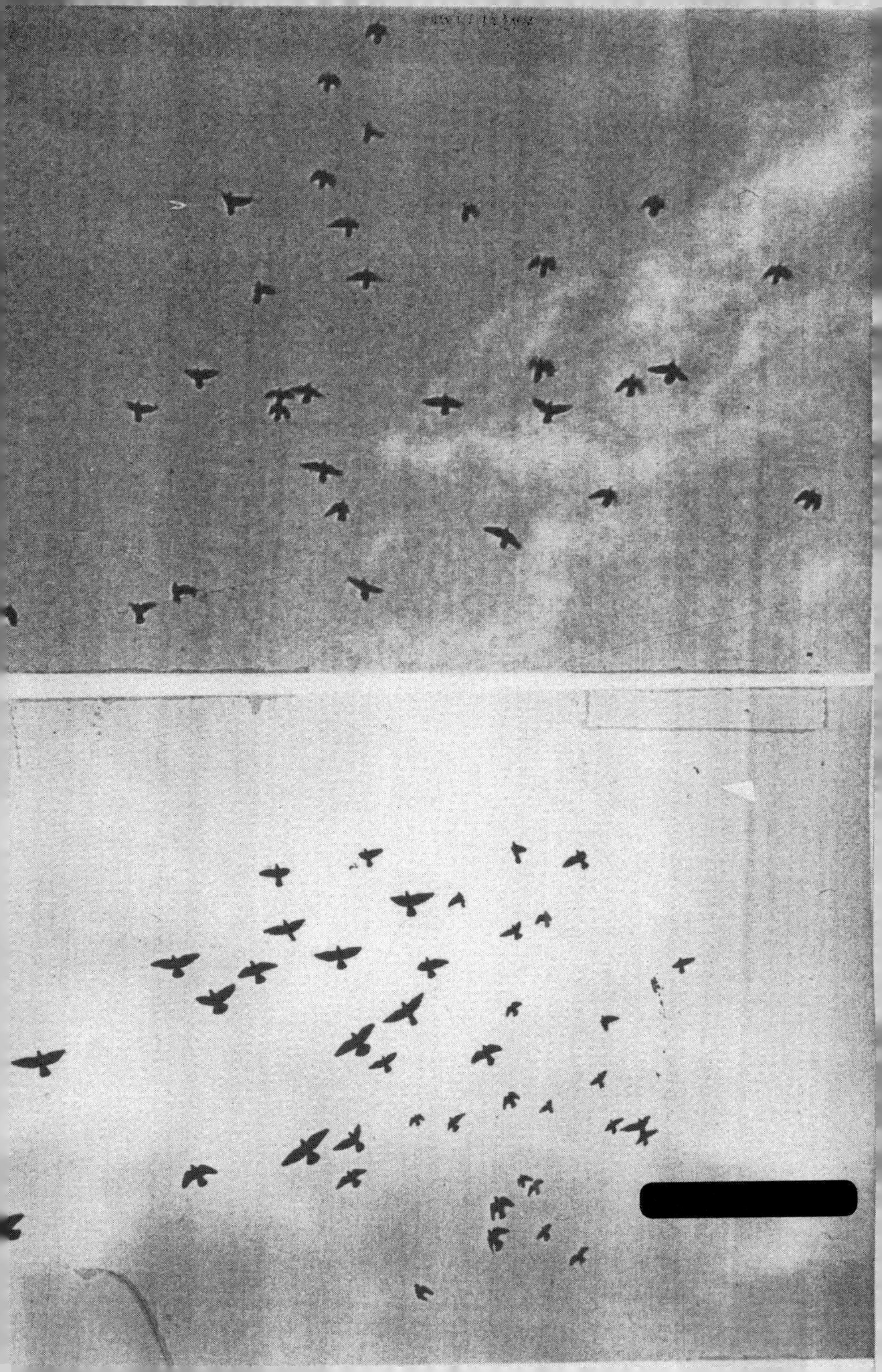

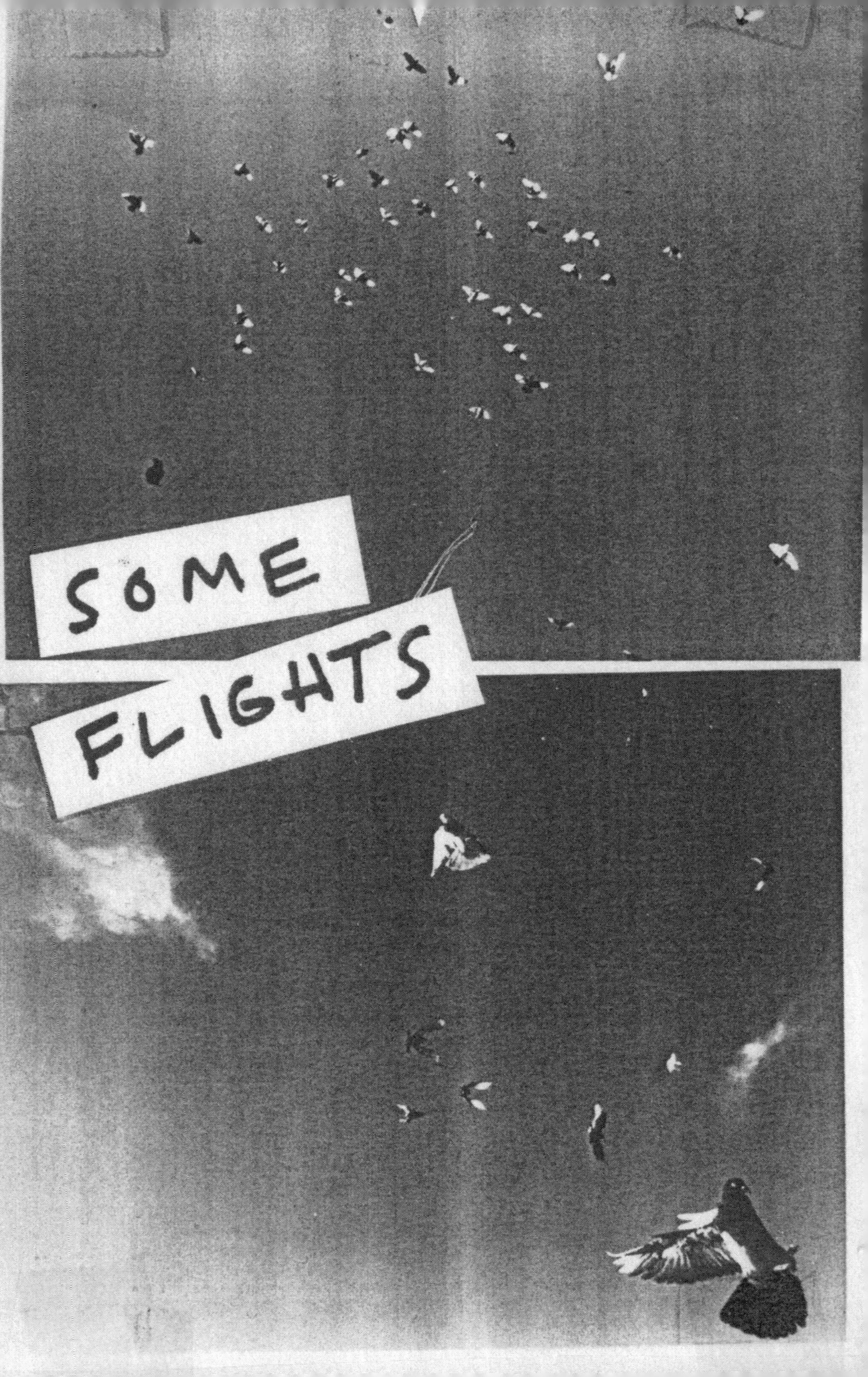

SOME
FLIGHTS

The fucking falcon..

AMATEUR RADIO !

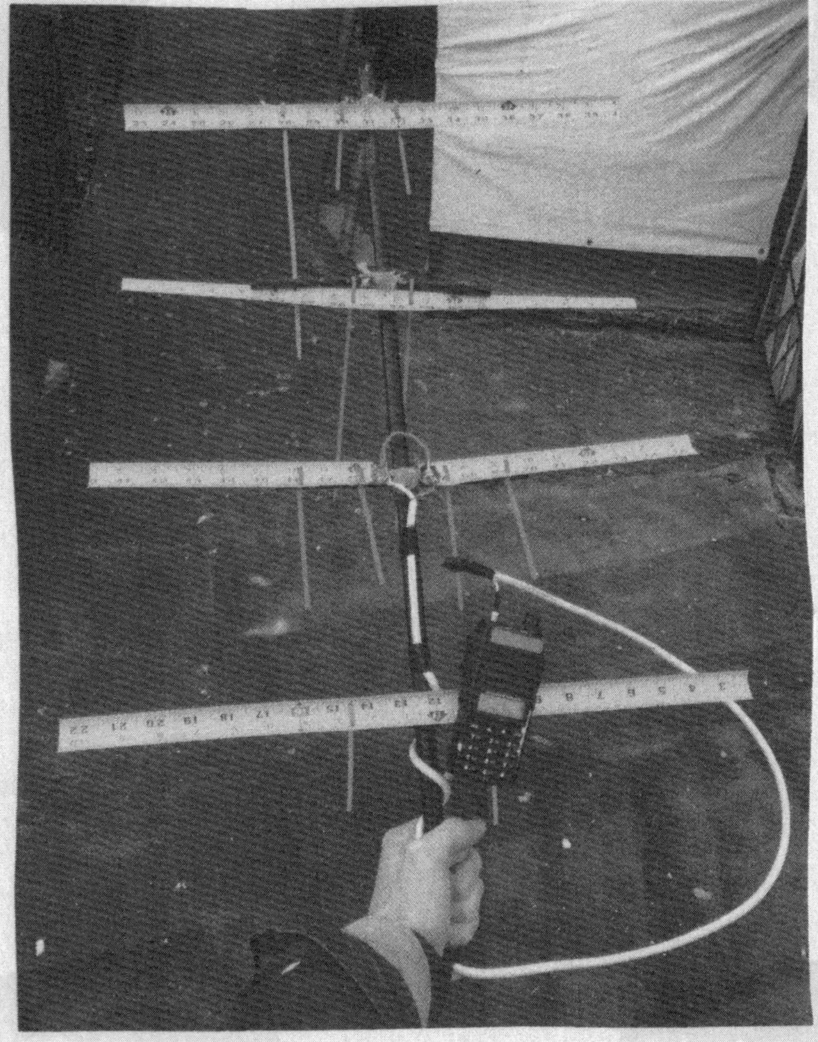

New York City is full of "HAM" radio enthusi[asts].
Nightly they take to their machines, often self built,
and talk with others around the city and beyond.
The air waves are there for the publics taking. Free
and open communication outlets. Literally any human
could be listening, but unlike the internet + cellular
phone calls, the powers that be are not cataloging
ones every correspondance. Pictured is our directional
"Yagi" style antennae, built of bamboo and tape measure.

NEW FLOOR SCRAPER !!

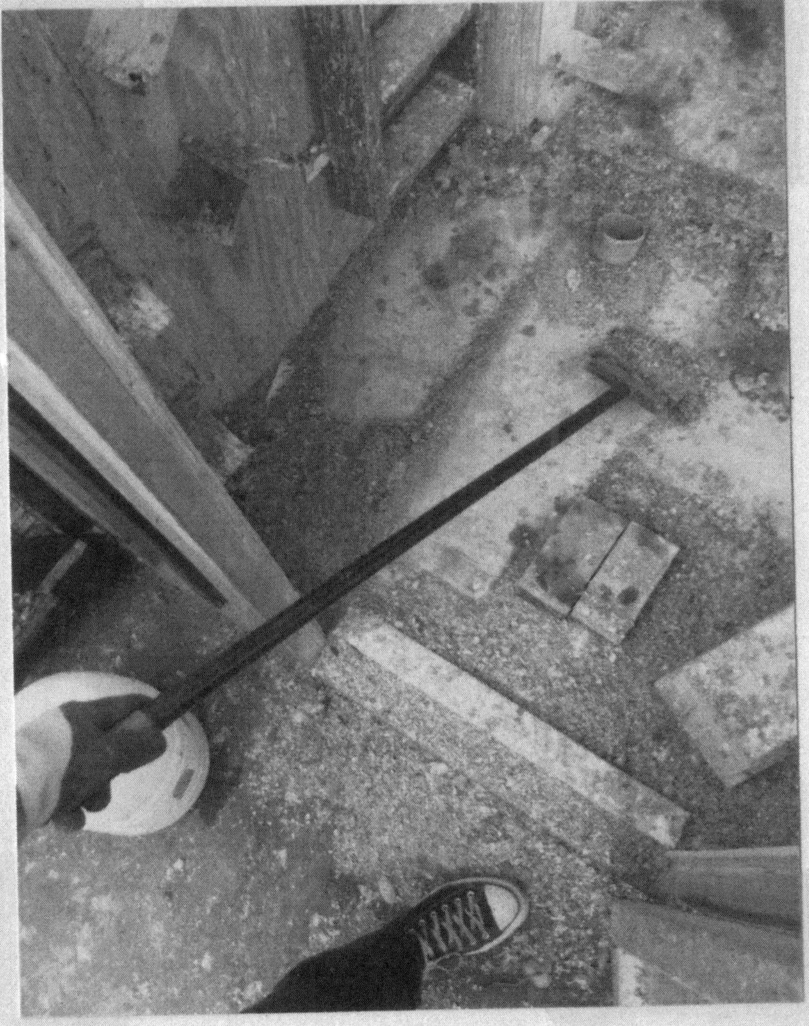

~~this~~ Now this is ~~an~~ ~~is~~ incredible
spade — a gift from Louie BatMan,
a ~~so~~ thick 12 gauge steel die threaded
onto a heavy steel rod, wrapped in
black ~~electrical electrici~~ elecchickens tape.
Just shreads thru the shit. ☆☆☆☆

DEFENDING THE FLOCK

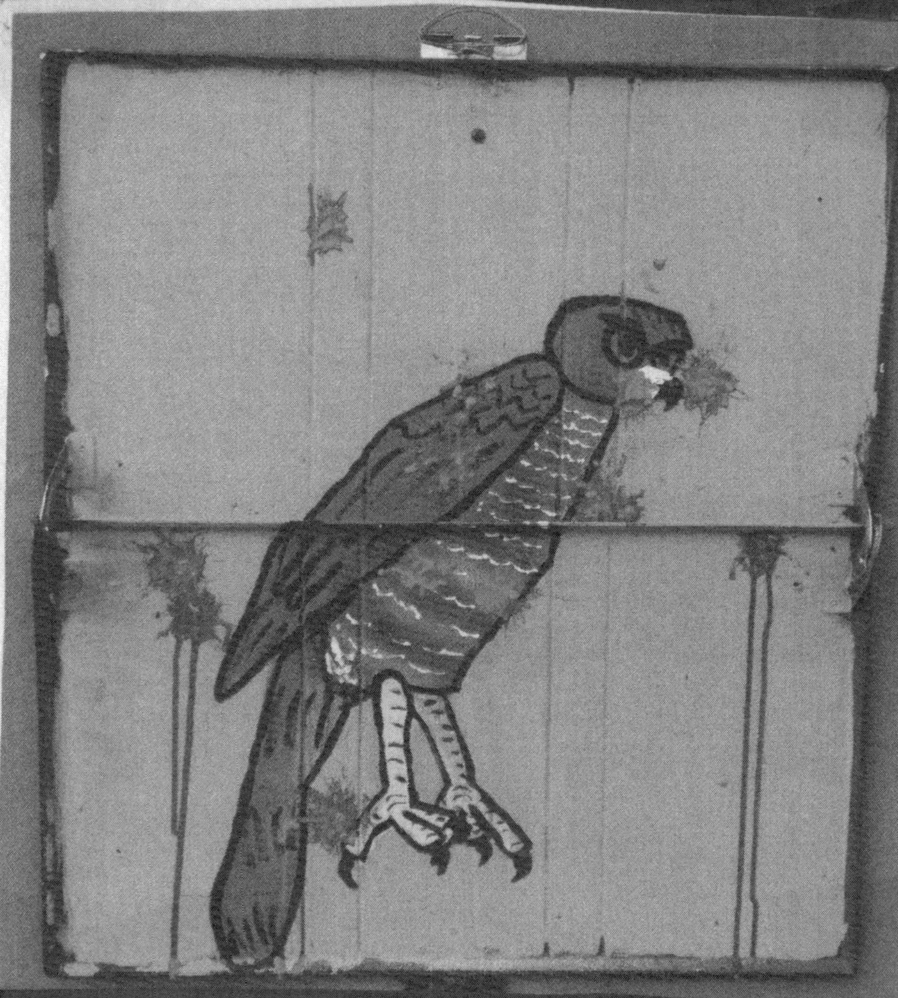

To be clear, I will not kill a hawk, I will not bring pysical harm in any lasting way to these monsters. But I will engage in pyscological warfare. I will strive to scare them from this community. We must protect our children. I cannot debate the hawks' right to fly these skies, no more than I can contest his or her right to live. However if and when I find them perched in our tree or worse standing on this roof, I will be forced to sling, at 100 meters per second, frozen beads of pigeon shit.

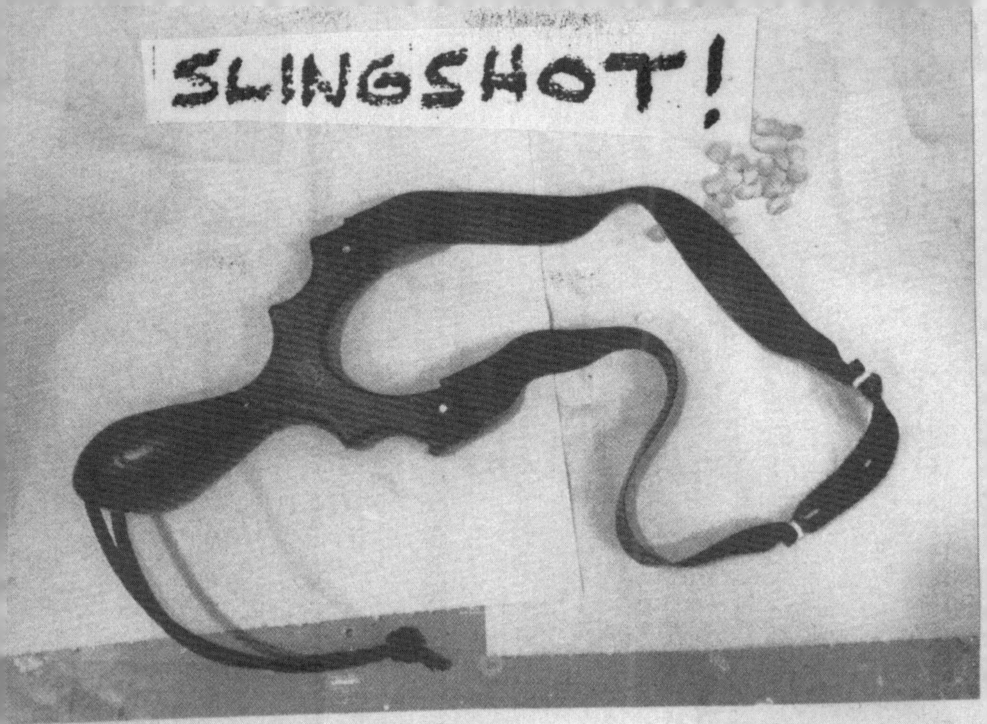

SLINGSHOT!

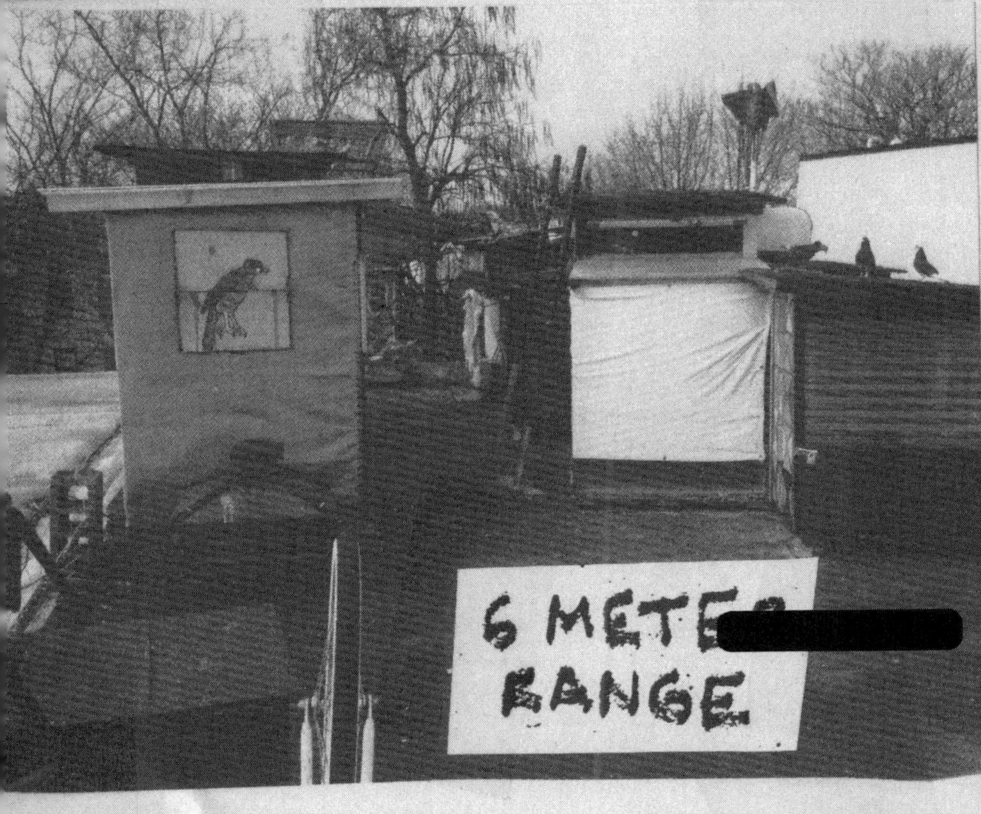

6 METE
RANGE

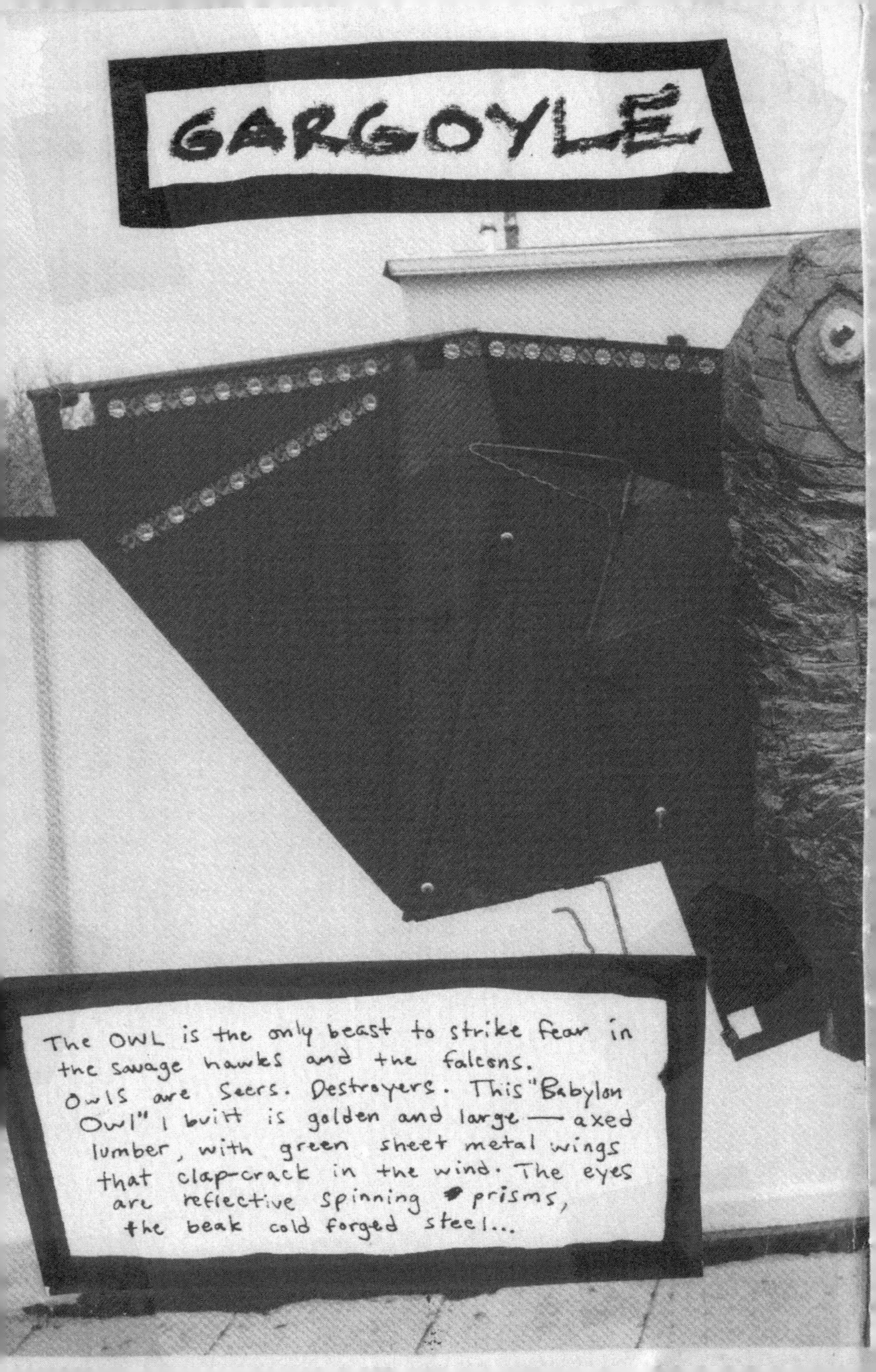

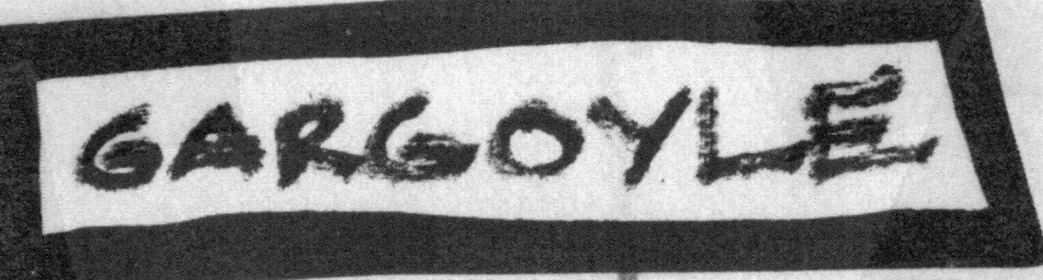

The OWL is the only beast to strike fear in
the savage hawks and the falcons.
Owls are seers. Destroyers. This "Babylon
Owl" I built is golden and large — axed
lumber, with green sheet metal wings
that clap-crack in the wind. The eyes
are reflective spinning prisms,
the beak cold forged steel...

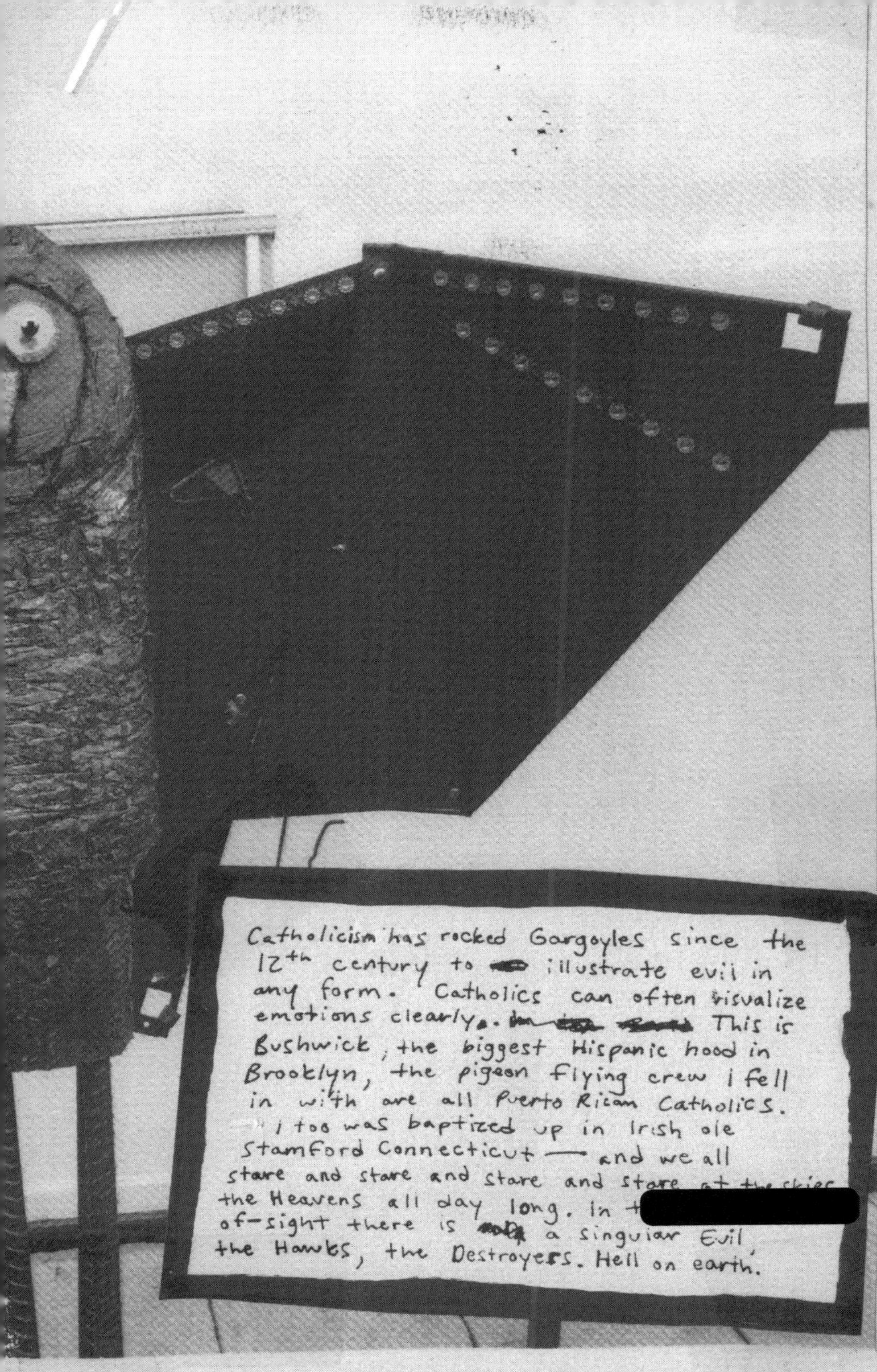

Catholicism has rocked Gargoyles since the
12th century to illustrate evil in
any form. Catholics can often visualize
emotions clearly. This is
Bushwick, the biggest Hispanic hood in
Brooklyn, the pigeon flying crew I fell
in with are all Puerto Rican Catholics.
I too was baptized up in Irish ole
Stamford Connecticut ——— and we all
stare and stare and stare and stare at the skies
the Heavens all day long. In
of-sight there is a singular Evil
the Hawks, the Destroyers. Hell on earth.

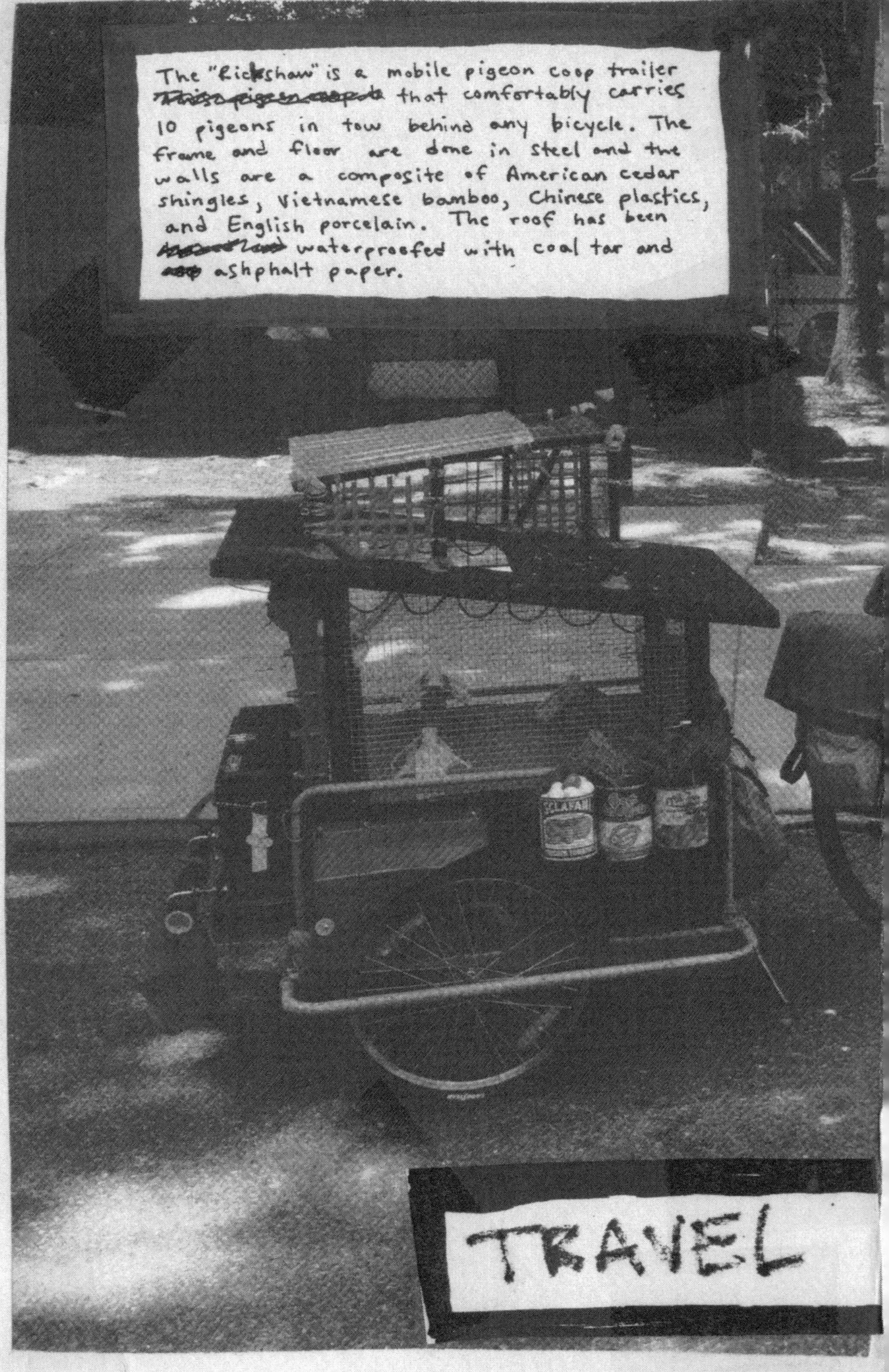
The "Rickshaw" is a mobile pigeon coop trailer
that comfortably carries
10 pigeons in tow behind any bicycle. The
frame and floor are done in steel and the
walls are a composite of American cedar
shingles, Vietnamese bamboo, Chinese plastics,
and English porcelain. The roof has been
waterproofed with coal tar and
ashphalt paper.

TRAVEL

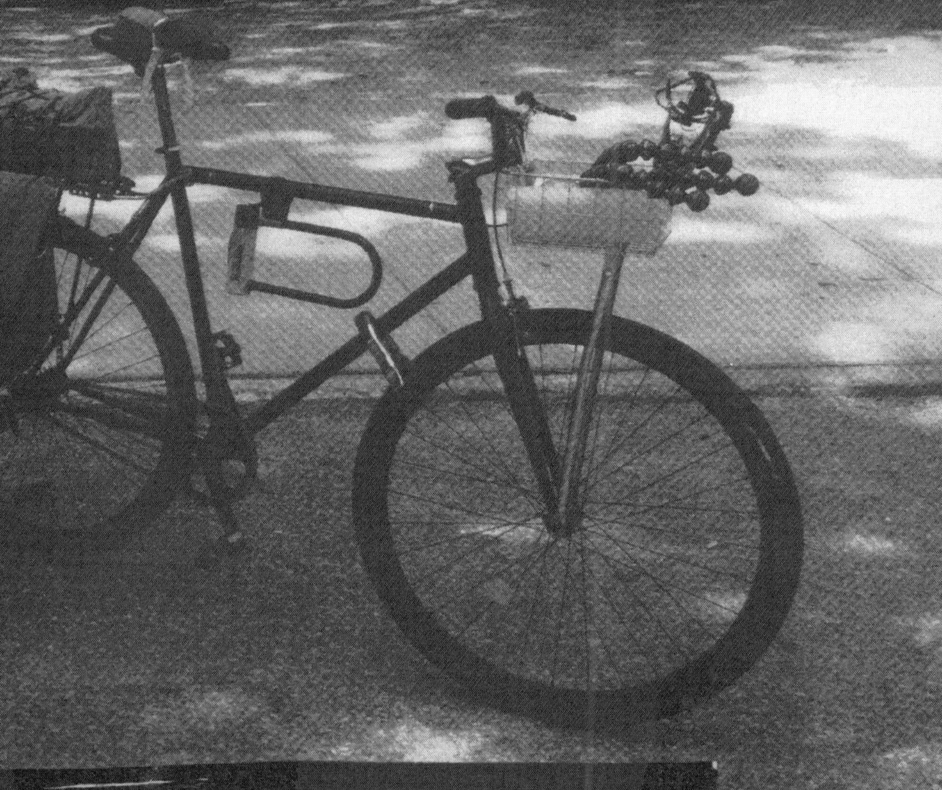

In August 2017 four pigeons were chosen from
Babylon Roof to embark on a long hard
journey to a promised land of leisure.
Two pigeons were elected for their athletic
prowess, one pigeon for bravery, and
one because she is the leader of our
greatest flight team — Queen Teeny.
Together we biked for 3 days and 3 nights
300 kilometer to Montauk beach, the
mythic end of New York. The beautiful
septic where all the varied great cultures of
"New Yorker" meld into the perfect party.

EQUIPMENT

VENETIAN PIGEON EGG AND CHEESE SANDWICHES

In the past short years the number of bed and breakfasts in Venice have quadrupled. Proud home owners are bullied into this b●soaring property values. Competition is high and the desperate Hoteliers seek sustainable living. Attic windows are flinging open across the city to take in the exiled pigeon flocks, refugees whom have been stripped of their feed, facing otherwise a nomad's peril damned to die in the sea. The Hoteliers feed these tenants the very best. Red milo, Yellow small-corn, White kafir, and fresh Farro, with Flax and Orange extract on top. The better the diet the tastier the eggs. Remember pigeons who feed in the gutter pop out horrid tasting eggs (and likely feel like a living hell themselves!)

- Pat McCarthy, Babylon Gardens Broadway Coop
May 2013

1) So always grab the eggs before day 4 There are always two in the nest, grab both.

2) Put them individually in your candler to confirm no babies dark spots

3) Toss a grilled cheese on the stove, a classic style, just 2 pieces of white bread and a slice

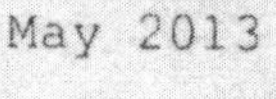

here.

4) Quickly crack em on high heat
Unlike a factory chicken egg, the
yokes here are super fragile,
they'll break. Fine.

5) Tricky to judge pigeon fried
eggs as the 'whites' never really
turn white, they remain clear
throughout Use the grilled cheese
as a timer, flip eggs when time to
flip sandwich

6) When firm, open the sticky cheese
and toss in the eggs.

7) Compress with spatula

8)A high-vinegar hot sauce on top

9) Presto! Perhaps best with a
stretto.

BUON APPETITO

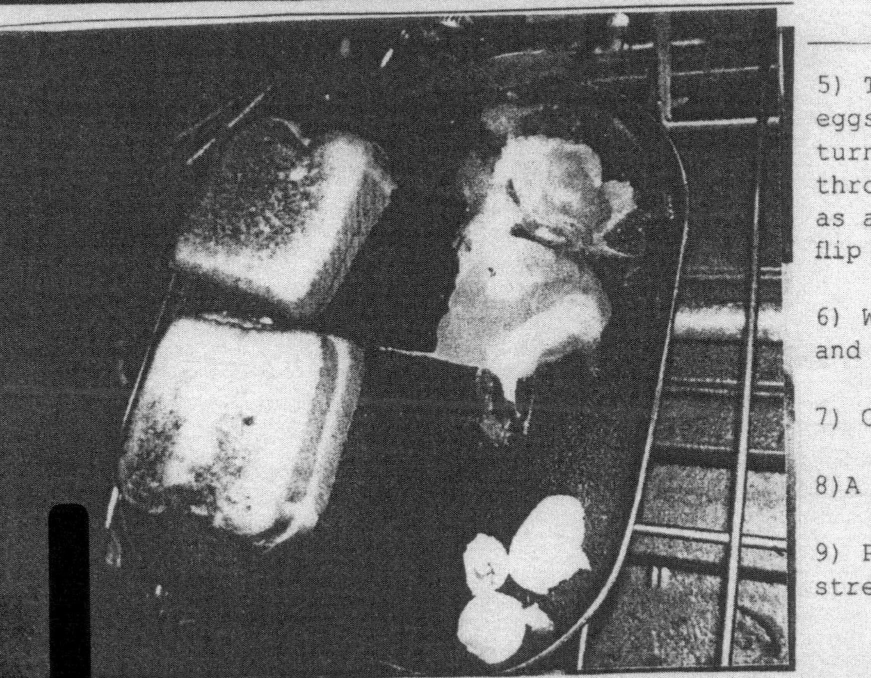

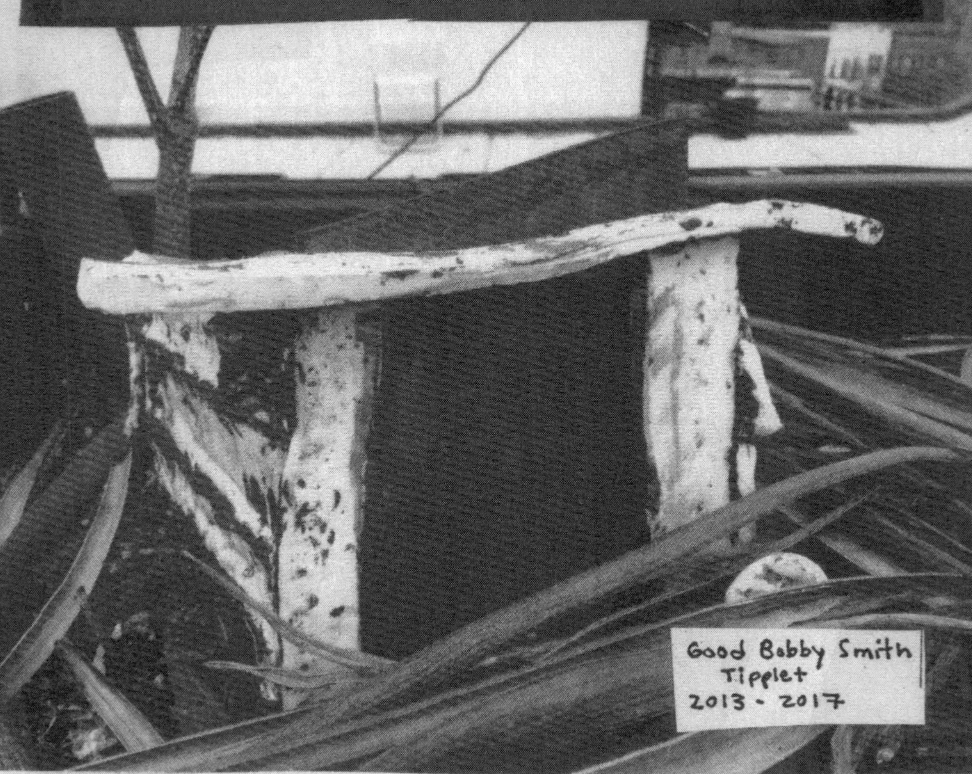

OBITUARIES

As it goes, another year we honor those we have lost.
They will be in our thoughts when our heads
hang and when our heads hook back. Fallen birds
are laid to rest in porcelain tombs.
There is a prayer by Walt Whitman,

    Sing on, sing on you grey brown bird,
    Sing from the swamps, the recesses, pour your chant
        from the bushes,
    Limitless out of the dust, out of the cedars and pines,

    Sing on dearest brother, warble your reedy song,
    Loud pigeon song, with voice of uttermost woe.

    O languid and free and tender!
    O wild and lose to my soul — O wondrous singer!
    You only I hear — yet the star holds me,
        (but will soon depart);
    Yet the lilac with mastering odor holds me.

Good Bobby Smith
Tipplet
2013 - 2017

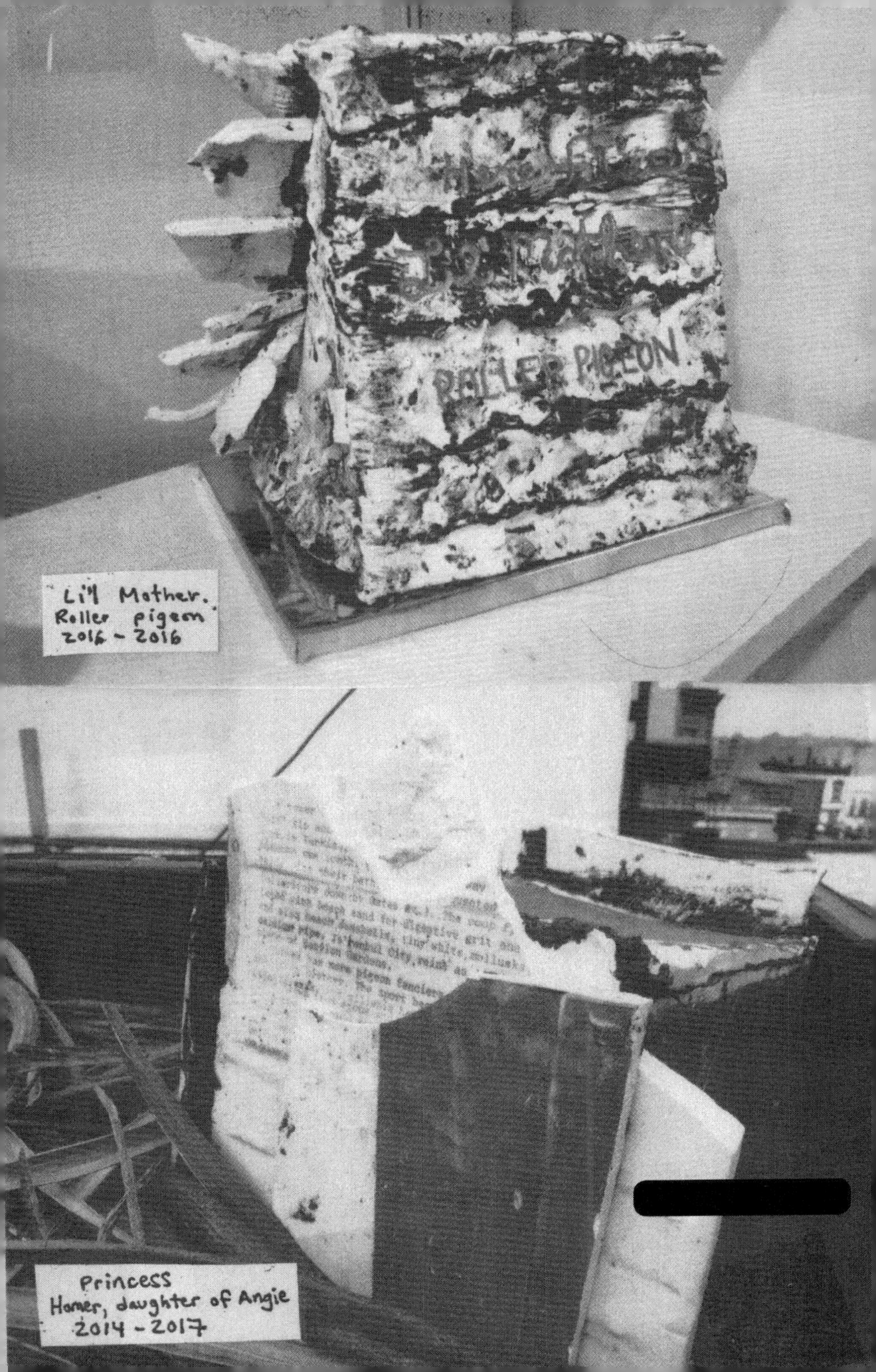

Li'l Mother.
Roller pigeon
2016 - 2016

Princess
Homer, daughter of Angie
2014 - 2017

Written for the project: Commonism

Two homer hatchlings.
Age 10 minutes ~~10 minutes~~ and 2 minutes
respectively.

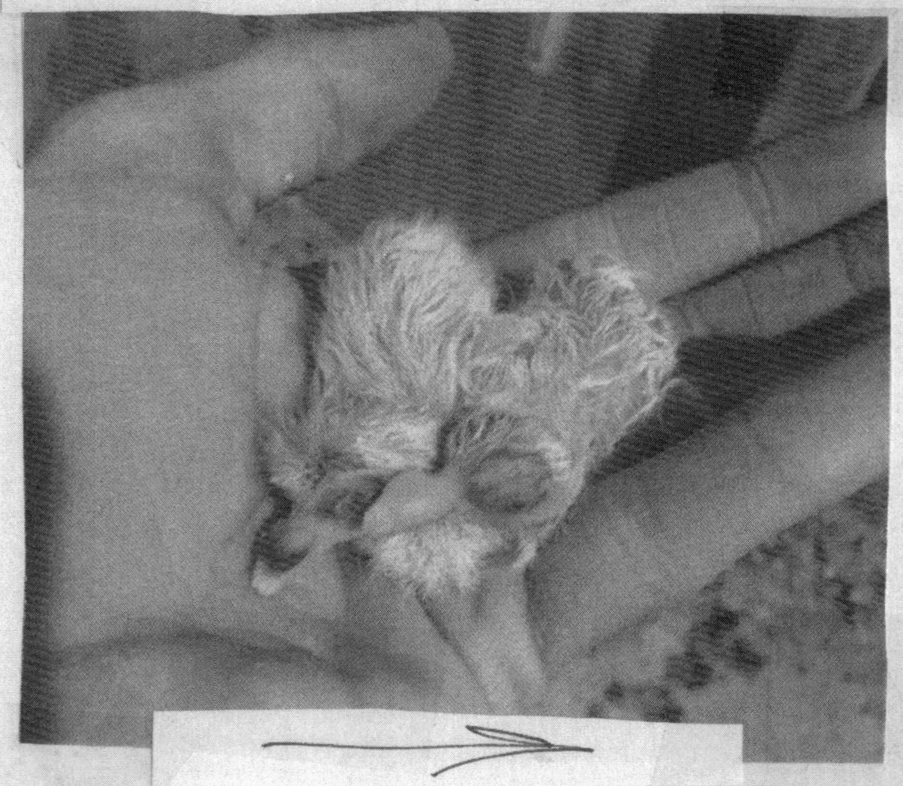

Born To Kill issue 93
"LE DRAME INCESSANT"
Brooklyn, NY
Winter 2017 - 2018
X Pat McCarthy →

Commonism
A New Aesthetics of the Real

Nico Dockx &
Pascal Gielen (eds.)

Antennae-Arts in Society
Valiz, Amsterdam

Commonism
A New Aesthetics of the Real

Nico Dockx & Pascal Gielen (eds.)

With contributions by
Michel Bauwens
Giuliana Ciancio
Santiago Cirugeda
Maria Francesca De Tullio
Nico Dockx
Futurefarmers
Harry Gamboa Jr.
Lara Garcia Diaz
Pascal Gielen
Liam Gillick
Eric Kluitenberg
Rudi Laermans
the *land* foundation
Sonja Lavaert
Peter Linebaugh
Matteo Lucchetti
Pat McCarthy
Antonio Negri
Hanka Otte
Elizabeth A. Povinelli
Jörn Schafaff
Stavros Stavrides
Evi Swinnen
Dennis Tyfus
Nomeda & Gediminas Urbonas
Walter Van Andel
Louis Volont
Judith Wielander

Contents

Introduction
Ideology & Aesthetics of the Real

Nico Dockx & Pascal Gielen

Every ideology is good at hiding the fact that it is one. That's what makes it an ideology. To paraphrase Mark Fisher (2009): Every ideology claims realism. So it claims that it is not an ideology, not a belief system, no false consciousness, but reality: just the way things work and just the way things are. By consequence, it is just how (we need) to do things and how (we need) to deal with things. Communism was an ideology, fascism was one also, neoliberalism certainly is one, and probably most religions function like one. They are all aesthetics of the real. They claim to be the only real truth and through this claim those belief systems give form to society as 'real'. Ideologies are very good in turning a belief into a reality, because they are make-believe and as such they function as self-fulfilling prophecies. Ideologies are performances of reality in name of what is real. But the *real* is unspeakable, it lies under the radar of the symbolic order, as we know from Jacques Lacan (1982). We know it is there and it affects our daily thinking and behaviour, while at the same time it is impossible to point at or to signify. The real functions as viscerality in decision-making processes in social relationships: we know it is there, that it is *real* and we know it influences our perception and even our judgements of others, but we do this without any rational ground. Or, it is like the 'what-you-cannot-speak-about' in an artwork, that which makes the piece or performance truly convincing, impressive, or even sublimely beautiful. But there is not one art-historical, art-theoretical analysis of, or rational explanation for why this work does what it does to us, why it is so convincing. And even when we can explain why an artwork 'works' at a certain moment in time, this explanation does not enable you 'touch' or 'feel' this (real) experience. It is like the feeling of falling in love, on which billions of words, millions of poems and quite a number of psychological studies and even neurologic analyses have been spent. They all cannot make you catch this real feeling. Love is blind, indeed. It precedes, and at the same time goes beyond rationality, it precedes and goes beyond the Enlightenment that gave us the light to see. And exactly those things that are impossible to signify, that we cannot but believe in, are the things ideologies build on.

It is no different for the ideology that is the central theme of this book. After half a century of neoliberalism, we are excited to welcome a new belief system. It is probably still in the margins, very often still under the radar, but we cannot ignore the fact that it is popping up everywhere: the commons. After the 'enclosure of the commons' by neoliberal politics, by privatization or simply by capital, it seems that the era of the 'disclosure of the commons' is now dawning. At least, that is what some people, mostly from the political left, believe in. What is this belief about? They believe that social relationships can replace money (contract) relationships. They certainly believe that we need more solidarity. And they trust in peer-to-peer relationships to develop new ways of production. Some of them think that economy sucks while others believe that only *this* economy sucks. Most of them agree that the contemporary political model of democracy does not stand for *real* democracy anymore, because representative democracies are becoming more and more the servants of a financial elite. So, we need another, more radical political system and some people even dream of direct democracy.

In this book, we want to map those new ideological thoughts. How do they work and, especially, what is their aesthetics? Just as communism, fascism, or neoliberalism, commonism is an aesthetic of the real. It is a belief, a make-believe that claims realism. At least it claims to stand closer to our contemporary ecological and social reality than capitalism. But it is also nearer to how social relationships really function, and much closer to what humanity in general is about. The former technocratic soviet communists, the German Nazis, the Italian fascists and the contemporary western neoliberals all share one characteristic: They neglect(ed) the human condition in their political and economic organization of society. Commoners, on the contrary, place this human figure in the centre again. That is why they think about the ecological, social, political, economic, and even the mental conditions of mankind. Commonism is concerned about the *total* person in his or her total context and global environment. And it is this total concern that makes commonism more and more convincing. At least, this new belief gives the impression that it stands closer to reality today than neoliberalism does. And we—the editors of this book—confess: we also believe in a more common future. We are sick of neoliberalism and its perverse mechanisms, and we believe that the proposals of the 'commoners' are much better aligned to the contemporary global reality, and to the human condition in general. But, probably unlike a lot of 'commoners', we also strongly believe that this belief is an ideology. That is why we speak about 'common-ism', a term perceptively coined by the Canadian Marxist Nick Dyer-Witheford (2007; Lemmens 2017, p. 173). We do this because we see that commonists too argue and operate in the name of realism while counting on the earlier mentioned 'real'. In that sense it is not really different from Friedrich Hayek's view, who started his neoliberal project in the 1940s in the name of reality. Just as commonism now, neoliberalism was, at that time, a very marginal project (Srnicek and Williams 2015), and just as with neoliberalism we do not yet know if commonism will grow and take up a dominant position, as neoliberalism did in the 1970s. We even do not yet know if we really want this, but just as with neoliberalism, that is out of our hands.

For us the main difference probably lies here: just as most historical ideologists, Hayek did not see himself as an ideologist, but as a... realist. Well, we do say we believe! We say that we believe in commonism and also that we know that it is an ideology. So, as a consequence, we are ideologists. And all commoners are, but maybe not all of them would agree. Probably they are distancing themselves from the quite negative image the concept of ideology has, as something that hides things, that works as an 'opium of the people', that masks reality in the name of reality. But maybe it is better to invert this way of reasoning. At least we try to do this here by saying: we are ideologists, we are conscious of our make-believe and we are very aware of the fact that we construct a reality. But we do this, because we are convinced it is a better reality and we also believe it fits better with the contemporary human condition. We could call it a self-conscious ideology, one that tries to convince others because it is convinced of the truth of another reality than the contemporary one. For those interested in the theoretical background of our heterodox twist: we follow the Gramsci-Laclau-Mouffe-Žižek line of reasoning in their re-articulation of the Marxist ideology critique. Especially Gramsci's rejection of the (economic) base vs. (cultural) superstructure model of ideology by stressing the role of culture in hegemonic and ideological constructions is inspiring for us. As argued in another book (Gielen and Lijster 2015), we see culture as the base (and not as superstructure), because culture stands for the whole process of giving meaning to ourselves and to the societal environment and its economies, ecologies, jurisdictions, and politics in which we are living. In that sense we follow the arguments of Ernesto Laclau and Chantal Mouffe, who stress the role of discourse in ideological constructions. We only enlarge the concept of discourse by using the notion of culture, which also gives a place to other cultural expressions besides language, such as visuals, sounds, smells, and touch or all the senses of aesthesis/aesthetics that contribute to processes of signification, ideological or not. Related to the commons, political economist Massimo De Angelis stresses also the importance of culture as a process of giving *meaning* to common goods:

> While any principle for selecting what constitutes a common good should be founded on strategic grounds, this claim cannot be made on the basis of some inherent character of the good in question. Rather, it must be made on the basis of the meaning that a plurality has given to that good...' (De Angelis 2017, p. 62)

Finally, to come back to our topic of ideology as a cultural product, with Slavoj Žižek we share his Lacanian emphasis on the role of the imaginary in the construction of ideologies. We find especially his articulation of ideology that 'has nothing to do with "illusion", with a mistaken, distorted representation of its social content' (Žižek 2012, p. 7) attractive. For Žižek,

> An ideology is thus not necessary 'false': as to its positive content, it can be 'true', quite accurate, since what really matters is not the asserted content as such but *the way this content is related to the subjective position ...*' (p. 8).

The pivotal thing that makes a belief system an ideology is that it hides and legitimizes the unequal power relationships for which it is functional, according to the Slovenian philosopher. It is from this tradition of post-Marxist re-articulations that we radically inverse the classical Marxist chronological chain of first economy, then state, then ideology, and then culture. You first need culture, its signs, its words, its traditions, its values, its ideas, its imaginaries to articulate and elaborate it as an ideology—like Hayek did with his think-tanks for neoliberalism. Only after ideology is translated in its broad range of (journalistic, scientific, political, et cetera) articulations, can it re-invent the state and its operational functions. And up till now, it is still the nation state that regulates or deregulates markets and economies. (The state is of course highly influenced by economies, multinationals, and 'revolving door politicians' who easily exchange their political position for

that of a CEO, but in the end it is the state or some other government institution that decides about laws and market regulations.)

However, this inversion of the classical Marxist chain will
be not our main speculative deed. When ideology is a 'melange'
of fictions and facts to legitimize and hide relations of social domination in hegemonic circles (or, we could add, in a hegemonic
'Empire', with Negri and Hardt), then a counter-hegemony can
only be articulated as a counter-ideology. Why? Because a counter-
hegemony always hopes for a better (utopian) future to come.
Its drive and energy come from a side we cannot know yet since
futurology is not an empirical science. So, we imagine a horizon,
a picture of a utopian social configuration that does not exist yet.
This means we have to rely very much on fiction and our imagination to render our goal lucid and to legitimize our walk towards it.
For such a journey we mix facts (e.g. statistical knowledge about
inequality) with possible solutions that hopefully will be realized
in an imagined future. Especially those projections on a future
horizon are built on artistic tools such as imagination, fiction
and creativity, and they use the artistic instruments such as play,
visualization, mimesis, and articulation to get there. Ideology is
in that sense for us the intelligent mixture of fact and fiction, science and (make-)believe to perform an acceptable future. And, it
is *in* the traveling that we make or perform this future reality. In
the 21st century, it would be quite strange to not see the Marxist
tradition of ideology critique—valuable as it may be—as a tradition that builds its own (counter)ideology. As Geörgy Lukács
took over the positive interpretation of the concept of ideology
from the Second Internationale as an expression of the proletariat, we also want to highlight the positive and constitutive character of the concept in this book. And for this construction we
will use the same strategies as all the other ideologists by saying
that this current reality is not true, it is fake, it is cynical and
opportunistic, but certainly not real. And just like other ideologists we do so in the name of realism. For us, this is a way to open
up the horizon for this book. Through contributions by artists,
theorists, and researchers we want to evoke a better understanding of the commons as an ideology. That means as an aesthetic
of the real: a way of giving form to society and our contemporary human condition. With Alexander Gottlieb Baumgarten we
understand aesthetics as 'the art of thinking beautifully' about
what could be beyond the horizon (Raunig 2015). For us it is a

way of thinking of a better, more beautiful world that manifests itself in the liminal zone between fiction and non-fiction, imagination and reality, utopianism and realism. In the aesthetic of the real, fiction can become reality and reality is constructed in the shadows of human imaginations. In this book we want to put a spotlight on those reciprocating movements for the commons in four chapters.

The Contributions

Perhaps, before you even started reading this introduction, you already browsed the communal practice of the American artist Pat McCarthy. Some of you did so with great curiosity, others hastily turning pages, slightly irritated. This is not unlike the experience of encountering communal practices: curious about what is going on, one jumps in full of enthusiasm and energy, only to soon become irritated by the unclear counter-voices and the sometimes excruciating and endless debates that come with dissensus and assemblies. It takes a while to become used to this and also to see the point of it. Whether Pat McCarthy's zines are 'useful' is a matter of opinion, but he does demonstrate to us with his work that the 'commons' is something inclusive and not exclusive. In the context of this book, he created a special issue of his ongoing series of *Born To Kill* fanzines. This serialized zine is at the same time journalistic study and poetic inquiry. To quote the artist:

> For the reader, it is a direct conversation with the private sphere of my 'field studies' which include raising domestic pigeons, travel on foot, selling food in the street, and studying gender and sexuality. And paper is the blankest stage on which to stand.

Liam Gillick replied to our invitation to contribute to this book by sending us a layout of many different prints he has made in the last few years and that somehow make sense to the theme of 'commoning'. He proposed to use the book as a space to reproduce a number of these varied prints—which are definitely not illustrations to the theme of our book, but rather possibilities contained in a sort of 'what-if' scenario. To quote curator Nicolaus Schafhausen: 'His work often demonstrates an uncanny ability to translate complex and abstract social situations into visual mise-en-scènes—that grapple with the functional mechanisms and the failures of post-industrial social models.' We decided to distribute these little works of Liam throughout the book... almost like a metronome (pp. 72-73, 88-89, 132-133, 196-197, 250-251, 342-343, 360-361).

In the first part of the book, 'Commonability & The Art of Assembling', we give the floor to artists and theorists on the subject of possibilities and form of the commons. To sociologist Pascal Gielen, that form is certainly the assembly. Against the abstract aesthetic of neoliberalism and the present finance economy the commons posits a social reality that is much more capricious and dissonant. Still, it is the dissensus of both love and friction that defines the warmth within the commons. The current finance economy represses this social reality, making it manifests itself only more fiercely. Commonism meets the desire for 'the social' and therefore it could very well develop into a new aesthetic for the real, even into a new meta-ideology. That is to say, one that, like neoliberalism, appeals to both left and right, progressive and conservative. That same 'social' also means however that such an assembly may take on a monstrous shape. The manner in which social control is organized can make or break the well-functioning of the commons, as social control can lead to either a utopian or dystopian reality.

The philosopher Antonio Negri, in his interview with Gielen and philosopher Sonja Lavaert, agrees with the notion that the commons may appeal to multiple political movements, but is wary of the term 'meta-ideology'. After all, the prefix 'meta-' implies a transcendental pretention. Negri—who together with Michael Hardt put the notion of the commons back on the philosophical world map—does regard commonism as a natural follow-up to that other ideology, communism. In their latest book, *Assembly*, they say that concepts appropriated by neoliberalism such as 'leadership' and 'entrepreneurship' must be reclaimed for the commons. For the purpose of our book we asked Negri how exactly this should happen and what role art might play in it.

The Futurefarmers also zoom in on the assembly in their contribution by asking: 'Who is part of *our* assemblage? Who is the other that co-determines or co-constitutes what is of importance? What provokes this pre-subjective process of commonization?' With projects such as the Flatbread Society, the Futurefarmers collective focuses on concrete practice. They conduct hands-on exploration of how people and things, neighbours and grains affect each other in an almost absurdist manner, and how art can play a role in the transformation of a 'public space' into a 'common place'. The objects they produce transcend the symbolic order, shaking up deep-rooted certainties, thereby generating new possibilities for communal practices. Futurefarmers demonstrate how the social-political assembly of the commons is arrived at in practice.

Rudi Laermans extends this analysis to the micro level of social interaction. The communication among dancers during rehearsals demonstrates how communal processes of co-creation actually work. Here too, the game of equal and unequal is played out: some dancers are always talking, others remain silent. This cultural sociologist neatly shows how to deal with such ambivalences pragmatically and thus arrive at the assembly of a singular choreography.

Elizabeth A. Povinelli of the Karrabing Film Collective applies an even stronger lens than Laermans, following his observation of micro-interaction with a look inside the individual. In an interview by Judith Wielander and Matteo Lucchetti of Visible, Povinelli stresses the importance of the social obligation to leave the individual (artistic) narrative completely behind. She does this by making the practice of common-ability central:

> the ability to become something in the crossing over to someone else while remaining where you are; rather than being something being a one or another. Within this way of imagining the common, the possibility that you will become or want to become something more or less different always hovers over the scene of the common.

The Karrabing Film Collective won the 2015 Visible Award for how they put that view into practice. The jury process that Visible applies in its selection procedure is also worth mentioning. The jury is not exclusively made up of art experts or cultural connoisseurs, and nominations are decided upon during a day-long, deliberative process in a parliament-like setting with experts and culturally interested people. In other words: an assembly.

The second part of the book, 'A-Legality & Commoning Economies' focuses on economic organization and working conditions in the commons. Artist and art theorist Lara Garcia Diaz, together with Gielen, explores the potential of the growing precariat. Could this precariat, like the proletariat in Marxism and communism, take upon itself the role of protagonist in the struggle for the commons? According to Garcia Diaz and Gielen, the situation and social composition of the present-day precariat are fundamentally different from those of the 19th-century working class. Still, they point to various strategies by which a creative class might play an important role in forming and shaping new autonomous organizations of and for the commons.

Evi Swinnen of the Ghent commons organization Timelab and Michel Bauwens, founder of the P2P Foundation, in their conversation in any case regard artists as the pioneers of this precarious class. Art, creativity, and culture play a crucial part as a foundation for the commons and commoning practices, although there is still a long way to go. Which is why Swinnen and Bauwens also advocate education about the commons.

How this precarious class actually functions is explored by artist Nico Dockx in an interview with members of the *land* foundation, a commoning organization in Chiang Mai. (the *land* foundation is also discussed from a different angle by Jörn Schafaff elsewhere in the book). Against mounting market and 'eventilization' pressure, this foundation organizes an alternative economy for artists—a no pressure economy that forefronts singular contributions and the autonomy of artists in how they spend their time.

The importance of such an alternative economy between the art market and festival frenzy also crops up in the conversation among the artists Nico Dockx and Dennis Tyfus. 'The Value of Squatting a Nipple' provides an historical insight into the Do-It-Yourself and squatter's culture in Antwerp in the 1990s. Tyfus shows how an exchange value that is different from the traditional Marxist interpretation was at work here and that squatting can be so much more than just occupying buildings. The squatting culture is an alternative economy in itself.

Economist Walter Van Andel and sociologist Louis Volont test a different economy for its alternative potential. Does the blockchain provide a true alternative for regular financial markets? To find the answer to this Van Andel and Volont unravelled the technology and social interactions that drive such economies. Whether the block chain really benefits the commons is ultimately an ideological choice, they conclude.

Choosing to develop a commonal economy is indeed not a technological, let alone a technocratic choice, but it is an ideological one. That much becomes clear in an interview by Garcia Diaz with architect and activist Santiago Cirugeda. This founder of the Spanish Recetas Urbanas is constantly navigating between creativity and criminality, between legality and illegality when he builds structures, often at the request of civilians and communities. Whether it is a house, a community centre, a school, or a curious cocoon construction for homeless people in a tree, the economy of his architectural firm works in a peculiar in-between space between market and government, often verging on the illegal. Striving for a fundamental right like equality, strangely enough often quickly leads to this 'a-legal' twilight zone, these days.

Whether economy-related or not, becoming involved in commoning practices means having to deal with politics. The third part of the book, 'Secrets & Commoning Politics', concludes with *Magna Carta Manifesto* author Peter Linebaugh's proposition that commoning practices had best remain secret or invisible if they are to survive. After all, both the market and the state are always looking for ways to occupy the commons, says Linebaugh in his interview with Louis Volont. Policy researcher Hanka Otte and Gielen make the same observation when looking at the history of community art, seeing how it has been used by governments to plug up the holes in the welfare state, ever since Roosevelt's New Deal in the 1930s. Unlike in the 1960s, community art's revival in the 1990s and 2000s can again be explained by government interest. The cost: community art can hardly express itself politically or ideologically anymore and must resign itself to the pragmatic social order where it mainly serves to maintain internal social cohesion or upholding a 'we'-feeling. *Commoning* art, by contrast, explores the unknown and the unknown other in the grey area between market and state. By paying attention to the social, commoning artists inevitably enter the realm of politics. This is exactly why both politics and market would rather ignore them. The only possible cultural policy for commoning art is a 'cosmopolitics', Otte and Gielen think. This is a policy that—like the practice of Recetas Urbanas—rests on inferential legality: a self-regulating bottom-up policy can only be evaluated according to a number of constitutional conditions but should otherwise be left as free or autonomous as possible. Only the commons can guarantee this.

Exactly how a commons policy would look like and might be organized is a question that the authors leave open, but the essays that follow fil the gap that Otte and Gielen left. Cultural manager Giuliana Ciancio and lawyer Maria Francesca De Tullio in their contributions both zoom in on Naples. Ciancio relates how this Italian city has historically arrived at an 'officialized' policy of the commons, which was politically embraced by the mayor and confirmed by actually appointing an alderman for the commons—probably the only one in the world. De Tullio then looks at the legal aspects of the issue. What do official regulations for the commons look like, how are they arrived at, and how do they relate to the constitution? Both Ciancio and De Tullio take the commons organization l'Asilo as their starting point. In spite of its impressive and highly innovative commons policy Naples is still plagued by austerity measures and micro-criminality, and (national) politicians as well as profit-driven entrepreneurs are looking for a chance to take over the city and occupy the commons. Whether the commonists will be forced to retreat into a secret, clandestine existence, as Linebaugh strongly suspects, is something time will tell.

In the fourth and final part, researchers and theorists explore the potential of commoning time and space. American Chicano artist Harry Gamboa Jr. emphatically shows how public space has become a rare phenomenon in Los Angeles. Privatization and even militarization rule the streets, squares, and public transport, creating a claustrophobic atmosphere in which there is preciously little room to move about freely. Uncommon Commoning paints a bitter, black story in which the public performances that Gamboa himself organizes, mostly with students, can create only small cracks. L.A., and perhaps the entire USA, are obviously in need of a radical reconquest of public space.

In his contribution, Athenian architect, activist, and theorist Stavros Stavrides is looking for the potential of commoning practices in order to break space open again. By regarding space as 'potenza' to think and act through space, Stavrides re-articulates the debate around pre-figurative politics in which dreams and desirable social relations are already tried out here and now. Or, as he says: 'In actual spaces people can experience the future and the means to reach it.' Perhaps this is the very thing Gamboa is testing with his performances: how to imagine the future space by performing it already in the present. Performances in public space as pre-figurative power, a practice of commoning that charges the 'potenza' of a space.

German art historian Jörn Schafaff returns to the subject of the *land* foundation, several members of which are also interviewed elsewhere in this book. This foundation not only develops an alternative economy, but the openness that it affords artistic interventions also continuates the commoning process. For example, Nico Dockx built a bridge that may be used in a functional sense by local farmers, but also by artists, and can even accommodate artistic activities such as film screenings and performances, but also social activities. Schafaff regards the *land* foundation primarily as a place for rehearsal: 'a space (and the time) to imagine, develop, test and train, but also to question and reject issues of social concern.' Thereby the *land* foundation becomes a project of continuous making and remaking of commons through shared practices.

Next, Nomeda and Gediminas Urbonas focus on the Protest Lab Project that started as a call to reclaim the public space in the city and in particular save the largest cinema theatre in Vilnius, Lithuania, from being demolished. With their hypothesis about 'emotional infrastructure' they further develop Stavrides' idea of space as potenza. Suggesting that in a search for alternatives to the rationale of economy, 'emotional infrastructure' could model cultural and critical forms of civil engagement, build on the senses, memory, human rights, dignity, safety, and certainty'. They regard play and art as alternatives for urban planning and development to bring back 'soul in the city'.

Instead of emotion, Dutch media theorist Eric Kluitenberg takes the unconscious variant 'affect' as a starting point for obtaining a grip on not space but on the current occupation of time. In doing so, Kluitenberg unfolds commoning practices—a true counter-ideology—to counter the immediacy of contemporary affect relationships. Affect-driven processes are after all easy to manipulate. The unspectacular, everyday aesthetics of the commons can interrupt such effect-laden real-time flows through the duration that all deliberative processes of commoning require. The essentially deliberative nature of participative art stretches time, as it were, thereby creating the contours of a counter-ideology. Kluitenberg completes the circle of this book. Because, whether meta-ideology or counter-ideology, both underline the ideological nature of an emergent commonism. After all, a counter-ideology is still an ideology, just as ideology critique is always part of another ideology. Through aesthetics, ideology *shapes* our reality, and the many contributions in this book offer a view of what this aesthetics looks like, how it sounds, and even how it feels: assembled, whimsical, dissonant, pre-figurative, not affect-laden but emotionally charged, mundane, unspectacular, but socially and politically involved. It not only takes time to produce the aesthetics of the commons but also to detect it. In addition, this is an aesthetics that is not imposed from the top down, as with the time-honoured civil *Bildung* ideal, but rises from the bottom up from the *communi* or is distilled from it. What is clear is that aesthetics cannot be claimed individually but only as part of a collective co-creative process in which ultimately any commoner can claim 'authorship'. Commonal practices are precarious, however, and extremely sensitive to recapitulation, gentrification, privatization, commodification, and even to 'nationalization' as in a romantic 'we'-feeling. In order to survive in the long run, commonal practices had therefore best remain invisible, 'secret', or clandestine. Perhaps commonism is most effective when it works like the wind: invisible, odourless, but nonetheless sometimes strongly felt, and chilling. Pushing against reality, shaping reality without pushing oneself to the forefront, without even claiming any right of ownership or ego. It is at least remarkable that quite a few commoning artists, like commoners, prefer to remain invisible or to disappear from sight in the long run. They do initiate processes and push the world in a specific direction, but they do so in the hope that others will appropriate, take over, and continue these processes. Stealthy, slumbering, underground, and under the skin: these are the characteristics by which an ideology spreads and persuades the best. It's called poetica.

Commonism—A New Aesthetics of the Real, like almost all publications in the Antennae-Arts in Society series, alternates theoretical analysis and almost empirical observations with wild and speculative, indeed artistic exercises in thought. As always, we try to push the envelope and broaden the sense of what may be. It is an increasingly marginal practice and approach in a world in which the borders between art and society, between fiction and reality, are being made ever stricter. Academics make only minimal progress because they have to safeguard themselves with endless references and verifications, while artists find it increasingly difficult to move beyond the neutralizing, standardized confines of fiction: the museum, the gallery, or the theatre. Let it be clear that with this book we sought out and invited especially those researchers, scientists, and artists who navigate these frontiers, taking risks in doing so. After all, a publication in the Antennae-Arts in Society series doesn't yield any academic credits and we very much doubt that it results in any artistic recognition or symbolic credit for artists. For that they would have to publish in an A1 journal or in *Artforum*. We are therefore most grateful to the contributors for their commitment and their at times wild images and speculative ideas and we also very much appreciate Valiz publishers for providing space for exactly this type of writing. We don't mind telling our readers that this is not a lucrative business by far. Thanks also to the Royal Academy of Fine Arts Antwerp for once again supporting a speculative study by an artist and a pseudo-scientist. This study 'Making Public Domain' has indeed been an idiosyncratic search for how we can think of and create public space today. Without the freedom provided us by the Antwerp Royal Academy to conduct this study we would perhaps never have arrived at commonism. Finally, we applaud ARIA (Antwerp Research Institute for the Arts) and the colleagues at CCQO (Culture Commons Quest Office) who—also with funds of the Flanders Foundation for Scientific Research—have had the courage to engage with this curious quest, with growing affection. But perhaps that is another commoning practice that had better remain secret (for now).

References

— De Angelis, Massimo. 2017. *Omnia Sunt Communia: On the Commons and the Transformation to Postcapitalism.* London: Zed Books.

— Dyer-Witheford, Nick. 2007. 'Commonism.' *Turbulence 1.* http://turbulence.org.uk/turbulence-1/commonism.

— Fisher, Mark. 2009. *Capitalist Realism: Is There No Alternative?* Winchester, UK: Zero Books.

— Gielen, Pascal, and Thijs Lijster. 2015. 'Culture: The Substructure of a European Common.' In *No Culture, No Europe: On the Foundation of Politics.* Edited by Pascal Gielen, pp. 19-65. Amsterdam: Valiz.

— Lacan, Jacques. 1982. 'Le symbolique, l'imaginaire et le réel.' *Bulletin de l'Association Freudienne* 1, pp. 4-13.

— Lemmens, Pieter. 2017. 'The Conditions of the Common: A Stieglerian Critique of Hardt and Negri's Thesis on Cognitive Capitalism as a Prefiguration of Communism.' In *Perspectives on Commoning: Autonomist Principles and Practices.* Edited by Guido Ruivenkamp and Andy Hilton, pp. 169-212. London: Zero Books.

— Raunig, Gerald. 2015. 'The Invention of Aesthetic Law: An Experiment on the Aesthetic Horizon and the Art of Living Beautifully.' In *Aesthetic Justice: Intersecting Artistic and Moral Perspectives.* Edited by Pascal Gielen and Niels Van Tomme, pp. 95-111. Amsterdam: Valiz.

— Srnicek, Nick, and Alex Williams. 2015. *Inventing the Future: Postcapitalism and a World Without Work.* London and New York: Verso.

— Žižek, Slavoj, ed. 2012. *Mapping Ideology.* London and New York: Verso.

Part 1

Commonability & The Art of Assembling

Quotidian

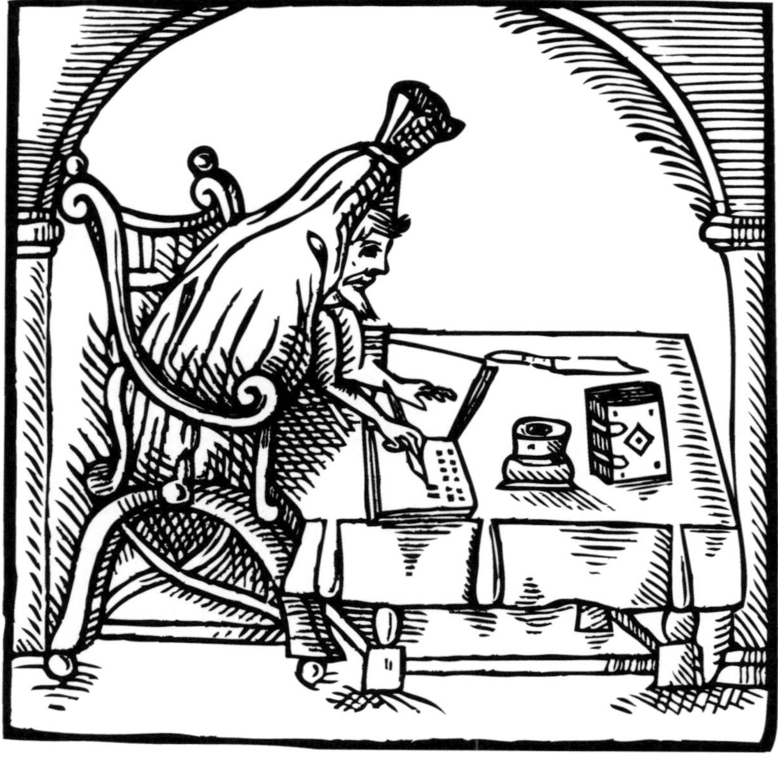

Quotidian, *Another Magazine*, London, 2010

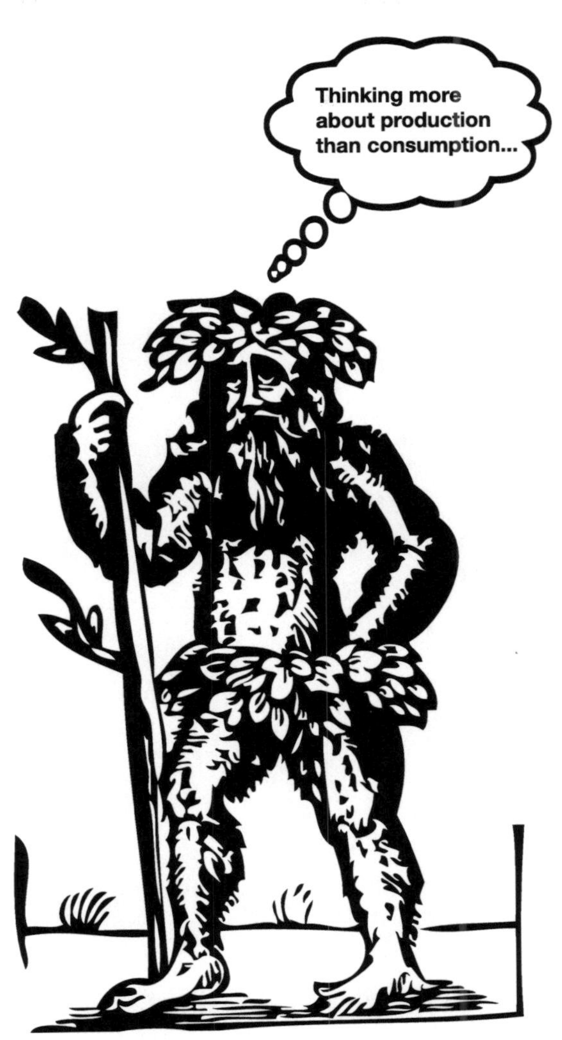

Thinking more about production than consumption, Artists Space, New York, 2010

Common Aesthetics
The Shape of a New Meta-Ideology

Pascal Gielen

The image in the original frontispiece of *Leviathan*, which Hobbes himself commissioned, shows the body of the king as constituted by the bodies of all the male subjects of the English nation—an elegant and ingenious depiction of the unity among people, the nation, and the sovereign. Imagine if we could re-create that image now with radically heterogeneous raced and gendered bodies in all their singularity, moreover bodies in motion, encountering one another, speaking different tongues, but nonetheless able to cooperate in both shared and conflicting relations. The image of such a multitude would depict how the processes of translation—taking the word—subvert the structures of sovereignty and construct the common. (Hardt and Negri 2017, p. 153)

Social Fiction

Émile Durkheim's (1912) greatest gift to the sociology of religion probably was the basic insight that all faith is the product of social construction. In rites, the tribe doesn't celebrate anything supernatural, but simply itself. Religious emblems or relics are nothing but symbolic materializations and rationalizations of what occurs among people—that which eludes the individual, is immune to it, but is still really there. Every social interaction, group dynamic, co-creation, even all visceral affect-communication does indeed have a surreal, ephemeral quality. All these things exist in an elusive 'in-between'. Or, in a well-known phrase: the whole is more than the sum of its parts, just as a community is more than a sum of individuals. The 'in-between' indeed produces a surplus, albeit one that is hard to establish in an empirical sense. Hence the production of religion to compensate for our lack of social understanding. And this is also one of the similarities between religion and ideology. Ideology too is in fact based on a social unawareness and like religion it promises to point the way to a utopian society. The difference is that the ideal of religious faith is usually located in the transcendental sphere, as in an hereafter. In an ideology, by contrast, the ideal world can be realized in this world. Utopia is immanent, not supernatural. However, this immanence always brings ideologists to paradoxical reasoning and rationalization: on the one hand, ideologists create utopian projections of an ideal society in the future, while on the other hand they claim that these projections are already there in the present reality. For example, all forms of nationalism imagine an ideal people while at the same time claiming that this ideal—'our' values and norms—is already present in that people's DNA. And although the presence of others, the 'unbelievers' or those that do not belong to the people, may muddy the waters somewhat, the people's true nature remains firmly rooted in blood and soil, sometimes deep underground. Durkheim didn't call nationalism a 'secular religion' for nothing. The same paradoxical reasoning dominates liberalism and neoliberalism. Both Adam Smith's and Friedrich Hayek's belief that the ideal society is grounded on a free market with competitive individuals assumes that people are in fact already competitive 'by nature', that it is in our genes. That is why from that point of view socialism and communism can be labelled 'unnatural' political solutions.

In any case, both religions and ideologies are tasked with closing the gap between dream and reality, between utopia and reality, and between fiction and non-fiction. In the interweaving of the imaginary and the real, culture and nature also become inextricably interlinked. But perhaps it is not so much the fictional or imaginary aspect that makes a religion the 'opium of the people' or labels an ideology as 'false awareness', but much more the fundamental suppression of social construction labour—including relationships of power—which brings them to life and by which they are ultimately sustained. Both forms of faith are in fact sponging off social processes. They come into being to explain an elusive surplus that is generated by every 'in-between' or every '*inter*-action', while at the same time suppressing the causal relationship with that social life. All the same, ideology is nothing but the fictional rationalization and legitimization of existing or desired social relations (or disparities).

The Aesthetics of Finance: Abstraction

The less you eat, drink, buy books, go to the theatre, go dancing, go drinking, think, love, theorize, sing, paint, fence, etc. the more you *save*—the *greater* will become that treasure which neither moths nor maggots can consume—your *capital*. (Hardt and Negri 2017, p. 103)

Perhaps neoliberalism is the ideology par excellence of social suppression. Margaret Thatcher's 'there is no such thing as society' not only confirms that notion, but her statement also suggests an aversion to the 'in-between'. It reflects neoliberalism's deep-rooted fear of social commotion. The intermediary space between individuals but also that between people and technologies may indeed generate an unexpected surplus of energy, uncontrollable, not to be rationalized outbursts in every direction. This is perhaps why the social is the neoliberal's greatest enemy: the social is the source of both unpredictable loves and alliances and of unpredictable irrationality and violent eruptions. Nevertheless, the free market and capital only exist by the grace of social life. The present-day finance economy anyway survives by abstracting and extracting commonal energy (Hardt and Negri 2017, pp. 162–166).

Abstraction is indeed the magical art of the present-day finance economy. The idea that exchange value is an abstraction of use value is an old Marxist insight (Marx (1867 [1984]). The denial of social production relations is however moved to a higher level by the current financialization:

> Industrial capital is territorialised, embodied in machines, factories and physical products. Financial capital, on the other hand, has no territory, no material assets; it is composed of pure abstractions, figures, algorithms, sings. (Berardi 2017, p. 159)

In the finance economy not only production relations, but just about all social relations are abstracted. More specifically this abstraction concerns the human factor, man as a bio-political being with production power *and* consumer potential *and* emotions *and* a biorhythm *and* social affects *and* religious or political beliefs. The notion of the so-called *homo economicus* reduces every complex and heterogeneous *and-and* being to a measurable unit whose behaviour is driven by and can be explained by equally measurable calculations. Perhaps this rationalistic view of mankind is precisely the reason why the current science of economics is failing. By relying too heavily on mathematical models, on chance and risk calculations, the economy is seen as a rational machine and the exchange among people is presented as only exchange value. As if making an abstract painting would be nothing more than bringing together mathematically calculable blobs of paint, so too social relations are nothing but measurable events. In this view, painting is only about the relations between forms on a canvas and the economy is only about financial transactions.

The abstraction craze is not limited to the field of economics. According to the French historian Pierre Rosanvallon, politics has also withdrawn from social life. Within the present day representative democracy, traditional ideals of rational government with universal suffrage and public management, as once formulated by Auguste Comte, lead just as well to an exceptionally high level of abstraction. Administrative techniques such as good governance, evidence-based policy and monitoring, including election polls, reduce the colourful social range of political and religious beliefs, of tensions, energies and affinities to a measurable whole of quantitative relations. This sterilized version of the social as a political majority, reduces a population to a 'voting mob' which, like consumers, must be persuaded to vote once every so many years. Citizens become customers, active participants become consumers of often privatized 'public' services. However, such a majority or consumer democracy denies the fact that the current social reality is of a completely different nature. It only consists, after all, of cultural, ethnical, and religious minorities and a 'minority is no longer the "small element" (that should resign itself to what the "large element" wants): it has become one of the many broken expressions of the social whole' (Rosanvallon 2012, p. 130). The negation of a radical pluriform social reality leads to political sovereignty becoming more and more detached from social sovereignty, says Rosanvallon. This is why the democratic ambition to close the gap between politicians and the people, between the representatives and the represented, is more and more easily exposed as a myth: there we have the traumatic experience of representative democracy. As with any trauma, the impossibility of bridging the gap with the citizen leads to the suppression of what causes it, which in this case is 'social reality'. The aesthetics of abstraction based on majority calculations and technocratic policy instruments attempts to solve reasonable social claims by rational calculation. But, as we know from psychoanalysis, suppression of trauma can come back to haunt reality like a boomerang. Perhaps that is what is happening today: social life reclaims its right to exist and to be recognized. All social eruptions are evidence of a hunger for expression, a thirst for concrete assigning of meaning and sense and therefore of cultural recognition (Gielen and Lijster 2015). This concerns a form of recognition that has been rationalized away by every audit, troika or budget of the last decade. According to Rosanvallon, in politics this leads to a counter democracy of civil activities, a vitalistic murmuring and commotion of an empowered multitude that is increasingly aware of the fact that its social well-being and quality of life do not coincide with the sterility of a majority, or a balanced budget.

Within the current speculation economy hyper abstraction evokes its own countermovement: an insatiable thirst and hunger for a real economy and, especially, concrete prosperity. In other words, an economy that serves the well-being of the entire social fabric, an economy that posits the all but forgotten other revolutionary ideals of equality and fraternity (or solidarity) against the liberal ideal of liberty. In short, it concerns a longing for an economy that serves social reality again. This generates a leaning towards a politics that resumes control of the economy in order to subject it to social reality. The currently booming debates, conferences, and studies about the commons and commoning can be interpreted as the expression of a desire for a future that is more socially equal. Like all ideologies, this one also looks towards an ideal based on claims about something that in fact already exists: people *are* already social, it's just that this social reality has been pretty much suppressed over the last few decades. Reality is now resurfacing, claiming its right to exist. In any case, the neoliberal suppression and abstraction of the social stimulate a growing longing for that social life, thereby constituting the breeding ground for a new ideology: commonism.

Common Aesthetics: Assemblage
Compared to the smooth and monochromic, marble aesthetics of neoliberalism and virtual capital, commonism at first sight seems to be giving birth to a particularly ungainly child. What it presents is truly a monster, reconciling everything that is in fact irreconcilable. Those who immerse themselves in social life for the first time indeed tend to miss the simplicity of numbers, the helicopter view of statistics, and the abstract beauty of sound mathematical proof. In addition, the working, stressed-out bodies that populate the social domain produce a bouquet of sometimes poignant odours. The financial economy can only maintain its clean pure form by keeping bodies and polluting practices at a safe distance. In the commons, however, economy and labour are reunited, as things are reunited with people, people with animals, culture with

nature, the young with the old, including colours and shapes that frequently clash. People sometimes engage in verbal fights, only to embrace each other intimately at other times. Perhaps the best analogy for commoning is forbidden love. One time lovers will embrace and then again reject each other, only to meet again later, filled with even more desire. Liberalism and neoliberalism have attempted to abstract and manage this social fickleness as well by banishing our love life to the private domain of the nuclear family. Or, as Thatcher continued in her notorious interview in *Women's Own* of 1987: 'There are only individual men and women and there are families.'

The traditional bourgeois family is indeed the only social unit that neoliberalism can handle, as it remains relatively manageable in the private sphere. However, with love being banished to private life, the entire social reproduction and care work—indispensable for economic production—was pushed outside the economic order by this patriarchal structure. Embracing the bourgeois family not only confines social reproduction to a monogamous contractual relationship, but this social model turns out to be also economically and ecologically suffocating nowadays. The *oikos* of the nuclear family has proven to be cost-inefficient and households with one or two cars constitute a too heavy burden on the environment nowadays. The point is that the limited social life tolerated by neoliberalism produces quite a narrow form of living. Therefore the more differentiated commonal love is not only stretching the limits of the living room because of emotional and social reasons, but also because of economic and ecological ones. The procreative love of the birds and the bees is exchanged for that of love for the sake of love of wasps and orchids, to paraphrase another book by Hardt and Negri (*Commonwealth*, 2009). Pulling and pushing and again pulling and pushing determine the social dynamics of the commons. The kinetic movements of the swarm determine friction and energy here. Collaboration in dissent doesn't make for a very joyous working or living environment. Or, rather, sometimes there is the intense joy of conviviality and solidarity and at other times an ugly hostile atmosphere. One thing is certain: unlike the cool abstraction of the finance economy, the endless movements of push and pull guarantee a pleasant warmth, even though things may become overheated at times. Whether it is intense love or heated debate, both provide commonal life with high temperatures. Let us therefore by no means romanticize the commons, as we once did with communities and community art. Commonism is a quest for new forms of living together and such changes rarely take place without fits and starts. Passion and suffering—like that of the growing precariat—go hand in hand, making the collective enterprise somewhat tragicomical. There is a lot of laughter in the commons, but also a lot of shouting, screaming, and... sweating.

However, let's not get ahead of ourselves. The suppression of social life by the abstracting finance economy may perhaps result in an eruption by that same social longing, but recent history teaches us that the growing longing for a social life does not automatically end in commonism. Religions, fundamentalisms, and neonationalisms, including some populisms and all kinds of neoconservative movements capitalize just as well on the social poverty created by late capitalism. In addition, there are perfidious political forces hedging their bets by casually combining a conservative 'edifying' nationalism with an underlying neoliberal agenda (Gielen 2015). While undermining the social fabric and the welfare state via the latter, via the former they promise more 'we'-feeling and to build a Big Society in David Cameron style. Such promises turn out to be paying great lip service to socially deprived segments of the population, but in fact they provide no structural measures that really strengthen the social fabric. The rhetoric of social norms and values remains stuck in a symbolic order, just as in the art world of today there is much debate about radical politics and the commons without anybody putting their money where their mouth is. It's all very fine to read from Marx at the Venice Biennial, and the documenta in Athens may well base itself on social and political themes, but in the end they continue to operate within the frameworks of the art market and the creative industry and only contribute to the aestheticization of the political. For Walter Benjamin (1936) this signalled fascism, today it is perhaps the ultimate legitimization of neoliberalism and neocolonialism. In both the art world and in politics, this rhetoric remains nothing more than well-marketed PR. Those who give their vote to such symbolic politics because of social expectations will be sorely disappointed, because the structural changes that are effectively brought about by neoconservative and neonationalist groups tend to follow neoliberal principles that pass off social responsibilities to the individual, to the 'active citizen', and to an army of volunteers. These are by now well-known political strategies that apparently work quite well, as they win votes in the elections. The question is, however, how long this success will continue in view of the festering social deprivation within such administrations and forms of organization. Just like individualization and heightened competitiveness are being promoted, and artists are still exploited within the prevailing artistic system, the neocons are promoting social change in that direction as well. And, as has meanwhile been established, neoliberal policy often enforces this by authoritarian and repressive means (Wacquant 2009). By doing so the foreseen backfiring effect can probably still be postponed for a while. After all, traumas can lie dormant in the social subconscious for a very long time. Still, the symptoms of increasing social isolation and hyper-individual competition can hardly be suppressed any longer: burnout, depression, suicide, but also discrimination, xenophobia, and racism, sometimes leading to violent eruptions in cities and suburbs. The demolition of the welfare state takes its toll and for that neither neonationalism nor neoliberalism offer structural solutions. The only thing they have come up so far is a strong, indeed authoritarian state with more prisons, more surveillance cameras, and more police in the streets. But even the repressive approach turns out to be increasingly cost-inefficient—even perhaps more expensive than maintaining a welfare state. And so political solutions to social problems threaten to also cut into the economic agenda of these conservative formations in the long run. Not only social, but also political and economic relations will have to be rethought fundamentally in order to break the circle of the snake biting its own tail. Which brings us back to the hypothesis of commonism.

The Commonist Monster

As the previous subheading suggests, assemblage is commonism's trope. Organizing and managing the commons requires a heterogeneous mix of practices fusing economics, politics, ecology, and social care and love. It is a mix that frequently turns the commons into a heterotopian environment where conflicting interests intersect. Divergent social strata and currents clash here, but all the same they have their gaze fixed on the same horizon, one where society is organized in such a way that equality and solidarity are balanced with liberty. Commoning sounds a bit like the noise rock of the band Sonic Youth. Melodic and dissonant sounds alternate against pumping rhythms. Everyone feels the energy, the will to move together, but the ominous sound also predicts violent clashes. Social change is an uphill struggle and can sometimes hurt, but it is especially in this heterotopian setting that social life is again experienced personally. One is immersed in it, as it were. And perhaps this also provides a sound foundation for commonism. Commoning practices start from the need to fundamentally change social life. Organizations of the commons are often born from crisis and real needs. As we know, the massive gatherings and assemblies in Syntagma Square in Athens in 2011 signalled the start of many alternative forms of organization, from solidarity bakeries and ditto farms and schools to free accessible medical centres (Varvarousis and Kallis 2017). The failure of the market and the state does indeed occasion a revival of the commons. The point is that such movements do not limit themselves to protest actions and occupations aimed against an existing political and economic order, but simultaneously present tangible alternatives. And in this self-organization new social relations are experimented with. Precisely through the real experience of and becoming habituated to alternative social life styles, more sustainable changes become possible. There is a lesson here for artists striving for real change. They cannot afford to limit their activities to the artistic and discursive domain. They can only hold on to their autonomy if they address the organization of the art world itself. Here too, only alternative self-organization of all social communication can generate sustainable change.

The patchwork of initiatives that resulted from the Syntagma occupation is still intact after more than five years and is still open to new initiatives and commoners, such as, recently, refugees and illegal migrants. Because of a hands-on attitude, many initiatives develop only slowly, by much trial and error and, typical of the assembly method, accompanied by lengthy discussions. At the same time, such pragmatism leads to fundamentally rearticulating and reorganizing the social fabric. This is perhaps a notable difference with most protest movements from the 1960s, but also with tea party actions from the 2000s, and even with traditional labour union actions. Such protests are usually limited to political actions demanding reforms within existing political and economic conditions. The communes in the 1960s may have been experimenting with new forms of living together, but they originated much more from ideological or spiritual beliefs then from practical necessity. Protests from conservative and neonationalist quarters in turn fall back on traditional lifestyles such as the family and the myth of 'our people'. The demands of labour unions, finally, such as wage increases, more days off, and reduction of working hours often remain reformist and purely economic. They may improve existing labour relations but at the same time they often affirm them.

Commons organizations may differ from the aforementioned protest movements in at least two ways: (1) their actions are not just inspired by an—often discursive— ideology but are pre-figurative in nature, meaning that they set up and test a future ideal of effective self-organization in the present (Van de Sande 2017, p. 25); and (2) their actions are not strictly limited to the domain of labour. On the contrary, initiatives may start from practical needs that concern social life in its entirety. In other words, commonism is a practice-based ideology. It differs from traditional unions by radically transcending the domain of the economy. In commonism the labour movement expands to a social movement or a highly colourful civil parade with a much more varied list of demands (Gielen 2017). During actions and within organizations not only working conditions are the topic but all living conditions, which means that traditional class struggle is combined with other issues, including gender issues and ecological, postcolonial, and transcultural debates.

In commonism all of social life manifests itself, in all its complexity. Perhaps this is why it has the potential of a meta-ideology. Just like the message of liberty of neoliberalism appeals to both left and right across party lines, so commonism's call for more equality and solidarity today appeals not only to the working class but also to an endangered middle-class, the proletariat and the precariat, people with and without jobs, students and pensioners, women and men, heterosexuals and holebis, legal and illegal aliens. Also, both progressive and conservative forces now regard social deprivation as problematic. Liberal and conservative parties alike hold debates about the commons these days, while not only the precariat but some billionaires as well advocate commonal principles such as a basic income. In short, the idea of the commons is being claimed and defended from the most divergent sections of society. Precisely in this aspect lurks the potential of a meta-ideology, but also that of a monstrous figure. The claims and projections of many contradictory forces can make commonism look like either a ravishing assemblage or one that is ugly as hell.

This concerns social forms that perhaps we may dream of today, but whose final realization we may not wish to face.

If the commons consists of material and immaterial sources that we may use under certain conditions and whose exchange value is diminished as far as possible in favour of the use value; and if commoning is the inclusive open source movement in which a maximum number of users have access to resources that can be reclaimed from the market and the state or that we protect from their control and exploitation through democratic self-rule—then we are faced with one huge issue: *social control*. The system of the commons is made or broken by how access is regulated and sanctioned, how free-riders and other abuses such as recapitalization are detected and corrected (Ostrom 1990). No matter how horizontal and democratic this system of social sanctioning may turn out to be, when the state and the market are no longer there all that is left are commoners who can and may sanction other commoners. Whether these are positive or negative sanctions, we know from historic experience of systems of social control that they can develop quite restrictive forms, and especially since the commons concerns every aspect of our being, such control may take biopolitical and claustrophobic forms. It is fair to say that this is the Achilles heel of commonism. In any case this aspect of social control is something that quite a few commoners and theorists of the commons are skilfully avoiding (Hardt and Negri, for instance), or repressing or sometimes even glossing over. But it is exactly the social aspect that makes commonism an ideology like any other, with both utopian and dystopian perspectives.

References

— Benjamin, Walter. 1936 (2005). *The Work of Art in the Age of Mechanical Reproduction*. New York: Schocken/Random House.

— Berardi, Franco 'Bifo'. 2017. 'Insolvency/Autonomy: What is the Meaning of Autonomy in the Semiocapitalist Age?' In: *Perspectives on Commoning: Autonomist Principles and Practices*. Edited by Guido Ruivenkamp and Andy Hilton, pp. 153-168. London: Zero Books.

— Durkheim, Émile. 1912 (1985). *Les Formes élémentaires de la vie religieuse: Le système totémique en Australie*. Paris: Quandrige Presses Universitaires de France.

— Gielen, Pascal. 2015. *The Murmuring of the Artistic Multitude: Global Art, Politics and Post-Fordism*. Amsterdam: Valiz.
—. 2017. 'The Global Civil Parade.' In *How To Gather. Acting Relations, Mapping Positions*. Edited by Bart De Baere et al., pp. 405-417. Moscow: V-A-C.
—, and Thijs Lijster. 2015. 'Culture: The Substructure of a European Common.' In *No Culture, No Europe: On the Foundation of Politics*. Edited by Pascal Gielen, pp. 19-65. Amsterdam: Valiz.

— Hardt, Michael, and Antonio Negri. 2009. *Commonwealth*. Cambridge, MA: Harvard University Press.
—. 2017. *Assembly*. Oxford: Oxford University Press.

— Marx, Karl. 1867 (1984). *Capital: Volume I, II & III*. London: Lawrence & Wishart.

— Ostrom, Elinor. 1990. *Governing the Commons: The Evolution of Institutions for Collective Action*. Cambridge, MA: Cambridge University Press.

— Rosanvallon, Pierre. 2012. *Democratie en tegendemocratie*. Amsterdam: Boom.

— Sande, Mathijs van de. 2017. 'The Prefigurative Power of the Common(s).' In *Perspectives on Commoning: Autonomist Principles and Practices*. Edited by Guido Ruivenkamp and Andy Hilton, pp. 25-63. London: Zero Books.

— Varvarousis, Angelos, and Giorgos Kallis. 2017. 'Commoning Against the Crisis.' In *Another Economy is Possible*. Edited by Manuel Castells, pp. 128-159. Cambridge, MA: Polity Books.

— Wacquant, Loïc. 2009. *Punishing the Poor: The Neoliberal Government of Social Insecurity*. Durham, NC: Duke University Press.

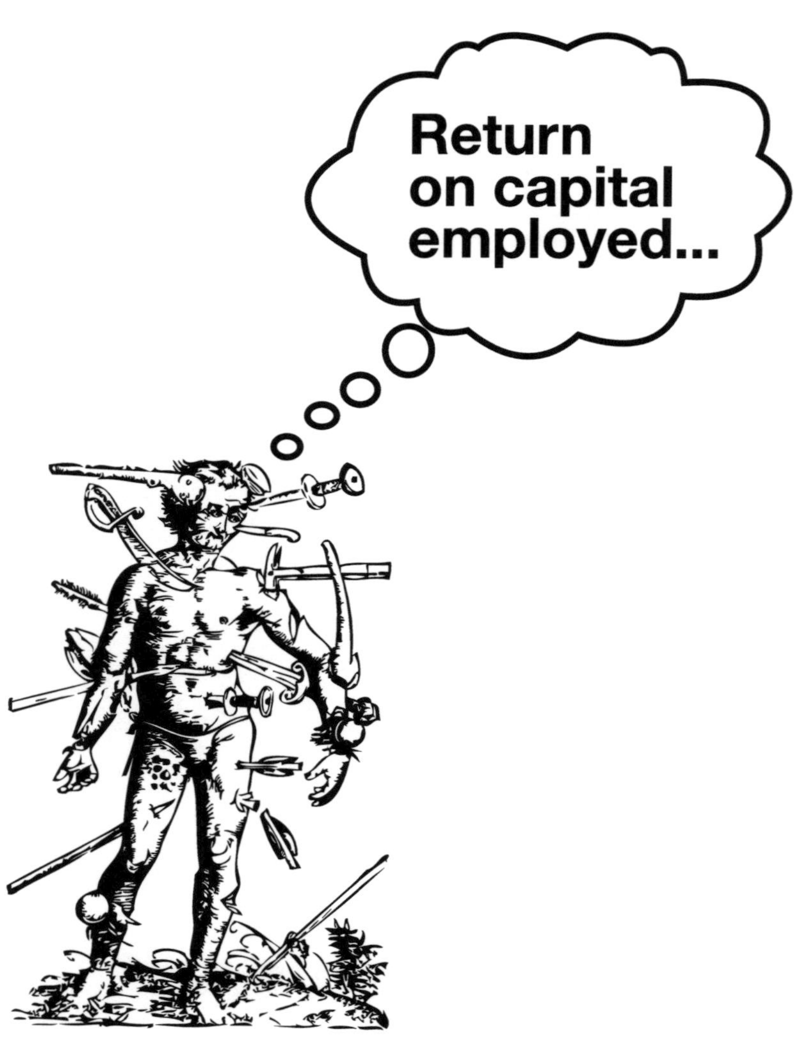

Shuttered, 2013

mmm... money pie

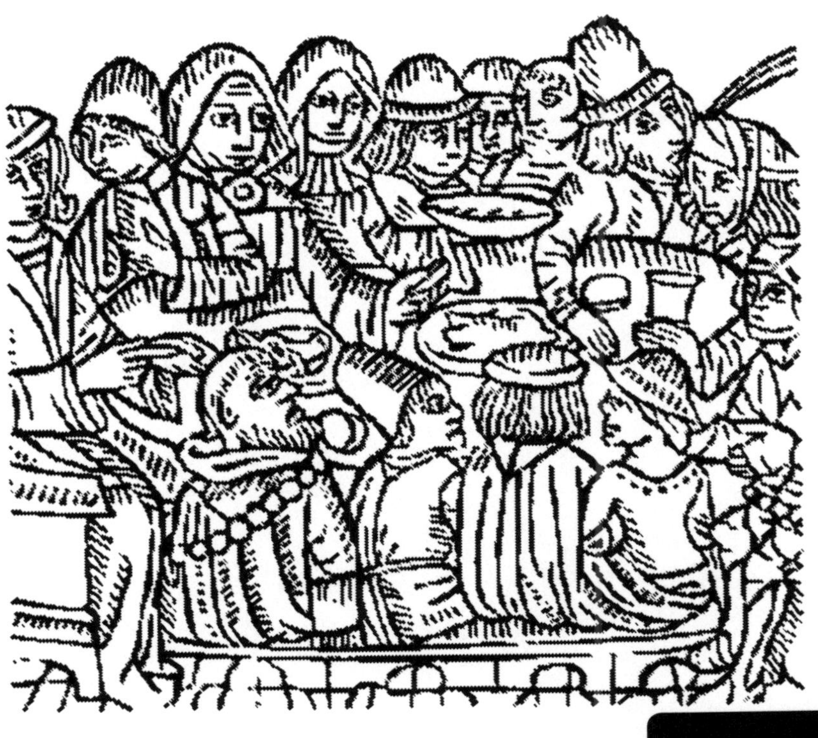

Money Pie, De Appel, 2009

The Salt of the Earth

On Commonism
An Interview
with Antonio Negri

Pascal Gielen &
Sonja Lavaert

With *Assembly* (2017), Michael Hardt and Antonio Negri have continued their trilogy *Empire* (2000), *Multitude* (2004), and *Commonwealth* (2009) into the new decade, in the process expending it to a tetralogy. In this fourth episode of their cycle, these advocates of commonism once again provide a critical analysis of the most topical developments in society. Their central issue this time is why the social movements that express the demands and wishes of so many and show that the common is a fact, have not succeeded in bringing about a new, truly democratic and just society. The question itself is already controversial, as are many of the propositions and concepts launched by the authors in *Assembly*. According to them we must confront the problem of leadership and institutions, dare to imagine the entrepreneurship of the multitude, appropriate old terms and, especially, reverse their meaning. We meet with Antonio Negri in his apartment in Paris, to try out this recipe of reversal and to discuss strategy and tactics, ideology and aesthetics, art and language.

Pascal Gielen & Sonja Lavaert – Our book *Commonism* is about the triangle of ideology, aesthetics, and the commons. Our tentative assumption is that commonism may be the next meta-ideology, after neoliberalism. We understand *ideology* not only negatively as a false awareness, but also positively as a logic of faith that connects fiction and reality and can make people long for and work towards a better form of living together. In *Assembly* you and Michael Hardt do something similar with notions such as 'entrepreneurship', 'institution', 'leadership'. What does 'ideology' mean to you and do you think it may also figure in a positive narrative?

Antonio Negri – In my experience, ideology tends to have mostly negative connotations, or, rather, I have regarded 'ideology' mainly in negative terms. This means though that we are speaking of something that is real. Ideology is a real fact. In addition, it is something real that embodies, shapes, and constitutes reality. What I see as positive in this embodiment of reality is critique—which can be critique of the ideology or of reality—and the dispositive, understood as the transition of the world of thinking to that of reality. In my view, ideologies make up reality, but I use the term preferably when discussing its negative aspect, whereas when I speak of its positive aspect, i.e. the critique or the dispositive, I prefer these latter words.

The ideological dimension is absolutely crucial when thinking about reality and in trying to analyze and understand it, but, again, it can be both positive and negative. Gramsci, for example, saw it this way. The ideological dimension is an essential part of any analysis of reality, but a discourse on ideology is therefore always both positive and negative. On the one hand there is the bourgeois ideology (which Gramsci opposed, as do we) and on the other hand there is the communist ideology (which we support). Today, I think it is better to call the communist ideology a 'critique' or 'dispositive'; 'critique' as in taking place in the realm of knowledge and understanding, and 'dispositive' in the Foucaultian sense of the transition of knowledge into action.

And well, there is the matter of meta-ideology... Again, I agree with your view that ideology, being something that belongs to the realm of knowledge and understanding, in a sense branches out into reality, feeding and shaping it, and that therefore ideology is always and everywhere present in concrete reality. However, I would be very reluctant to speak in terms of 'meta', 'post', or 'after', as if it were something transcendent or as if there is such a thing as a space of transcendence at all.

PG & SL – When we speak of meta-ideology, we refer to the tendency of transcending the traditional party political differences between left and right. It is a trend that can be seen clearly today, wherever the theme of the common is picked up or where common-initiatives are being developed. And elsewhere as well: liberal politicians write books about the importance of the basic income; neonationalism presents itself as a longing for social cohesion; religiously inspired political parties emphasize communion and the community, et cetera.

AN – Common is not the exclusive property of the left, that much is clear. Looking at history from a Marxist perspective, we see how it was precisely the commons that were transformed by capitalism to be financially profitable. Capitalism's attitude towards the commons is about expropriation, exploration, creating surplus value, and the dominion that is founded on these things. The common exists in two major forms: there are natural commons and social commons and, as Michael and I put forth in *Assembly*, these can be subdivided into five types: the earth and ecosystems; the immaterial common of ideas, codes, images, and cultural products; material goods produced by cooperative labour; metropolises and rural areas that are the domain of communication, cultural interaction, and cooperation; and social institutions and services that provide housing, welfare, healthcare and education. Now the essential characteristic of the present-day economy and society is that the social production of the commons is being exploited by capital. The struggle of the commons therefore is working people re-appropriating that of which they were robbed by capital. Re-appropriating what was taken from them and putting it to work for the benefit of the common: that is the meaning of liberation and emancipation. This also means that the fiction of 'post' or 'meta' is debunked and eliminated. There is no meta. The struggle of the commons is the possibility of eliminating an 'outside' (meta [above], post [after]). This struggle is exclusively fought in the domain of immanence, meaning: here and now, at the heart of the reality in which we find ourselves, because there is no 'outside'. By the way, we can only speak in the abstract about common as a general unitary, singular, and exactly definable concept, because in reality the common is always twofold, just like labour is.

There is much talk about 'common' nowadays; studies are undertaken, and various movements and schools of thought have emerged around the theme. Here in France, for example, there is the school of the economist Benjamin Coriat, editor of *Le retour des communs* (2015); we have Pierre Dardot and Christian Laval, who posit the common as a demand and alternative in their *Commun* (2014), and Carlo Vercellone and other comrades—and Michael and myself are two of them—who regard the common as something that can be used ontologically, can be annexed, and for whom the struggle therefore consists of reappropriating the common. This also ties in with David Harvey's reading of Marx. In *Assembly* we concern ourselves in great detail with his analysis and for the most part we agree with him. However, whereas Harvey focuses on capitalism as a continuous primitive accumulation, we see it as a developmental phase and therefore prefer to speak of formal and real subsumption, but this perhaps is a different theme.

What I'm trying to say is: my distrust of the term 'meta' is that it suggests that there is no difference or antithesis anymore between left and right. Well, of course left and right are inaccurate concepts, but to put it more plainly: it means that capitalism is no longer recognized and that being liberated of capitalism is regarded as something that could easily happen or would even be a battle that is already won.

PG & SL – To give a concrete example of how we use the term 'meta': the occupation of Syntagma Square in Athens in 2011 was predominantly organized by the left, but people from quite different ideological backgrounds are also joining the movement and are developing new initiatives, out of necessity, for their daily survival. For that reason, this movement—which is really more of a patchwork of initiatives—is sometimes 'accused' of being apolitical. In that sense we call commonism a practice-based ideology and we call it 'meta' because it brings together people from various, traditionally opposed political currents, and does so out of necessity.

AN – I fully agree with that conclusion and analysis, but I would still be wary of using such an ambiguous term. The word 'meta' covers a political concern aimed at reconciliation with regard to the profound rift between—to put it bluntly—the bosses and those who are exploited.

PG & SL – What do you think of the fact that liberal or neoliberal parties organize conferences about the commons as apparently they think it is important, without necessarily wanting to capitalize it but, as things look now anyway, because they are genuinely interested or find something lacking in their liberal system.

AN – It is obvious that we are facing enormous problems nowadays. We see a general transformation of the system of production as it is being automated and robotized. These are things that we thematized and analyzed in our *operaismo* movement, some forty years or longer ago. In the first issue of *Potere Operaio*, in 1969, we demanded the 'civil income' (*reddito di cittadinanza*) and this was because we already foresaw this process in which labour would be reduced to a completely secondary element. The question is how to respond to this revolution and reality and as far as that is concerned I see an urgent need to create spaces for developing initiatives outside of capitalism.

There are a number of interesting initiatives in Belgium: the start-ups, with already 50,000 participants, and Michel Bauwens, the founder of the P2P Foundation. And yes, the commons is a domain that very much interests 'the right'. The same goes for socialdemocrats, by the way. So, the entire problem consists of understanding what the alternative could be, how to respond, what to do, and this is in fact the very theme of autonomy.

PG & SL – In our research and book we speak of *aesthetics* not only in regard to art but also in relation to society. We understand aesthetics as the shaping or design of both material and social things, of people. In your book *Assembly* we detect a similar idea: assembly characterizes the aesthetic style and strategy of the commons. Likewise, in *Commonism*, we oppose the aesthetic figure with the abstraction that we associate with exchange value, finance capitalism, and neoliberalism. What does the ideal assembly look like, in your view? What are the conditions for its realization? How can non-humans (things, nature) be involved in an assembly? What instruments or strategies are needed? In short, how should assembly be practically organized in order to function well, in your view?

AN – We argue that the assembly is already there. It is already there in the structure of the present-day economy in which labour has transformed itself in language and in cooperation that is largely autonomous. The assembly is what we are confronted with. The problem therefore is how these labour forces or subjects/people who produce subjectivity can become political subjects. This is demonstrated by the recognition of the common, by the transition to the common and being together, by the transition of the mere finding of being together to being aware of it. The transition of collaboration and being-in-common to the production of common subjectivity is the central element of the assembly.

The comrades and activists who take part in the fight of the movement, from Occupy Wall Street to the Indignados in Madrid, have attempted to bring about such a transition, especially from the condition of people producing under capitalism and whose situation simply happens to them to a free condition in which the common is built and formed. This transition is fundamental and in addition it demonstrates that commonism is much more feasible today than in the previous situation, in which the workers were organized and brought together by capital. Before, the workers were brought together, they did not come together of their own initiative. This is no longer the case and precisely this means an enormous boost for the possibilities. The possibility for liberation is infinitely larger and wider today, because there is this being-together, an ontological fact that is also a point of departure.

The assembly is an ontological fact that must become political, that is the heart of the matter.

Marx has said of the working classes that they were made by capital and that therefore it was necessary for them to become aware of their situation through a political party, an external organization, an ideology, et cetera, in order to become political. Today we see a maturity and an original organization, so to speak, thanks to the transformation that occurred in labour and society. Labour today is no longer a labour under command. The aspect of the command is becoming increasingly alienated from the possibility to work together subjectively. What is important, is that the language that is formed by the worker comes before the command, precedes it. The importance of neoliberalism, by the way, is that it understood that this autonomous use of language can be reversed and can be made use of by capital. This is why the most important political work of today is to recognize this subjective and special use of language and to reverse again what capitalism and neoliberalism have reversed, and to bring about the liberation.

PG & SL – We are still not quite convinced, in the sense that we miss a concrete definition of what assembly exactly is. Looking at this as sociologists, we look at examples of assemblies such as the Ex Asilo Filangieri in Naples, and we think: assembly is a tool, a meeting method, a more democratic way of organizing things, of taking autonomous decisions, of achieving self-governance. Can we say that assembly is a formula for organizing direct democracy?

AN – What Michael and I have in mind is exactly the type of phenomenon like l'Asilo in Naples, where sovereignty has been reversed: to the common, to a space and a series of shared goods (*beni communi*) in the widest sense, both material and immaterial goods. In other words, where a series of remarkable initiatives is undertaken for the common good. The concept of common is always a production, something that is invented, made, shaped. The assembly is this: a body of people, a small multitude that manages well the shared (material and immaterial) goods and thereby constitutes a common. The fundamental concept of assembly is that the political and social are again joined and today we have a chance, an opportunity to do this. Unlike Lenin, we no longer find ourselves in exceptional conditions like it was with the Russian Revolution when there was only hunger, war, and catastrophe and everything had to be torn down in order to create a new force. Now, today, we have the opportunity to transform the assembly into a force. Because that is politics: lending force. Or, that is aesthetics, if one wishes to use that term: lending form and force. There is no form without force. Politics is force, power, and that includes the aspect of violence. In politics it is about the force (the power, sometimes violence) to construct peace.

PG & SL – What we see in the practical functioning of assembly, for example, is that the practice of language becomes very important. After all, people have to speak to each other and try to convince others through dialogue.

Now this mechanism has two problems: 1) those who speak more and better have an advantage in winning the debate, and 2) there is a class phenomenon. In the situation of an assembly the middle class becomes dominant: those who are white, educated, and can speak well have the floor. So there is an element of selection. My question to you is: how can the assembly be organized in such a way that there is no such selection or that this shortcoming is compensated for by letting basis-democratic principles prevail? How does one give a voice to those who remain silent?

AN – We are of course discussing examples and I think that especially in Naples, if one looks at the periphery, in the surrounding region, in all those places where the *case del popolo* are strong and many initiatives are taken by the people, one definitely sees a direct proletarian use of language, and in quite dominant forms. And of course there are also initiatives such as l'Asilo that already have quite a tradition, that have statutes and a legal structure. And yes, in those cases a certain political class is involved. However, I think that the assembly is both cause and product of a break with class distinction. The obvious objection one could have against these assembly initiatives is of course that not everything has been properly defined. We are after all speaking of a process that is not free of contradictions and downfall, but it is an extremely important process and it has begun.

The problem is that we have to develop a different model than that of parliamentary democracy, or, rather, we need a post-parliamentarian model of democracy.

PG & SL – What do you think of the fact that in Naples a commissioner for the commons (*assessore dei beni communi*) has been appointed? We ask this specifically with regard to your rejection of state institutions.

AN – We cannot have this discussion with Naples as an example. The situation there is quite ambiguous. What is happening there now was achieved with great effort after an immense political crisis: the PD (Democratic Party) in Naples is divided into four or five factions, the 5 Stelle movement is weak, and there is this incredible Mayor Luigi de Magistris, a former magistrate-very straight and tough—who is open to what according to him might constitute the majority. So all this makes Naples a rather unique case, a confluence of events. There are so many contingent factors playing a part there. The first concern of the comrades who occupied buildings was therefore to obtain a guarantee, an anchoring in the institutions.

But to return to our point, the institutions are indeed a major problem, but we should not concern ourselves with the case of Naples as it is very much a separate case.

PG & SL – In *Assembly* you regard the new leadership of the commons as a possible strategy of the multitude and as a tactic of the *leader*. The leader can only temporarily—and depending on her or his expertise—make certain tactical moves in the general strategy of the multitude. How can this be organized and in how much is your reversal of attribution of the strategy (to the multitude) and of tactics (to the leader) different from a representative democracy where leaders are also only appointed temporarily?

AN – I think that we are faced with the problem of removing or eroding the political relationship between movement and leader. What is at stake is decision authority. What exactly was the formula of political parties? A party gathered a great number of people along a certain political line that was decided upon by the top, by the leader, and which was literally imposed on or taught to the people in a top-down fashion. In our work, Michael and I take the critique by movements as our starting point, because these movements reject the existing institutions. Today, we have to reject leadership but not necessarily institutions as such. So we are now faced with the problem of the institutions and we have to solve this, we have to face this, and study it together. Or, in other words: we have to bring back the leadership to the movement and it is within the movement that the hegemonial strategy of leadership must be developed. We have to take the decision authority away from the leader, or rather, take the abstraction and transcendence of the decision away from the leader.

PG & SL – But how does one choose the leader, and how do the commons differ from representative democracy?

AN – The problem is not how to choose, as this can be done in any number of ways. The problem is that of the power that is given to the leader. Often though, the leader will spontaneously emerge from the multitude.

The power of the leader must be limited to the tactical level and this usually means the power to make proposals.

Anyone who has been active within the movement knows the phenomenon of the leader who spontaneously comes forward. It has to do with the actual needs and problems the movement faces and into which the leader has more insight than anyone else. One often sees how a leader's power is acknowledged at some point and then begins, works out well, and thus becomes a reality.

Let me give an example. During the 1917 revolution, Lenin succeeded in becoming the tactical leader because he could instantly, in a very direct manner, provide answers to two problems that presented itself at the time: peace now, and land to the farm labourers. However, on the other hand, the powers representing the military and the farmers were convinced that neither the soldiers nor the farm labourers were ready for these changes and so they didn't undertake any action. It was a paradox: the leader, Lenin, saying No to the ruling institutions because he understood what the soldiers and the farm labourers needed. This is a tactic that becomes power and force (*forza*).

The leader is always temporary, tactical. He steps forward in a struggle of the people/subjects who have demands and needs.

PG & SL – But then how does the leader know what those needs are? Simply because he stems from the people?

AN – Quite so. He knows what is needed because he is part of it, because he is in the middle of it, but, again, this is a paradox. According to the official history books Lenin was a demagogue who played games with the people, but I know that the reverse is true: the revolution succeeded because Lenin understood that these were the real needs and because he immediately articulated an answer to them, without all the compromises, crippling detours and institutions as created by the parliamentary system. Those real needs to which he provided an answer were peace now, immediately, and giving the land to those who worked the land, without any compromise.

The same is true for many leaders. Churchill, for example, took a direct decision to fight against the Germans in World War II. This is the point: the leader who immediately and directly coincides with the needs and wants of the many/the common.

PG & SL - In *Assembly* you defend the hypothesis that the institutions or the leader don't need a centralized rule but that they can be realized by a multitude in a democratic manner. The examples you provide for the future of the movements are in line with this hypothesis: for example Black Lives Matter. But isn't this notion and aren't these examples at odds with or even contrary to your criticism of the 'horizontal leader-lessness'?

AN - Well, many movements are leaderless, but that is not the issue. What is problematic, or what these movements need, is: institutions. What we are trying to say is not so much that movements need leaders—as, again, they should take charge of leadership themselves—but that they do need institutions. It is a mistake for these movements not to have an institution, to not adopt an institutional frame-work. However, Michael and I are convinced that within the movements there is a tendency to do this, to form insti-tutions—these are not anarchist groups—and thereby real-ize this horizontal hegemony. Our work is about searching for a type of institution that is not sovereign and is not connected to ownership. How this works out in practice, well, that is exactly what we need to discuss, think about, try out...

PG & SL - This leads up nicely to our next question. You advocate complementarity of the three political strate-gies: pre-figurative politics, antagonistic reformism, and hegemony. Existing institutions are abolished and new, non-sovereign institutions are created. What exactly needs to be abandoned when it comes to existing institutions?

AN – We are currently witnessing the death struggle of the concepts that have dominated political thinking and practice in the 19th and 20th century. The most important of these dying concepts are national sovereignty and property, both private and public. National sovereignty has been beaten by globalized capitalism, but at the same time actual capitalism is founded on those same barely surviving concepts that influence and mutually confirm each other. The concept or principle on which national sovereignty is based, in particular the 'border', has really become absurd. We transcend and cross borders constantly. Our brains are globalized and have no more use for the concept of border, so we need to get rid of it. That is the theoretical work that needs to be done: giving short shrift to moribund principles and concepts such as the border. As abundantly clear as this is for national sovereignty, so it is for ownership, both private and public: ownership is based on the same logic as the border, an obsolete concept that is at odds with reality. Even more so: property and border are one and the same thing.

The concept of the common, by contrast, is not one of ownership. In thinking about this issue it is extremely important to make a distinction between 'common goods' (*beni comuni*), which can be the object of ownership, and 'the common' (*il comune*) as in 'commonwealth', which is a production, something that is formed by the common from within and which consequently cannot be owned.

PG & SL – Is there anything positive you could mention about what these new 'non-sovereign' institutions may look like? How should the three political strategies—pre-figurative politics, antagonistic reformism, hegemony over the institutions—work together exactly? Is there a sequence that these three strategies should follow, or should they be deployed in parallel?

AN – That is a question of the political practice. I simply can't answer that, as it is too hard to do this sitting at a writing desk. It is both impossible and undesirable. I don't see it as part of my work, which is studying, philosophizing, providing general frameworks in a critical manner, studying the foundation of the discourse, questioning the principles and concepts. And then there is the practice of the struggle and it is within the struggle that debate and consultation should take place, among each other, about what should be done. We cannot be expected to predict the future, and it is not our ambition to do so. To me this is one of the core issues: we will have to wait until the future announces itself, breaks out. That takes place in practice, whereas in my work I wish to point out directions, and formulate a critique of the principles of ideas and structures.

PG & SL – In *Assembly* you quote Hegel: 'Everything turns on grasping and expressing the True not only as a Substance, but equally as Subject' (PhS, 10). What exactly is *subjectivity* to you? Does subjectivity take on a different form today and if so, what does it look like?

AN – To Hegel, subjectivity meant synthesis and overcoming. Think of Kojève's interpretation of the master-slave dialectic: the slave overcomes the master in as far as he serves him and at the same time constructs him. Also think of the concept of the proletariat in relation to capitalism in the work of the young Marx: the proletariat forms itself and realizes its project in as far as its becomes a fully integrated part of the bourgeois society. In *Capital* we no longer find this interpretation, and it is also gone from or at least nuanced in our analysis of the reality of workers today. Today, the subjectivity of the worker is that of singularity, of a particularity that is being produced in the construction of the common. This particularity is invention, is immaterial and serves to construct the common, that is, a bringing together of all these things. The (worker's) subjectivity of today is a production of 'being', as it is an innovation and a surplus. It is a practice of freedom and therefore the production of subjectivity is something that transcends any identity. The subject is non-identic, is not an identity (hence the impossibility of providing exact definitions for it). The subject is formed in the collaboration, in being social, and it is something historical.

PG & SL – How do you see the role of *art* and the art world in the organization of assembly? On the one hand we state that the art world today indeed has a role by creating a space for exchange and debate, which is lacking in mainstream media, at exhibitions and during biennales. On the other hand we conclude that it doesn't go any further and that these initiatives remain limited to the domain of the discursive. Also, these initiatives are often used as a PR tool, turning the debate into a commodity. In light of this, what role can the art world—and art itself—play according to you, and can it have a role at all in shaping and strengthening the commons?

AN – As I have tried to clarify in my book *Art and Multitude*, art can always be linked to its mode of production. Art is production. Its dignity is derived from the fact that it is production of 'being', of meaningful images. In other words, of images that shape 'being', that take 'being' out of a hidden condition and transform it into an open and public condition. This always happens during a process of production. This is why there is an analogy between how goods are produced in general in a certain historical context and how art is produced in that same context. In art there is always a 'making' in the sense of constructing something. Art is always a form of building, a bringing together, a productive gesture. When looking at things from this point of view, it becomes clear that it is all about making distinctions within this world. There is beautiful art and there is ugly art, useful art and useless art; likewise there is art that markets itself as a commodity and there is art that is a form of productive artistic making.

Like language, art produces communication, it makes connections. Especially nowadays, art is like the practice of language in constructing connections, becoming event. Art is getting rid of materiality and is increasingly linked to immaterial production. It follows the same trend as the immaterial production and makes connections in fluid, unstable, and new images, in unexpected forms and figures. In this way art affiliates itself with the present-day mode of production and, like this mode of production, it interprets behaviour that is related to special events and passions. We are in a phase of metamorphosis of art, just like we are in phase of the production mode in which labour is completely transforming itself.

With regard to art I would like to underline two things. First, I assume that art is a form of making and working that is therefore completely linked to the production mode of a specific historical situation. Secondly, I assume that art has the capacity to produce 'being'. Of course not all art always produces real 'being'. By this I absolutely do not mean that there is good and bad art; that is not for me to say. But I do think a distinction can be made between art that serves the market and that is produced and circulates within the market, and art that is absolute production, meaning that it produces 'being'.

PG & SL – One year ago, at the Venice Bienniale Marx was read and at the documenta in Athens so much engaged political art was shown that it looked like a 'stage for the revolution' [Dutch national newspaper *NRC Handelsblad* of 12 April 2017]. At the same time, however, these revolutionary platforms stay within the confines of Biennales and documentas, which reminds one of what Walter Benjamin has called the 'aestheticization' of politics, which according to him was also a sign of fascism. Is there a way out of this for art? Can art escape from institutions that maybe do not affirm fascism as such, but certainly neoliberalism, and that turn art into a commodity?

AN – There is always an escape route! Obviously these places must be regarded as battlefields, as places of confrontation and collision, of conflict and rifts. One can always escape that which Biennales and documentas represent, that is, one can and should try to escape their control function—these big art institutions of the state or the market do function as control mechanisms—and artists therefore find themselves in exactly the same condition as the workers.

In my view, the problem with art institutions is this: they are arenas, more specifically arenas of a fight for the truth, of critique of ideology and production, places where the discourse of power is exposed, but they are always also marketplaces. The point is to break out of this cage of control by the state and the market and this has always been part of the development of art as it has manifested itself in many different forms, each time in a different manner. For example, at one time we had patrons of the arts who had the same role as the art institutions of today; it was no different then.

And so we have this whole history of constant artistic resistance against these conditions. I don't think that art has ever been in line with power in any way. The great Italian Renaissance painters and sculptors were not, nor were the painters of the Golden Age in the Lowlands. On the contrary, there have always been breaking points in art that become evident in the artistic production, while these painters and sculptors were nevertheless an integral part of their specific social context. Because of these breaking points one can regard art as a way of unearthing the truth. They qualify art as a mode of truth.

I often talk to friends-comrades who make art and they are becoming increasingly critical of the market. There is a general resistance against the market these days in the actions of those comrades who believe strongest in or empathize with the class struggle; a rejection of the market that is becoming more and more radical. The protest is expressed in this negation, which is quite strong, and it leads to a radical criticism without compromise and without market possibilities.

There is of course also, and quite often, a strong temptation of 'nothing', of not doing/making, or of presenting art works that express a not-doing/not-making.

Anyway, I tend to be cautious with regard to these issues, and I think that in every action—and therefore also in art actions—a material composition is required and therefore a composition with reality as well. What I mean is: one should neither look for purity nor demonize the power/force.

PG & SL - In *Assembly* you emphasize the importance of *language* and communication. You mention the changing

of meaning of words, speaking, translation, and the appropriation of words as important political action. In this
context you posit the idea of entrepreneurship of the multitude. Is this at all possible with a term like 'entrepreneurship', which has been associated with capitalism in all its
guises for over 200 years? Is there not a risk that critique
will wither and distinctions become blurred with such an
act of appropriation?

AN – I don't think so, and frankly I don't understand why
such a polemic arose around specifically this issue as soon
as our book was published. We, Michael and I, have always
recuperated and reused words, and reversed their meaning in our work. For example, 'empire' may be the most
academic and traditional term in the history of political
science. Not that we were the first to do so: the word 'capital' as the title of Marx's three-part book on the critique of
political economy is about as capitalistic as can be. There
is nothing wrong in appropriating words that are part of
the tradition and ethics of the capitalistic bourgeoisie and
assign them a new meaning. On the contrary, this is what
we should do. The problem with regard to this form of language practice is to understand the force of reversal.

As to the semantic series of words such as 'entrepreneurship', 'enterprise', 'entrepreneur' in relation to the common—because we never just speak of 'entrepreneurship'
but about the 'entrepreneurship of the common'— the word
'enterprise' admittedly is rather ambiguous. Enterprise is
something like Christopher Columbus who crossed the
Atlantic Ocean and demonstrated a huge capacity for
invention. So on the one hand the word refers to a heroic,
fantastic project. Columbus engaged in an improbable and
completely new undertaking in the space of his time. On
the other hand, the term 'enterprise' also refers to that with
which it is commonly associated, namely a project aimed
at financial profit and at generating income.

What we try to do in *Assembly* is to appropriate
words that belong to tradition. We see it as our task to gain
words for the common, to recuperate the words. Again, we
do not speak of entrepreneurship *tout court*, but of entrepreneurship of the common. Speaking of the entrepreneurship

of the common has the same potential and power as speaking of refusing to work: it leads to a reappropriation of the common. So the power of this language use lies in this action of reappropriation and in this the reversal is crucial.

PG & SL – In *Assembly* you imply that revolution is ontological and not a contingent event. That revolution is not aimed at seizing power, nor that it brings you to power, but that it changes power, or that it can bring you to power but that it changes the nature of power in doing so. You call upon the multitude to seize power in the sense of Machiavelli at the end of *Il Principe*: a call for a new leader who emerges from the multitude, and to not waste the opportunity. What is essential here is the phrase 'to take power differently', by which you mean, with Spinoza, that the 'common' or 'freedom, equality, democracy, and wealth' are guaranteed. 'Differently' here does not mean repeating the hypocrisy of freedom (without equality) as a concept of the Right, nor that of equality (without freedom) as a proposal by the Left. The formulation therefore is inspired by Spinoza to whom the 'common' was the basic idea that can also be summarized as: there is no freedom without equality and there is no equality without freedom. Common is an ontological and logical category that assumes and unites an internally contrasting multitude of singularities. Our question is twofold. Why speak of 'commonism' instead of simply calling it 'communism'? And where is *solidarity* in all this?

AN – Why we don't call it 'communism'? Perhaps because that word has been all too much abused in our recent history. In Italy, in the 1970s, there was a group of situationists who called it 'commontismo' (rather a sympathetic lot, these situationists, but it all ended very badly: they turned out to be activist robbers, went to prison or became drug addicts; it all ended tragically).

I have no doubt that one day we will call the political pro-ject of the common 'communism' again. But it's up to the people to call it that, not up to us.

Where is solidarity in our discourse? In everything we say there is solidarity because solidarity is in the principles of our discourse. To say it in Aristotelian terms, there is solidarity as in three of the four types of causes: as material cause in the rejection of loneliness, as efficient cause in the collaboration to produce, and as final cause in love. In other words, everything that we propose, our entire theoretical building, has its material, efficient and final cause in solidarity. The 'commontism' is drenched in solidarity. One cannot live alone, in loneliness, one cannot produce alone, and one cannot love alone.

Our proposals cannot be read in any other way but as proposals of solidarity, or how to escape from loneliness. We have to escape from loneliness in order to define a solidary, close community, as we cannot survive alone in a barren desert. We must escape from loneliness in order to produce, because alone we would never have the means or the time. We must escape from loneliness in order to love, because on your own and without someone else there can be no love. This is the only way to understand this radical transition of/ to the common, a transition that we are evolving towards, by the way. There is truly a developing tendency towards solidarity and towards an escape from loneliness.

We live in times of great crisis and terrible emptiness but at the same time these are also times of great expectations. We are facing a void between that which is finished and that which still has to begin. Especially in talking to young people one becomes aware of this terrible loneliness, but also of this great longing. The desert caused by neoliberal capitalism is insufferable in every regard.

PG & SL – Our next question is about that. As in your previous writings, in *Assembly* you start from the optimistic thought that the Occupy movements demonstrate a rebellion of the multitude, that the 'possible is a given', that the 'common is a given'. But in *Assembly* you also pose the question, perhaps for the first time, why the revolution of the Occupy movements failed. Does this indicate a turn in your work, a turn away from the earlier *optimism*? And what does this mean for the idea of revolution?

AN – There is no turn from optimism to pessimism in our work. What we attempted to do is to understand the problem in a realistic manner and to think about possible solutions. The problem as we see it is that of the limits and limitations of movements, both of Occupy and other movements we have seen over the past decade. The most important limitation, in our analysis, is that these movements have not been willing or not been able to translate themselves into institutions and that where they did attempt to do so and in those cases where they actually formed institutions, it all ended in a betrayal of the movement. We see this for example in a part of the Indignados that founded Podemos, who eventually betrayed the situation from which they departed. Having followed all the debates from close up, my opinion of Podemos is negative. They have not succeeded in maintaining the reversal of the relation between strategy and decision or between tactic and strategy, leaving only the tactic.

So it is not about being more or less optimistic, but about grasping the problem in a realistic manner and about thinking of ways to solve the problem and this is what we try to do in our work. We try to see the limits and limitations of the political common-movement. Our conclusion is that power should be seized, but that in and with that operation power should be changed. Therefore, as you quote and as we expressed it in *Assembly*, it is all about 'to take the power differently' and then maintain this radical transition/reversal.

PG & SL – You also deal with populism in *Assembly*. Shouldn't we discard the term '*people*' anyway?

AN – Yes, that's what the common is all about. The term 'people' stays within the logic of Hobbes and the bourgeois line of sovereignty and representation. It is a fiction that violates the multitude and has only that purpose: the multitude should transform itself into one people that dissolves itself in forming the sovereign power. Think of the original frontispiece of Hobbes' *Leviathan*, which perfectly illustrates this. But it was Spinoza who, against Hobbes, emphatically used the concept 'multitudo' and underlined that the natural power of the multitude remains in place when a political ordering is formed. Actually, Spinoza, in elaborating these concepts of *multitudo* and *comunis* encapsulates the entire issue of politics and democracy, as I have attempted to demonstrate in my book *L'anomalia selvaggia* and to which we refer again in part in *Assembly*. Crucial in the transition of singularity to the common, Spinoza teaches us, are imagination, love, and subjectivity. Singularity and subjectivity becoming common and translating themselves into newly invented institutions, is one way of summarizing commontism.

PG & SL – With regard to the current digital and communicative capitalism you also dwell on *critique* and what you call Horkheimer's and Adorno's techno-pessimism. You state that in order to arrive at an evaluation of modern technology it is necessary to historicize the arguments of critique. The position of Horkheimer and Adorno only relates to the phase of capitalist development that is controlled by large-scale industry. This constitutes a serious limitation of their critique. My question is: is this restriction of their critique related to the counter image of Enlightenment and modern thinking as forged in the Romantic period by opponents of revolutionary ideas and emancipation and in which their *Dialektik der Aufklärung* is also caught? Or, to put it differently, is it due to the fact that they do not make an explicit enough distinction between emancipatory modern thinking and capitalism? What is your view on this, also in the light of your thesis on the alternative modernity of Machiavelli-Spinoza-Marx, in which the first two are regarded as the main suspects by Horkheimer and Adorno?

AN – I grew up against the background of the critical theory of the Frankfurter Schule and it is evident that operaismo is indebted to their critical work, but the same time the entire development of operaismo can be seen as opposing the conclusions of *Dialektik der Aufklärung*. Horkheimer and Adorno's work leads to extremes and extremism, it takes you to the border and then you can't go any further. It is the conceptualization of a hermetic universe. In operaismo we asked ourselves, departing from this hermetic universe, how one could break it open. Instead of ending where they did, in operaismo we took the hermetic universe as a starting point, that is the universe of capitalism, of the excesses of instrumental rationality, and of the logic of control and repression, and we asked ourselves how we could break open this hermetic universe. We looked for ways to force open this hermetic universe, which had deteriorated into commodity and was heading for catastrophe. Introducing subjectivity is the central element in this, the crowbar.

So we are the children of the *Dialektik der Aufklärung*, but also rebel against it.

What we rediscovered in operaismo (and also in *Assembly*) against the positions of Horkheimer and Adorno's dialectics is ontology, the class struggle, and the possibility of subjectivation. Our interest in the pre-1968 Herbert Marcuse can be seen in this perspective, and what has been especially important, according to us, is the work of Hans-Jürgen Krahl. He was a young student of Adorno who was killed in a traffic accident in early 1970, but he wrote a very important work about the formation of the class struggle, *Konstitution und Klassenkampf* (published posthumously in 1971). His discourse was similar to what we tried to do in Italy. It involves the discovery of the immaterial and intellectual labour that had the potential for political action, for liberation, and for breaking with the total exploitation. Georg Lukàcs also played an important part in this discovery, as did Maurice Merleau-Ponty in France. In the intersection between phenomenology and Marxism we find the fabric in which our movement originates.

PG & SL – If you, as an intellectual, thinker, researcher, critical theorist, were to give an assignment to the future generation, what would it be?

AN – What I see as most important, as fundamental in my life, and what I experience as unique in my life and something that connects everything and is positive, is the fact that I have always been a communist militant. Throughout my life I have never done anything, not as a philosopher nor in any of the many other professions or occupations I engaged in, not as a sociologist or sometimes

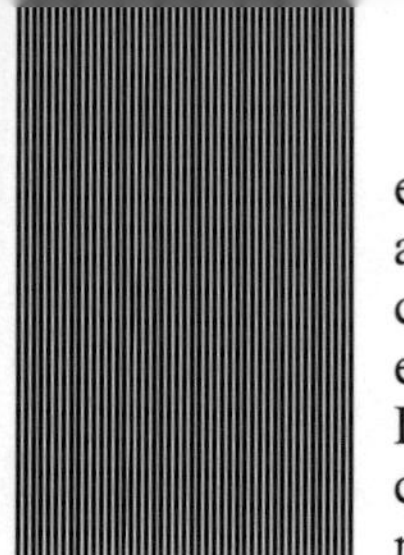

even as professional politician, never have I undertaken anything that wasn't completely driven by my communist commitment. I have always been a communist militant in everything. That is what I would like to leave to the future. I would like for communist commitment to become the central element again in people's lives. Because the commonist militant is the salt of the earth.

Bread Kneads Hands

Futurefarmers

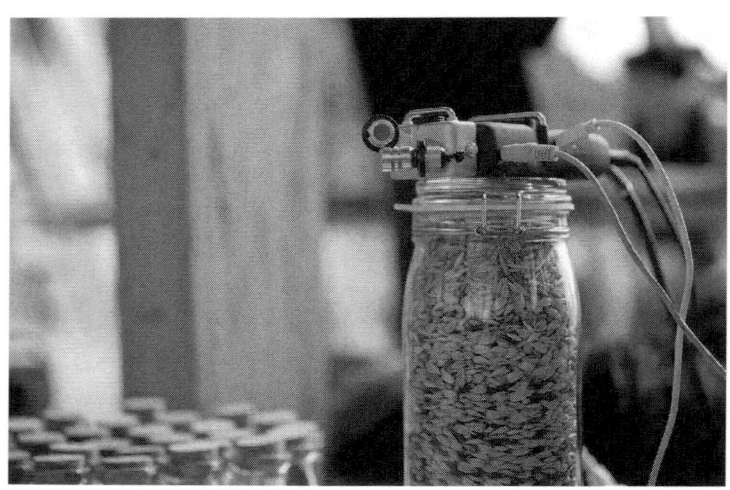

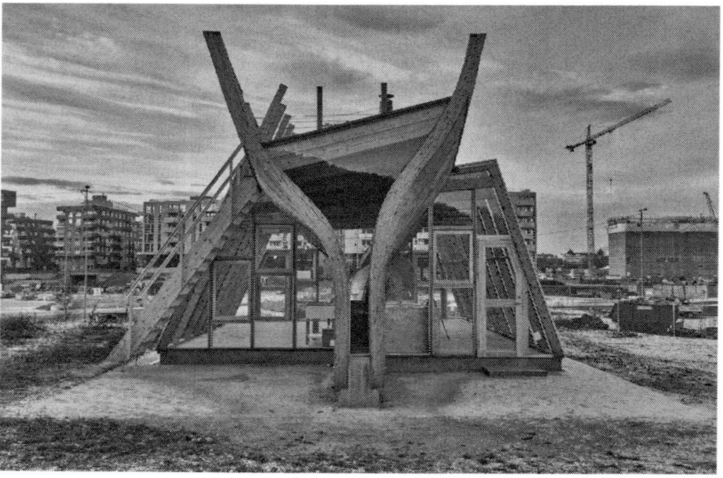

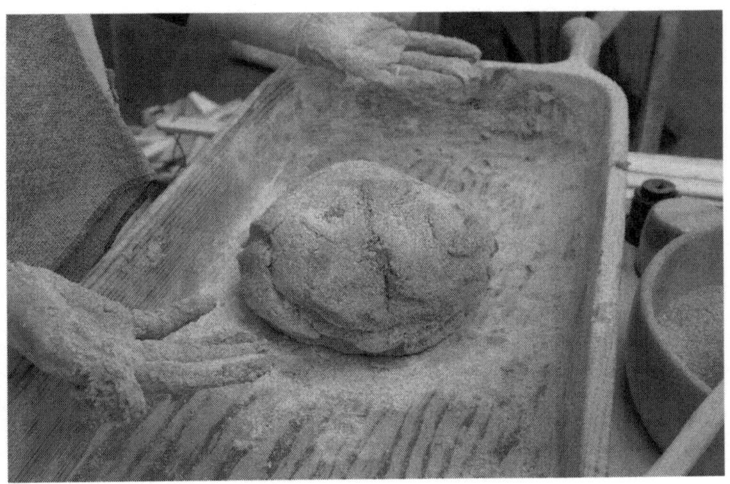

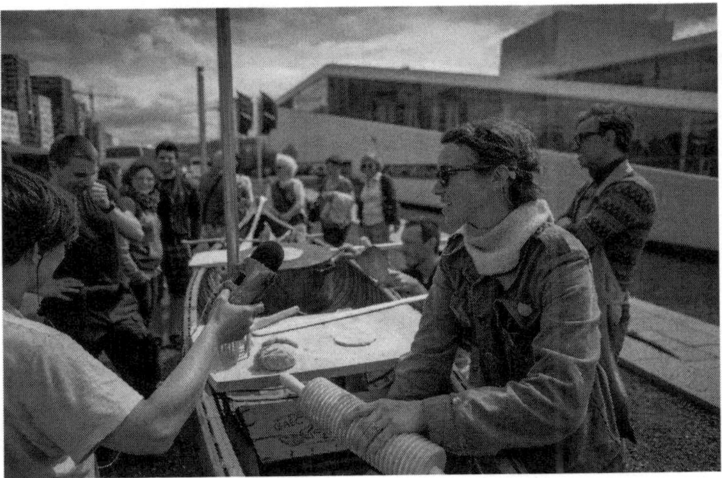

— Radio Ramona and Vavilov Barley.
  Photo: Max McClure, 2013
— Flatbread Society Bakehouse.
  Photo: Monica Løvdahl, 2015
— Form and Function Workshop,
  Max McClure, 2013
— Radio Ramona (in baguette).
  Photo: Max McClure, 2013

Sublime

Aesthetic judgement has to do with personal taste and defines the paths of our actions. Through aesthetic judgement we distinguish nice from ugly, tasty from rotten, what we like and don't like, what we want and don't want. In experiencing beauty, however, we lose these judgements. Beauty brings us into a state of 'not knowing any more'. We become speechless.

> *What is this?*
> *What do I do with this?*
> *Can I still judge here?*

Beauty is strange. Beauty amazes. It brings people in a state of disinterest, where they are deprived of their aims and freed from the drives that direct them. It brings them a feeling of love, rather than desire.

Immanuel Kant told us that beauty brings the subject beyond its preferences, but simultaneously with the experience of beauty one gets the feeling of something grotesque and incomprehensible. The state of having no thoughts or goals, caused by the experience of beauty, brings the subject in a condition of discomfort, which characterizes the pathos of the sublime.[1] At the edge of this anxious state the question of the meaning of life presents itself. But with that the insight also reveals that in this state of 'not knowing any more' we can set our own goals. Kant's main question was: 'What must I do?' In the queerness of the sublime, reason appears. In this moment of the loss of drives the subject becomes free and needs to set his own drives, give reason to his own acts.[2]

Beauty

A boat is at sea, going from Norway to the Middle East, collecting variations of heritage grains from different places along the way. Collecting stories of relationships between and among living beings—relationships between cultural groups, but also between human and non-human life forms such as seeds, sea-life and the terrestrial species from the various places and times it traverses.

> ... we can speak of this journey as return or a re-tracing of a very ancient route combining human and

non-human initiative by which wheat was domesticated from the wild and then slowly made its way through gifts, trade, winds, and sea currents, from the highly cultured Middle East to the barbarians of the north.
– Michael Taussig[3]

A canoe with legs walks around in Oslo. Human legs. Two pairs. Where it stops, people start to bake thin flat bread on the small oven on top of the canoe. The smoke, the melted butter, and the warm bread fuse into a familiar and welcoming atmosphere, while the sight of a four-legged canoe and the old-fashioned baking device are uncommon enough to slow down traffic and spark questions.

It is absurd. I suppose it's art? But then what is art? Something ungraspable, just beyond one's understanding? It's beautiful! Real Beauty!... but weird.

The emphasis in Futurefarmers' project has been on developing self-generating works that find their own meaning. Astonishment has always been a central topic in their work, in the sense of making people aware of contemporary ethical questions, but even more as generating processes that bring with them conscious awareness. By installing unconventional constellations in public space they bring about wonder and activate public questioning, sharing, and exchange of knowledge, creating common thinking and acting ... a common sense.

Unreasonable

Kant brought us the insight that through beauty and the sublime we come to giving reason. However, the grounds of our actions are not always clear. Freud showed us the existence of unconscious complexes that structure the subject. But these structures are not stable. Our drives seem more regulated by a multiplicity of discourses that discipline the subject, rather than by innate unconscious urges.

The public sphere is like a space of conflict where different subjective positions compete, and in which the subject tries to define its place.

With what position do I identify myself?
Which discourses do I include as part of the self and
which do I exclude?
Who or what is important and what do I exclude?

In this way, the subject is always in search, never stable, always out of place, dislocated. It is always situated between the discourses and the self, trying to define its unity, always changing, never capable of final self-determination or self-organization.

Flat Bread Society – a Common in the Making
'There is no reason for the Bakehouse.
The Bakehouse gives reason.'

A cosy shed giving shelter to three ovens somewhere on an empty, idle plot of land in the former industrial harbour of Oslo—between the rail tracks of Oslo's station, the central business district, a huge building site and the Oslo fjord, on top and under the shafts of a highway tunnel. There is no reason for this bake house to be there. Strange... but beautiful!

> This strange site, named Losætra, is one of the commons near the fjord in Oslo. At this site, Futurefarmers formed Flatbread Society as a proposition for working with local people to establish an aligned vision for the use of this land. Flatbread Society uses grains as a stimulus to meditate on the interrelationship of food production and knowledge sharing, cultural production, socio-political formations and everyday life.[4]

Public programmes, the building of a bake-house and the installation of a cultivated grain field attracted and activated the imagination of bakers, soil scientists, oven builders, farmers, artists, and city officials, which resulted in the formation of an urban gardening community called Herligheten. New layers of soil and stories were spread over the site, and a polyphonic choir of voices gathered: insects, people, soil, sea, birds, buried Viking ships, cars, mycelia, microorganisms, plants, and seeds. They were all kneaded together, contributing to the emerging narratives and goings-on on this land. Losætra is a 'porous world always in the making',[5] transforming the public space into the common place.

Bjørvika, the bigger area surrounding Losæter, is currently being transformed into a new and central area for residential housing, commerce, and culture. The question of doing a project in this new development of gentrification and the ethical issues that come with it, brings the artists in a precarious situation.

Which position to take in this debate?
Are we a sort of disturbance in this new capitalist development
or rather promoting and beautifying this process?

Can we, as foreign artists, start a public trajectory?
Should it not be local artists, who know the people and the site?
Aren't we out of place?

If we are already out of place, should we then not try to focus on a process that activates new local narratives instead of trying to find our position in the existing debates?

Constellations

The individual is rather a *dividu*-al,[6] fragmented rather than whole. It is not a stable unity, but more like a knot of different mechanisms that structure it, a constellation, or, even better, a superposition of constellations of processes of subjectivation. It is subject to continuous discipline by cultural systems, discourses, and the self. It is in this sense always already non-personal, beyond the self, collective. The term collective should be understood in the sense of a multiplicity that deploys itself as much beyond the individual, on the side of the *socius*, as before the person, on the side of preverbal intensities, indicating a logic of affects rather than a logic of delimited sets.[7] Consequently, we can't speak any more of a subject that gives reason to its own actions. Kant thought we could define our final goals by reason, but it seems that what drives us are desires, and these desires are produced by mechanisms that are to the utmost extent exterior to the subject. The subject is undetermined and never stable. It is a continuous changing 'assemblage' moved by what Guattari would call abstract machines.[8]

These abstract machines are not mechanisms like natural laws, but processes of mutation and adaptation that one can find in all organic, but also in social life. Since Guattari sees the subject as a knot or a bounding entity, these processes are always relational. They are autoproductive systems of connecting and interweaving, of interaction. The subject, driven by these 'machinic' processes, is no free self, nor a knot of human co-existence or co-constitution, but a rather a space where subject and object fuse in an animist nucleus.[9] Things, humans, plants, and animals interweave to become collective entities, half-thing half-soul, half-man half-beast, machine and flux, matter and sign... In this way, the subject seems more like a dynamic ecology.

These nodes of connection assign what is linked, what is of importance, here and now. In fact, the subject defines time, space, and value, and as Guattari shows, this is not only a human decision to make. What defines the subject is partly exterior to us, outside our conscious, outside our reason, inhuman.

The question that then comes up again, is if there is a way of self-organization if the subject is an ecology driven by abstract machinery? 'How do *I* act?' is not a valid question anymore. In fact, what we should ask for is what is of common interest to the subject as an ecology. Or rather: What *is* the subject-matter, here and now? Who is part of *our* assemblage? Who is the other that co-determines or co-constitutes what is of importance? What provokes this pre-subjective process of commonization?

'Bread Kneads Hands'

The bake-house and grain field are a junction rather than a space. A node where people meet, think and act together. But it is not only a place of people. The ovens make room for thinking. The soil that is spread over the site speaks. The swallows that suddenly appeared in this strange industrial place say something. The bees and artists, the farmers and the horse, seeds and grains, herbs and vegetables, neighbours and sea-weed: they all participate in the writing of the story. This story is not a political one. The bread, the birds, the grains and soil, the air pollution and building site co-determine the narrative of the site. The artwork is a knot that brings the political agenda to a common ecological agenda where things and plants and animals are not objects anymore, but co-subjects in a common auto-productive story. The narrative is not a human but rather an inhuman one.

Adorno always said that the artwork never should have an explicit content, but rather be an object that promises content.[10] Deleuze speaks in this way about the *figural*[11] of an artwork, its ability to make a gesture. The figural is always sort of recognizable and at the same time never clear. It gives no explication, only hints that ask for possible explanations. The final meaning stays away. The weird practice of baking bread in the middle of the industrial zone of Oslo is such a gesture, at the same time common and beyond understanding. It produces estrangement and curiosity tinged with fear and wonder. The growing constellation of Flatbread Society, moved by this weirdness, is super normal and at the same time sublime, almost ordinary and without ideological statement. All of that is subsumed in the object, the object *out of place, in place*.[12] The bake-house and grain field installed an alternate local reality that through gentleness and humour, cleverness and absurdity, defines new *processes to revalue the common subject of this space at this point of time.*

This dynamic of absurdity, where humans and things collaborate, becomes visible in the belly of the temporary bake-house that was built at Losæter in 2013, but also at other moments. A workshop organized by Tenthaus whereby a group of immigrant teens were invited to bake flat bread ignited the space. First some of the youngsters were observing the stupidity of the situation from the sideline.

What position should I take in this weird *uncommon* social constellation?

Proper attitudes do not work here. Soon everybody was sharing recipes from their own homeland, explaining how to roll the bread and how to use the different ovens. The whole *body* became engaged by Flatbread Society. Baking flatbread brought people to a *level* of losing their normal behaviour and connecting.[13] The baking workshop highlights the elegant and precise methods of Futurefarmers where people find potential in flatbread, letting it become a 'guide' to moments of sharing knowledge, memories, and imagination: a thin piece of bread that facilitates vital connections between objects and people, matter and mind, installing an ecological happening.

Cross-pollination between the new actors emerged; anti-GMO activists, climate change scientists, soil scientists, fermenters, maritime cultural unions, gardeners...

On June 13, 2015, a procession of farmers and citizens carried soil from their farms through the city of Oslo to its new home at Losæter. Soil Procession was a Ground Building Ceremony that used the soilcollected from over fifty ecologically run farms as far north as Tromsø and as far south as Stokke to build the foundation of the Flatbread Society Grain Field and community. A procession of soil and people, a donkey, goat and chickens, going through Oslo drew attention to the historical, symbolic moment of the transition of a piece of land into a permanent stage for art and action related to food production.

The soil was mixed into one social body and spread out over the site. A Declaration of Land Use was written and signed to secure the site as a space for growing grains and for food production.

> With the establishment of Losæter at Loallmenningen, we mark our commitment to support and highlight agriculture as a central part of the Bjørvika cultural landscape. We hereby declare Losæter a cultural commons. ... 'The Flatbread Society Grain Field' is an expression of this agreement.
> – Excerpt from the Land Declaration[14]

The amazing act of shining the spotlight on something as basic as soil (remember, the word 'human' derives from 'humus'), the common matter that we depend on for our nutrition, life and death,[15] shows how Futurefarmers, trough wonder, reconnects animals, things and humans in one ecology and one common narrative we have to walk together.

Futurefarmers' working sessions have been happily called 'psychotherapy craft parties' because the people making things together have tended, through the weirdness of the project, to open themselves up to one another.[16] Simultaneously, the distinction between artist and audience starts to fade.

From the moment the projects started, the artist had to let go. The art that Futurefarmers makes can often be thought of as performance objects; they are a type of objectified process, and they are best entered into with the spirit of 'Join us in making this'. The re-arrangement of things of this world invites people to join the play.[17] The only possibility left for the artist then is to push and pull these auto-genetic dynamics of co-creation a little as it slowly starts to go its own way.

That is why the medium Futurefarmers works with is sometimes considered as the participants itself. But this co-constitution of the world is never a human privilege. The soil, the birds, and the ovens are also *at play*. These actors are as essential as the participants. They form a bridge for participation; they are co-storytellers and co-writers, the *subject* of their own and the common story. They are co-protagonists in the narrative processes shared by everyone and everything of importance in this specific location and this particular time.

The Other

Actually, one cannot speak of the *other* in assemblages. The subject is always already the *other* of it-self. There is no terrifyingly great incomprehensible other. What is sublime is the subject itself. We should rather speak of the subject as a superposition of others and *selfs,* where the distinction between both always remains hazy. The *other* seems as unstable as the *self* in this continuously shifting multiple universe of subjective production. The subject seems more like a process. A process of constant reframing of what is the case here and now, of finding out what is in common, a process of re-commonization or re-ecolization, of *Aufhebung* of the other and the self. The subject seems to be the on-going enquiry and questioning of the self, not having as a goal to find an answer, but rather having as its nature this practice of adapting, mutating, adjusting, ... in short, searching for the common, *how to live together as one body.*

> We don't need a museum for conserving varieties, what we want is to grow them.
> - Johan Swärd of Vestre Aschim Farm

What is this locality, this here and now in the works of Futurefarmers? It is not a museum.

> Unlike museums that collect and preserve works of art, 'The Flatbread Society Grain Field' is a museum without walls that preserves through sharing and distribution.
> - Excerpt from the Land Declaration[18]

While workshops were being organized on the site, the Canoe Oven emerged out of the water, connecting people who in turn became protagonists in the story of the Flatbread Society. On board and on land, Radio Ramona spread the polyphonic voice of the new society.

'She is the radio of the town.'

> Since the beginning, Ramona has been a voice, a tune, interviews, concerts, field recordings, compositions ... dealing

with strange affairs between bread, astronomy, migration ... a character that witnesses, interacts, bread-casting stories; a constant collective becoming in Flatbread Society, sowing seeds on the electromagnetic grain field of Losæter. Radio Ramona is a living archive in lots of different languages, ages, gender, a hybrid between a body and a living organism intra-action.[19]

Where the project started as an artistic intervention in a planned recreational area as part of the new housing development near the water, it evolved into a process of connecting hundreds of families from the surrounding neighbourhoods, city officials, farmers from the region, existing projects around food production and alternative economies active in the city, activists, the bakers union, farmers union, banks, the university ... There is no fixed scale of this project. One would rather speak about a superposition of localities in time and space.

On the Flatbread Society Grain Field a variation of heritage grains were sown, including Forest Finn Rye, one of the first grains ever cultivated in Scandinavia. These heritage grains tell stories about the region, the habits and customs of the Vikings, but also about the site as a former Royal Farm... Another grain that grows on the field is Ardre Emmer. Emmer is one of the oldest grains in the world and brings us back to the first farmers in the Fertile Crescent, the first human settlements, and the appearance of the polis. But the field is also about producing your own food as citizens, and the right to do this in an urban environment as local residents. Along with this topic another story comes to the surface. The race between multinationals trying to develop genetically modified grains, to patent them, and take control of our basic food production. By contrast, there is also the story of the fifty farmers who brought their soil, and the appointment of the first Urban Farmer in Norway.

It seems that the work does not have a single narrative but is multi-layered and that its stories go in all directions, sometimes even in an opposite and contradictory sense. There doesn't seem to be one true story, and if the artwork cannot provide direction, its only task can be task to give the means to help the subject, as a multitude, to continuously redefine itself and its sense. It is not the goal that is important, but the possibilities to adapt to the ecology of importance.

> Always changing to remain the same
> - Didier Demorcy

The Oslo municipality, charmed by the local dynamics, changed their plans for the site as a recreational area to a common place for food production, adjusted the building regulations for the site, and raised money to build a permanent neighbourhood bake-house. In 2016, this permanent bake-house, in the form of an old lifeboat, was erected by the people of Flatbread Society.

The urban garden expanded into a communally farmed field, with Andreas Capjon being employed as Norway's first urban farmer. A core of residents, non-eventful projects, institutions, bakers, the government, and artists was founded to horizontally organize the site: Growlab, Jørund Aase Falkenberg, Herbanists, Food Studio, Emmanual Rang, Oslo Apiary, Herligheten and Northern Company. The project was taken out of the hands of the artists. Where they had started with initiating some gestures for this vacant space, now the place was defining the direction of the artwork.

Setting in Motion and Being Moved

Being touched, being in intra-action[20] or connected, is being common, and being common is being on the move, becoming.

Jean-Luc Nancy speaks about being touched as getting in a state of adoration.[21] Adoration, he writes, is a state of wonder that leads to a state of flooding. It is not a state of adjusting and adapting, of getting boxed or limited, but rather a moment of surplus. As in wonder one loses oneself, this experience is the moment of becoming opened and receiving. But as Edmund Burke says it is also a moment of love,[22] of unconditional giving, of overflowing, connecting, growing, moving others, and being moved by others.

But this being touched and being moved is an ecological happening. This being moved is sublime in the sense of un-human. It is unhuman because it is not only humans that can be touched and moved by another being. In an ecology everything moves everything: birds, mountains, neighbours, grains, paintings, sunsets, paper and food. Making the world, setting things in motion, is not a human privilege. It is always an ecological happening.

Consequently, one cannot speak of a human story anymore. The narrative will be an ecological one in which everything speaks, and this narrative will never have a clear ground since it has only a *sense*, no goal, and this sense is multi-vocal and has different directions. At the same time, this narrative will always be super-grounded since it is unhuman and everyone and everything participating in the subject of the story is also defining the story. Maybe Leibniz was right in saying that everything has a ground, but only in the sense that this ground is a common ground.

The Artwork as a Tool

Futurefarmers' Flatbread Society never had the intention to tell a story, to direct people, or to make them take the *right* decision in on-going political debates. Futurefarmers work is more a set of DIY tools provided to generate processes that bring conscious awareness. What are the subjectivating processes that direct us? And is there a space where we can, for a short while, be free of the discourses that define us, of the habits and believes that drive us?

Flatbread Society Bakehouse and Grain Field are not just symbolic objects. These objects work, make wholes in our certainties, generate possibilities and dynamics. They are *living tools* that don't only make room for thinking. They especially make room for action, for baking, walking, planting, ploughing, and kneading. Flatbread Society as a sublime and beautiful *thing* gives this openness, generating 'not knowing' through weirdness. But at the same time, it is a practical facility creating the possibility to act. And since in the work of Futurefarmers the audience—being shovels, people, fire, institutions, worms, and rolling pins—is always co-creator, the sublime becomes a common place of action and self-organization.

Notes

1 Jean-François Lyotard, *Het onmenselijke: Causerieën over de tijd*, transl. Ineke van der Burg (Kampen: Kok Agora, 1992), p. 104.

2 Immanuel Kant, *Kritiek van het oordeelsvermogen*, transl. Jabok Veenbaas and Willem Visser (Amsterdam: Boom, 2009). In the *Critique of Judgement* Kant goes into the analytica of the beauty (book 1 §2) and the sublime (book 2).

3 Michael Taussig, *Let Us Praise Famous Seeds*, Internationale Seed Journey.

4 Elizabeth Thomas, curator.

5 Karolin Tampere, *Flatbread Society Grain Field and Bakehouse: A Common in the Making*, 2017.

6 Gilles Deleuze and Félix Guattari, *Rizoom*, trans. René Sanders (Utrecht: Spreeuw, 2004). *Dividu* is a concept used by Deleuze and Guattari to describe the individual as a knot. From French, *divisé* (divided).

7 Félix Guattari, *Chaosmosis: An Ethico-Aesthetic Paradigm*, transl. Paul Bains and Julian Pefanis (Bloomington, IN: Indiana University Press, 1995), p. 9.

8 Ibid., p. 35.

9 Ibid., p. 102.

10 Theodor W. Adorno, *Aesthetic Theory*, transl. Robert Hullot-Kentor (London: Bloomsbury Academic, 1997), chapter 8.

11 Gilles Deleuze, *Francis Bacon: Logica van de gewaarwording*, transl. Sjoerd van Tuinen (Den Haag: Octavo, 2015).

12 Gloves and Bread.

13 Tampere, *Flatbread Society Grain Field and Bakehouse*.

14 Excerpt from the Land Declaration, www.flatbreadsociety.net/stories/view/31.

15 Tampere, *Flatbread Society Grain Field and Bakehouse*.

16 Cooley Windsor, *Futurefarmers Psychic Library*, 2017.

17 Ibid.

18 Excerpt from the Land Declaration, www.flatbreadsociety.net/stories/view/31.

19 E-mail from Marthe Van Dessel, April 2017, http://flatbreadsociety.net/ramona.

20 Karen Barrat, *Meeting the Universe Halfway: Quantum Physics and Entanglement of Matter and Meaning* (Durham, NC: Duke University Press, 2007), p. 132.

21 Jean-Luc Nancy, *Adoration: The Deconstruction of Christianity II*, transl. John McKeane (New York: Fordham University Press, 2013).

22 Edmund Burke, *Een filosofisch onderzoek naar de oorsprong van onze denkbeelden over het sublieme en het schone*, transl. Wessel Krul (Groningen: Historische uitgeverij, 2004), p. 148.

POURQUOI TRAVAILLER ?

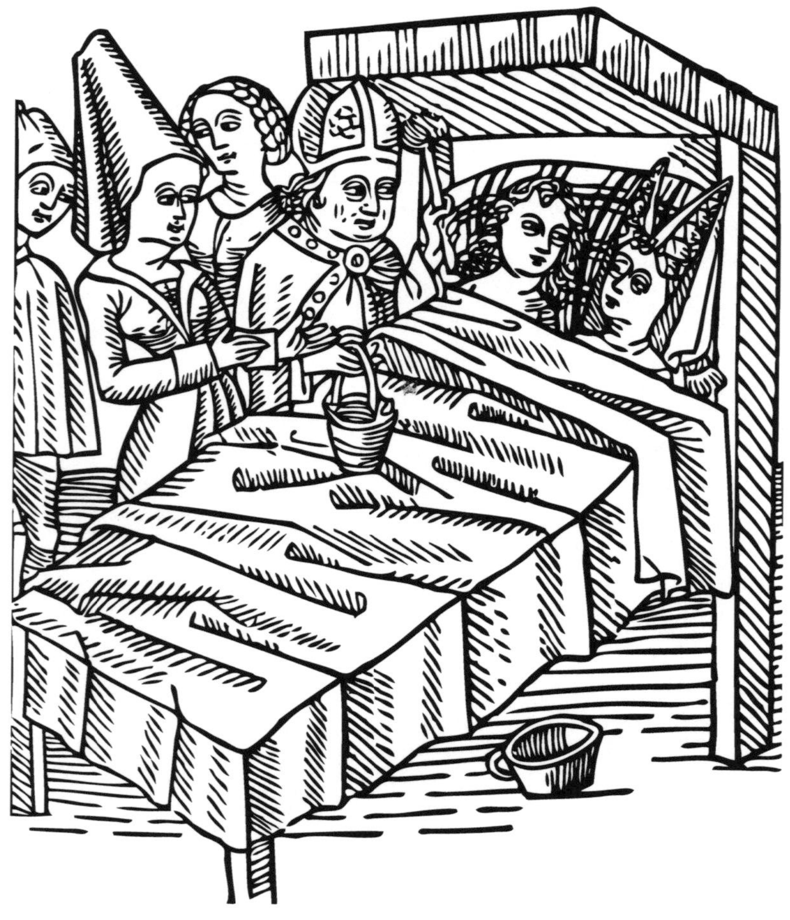

Pourquoi Travailler, Three Star Press, Paris, 2015

Sostenuto!

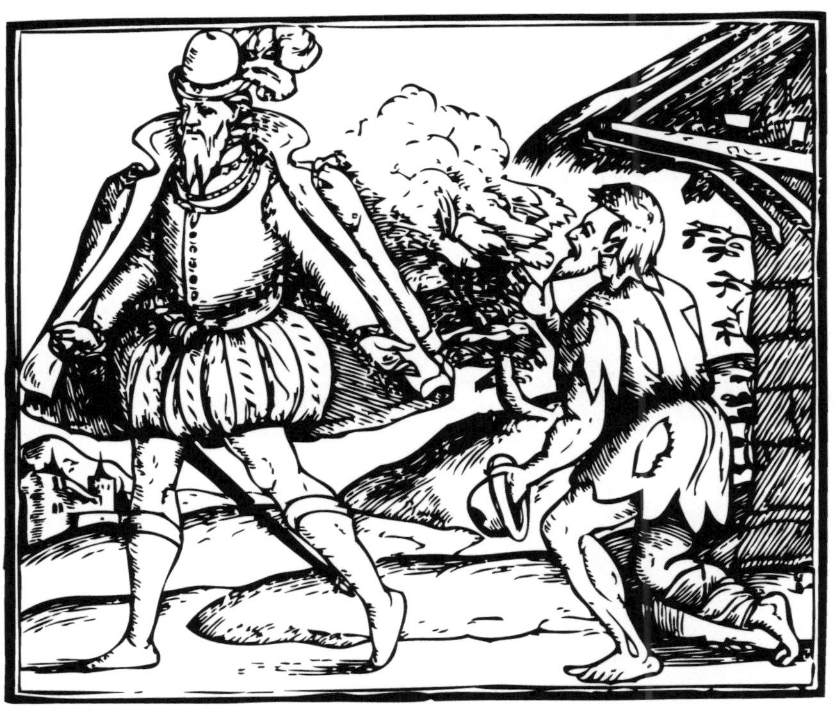

Sostenuto!, ICA, London, 2011

Notes on Artistic Commoning

Rudi Laermans

1.

'The progressive composition of the common world ... is the name I give to politics', Bruno Latour contends.[1] Although he himself does not use the verb, the implied activity can be termed *commoning* and given a broader twist in at least two directions. The first one regards the created common world. It may solely consist of humans or is made up of both humans and non-humans (such mixed, hybrid, or heterogeneous assemblages are the focus of Latour's Actor-Network-Theory).[2] For example, the shared reality that emerges during a dance performance does not only include the actively moving dancers and the passively on-looking audience but also comprises the music that is played and the well thought-out lighting. Yet, it is also possible that this collaboratively created reality has a primarily communicative, textual, or discursive nature (negotiated treaties are an evident example) or is both meaningful and genuinely material (such as the jointly produced movement vocabulary for a dance work). In light of this plurality, it is fitting to speak of the composition of a commonality or a common, in the broad sense, and also necessary to contextually specify the kind of common that is collectively performed through a practice of commoning.

The second broadening has to do with the relationship between the social, the common, and the political. Evidently, commoning involves social acts or operations, ranging from simple statements to discussions, to doing various things together in silence, either face-to-face or in a mediated but nevertheless coordinated mode. However, the social and the political do not form two sides of the same coin, quite the contrary: Although the reverse may be true, not every social act is a political one. In order to clarify the relationship between both, we can once again invoke Latour's simple but inspiring definition of politics, which in fact contains three suggestions. The first one states that commoning, or the collective production of any kind of commonality, is the essential practice through which the social instantiates the political. Understood in this way, all social acts acquire a political character when they involve the joint creation of something. However, a second, rather implicit but crucial presupposition informing Latour's idea of politics-as-commoning stipulates that the implied relationships do not testify of rigid hierarchies or segmentations but, on the contrary, tend towards a collaborative mode of social self-organization. The third and last suggestion stipulates that the politicizing of the social is neither intrinsically connected with a particular kind of shared activity nor implying a certain scale. The social and the political not only meet in deliberations over the common good (*pace* Aristotle, indeed); and commoning is also not only a societal affair but happens on the meso-level of organizations and the micro-level of interaction as well.

To understand commoning as a plural practice denaturalizes it figuratively and literally: This very verb points to a multiplicity of collaborative activities tending towards self-organization and is not synonymous with a focus on the common good or a common nature (the so-called ecological commons). A similarly broad and activity-oriented approach is advocated by the intellectual proponents of Italian autonomous Marxism such as Antonio Negri or Paolo Virno. However, in their considerations on the joint production of 'common wealth', they clearly tend to reproduce the traditional infra-structuralism or economist bias of Marxism through their focus on immaterial labour.[3] Conversely, Pierre Dardot and Christian Laval defend a truly encompassing and practice-based approach in their admirable study *Commun*. 'The common must be thought of as co-activity, and not as co-membership, co-property or co-ownership', they rightly emphasize, adding under the title 'common as praxis': 'Against the modes of essentializing the common ..., one has to affirm that *only* the practical activity of humans can bring forth common things, in the same vein as it is *only* this practical activity that can produce a new collective subject ... .'[4]

2.

Artistic commoning entails the co-creation of any kind of aesthetic commonality, ranging from the co-production of an exhibition by a curator and several fine artists to the joint production and performance of a new piece by a theatre collective, to the kind of relational or participatory art that very much engages audience members. Again we stumble upon a very broad palette of practices that to a certain extent resemble each other but also look strikingly heterogeneous. What they effectively do have in common and therefore lies at the heart of every mode of commoning, is a varying degree of a relatively symmetrical collaboration between all those involved.[5] Indeed, no commoning without a minimum of self-organizing cooperation—but the reverse does not hold, at least not in general. Even when having a self-organized nature, collaboration—or cooperation, or coaction: I use these words as interchangeable—only instantiates the praxis of commoning when driven by a common cause.

Notwithstanding the fact that in the course of the deployed joint action it will be further refined and re-interpreted, or may even become drastically re-articulated, the common cause produces a collective focus underlying and framing the joint artistic action. It therefore acts as a true subject, in the literal sense of the Latin word *subiectum*: a bearing surface or sustaining ground. This quality also comes to the fore through the fact that in genuine collaborations the subjacent common cause opens up one or more shared matters of concern that prompt the personal commitment of those taking part. The collaborators invest in the collectively done artistic labour, and this also in a quasi-libidinal sense: They are individually attached to the stakes of the project at hand and feel responsible for it. Artistic—and more generally: creative—work may start from a consensus on the collaboration's common cause, yet it frequently happens that this condition for commoning is produced through long talks and perhaps heated discussions before the mutual sealing of an actual cooperation, so through acts already exemplifying the practice of commoning. In other words, one already 'makes common cause' in order to define a common cause: no future commoning without an implicit commoning laying the foundations for this commoning-yet-to-come.

There are yet other, primarily discursive commonalities that are at once vastly informing artistic commoning and are simultaneously created through that very practice. Contemporary aesthetic practices have an open, explorative nature and are no longer regulated by constraining norms or axiomatic principles. Hence the well-known valuation of originality or newness since the breakthrough of modern art. When collaborating, however, the fact that the artistic is generally not fully defined necessitates the development of a shared discourse or language tailored to the specificities of a project or a particular task. In fact, the required vocabulary is layered and in essence doubles the traditional distinction between facts and values. Artistic cooperation first and foremost requires the co-definition of a descriptive common, a set of terms—be it concepts or metaphors, well-defined theoretical propositions or loose images—allowing mutual understanding and facilitating communication during work. Yet of even greater importance is the joint production of a value common, however contextual or temporary.

Appraisal is the core operation within the artistic field. Every work of art is appreciated in multiple ways since various value registers or standards of justification may be invoked: the traditional aesthetic distinction between beauty and ugliness, the political code 'progressive versus conservative' (or a more recent variant such as 'socially relevant versus autonomist art'), the notion of emotional expressivity, the standard of conceptual originality, and so on. But producing art also continually involves making value judgments. Thus, the young poet jotting down a still isolated sentence reads it over and over again, trying to determine its possible aesthetic worth before moving on to a next line. In a similar way, the collaborative creation of an artistic work again and again demands coactively made appreciations of interim results, potential materials, possible routes... Collaboratively creating artistic value requires a common valuation activity, the collective negotiation of shared judgments that may contribute to a situated common culture or project-embedded discourse. In sum, producing artistic value together necessitates constantly valuing the active production together. This is anything but an easy activity. Assessing together the worth of what has been jointly produced makes up the core of artistic commoning (and again, more broadly, of creative collaborations)—yet it is also a practice in which value dissonance may prevent the co-creation of a value common.[6]

3.

When materials or underlying notions are inter-individually appreciated, pluralism is predictably harder to deal with than in situations focusing on the 'thick description' of their crucial characteristics. Dissonance is indeed often more outspoken, in the literal and the figurative sense, when it comes to divergent or somewhat contrasting conceptions of the desirable or the discursive fine-tuning of a general value's 'real meaning'. Normative positions tend to be more personally engaging: what people find worthy directly implicates their self, that which they stand for as an artist—or even as a human being or individual—and identify with in a partly conscious, partly unconscious way. In a process of artistic collaboration, differences in opinion on the worth of interim results therefore always risk hardening into difficult to settle disputes, if not into an open strife endangering the minimal social cohesion every productive coaction must rely on.

Collectively resolving questions regarding artistic, political, conceptual or whatever sort of value when incommensurable frameworks are at play, is a markedly difficult mode of commoning. Polyphony has to metamorphose momentarily into a relative unison without having any solid ground to build up the necessary accord. Judging in the collective mode indeed usually creates a semi-public space, however small or encapsulated, in which divergent appraisals relate to each other. Differences are explicitly addressed, spelled out through an at times detailed argumentation and underpinned with various references to 'facts'. The actual conversational dynamic and its possible outcomes greatly depend on the very value that each party imputes to its value position since this strongly calibrates the effective chances to negotiate a middle ground judgement, to make 'an honest compromise' or to become convinced.

As said, commoning stands at the junction of the social and the political, and simultaneously premises a relational dynamic undoing linear hierarchies and promoting an open public reasoning. Within this practice, the composition of a common value judgment is in fact the political act par excellence. That much is at least suggested by Hannah Arendt, who considers collective judging as constituting the generic base of political action. Her perhaps astounding thesis comes with some crucial qualifications. Judging is political insofar as it relates to other opinions in an essentially twofold way: one tries to persuade others of one's standpoint, and simultaneously one takes into account their judgments in view of a possible agreement. For every judgment's validity hinges on its possible social generalization or capacity to become shared. In a situation of value dissonance, this potential will be furthered when those involved act 'representatively': they openly acknowledge the perspectives of others by representing them in individual thinking or speaking. Or, as Arendt writes: 'The more people's standpoints I have present in my mind while I am pondering a given issue, and the better I can imagine how I would feel and think if I were in their place, the stronger will be my capacity for representative thinking and the more valid my final conclusions, my opinion.'[7]

Within the context of creative collaboration, a value common only emerges when the different collaborators quasi-ethically unite in a shared willingness to think and communicate 'representatively', to construct shared appreciations through the discursive interlacing of a plurality of opinions, thus at once condensing and superseding the initial pluralism. In a word, the various participants must be willing to broaden their personal viewpoints through the mutual incorporation of those of their direct peers. Without this attitude, individual judgments remain only subjectively valid.

However, in reality artistic commoning is frequently blocked—if not made altogether impossible—by a public exchange of opinions not directed towards the active communalization of one or more value judgments but rather marked by a pure self-congratulatory, even narcissistic affirmation of individual standpoints. At stake is a more general, also central ambiguity informing any instance of commoning. There is the desire to collaborate or to co-create, which is usually driven by the hope, and particularly the actual experience that one or more others inspire because they help to re-orientate, deepen, or expand one's capacities, thus eliciting processes of de- and re-subjectivation; and there is the contrasting desire for personal recognition by these very same others at the expense of recognizing them, resulting in frozen standpoints marked by the incapacity to represent one or more different opinions. Where collaboration and a fierce competition for recognition intertwine, the reality of 'co-opetition' emerges.[8] Indeed, collaboration is not by definition a non-contradictory or equal practice, quite the contrary: even when clearly tending towards one or another mode of social self-organization, commoning in the neutral sense equals the unity of the difference between harmonious working-together and inharmonious competition.

4.

How to avoid the tipping point where evaluative dissonance becomes unproductive noise? What strategies or tactics are deployed in processes of artistic collaboration to settle fierce disputes? I will not answer these and related questions in the abstract but through a brief excursion in the Brussels contemporary dance scene. I am acquainted with it through my teaching at P.A.R.T.S., regular studio visits, various coaching and mentoring activities, numerous informal talks, and some dozens of open interviews organized within the context of a research project on artistic collaboration.[9] Hence, the following observations are primarily intended to invite comparisons with practices of commoning in different artistic fields and, even more broadly, in non-artistic spheres where co-creative modes of thinking or doing are important.

In the world of contemporary dance, the work settings quite frequently display a peculiar form of communicative self-organization, not explicitly agreed upon, that facilitates the social generalization of value judgments. Three positions or roles actually stand out. The 'talkers' visibly enjoy the exchange of divergent viewpoints and are skilled language users: they excel in rhetoric and can relatively easily win over others. The 'listeners' regularly voice an opinion, now and then raise clarifying questions and sometimes formulate an apt remark or argument—but they primarily take the time to sort out the pros and cons of the discussed judgments by listening silently before publicly taking sides with a singular value position. The third role also involves a primarily listening-oriented attitude, yet the 'diplomats' overhear the different opinions precisely in view of their possible mediation. Generalizing viewpoints is the diplomats' genuine standpoint: they verbally create building blocks for potential compromises, dampen heated discussions and have an overall well-developed sense for the possibly unifying melody resounding in a polyphony of judgments. Above all, diplomats know that a singular view never contains generality in itself—it is not of the order of truth—but this quality is exactly the task to be performed: the value common has to be constructed. In dealing with value dissonance, those collaborating may of course also negotiate or compromise, thus in fact exemplifying an established cliché image of politics. However, making dance together also rests on two decidedly particular modes of overcoming individual differences in both descriptive interpretation and normative appreciation. Work-oriented commoning is the first one: the piece in the making and the varied activities it demands function as the primary locus of collective attention. This also applies when discussing together the actual value of a particular proposition or the potential worth of an unusual idea for a possible task. A distinct ethos is involved, one that does not systematically attribute sometimes vast differences in opinion to a self or subject but assumes that proficient collaboration requires a distanced, rather impersonal orientation to work. In this way, disagreements are thoroughly de-individualized. 'My viewpoint' is not counteracting or buttressing 'your opinion' because we both first and foremost address an external referent, including at once work (labour) and the work (the envisaged final piece, the task at hand contributing to that object's coming into existence).

Being centred on work frequently spills over into the kind of pragmatist commoning that truly defines the immanent micro-politics of artistic collaboration. Pragmatism is the loose denominator for the philosophical stance that consistently substitutes the metaphysical desire to attain representative accuracy for the mundane idea that the actual value of any action or thought primarily resides in its empirically testable capacity to solve a particular problem or to further new practicable possibilities. In artistic collaborations, this ethos underlies the marked attitude to cut short discussions animated by difficult to reconcile judgments with an appeal to action: 'OK, let's try it!' The individual opinion repeatedly defended by one collaborator or the singular viewpoint backed by some but not all thus changes into a hypothesis, the possible value or generalizability of which is no longer only a discursive matter but should be assessed in the light of the visible outcomes of its empirical translation.

Confirming the notion of performing research together, the question 'What is it worth?' is displaced from the realm of language to the domain of doing and observing, yet the pragmatic test in turn predictably elicits various descriptions and divergent appraisals. This brings about the distinctive dynamic and self-propelling cycle that characterizes the pragmatist politics of commoning, which also helps to settle value disputes and significantly re-articulate their stakes. Inspired by the overall problematic that frames the collaboration, a particular proposition is, for instance, first tried out and then collectively judged and discussed. This contextual debate generates differences in individual or collective judgement, which are pragmatically rendered into new proposals to examine this and to explore that. Experimentation rules: a judgment is neither true nor untrue but opens up a potential to act, speak or otherwise re-activate the work—again in the double sense of labour and artefact—which may be beneficial and create a relatively complex common world asking once again to be reduced through selective assessment.

5.

Yet another central ambiguity vastly informs artistic commoning. As a rule, collaborative practices of the more creative kind are explicitly inspired by the democratic ethos of equality and symmetrical self-organization but frequently cannot fully live up to it. Even with artistic collectives, these practices are often structurally marked by the partly economically and materially underpinned imbalance between, for instance, a curator and 'the invited artists' or between the choreographer initiating and financing a project on the one hand and the collaborating performers on the other. Hence the tension between the performative fiction of equality, symmetry, or collaboration-as-self-organization and the more or less visible social imbalances or differences in decision making in actual processes of collaboration. Within contemporary dance, this ambivalence is frequently temporalized. A long intensive phase of movement creation and exploration in which the working relations are (relatively) equal is followed by a shorter, often much less symmetrical one during which the principal choreographer makes the final selections and weaves them together into a singular composition. However, the equality apparently framing the initial working process in fact conceals a more complex reality, one that both reproduces and dialectically resolves the signalled ambivalence between 'leader' and 'follower' through the continual shifting of both positions.

All parties involved in a dance collaboration's first phase again and again take the initiative by making proposals, developing material, judging the results of tasks, and so on, with always uncertain, unpredictable outcomes. Initiatives are often counter-initiatives in response to an already created situation or previous activity. Within this dynamic, the leader is merely the one creating an opening 'now, here', through the contextual definition of a promising potential to further the work at hand. The temporary leader produces an event in the course of the joint action that one or more of the others will actively appropriate and re-articulate, discuss, and value. They can relate to it, or rather: a singular relation asking for social confirmation and continuation is brought forth within the overall labour setting. Subsequently, and regardless of its distinct status, a second collaborator may take the lead by responding to the proposition with a counter-movement, re-creating the temporal horizon of virtual possibilities, which all those partaking are collectively sustaining and individually assessing. In a word, a genuine inter-action unfolds in which the operations of leading and following are constantly re-distributed. In this way, the collaboration instantiates, in a micro-context, the peculiar political configuration of an a-personal 'leadingfollowing' (or 'followingleading') that provisionally displaces and de-segments the eventual general line(s) of inequality informing a work relationship (the expression 'leadingfollowing' is from André Lepecki).

Cooperating in the mode of 'leadingfollowing' creates an enigmatic kind of social subject. For each collaborator's actions are now grounded in an interpersonal dynamic, not reducible to only individually accountable initiatives or proposals. Nobody commands or really has authority: there is just the constant altering of leading and following, in which leading also includes following and the latter activity permanently passes over into the first. This Gordian knot functions as a 'choreopolitical plane of composition', André Lepecki observes, adding that 'following-as-leading-as-following requires a kind of *a-personal agreement*', 'a kind of shifting adherence, an immanent yet precarious, always renegotiated a-personal suturing'.[10] The work, in the already emphasized double meaning, must be the activity's direct focus: subjectivity has to be bent or curved, away from the personal self and in the direction of the anonymous one-ness underlying the singularization of any human potential whatsoever: 'one acts', 'one thinks', 'one experiences', 'one speaks', 'one judges'...

Overall, the issue of de-personalization and a concomitant suspension of subjectivity seems crucial in artistic commoning and its bending in the direction of a truly self-organizing practice. A distinctive ethos is demanded that relativizes the self in favour of various doses and different forms of anonymity. Impartiality, non-moralizing and being reasonable (in dealing with one's own viewpoints and the opinions of others), responsibility and loyalty (in relation to the work), openness and the readiness to test individual proposals pragmatically (with the risk of being refuted), humbleness, and the ability to lose both authority and authorship (in regard to 'leadingfollowing'): these and related stances very much underlie the practice of artistic commoning. In light of the history of art, most of them sound decidedly modern, even downright modernist: they are indeed reminiscent of of the aesthetics of impersonality ranging from rationalist architecture or Russian constructivism to the inexpressive, task-oriented movement research of Judson Church to generic conceptual art. Perhaps this at once self-contained and plural tradition must be revisited from the point of view of the kind of a-personal— or at least: a-personalizing—ethics and politics presupposed in practices of commoning.

Notes

1   Bruno Latour, *War of the Worlds: What about Peace?* (Chicago, IL: Prickly Paradigm Press, 2002), pp. 8–9.

2   See Bruno Latour, *Reassembling the Social: An Introduction to Actor Network Theory* (Oxford: Oxford University Press, 2005)

3   See especially Antonio Negri and Michael Hardt, *Commonwealth* (Cambridge, MA: Harvard University Press, 2009).

4   Pierre Dardot and Christian Laval, *Commun: Essai sur la révolution au XXIe sciècle* (Paris: La Découverte, 2014).

5   Not on principle but for the sake of argumentative convenience, I leave out the collaboration with non-humans, thus reproducing a traditional view of the social. For a more symmetrical approach of art—read: the field of contemporary dance—that takes into consideration the interactions between human and non-humans, see Rudi Laermans, '"Dance in General", or Choreographing the Public, Making Assemblages', *Performance Research: A Journal of Performing Arts* 13, no. 1 (2008), pp. 7–14.

6   For an inspiring sociological account of the way collaborative valuing activities inform various forms of creative work, see the case studies assembled in David Stark, *The Sense of Dissonance: Accounts of Worth in Economic Life* (Princeton, NJ: Princeton University Press, 2009).

7   Hannah Arendt, 'Truth and Politics', in *Between Past and Future* (London: Penguin, 2006), p. 241.

8   I owe the expression 'co-opetition' to Luc Boltanski and Eve Chiapello, *The New Spirit of Capitalism* (London: Verso, 2005), p. 110.

9   The results of the research are reported in Rudi Laermans, *Moving Together: Theorizing and Making Contemporary Dance* (Amsterdam: Valiz, 2015), pp. 285–396.

10 André Lepecki, 'From Partaking to Initiating: Leadingfollowing as Dance's (a-personal) Political Singularity', in *Dance [and] Theory*, eds. Gabriele Brandstetter and Gabriele Klein (Bielefeld: transcript Verlag, 2013), p. 34.

Indigenous, Not Homogenous
An Interview with Elizabeth A. Povinelli

Matteo Lucchetti &
Judith Wielander (Visible)

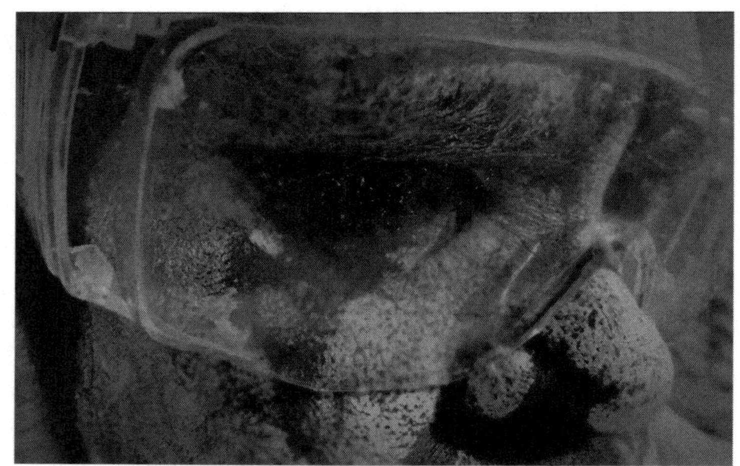

— *The Mermaids, or Aiden in Wonderland,*
2018. Karrabing Film Collective
— *Windjarrameru: The Stealing C*nt$,* 2015.
Karrabing Film Collective
— *Wutharr, Saltwater Dreams,* 2016.
Karrabing Film Collective

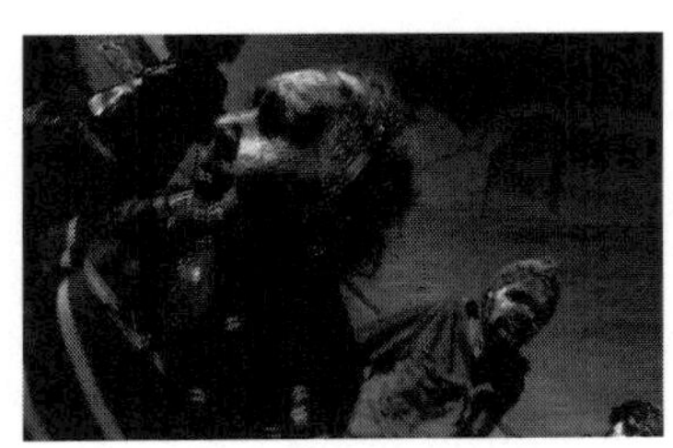

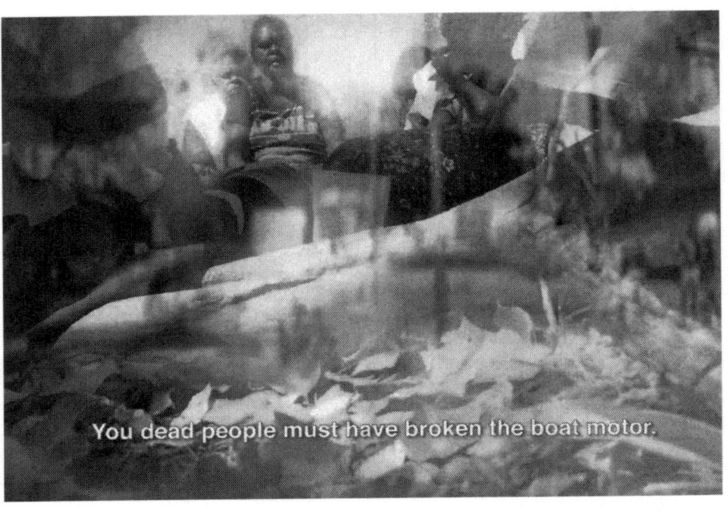
You dead people must have broken the boat motor.

Matteo Lucchetti & Judith Wielander (Visible) – In a conversation with Kim Turcot DiFruscia, in *eflux journal #53*, in discussing your practice with the Karrabing Film Collective, you introduce the notion of obligation. Specifically, in the act of entering the Karrabing community, you refer to the importance of leaving individual narratives behind, and pre-existing, even seducing forms of identity, in order to commit to immanent forms of social obligations. Could you elaborate on this notion and on how it may become a binding element in shaping common spaces to inhabit with others?

Elizabeth A. Povinelli – I first used obligation in a conceptual sense in *Economies of Abandonment*. I was grasping for a word that would conjure the belated nature of social and ethical commitment—a form of politics and ethics that breaks the transitive grammar of liberalism that assumes a subject and action and an object on which I act. I am not obligated to someone, something, some mood or action. I find myself already bound to a formative outside in the moment of encountering that someone, something, some mood or action. I wanted a term that captured this bondage of ethical and political being. I am obliged to do such and such. But the reverberations of finding oneself in encounter are crucial here. I find myself. I find myself in encounter. The subject is in continual disturbance as she continually confronts the nature of her extimate body as a body built out of materials outside and before its self. Arendt's concept of action and disclosure are close to what I mean here, as are Édouard Glissant's notions of relation and opacity.

In *Economies of Abandonment* I pivoted part of my argument about obligation on two pieces of fiction, Ursula Le Guin's 1973 'The One Who Walked Away from Omelas' and Charles Burnett's 1978 *The Killer of Sheep*. 'The Ones Who Walk Away from Omelas' imagines a city in which the happiness and well-being of its inhabitants depend on one small child being constrained and abused forever in a small dark closet. I read Le Guin as rejecting an ethics of liberal empathy. Instead, the ethical imperative is to know that your own good life is already in—obligated to—her constraint and abuse, and as a result, you must either relinquish your perfect health and happiness (and the idea that the health and happiness you experience is yours) or recommit to the current organization and distribution of powers and affects. At the end of the story, some people walk away from Omelas and its paradox. Burnett's film, and his body of work more generally, castigates liberal empathy from the perspective of those assigned to the closet, in this case African-Americans living in the wake of the Watts Uprising in Los Angeles. Across a multitude of loosely coordinated neorealist vignettes and plots we enter the life of Stan, and African-American man working in a slaughterhouse, and the fantasy that everyone could simply walk away from injustice. Throughout, viewers witness a level of exhaustion and endurance rarely captured in film as Stan navigates and confronts white privilege and its consequences across his world; and at the end of the film Stan remains where he began, pushing a group of sheep down a metal corridor to their slaughter. Burnett has characterized his film as hopeful insofar as Stan perseveres—he 'has decided to persevere and fight on despite society's place for him'. We can see Stan's supreme exhaustion as an index of the social body struggling to pull down its closet of abuse while others are straining to keep it in place so that they may stay in their benighted city. And we can understand his endurance as a heroic refusal not to be obliged to their distribution of health and happiness. The First Nation Anishinaabe theorist Gerald Vizenor called this form of persistence 'survivance'.[1]

I think these two pieces of fiction capture a feature of my attraction to obligation, namely that the belated reverberations of being are merely one moment in a more complex material unfoldings of ethics and politics. Okay, so I find myself already obligated to a formation and distribution of existence. And in finding myself there, I am pleased or disturbed, enraged or quieted. I may be enraged to find that I am being used as other people's liver or sewage system. Or I might be enraged to be told that I am using people in this way. Think here of wages and rages of whiteness (white heteronormativity) in the era of Trump and the alt-right in the US, of various new fascisms emerging in Austria, Germany, Poland, and other European regions. The point is that in finding that I am not inside myself but a result of a complex terrain of distributed extractions and surpluses the question remains how can I and how will I shift the distribution of materiality and identity. Again, the complexity of obligation as a reverberating extimacy[2] of existence means that persons can find themselves obligated across existing modes of identity and difference and still be gaining from or be denigrated within the broader terrain.

It might be useful to note that I am not overly attached to concepts in a nominal form. Because obligation means to conjure a state of existence in which one is always already bounded to others and other modes of being without being identical to them. I wrote two pieces[3] for Ashkan Sepahvand that try to conjure the complex obligations of this extimate body. One, 'Fires, Fog, Wind' thinks of desire from the perspective of toxicity and its distributions across race, colonialism, and class. In it, I describe a game my siblings and I played, a game played by generations of kids in the American South. In the 1960s, trucks filled with DDT would drive down residential streets discharging the chemical in clouds of toxicity. My siblings and I would run behind them, the game being how long you could hold your breath before your lungs gave out. The question now is: what were we thinking? What was anyone thinking? But I find myself obligated to this past in multiple ways, several of which are: the continued jubilance I feel when remembering our madness; the toxic remainder that has long settled into my flesh; the profit made from these contaminants that added to the accumulation of wellbeing in some regions rather than others.

In the long run, the circuits of harm run through what originally was sealed off. Aimé Césaire similarly argues 'colonization works to decivilize the colonizer, to brutalize him in the true sense of the word, to degrade him, to awaken him to buried instincts, to covetousness, violence, race hatred, and moral relativism'. '[E]ach time a head is cut off or an eye put out in Vietnam and in France they accept the fact, each time a little girl is raped and in France they accept the fact, each time a Madagascan is tortured and in France they accept the fact, civilization acquires another dead weight, a universal regression takes place, a gangrene sets in, a centre of infection begins to spread; and that at the end of all these treaties that have been violated, all these lies that have been propagated, all these punitive expeditions that have been tolerated, all these prisoners who have been tied up and "interrogated", all these patriots who have been tortured, at the end of all the racial pride that has been encouraged, all the boastfulness that has been displayed, a poison has been instilled into the veins of Europe and, slowly but surely, the continent proceeds toward savagery.'

All of this is to say that the consequences of finding oneself in a material terrain of obligated (extimate) existence cannot be resolved in such a way that anyone in the terrain simply remains in the same form. This is the point of Le Guin's and Burnett's fiction. But we need not turn to fiction to see this. We can look at some typical liberal responses to the concentration of toxic dumps in places where persons of colour, indigenous people, and the poor are concentrated. We must clean up these spaces. And indeed, we must. But the question should be: clean up to where? Not where to clean up but where to the clean-up? I know this is awkward grammar. But many calls for toxic clean-ups assume that they can help others by cleaning up what is in the other (or proximate to her) and outside themselves. But obligation in the sense I mean forces us to understand ethics as extimate—your insides are outside. If you want to help clean up then inhale some of the toxic clouds so others will not have to inhale as much. You will change physically, mentally, and affectively in doing so, and not in a singularly positive way. This is the wage of understanding obligation as a form of constitutive material formation that predates you encounter with its.

The common space is thus always a space that is distributed and outside itself.

V – Can the toxic dumps, literally and metaphorically, therefore become places for intersectional practices that involve obligation-like forms of commitment rather than a 'Kyoto-protocol' liberal understanding of commonality? This, considering also the rising number of these tainted environments, as a legacy of modern industrialization, and the growing conflicts between white heteronormative lifestyles and the neighbouring oppressed communities. Moreover, this scenario comes close to the concept of toxic sovereignty that is introduced in Karrabing's *Windjarrameru: The Stealing C*nt$* film. Especially in the scene where a group of young men seek refuge from the police in a toxic swamp, and in settling in, one of them, Kelvin, pronounces the sentence: 'We're safe, too much radiation here; we're safe.' Could you elaborate more on the paradigm of toxic sovereignty through the work with Karrabing?

EAP – Yeah, toxicity seems the right context for testing the power of obligation to disrupt late liberal, post-Kyoto notions of the common. In his recent Tanner Lectures, Dipesh Chakrabarty sought to understand the possible meanings and implications of the words 'common' and 'distributed' in the wake of the 1992 Rio Earth Summit and 1997 Kyoto Protocol 1997.[4] He asks what these terms might mean—what they *call* into being—when they are linked in the phrase 'common but differentiated responsibilities'. And I think it's important to note that those statespersons and technocrats huddling around tables trying to save their specific and different present conditions by contracting each other to specific and different future actions acknowledge that while we have a common plight from anthropogenic climate change and toxicity, our relationship to this common fate is not of the same, immediate intensity or kind.

The form in which nation-states show their commitment to this common plight is the international treaty. We-the-People of this nation-state agree to commit ourselves to doing such-and-such to achieve a common future built out of our differentiated pasts and present. I think it is right here that the concept of obligation might disrupt this contractual imaginary and the specific ideology of common and different that underlies it. Liberal contractualism creates a situation in which one party is obligated to do something in relation to another party until the delineated terms of the contract have been completed or expired. In doing so the contract *creates* the one party and the other party. In other words, it *creates* the discursive situation in which parties can feel and act as if they were separate things. Rather than common and differentiated, anthropogenic toxicity shows us a world of blocked and disavowed networks—it gives us the answer to what causes what physicists call 'spooky action at a distance'.

On the one hand, it is widely axiomatic that some regions are built up and sustained by ripping and disembowelling other regions while, in the process, leaving behind the chemicals used to separate metals and ores, the fungi that thrive in machine-friendly fields, and the winds and waters that flow differently when the trees have been uprooted. On the other hand, those who benefit from this uprooting act as if their lives were not obligated to these ravaged spaces—that what happens to them is only related to what is happening to me by some spectral connection. Rather than spooky action at a distance we can say they disavow their relationship to devastation at a distance; to the linkages between their healthy food, clean water, and fresh air, and the toxic dumps elsewhere. The answer from the white heteronormative households when (once again) forced to acknowledge that there is nothing ghostly at all about the circuits and transpositions connecting the 'common' body in one region of the world to another is that adequate infrastructure should be built for those who have none. In other words, the common body is still not acknowledged to be common. The rich cities and suburbs dig their psyches deeper into the disavowal. They refuse to acknowledge that new infrastructure would need to be built from materials found far away from their own neighbourhoods, ripped from someone else's land, manufactured in such a way that still another set of lands and peoples are contaminated. What they will never do is allow others to move into their suburbs or agree that some of the shiny lead-free pipes be ripped up and exchanged with others. And this too is true of nation-states signing climate change treaties. The very action of signing, or not, disavows that they could not be what they are without the surface and subterranean passages ravaging one area for the benefit of another. As Césaire, Arendt, and Mbembe all argued, the sewers will start overflowing at some point and then there will be nothing left to consume but one's own spoiled self.

But the common fate will never be experienced in a common time, intensity, or kind. *Zero Water Day* will occur somewhere first—looks like Cape Town. Specific Island nations will go underwater before other coastal cities. And what happens after this, somewhere else, will not be the same kind of thing. As the material effects ramify and then shift, so will the kinds of crises—new and unexpected forms of calamity or rescue. That's why it is right and wrong to say that if northern climate change policy makers want to see the future they should go look at places where it is already happening. What will happen to them will not be the same although it might be as hideous. Native and Indigenous lands are one of the places that are, and have been, the parallel future of the west. In these lands, Indigenous people are, indeed, grappling with unexpected forms of calamity and rescue. For instance, as you say, the young men in *Windjarrameru* carve out a toxic sovereignty in their chemically contaminated lands. To understand the paradox of this form of sovereignty we can turn to several Indigenous scholars who have been grappling with the toxicity of the concept of sovereignty. Aileen Moreton-Robinson, a member of the Quandamooka Nation from Stradbroke Island, Queensland, Australia, has systematically critiqued the 'white possessive' underlying the Western concept of sovereignty. The lands of Indigenous people were never empty (*terra nullius*), nor saleable (via treaty), nor subdue-able (through conquest).[5] Rather, people and land were in a relation of co-obligated bodily belonging. When Indigenous people claim sovereignty, they are swallowing a poisoned pill.

Rex Edmunds, an Emmiyangel member of the Karrabing Film Collective, makes a similar critique in a Karrabing film commissioned by Natasha Ginwala for exhibition at the IFA-Berlin. Not content to violently appropriate lands through the concept of British sovereignty, settlers insist Indigenous people internalize the same concept as if it were their own. For Edmunds, this symbolic form of equivalence—Western and Indigenous people communicate through the common concept of sovereignty—is a pipeline through which settlers can pump their discord and violence into and through Indigenous communities. By separating Indigenous people on the basis of Western imaginaries of traditional sovereignty, capitalists can pit them against each other. Business extracts billions as Indigenous people fight each other for the scraps left behind. 'Then that little part of the family gets that money for mining there, or running tourists....and that's why Indigenous people are fighting.' In his powerful analysis of capitalism and Indigenous dispossession, the Dene theorist Glen Coulthard writes:

> Aside from the inevitable debt trap that land claims lock many First Nations into, which can in turn compel these communities to open up their settlement lands to exploitation as an economic solution, it appears that the land-claims process itself has also served to subtly shape how Indigenous peoples now think and act in relation to the land ... I would suggest that one of the negative effects of this power-laden process of discursive translation has been a reorientation of the meaning of self-determination for many (but not all) Indigenous people in the North; a reorientation of Indigenous struggle from one that was once deeply *informed* by the land as a system of reciprocal relations and obligations (grounded normativity), which in turn informed our critique of capitalism in the period examined above, to a struggle that is now increasingly *for* land, understood now as material resource to be exploited in the capital accumulation process.[6]

Of course, the scraps are not merely the small amounts of money companies pay Indigenous owners to create billion-dollar profits for investors, but the toxicity that remains—affective toxicity as Edmunds notes, but also material toxicity. It is this latter form of toxicity that seems to create a new kind of sovereignty for the young men in the swamp, a form of toxicity that turns and bends away from its settler origins but without exactly purifying it of harm. Kelvin's statement seems to point to a horrifically unsettling truth, namely that it is only within utterly contaminated spaces made and then abandoned by settlers that he and his family can belong to each other and their ancestors without threat of settler interference. But note, unlike the cocooned white suburban heteronormative subject who refuses any real encounter with the common but unevenly distributed body, Kelvin doesn't offshore the ramifications of toxic present. He notes, pointing to a green glowing liquid the young men find in a contaminated swamp, that this is a gift from their ancestors, holds the substance of their ancestors (lips kissed this bottle), even as their ancestors are themselves making their way through the same contaminated land as the young men themselves. One of their sisters notes this mutual inhabitation of contamination when she says 'the old people'—the ones who she knew when they were alive—'said that grog is supposed to be red dark purple, not green'. But if the ancestors are indeed composed of the land, as Kelvin says, then the gifts they gift to sustain their descendants will be glowing green. What world comes—what is the traditional future—when material composition of the common is other than what is common?

V - The group's film-making unfolds a genre of 'Improvisational Realism,' an aesthetic that carries over from the Karrabing's everyday strategies of living within contaminated spaces, but it represents also 'returns to ancestral land, performances of heritage, and maintenance of diasporic ties' as 'strategies for moving forward, ways to articulate what can paradoxically be called traditional futures'. Could you develop this concept?

EAP - I think this takes us directly to the ideology of commonism in the shadow of obligation and aesthetics. The introduction to this volume argues that commonism is an ideology and like all ideologies assumes a 'one'; hides crucial features of power rather than reveals all features; and works by aesthetic (rhetorical) rather than propositional force. It dazzles rather than convinces. I think these observations are helpful in light of our discussion, although, of course, I would make amendments and footnotes.

First, I agree that the common must by necessity create and foreclose forms of power as it reveals the same. This is in the nature of all grids. They create a difference from what existed before as they cover it over in their analytics. But—or maybe just *and*—what they reveal and cover is as multiple as the terrains into which they are laminated. Here again we get to the common and differentiated, the blocked and disavowed. For instance, settler colonialism has attempted to govern my Indigenous Karrabing colleagues through a variant of Commonism, namely, the classical anthropology of Culture. The truth of Indigenous being lies in an unchanging, precolonial, culturally homogenous commonism. And the measure of their truth in the present is whether they still compose a homogenous commonism and how much or little they have changed from their supposedly original homogeneous commonism. Parul Sehgal quotes the Canadian Ojibwe author David Treuer in ways that are illuminating here. 'We function', he says in 2006, 'the way ghosts function in ghost stories.' 'We sort of hover around to admonish people about what they should be doing, what they're doing wrong, how they're destroying nature. We're always there, but chained to our own deaths, not really alive and active and engaged.'[7] Late settler liberalism functions by claiming the role of spiritual arbitrator: which ghosts do or don't deserve recognition, rights, and goods.

Secondly, I am not sure then that commonism would be the term my Karrabing colleagues would choose—though we not exactly disavow it. A group of us published a short conversation in Specimen on original linguistic multiplicity.[8] The conversation pivoted around the biblical story of Babel that imagines the original world as linguistically one and the cause of fall of man as linguistic diversity. My colleagues refuse this narrative, arguing that linguistic and social multiplicity was the foundation for a form of mutual co-substantiating respect. This is Cecilia Lewis and Linda Yarrowin.

> **Cecilia Lewis** – Yeah but here where you talk to det person [in their language] le you joinimupbet det tubela—and det nuther language where you speak le, that other person dem inside you again. You think bla det person.

Linda Yarrowin - Through marriage, ceremony, sweat you joinim but you also keep your roan roan strong. Det why people bin strong then. They bin respect that nuther person because they also bin connected like inside outside.

Thus, commonality is as Linda puts in the tension between the 'same but different' and the 'separate by connected' that emerges out of common-ability rather than common-ism, the ability to become something in the crossing over to someone else while remaining where you are; rather than being something being a one or another. Within this way of imagining the common, the possibility that you will become or want to become something more or less different always hovers over the scene of the common. The one is always under inspection by the other and vice versa. The same politics hovers over Karrabing: how are we same and different, separate and connected? What is causing the redistribution of powers on each side? what is causing the loss of the ability to have this form of the common? For Linda and Cecilia, the settler state imposes the one and the same to destroy the grounds of common-ability. As Linda says,

True. That land claim way same like language one. Magim meblea one, separate, separate mebela even though everyone same coast. What I was saying before, sis, many ways but berragut im magim just one thing and no connecting.

> True. Land claims operate the same way white language policy works: make everything one kind of thing and isolate people no matter that all come from the same coastline. It's what I was saying before, sister, we have many different ways, but white people make them all one thing with no connections across groups or lands.

We can ask the same sorts of questions about Karrabing itself. What provides the possibility of fashioning a common in the conditions of the toxically distributed present? One of the most obvious differences is that I am in Karrabing but not Indigenous. And the extimate circuits of wealth and impoverishment that fashion this difference beyond anything I could claim as *my intention* long before I arrived at Belyuen in 1984. Thus, my common-ability with my colleagues must respect, to use Linda's term, this fact—with respect a form of action rather than mentality. As I said above, the point is that in finding that I am not inside myself but a result of a complex terrain of distributed extractions and surpluses the question remains how can I and how will I shift the distribution of materiality and identity. This is not something I think about by myself, but something we as a group explicitly discuss and struggle with. The infrastructures that enhance me must be redirected to them and thus how to do this. But other members of the Collective insist that just because they are Indigenous does not mean that they are a homogenous one. Members of Karrabing have an insistent pride in their individual style within their constant practice of producing a mutual poetics.

Karrabing political 'strategies of traditional future' do not extend a precolonial oneness. They attempt to extend an analytics and process of common-ability.

Notes

1   Gerald Vizenor, *Manifest Manners: Narratives on Postindian Survivance* (Lincoln, NB: University of Nebraska Press, 1999).

2   Jacques Lacan coined the term 'extimacy' in order to signal linguistically the problematic of the topology of the external internality of the psyche. Here I extend this to material of existence more generally.

3   'Fire, Fog, Wind', in: *Elements for a World: Stone, Sky, Wood, Water, Fire*, ed. Ashkan Sepahvand, five volumes English/Arabic, as part of the exhibition *Let's Talk About the Weather: Art and Ecology in a Time of Crisis*, curated by Natasa Petresin-Bachelez and Nora Razian (Beirut: Sursock Museum, 2016). 'Breathing In, Breathing Out (Essay & Image)', in: *Grain Vapor Ray: Textures of the Anthropocene*, eds. Katrin Klingan et al. (Berlin: Haus der Kulturen der Welt, 2014).

4   Dipesh Chakrabarty, 'The Human Condition in the Anthropocene', lecture at Yale University, 18–19 February 2015.

5   Aileen Moreton-Robinson, *The White Possessive: Property, Power and Indigenous Sovereignty* (Minneapolis, MN: University of Minnesota Press, 2015).

6   Glen Sean Coulthard, *Red Skin, Black Masks* (Minneapolis, MN: University of Minnesota Press, 2014).

7   Parul Sehgal, 'Heart Berries' Shatters a Pattern of Silence', *New York Times*, 30 January 2018, www.nytimes.com/2018/01/30/books/review-heart-berries-terese-marie-mailhot.html

8   'Australian Babel: A Conversation with the Karrabing', www.specimen.press/writers/karrabing/.

Part 2

A-Legality & Commoning Economies

Precariat— A Revolutionary Class?

Lara Garcia Diaz
& Pascal Gielen

Multiple Precarization

The promotion of entrepreneurship by neoliberal policies has extended a new model of labour subjectivity based on risk-taking individualism (Berry 2016). Such subjectivity manifests itself in a growing precarization of a creative middle class on at least four levels. First, on the economic level, we see a growing competition that makes many freelancers take on commissions below cost price or even for a purely symbolic compensation. In addition, people incur more and more debts, also because the dismantling of the welfare state degrades other services too, such as free or cheap education and study grants. This means that the recently graduated often start their first commissioned work while still paying off their study loan (Graeber 2011). Freelancers take big financial risks as well because they take out cheap health insurance or none at all and postpone saving for their pension as long as possible. In doing so they effectively take out a mortgage on their future economic situation. Second, on the social level, increasing flexibilization and high mobility take their toll on social and private life of freelancers. As Richard Sennett stated in *The Corrosion of Character* (1998), freelancers and project workers are often forced to travel a lot and to move house frequently. This means that they have less time to engage in profound friendships or invest in family relationships. Professional network relations may increase strongly, while at the same time the quality of those relations decreases. Finally, the competition among freelancers and team workers is also not conducive to establishing trusting relationships. On the third, mental level, we can detect the increase of stress, more burnouts, and depressions. The combination of economic insecurity and social deprivation on the social level, as argued, makes a growing number of creative entrepreneurs seek psychological support and engage in all sorts of therapeutic coaching. And, finally, on the political level, freelancers and project workers are quite underrepresented politically. In order to obtain commissions, they had best not voice their ideological preferences. Especially unions are relatively taboo in the world of artists and creative workers.

This multiple precarization generally leads to a heightened sense of insecurity. Freelancers are never sure where the next commission will come from, they don't know whether they can confide in their competitors, and they can to a far lesser degree rely on the structural solidarity that was once safeguarded by the welfare state and its unions. This state of insecurity and precarity seems to have come to play a pivotal role in today's hegemonic mode of governance. Important to highlight is how, and this is different from the misery of the traditional proletariat, for whom the means of subsistence were often completely absent, our current precarity arises when the necessities for living are available but just not at one's disposal (Weareplanc 2014). In other words, if precarity works as a mode of governance, it is because the subjects governed live in a permanent state of dependency. By praying to an apparent 'protector', the precarious seek to end insecurity and hence diminish their vulnerability. However, vulnerability acquires a double logic here. On the one side, the precarious feels vulnerable and thus prays for security. On the other side, once the precarious obtain what they prayed for, they become extremely dependent on the power, or the protector, that secured them in the first place. If the counterpart of being precarious is protection and immunization against social and political instability and vulnerability, the result of such protection comes with processes of domination (Lorey 2010) and instability.

Supported by the concept of Michel Foucault's governmentality, political theorist Isabell Lorey brings forward the idea of *self-precarization* (2015). The figure of the entrepreneur relies on one's life as the enterprise of oneself and thus becomes responsible to provide for both the means of production and reproduction of one's own human capital (Lorey 2015; Gordon 1991). Accordingly, the entrepreneur is responsible for self-controlling, self-economing, and self-rationalizing his or her own labour time (Bröckling 2015). The entrepreneurial self becomes the only one responsible for embracing risk and insecurity, being the source of exploitation and the producer of existential anxiety. Equally, the entrepreneurs themselves becomes responsible for work security and insurance, for self-caring, self-curing and self-providing themselves in order to keep the production going. Asking for both professional and personal help, that is, not being able to perform individually, is a sign of weakness and of not being able to produce anymore in a neoliberal society. So, self-precarization has become the new type of oppression for the creative worker.

From Creative *Klasse an sich* to a Creative *Klasse für sich*
At first sight, the remedies for this existential anxiety and specific growing precarization seem to lie in solidarity and collectivization

(Neilson 2015). Like Karl Marx, who advocated the (international) organization of the proletariat, which required the change from a *Klasse an sich* (class-in-the-making) to a *Klasse für sich* (class-for-itself), we may ask ourselves whether the solution for the precarious creative class today also lies in forming such a collective class-consciousness. However, a number of fundamental differences between the proletariat and the precariat make it unlikely that similar solutions for improving their social position are available. Already in 1982, André Gorz declared the end of the proletariat and of the work society. For Gorz, just like the working class was shaped by the rise of capitalist production, so the 'non-class of non-workers' (Gorz 1982, p. 68) are the results of its crisis and decay. Indeed, the global economic crisis has eroded the security of the Fordist model, initiating a restructuring by the state limited by austerity measures that have affected every aspect of our lives. Still, it is necessary to recognize how as the result of the labour struggles of workers in the industrialized economies, the generations of the post-war boom were able to enjoy a higher degree of security and enjoy a decent education. We are talking here of the unique growth of a middle class, who, for the first time in history, could coexist between a higher and a lower class. This was accompanied by a welfare state that was able, temporarily, to support their emancipatory project. In that sense, one of the first divergences between the proletariat and the precariat is precisely the difference in origin and education. Whereas the proletariat of Marx' days, or the working class at the time of Pierre Bourdieu (1984), consisted of semi- or unskilled workers whose parents also lived at the lowest social level, the present-day precariats' origins are more diverse. This group includes both the skilled lower class and certainly also the so-called creative class, which have a mostly middle-class background and higher education. It seems that the internal division of the creative class of today is too great a hindrance for developing solidarity structures like trade unions. A cultural entrepreneur may, for example, be totally deprived socially and/or mentally but still do very well economically. And this while someone else may be living on the edge of poverty for years but still feel mentally healthy and creatively dynamic. It may be thus difficult to reconcile the wishes and demands of these two creative precariats. Moreover, it is important to note that the process of growing precarization occurs as an effect of the disintegration of different secure class positions, including mostly here the middle class. As a clear example of how self-exploitation has become, as argued, the new type of oppression, economist Joseph Brusuelas (2016) keeps insisting on how it is the middle class that has to undergo fundamental changes in order to restore the economy's most important growth engine. It is not that neoliberalism uses precarization as a mode of governing to keep the poor poorest and the rich richest, but rather it is the middle class that needs to improve, keep competitive, and become profit-obsessed if they want to conserve their middle-class position. This translates as: economy determines society and not the other way around (Polanyi 1944). Again, although the members of the creative middle-class precariat have completed a decent education, they are not conscious of themselves as an object and thus, in Georg Lukács (1923) terms, they lack 'true class consciousness'.

Finally, one of the most fundamental differences is that a working class of employees may confront their employers jointly and that the class of creatives of today, who, because of the prevailing freelance statute, are the employers of themselves as employees. This creative employer–employee has no other social class to point an accusing finger at. After all, the reason for their precarization lies partly in the risks that the creative entrepreneurs take upon themselves nowadays. Within the creative class the cause of precarization therefore partly lies in what we have addressed above, by using Lorey's terminology, as 'self-precarization' (2015). Each of us is only responsible for oneself, and as philosopher Judith Butler argues, 'that responsibility is first and foremost a responsibility to become economically self-sufficient under conditions when self-sufficiency is structurally undermined' (Butler 2015, p. 25). By placing the full responsibility on the entrepreneurs to fulfil their own demands, overwork, frustration, and anxiety become naturalized and overshadowed by a state of 'chronic insufficiency' (Bröckling 2015, p. 201).

The difference between the proletariat and the precariat, between the working class and the creative class, does thus suggest that the political challenges that this current moment presents seeks other revolutionary agencies and new methods of organization. These forms will need to go beyond trade union solidarities, Fordist economic structure, and more generally, the social state model and its welfare state. As pointed out before, one possible remedy, especially collectivization and mutual solidarity, may nonetheless be quite similar. Obviating current politics of pure victimization, Lorey suggests to counter-act constituent power through 'political practices based on the multiplicity of the precarious' (Lorey 2015, p. 109). Resonating Butler's proposition of precariousness as an ineradicable condition, and thus as a common condition, Lorey suggests precarity as a 'unifying factor' as opposed to a depoliticizing characteristic. In other words, the individual, independently of social group or class, becomes part of the precarious collective and hence acquires political agency. The common is produced through the communication among singularities (Hardt and Negri 2004) and precarity becomes a unifying and empowering commonality; a fearsome mode of constituting that allows searching for alternatives and inventing new forms of immunization that directly negates vulnerability and contingency (Lorey 2015). Crucial to emphasize here is how both Butler and Lorey understand 'composition' as a resistive moment, forms of coalition in the contemporary politics based on 'bodies in alliance' (Butler 2004) against a common economic precarity. Following this idea, we henceforth propose that rather than understanding the Precariat as a 'class in the making' (*Klasse an sich*), we understand precarity as *a point of articulation*, a negative moment of insubordination, towards the formation of a society based on common principles. Put another way, a common precarious condition becomes a starting point from where to start testing new collective identities and forms of organization, creative platforms of resistance and more collaborative social forms, which brings us to principles of commoning and commonism.

Articulation, Self-organization, and Commoning

Continuing with Marxian class theory, ideology has an important role in the process of class consciousness. By relating ideology to the goals of classes, Marx observed how dominant classes could maintain and reinforce their interests through the use of a concrete ideology. Following Marx, Lukács made a distinction between, on the one side, a 'false consciousness' derived from the upper classes, which presented economic laws as universal. While on the other side, and as indicated before, Lukács also signalled a 'true consciousness' coming from the proletariat, that was able to perceive itself as a consequence of historic capitalism. In this line of thought, ideology serves the upper class to establish a concrete system that, when internalized, becomes 'false consciousness'. The social consciousness promoted by dominant ideology, enforced in capitalism by alienating human labour and marketing human productive capacity, does not encourage the discovery of reality and thus promotes an inaccurate, or false consciousness. But what then promotes 'true consciousness'? It seems, within this logic, that the proletariat's 'true consciousness' was possible by actually not having any ideology beforehand and somehow acquiring such revolutionary knowledge once the revolution was already there. Therefore, as a precondition to communism, which was to be the result of the proletariat's rejection of capitalism, Marx described a transitional socialist state that would be able to create a reified reality that would uncover the essence of capitalist reality and bring about an 'anticipatory class consciousness' (Jakubowski 1936, p. 117). Overcoming this class reductionism, Italian theorist and politician Antonio Gramsci (1971) broke up and opened up Marxist understanding of ideology by including the idea of hegemony and, in particular, the concepts of 'organic ideology' and 'organic intellectual'. Within this framework, ideology does not belong to a concrete class structure, but instead, ideological systems navigate between different social classes through ideological discourses and elements. Such different ideological elements are organically arranged in a social system in which a class not just holds economic supremacy but also has successfully articulated essential elements of its ideological discourses through the civil society, ultimately achieving social hegemony or power. Gramsci's concept of hegemony is therefore based on the success of the dominant classes in presenting their definition of reality and in the acceptance of that reality by other social classes as 'common sense'. Thereafter, social institutions and structures such as the family, universities, churches, or trade unions become sources from where organic ideology is diffused, coexisting between different class interests and finally creating a concrete hegemonic system with its own concrete socioeconomic relations.

What Gramsci's theory of hegemony brings to the fore are two very important points for our discussion. On the one hand, it insists again on how heterogeneous collaboration and social solidarity between different social classes and interests are necessary. Far from perceiving one single dominant class, Gramsci describes an unstable and shifting system in which social classes are in a permanent 'war of position'. It is not enough to struggle for the control over the means of production, as it is equally important to struggle over the deconstruction of ideas and beliefs. On the other hand, the introduction of the figure of the 'organic intellectual' in the hegemonic approach brings forward how artistic and cultural practices can provide spaces for resistance as they contribute to the disarticulation of previous ideological principles and the re-articulation of new forms capable of inaugurating a new consciousness for the precariat.

Following this, we would like to propose here how this new consciousness for the precariat can be constructed on a number of levels. In the first place, there is the level of the *articulation* in which the current economic and political system is criticized and alternatives are formulated. Articulations mainly take place in the public and discursive space, where ideas are confronted with each other in dissent. Theatres, museums, festivals and biennials are nowadays an important platform for such articulating practices. However, ideas alone cannot produce real social changes. In the second place, therefore, citizens need to take action and start experimenting with forms of self-organization, or, in the parlance of Butler and Lorey respectively, building *compositions* (Lorey 2010) based on 'bodies in alliance' (Butler 2004, pp. 66–98). Self-organization, however, is usually initiated locally. In this case, economic and political problems, such as precarization, are addressed for a relatively small and primarily closed community but do not build an effective counter-hegemony, which, after all, requires structural interventions. In order to build an effective counter-hegemony—i.e., one that can really overturn the present neoliberal hegemony of precarization—alternative models must be distributed and, especially, shared beyond local borders. This is, in the third place, what we call the process of *commoning*. Alternative economies and forms of self-organization must demonstrate their effectiveness to others if they are to generate structural effects. This necessitates the preferably free or very low-cost sharing of information and knowledge, of materials and logistics, but also of business models and new solidarity structures based on trust and mutual support. A counter-hegemony strategy that fundamentally addresses precarization should also influence institutional bodies. It is only when actions take place on this political and legislative level that counter-hegemony reform may actually take place and the current precarization can be addressed in a structural manner. So, artists and creative workers who want to escape the contemporary precarious condition need to develop at least three different activities: (1) *articulation*, (2) *composition*, and (3) *commoning*.

The Commonist Creative Precariat

It seems obvious that creative professionals and the precariat in general are in need of new forms of collective protection. It's probably one of the reasons why more and more artists literally 'collectivize' their activities. They then form collectives in which they share materials and studio space as well as social contacts, thereby cutting costs. In some cases, this even leads to more complex systems of solidarity in which participants in, for example, cooperatives set up an alternative health insurance and provide other forms of social security. For this reason, young, sometimes still budding initiatives explore the wasteland between market and state, between commercial value and political-cultural value. Overall, what these commoning initiatives have in common is that they set up alternative exchange systems (e.g. a sharing economy) and solidarity structures in which, under certain conditions, goods and services are exchanged for free or at least cheaper than in a free market economy. This also concerns ways of working that require designing and enforcing copyleft and other legal regulations, such as the Creative Commons licence.

From Wikipedia and Peer-2-Peer foundations on the Internet to off-line organizations such as Culture 2 Commons in Croatia, Recetas Urbanas in Spain, or Fora do Eixo in Brazil and Ex Asilo in Italy, they all confirm a growing number of creative initiatives that generate completely different forms of working and organizing. Despite their great diversity, what all these initiatives have in common is that they are built within the civil domain. That is to say, they all start with a civil initiative for which a government has not or not yet designed regulation or subsidies and that is not or not yet of commercial interests to a free market (Dietachmair en Gielen 2017). From there they develop commoning practices which trickle into the studio at home (for example, open source projects such as Wikipedia and Linux) where they make free knowledge and free creative tools available. This sort of commoning practices generate free knowledge by launching debates and sometimes activists' discussions in art academies, during artist-in-residencies, and open studios where they analyze their social position from an economic, political, and social perspective, as well as from an ecological one. In addition, they penetrate the market itself by introducing alternative economies (via, for example, cooperatives) and alternative laws or regulations (such as the already mentioned Creative Commons licence) (Lessig 2004).

Commoning organizations do not only have in common that they develop, simultaneously, activities in the most divergent fields. They also freely mix formal and informal relations, public and private, politics and labour in how they are structured. Just as in mixed farms or the traditional circus, family relations and friendships are combined with professional roles, and commercial and civil activities merge into each other to the point that they can no longer be distinguished. Also, whereas many services are exchanged for free, others are strictly regulated and formalized in contracts. Precisely because of this heterogeneity our hypothesis is that their organizational form may be more suited to the creative labour model in which individuals are involved as a whole. In contrast with the traditional union they at least respond to the different layers of precarization mentioned before (social, mental, economic, political). Organizations of the commons attempt to solve very practical and daily problems through mutual agreements and a division of tasks. To illustrate this with a concrete example: when one artist 'works the market', another artist within the same organization has time and space to experiment and develop new work, since the latter is temporarily exempt from earning money, through a system of reciprocity. It is evident that social relations or the collectivization of activities make it possible to establish more sustainable practices. In any case, the collective labour model provides better opportunities and also more security than the dominant freelance model of the creative industries. After all, this latter, post-Fordist labour model only pays for production time, while other things necessary to produce, such as education, intimacy, reproduction, or reflection time are more and more shifted to the private sphere and the personal responsibility of the creative worker. By contrast, a collective and heterogeneous commoning labour model tries to meet the needs of both production and reproduction. That is, it also contemplates the important sphere outside of labour and the market.

The potential advantages of the heterogeneous and collective organization that we have brought forward, however, do not protect it from certain serious problems. For example, the typical heterogeneity and hybridity of its social organization can also carry the seed of dysfunctions we are familiar with from traditional mixed (family) businesses, such as nepotism and fraudulent tendencies. Moreover, such organizations are not only threatened from the inside, but from the outside as well. Self-organizing makes it easy for (neoliberal) governments to relieve themselves of public tasks that were originally theirs. Governments may find it easy to ignore their cultural and educational responsibilities, if these tasks are already spontaneously taken care of by volunteer initiatives. However, less government involvement also means that it becomes more difficult to develop a broader social support base in the civil domain. Organizations of the commons—especially in the art field—are therefore at risk of becoming relatively closed peer communities of insiders or 'connoisseurs'. In addition, commercial parties can then pass on a large part of the labour costs to these commons and only reap the lucrative benefits. Commons organizations have always run the risk of attracting 'free riders' (Ostrom 1990), individuals or organizations trying to walk away with the profit without investing in the commons proportionally. Further research will have to reveal what are the values and traps of these creative collective labour models. What, for example, are fitting legal and political conditions for an optimal functioning of the institutions of the commons?

As long as futurology is not an empirical science, it will be hard to predict whether this advent of commonism will continue. However, we would like to conclude with what has been exposed before, i.e. how the precariat is definitely using different revolutionary strategies than the old proletariat. While the latter mainly concentrated on labour relationships (via the union) and wage industrial work as the main source to improve its life, the commoning precariat is nowadays concentrating on the heterogeneous conditions of all of life to improve that life itself. It's probably this heterogeneous undertaking, and the implications of creating forms of organization that decentres the interests of the market and puts instead the sustainability of life at the centre, which also makes commonism look quite different from its communist predecessor.

References

— Berry, Josephine. 2016. 'Agents of Objects of Discontinuous Change? Blairite Britain and the Role of the Culturepreneur.' *Cultural Policies: Agendas of Impact. Kunstlicht* 37 (1-2016 Volume), pp. 25-36.

— Boltanski, Luc, and Eve Chiapello. 2006. *The New Spirit of Capitalism.* London and New York: Verso.

— Bourdieu, Pierre. 1984. *Distinction: A Social Critique of Taste.* London and New York: Harvard University Press.

— Bröckling, Ulrich. 2015. *The Entrepreneurial Self: Fabricating a New Type of Subject.* Los Angeles and London: Sage.

— Brusuelas, Joseph. 2016. *The End of the Middle Class: What Went Wrong and What We Can Do About It.* New Jersey: John Wiley & Sons.

— Butler, Judith. 2015. *Notes Towards a Performative Theory of Assembly.* Cambridge, MA: Harvard University Press.
—. 2004. *Precarious Life: The Powers of Mourning and Violence.* London and New York: Verso.

— Foucault, Michel. 1991. 'Governmentality.' In *The Foucault Effect: Studies in Governmentality.* Edited by Graham Bruchell et al., pp. 87-104. Chicago, IL: University of Chicago Press.

— Garcia Diaz, Lara, and Pascal Gielen. 2017. 'Precarity as an Artistic Laboratory for Counter-Hegemonic Labour Organization.' In *Precarious Work, Precarious Life: Frame Journal of Literary Studies,* Issue 30.2 (December).

— Dietachmair, Philipp, en Pascal Gielen, eds. 2017. *The Art of Civil Action: Political Space and Cultural Dissent* (Antennae-Arts in Society). Amsterdam: Valiz.

— Gielen, Pascal. 2015a. 'A Caravan of Freedom. Mobile Autonomy beyond "Auto-Mobility".' In *Mobile Autonomy: Exercises in Artists' Self-Organization.* Edited by Nico Dockx and Pascal Gielen, pp. 63-84. Amsterdam: Valiz.
—. 2015b. *The Murmuring of the Artistic Multitude: Global Art, Politics and Post-Fordism.* Amsterdam: Valiz.

— Gordon, Colin. 1991. 'Govern-mental Rationality: An Introduction'. In *The Foucault Effect: Studies in Governmentality.* Edited by Graham Burchell, Colin Gordon and Peter Miller, pp. 1-54. Chicago, MA: University of Chicago Press.

— Gorz, André. 1982. *Farewell to the Working Class, An Essay on Post-industrial Socialism.* London: Pluto Press.
—. 2004. 'Économie de la connaissance, exploitation des savoirs.' *Multitudes,* 15, www.multitudes.net.

— Graeber, David. 2011. *Debt: The First 5,000 Years.* New York: Melville House.

— Gramsci, Antonio. 1971. *Selections from the Prison Notebooks.* London: New Left Books.

— Hardt, Michael, and Antonio Negri. 2004. *Multitude.* New York: Penguin Press.

— Harvey, David. 2011. 'The Future of the Commons.' *Radical History Review* 109 (Winter 2011) MARHO: The Radical Historians' Organization, Inc.
—. 2005. *A Brief History of Neoliberalism.* New York: Oxford University Press.

— Jakubowski, Franz. 1936 (1978). *Ideology and Superstructure in Historical Materialism.* London: Pluto Press, 1978.

— Laclau, Ernesto, and Chantal Mouffe. 1985. *Hegemony and Socialist Strategy: Towards a Radical Democratic Politics.* London and New York: Verso.

— Lessig, Lawrence. 2004. *Free Culture: How Big Media uses Technology and the Law to Lock Down Culture and Control Creativity.* New York: Penguin Press.

— Lorey, Isabell. 2006. 'Governmentality and Self-Precarization: On the Normalization of Cultural Producers.' In *Transversal:* http://eipcp.net/transversal/1106/lorey/en.
—. 2010. 'Becoming Common: Precarization as Political Constituting.' *e-flux* #17, www.e-flux.com/journal/17/67385/becoming-common-precarization-as-political-constituting/.
—. 2015. *State of Insecurity: Government of the Precarious.* London and New York: Verso.

— Lukács, György. 1923 (1971). *History and Class Consciousness: Studies in Marxist Dialectics.* London: Cambridge University Press.

— Marx, Karl. 1874 (1974). *Capital: A Critique of Political Economy. Volume 1.* Translated by B. Fowkes, New York: Vintage Books.
—. 1846-1847. *Das Elend der Philosophie.* In *MEW,* Band 4, pp. 63-182. Berlin: Dietz Verlag.

— Mouffe, Chantal. 2013. *Agonistics: Thinking the World Politically,* London and New York: Verso.

— Neilson, David. 2015. 'Class, Precarity, and Anxiety under Neoliberal Global Capitalism: From Denial to Resistance.' *Theory & Psychology* 25, no. 2, pp. 1–18.

— Ostrom, Elinor. 1990. *Governing the Commons: The Evolution of Institutions for Collective Action.* Cambridge, MA: Cambridge University Press.

— Polanyi, Karl. 1944 (2001). *The Great Transformation: The Political and Economic Origins of Our Time.* Boston, MA: Beacon Press.

— Power, Michael. 1994. *The Audit Explosion.* London: Demos.

— Sennett, Richard. 1998. *The Corrosion of Character: The Personal Consequences of Work in the New Capitalism.* London: W.W. Norton Company.

— Srnicek, Nick, and Alex Williams. 2015. *Inventing the Future: Postcapitalism and a World Without Work.* London and New York: Verso.

— Standing, Guy. 2011. *The Precariat: The New Dangerous Class.* London: Bloomsbury Academic.

— UNIZO.2015. *Freelancers Focus.* Brussel: UNIZO. www.unizo.be.

— Virno, Paolo. 2004. *A Grammar of the Multitude: For an Analysis of Contemporary Forms of Life.* Translated by Isabella Bertoletti, Andrea Casson, and James Cascaito. Los Angeles, CA: Semiotext(e).

— Weareplanc. 2014. 'We Are All Very Anxious'. *Plan C.* www.weareplanc.org/blog/we-are-all-very-anxious/.

Commoning Art, Democracy, and the Precariat, a Dialogue

Evi Swinnen
in Conversation with
Michel Bauwens

Michel Bauwens – Dear Evi, I look forward to a discussion with you that explores the intersection between the commons, the world of art and culture, and the situation of artists. I would then like to expand the conversation to also address the kinds of cultural and artistic expressions that are emerging alongside the new commons.

Let me begin by presenting the evolution of the P2P Foundation's work with regard to the commons. About ten years ago, we started our work by focusing on the dynamics of peer production communities. Specifically, we looked at the interconnections between global open-source communities, their relationship to entrepreneurs active in markets, and their governance and property mechanisms. What we found was a working ecosystem at the micro-level that contained lessons for the political economy as a whole. So, we started working on institutional design issues, focusing first on the relations between commons and the markets, and how to generate ethical, non-exploitative livelihoods that would recognize not just market value, but all value contributions. We then shifted our attention to public-commons cooperation with projects about generating nation-state level productive knowledge commons in Ecuador, and a commons transition plan for the city of Ghent. This is where we met and where I asked you to be our new chairperson.

Evi Swinnen – My dear friend, more than a year has passed since we met and felt a strong connection in our ambition; me as a practitioner, you on a visionary theoretical level, both striving for a better world. Contemplating your words, I think back to ten years ago, and recall the atmosphere that set the stage for the founding of the P2P Foundation and, probably not by coincidence, for the first steps in the development of my organization, Timelab.

In 2008, when I got involved in the upcoming peer-to-peer movement, ideas about open-source and inclusive production were beginning to influence the international art scene. Important influencers at the time were the Pixelache/Mal au Pixel/Bricolabs network and hacker spaces popping up in Berlin and Brussels, and a short time later also in Ghent.

In many ways, the expansion of this movement to the art world was not so surprising. The open-source ideology began in the digital world but came to life through the hacker class, a politically engaged community of people who were forced to address the system collapse that resulted from the 2008 financial crisis. Hackers are motivated to take action based on critical thinking and shared expertise. Enabled by the World Wide Web, individual ICT companies were booming as a result of smart and fast open-source networks. They experienced the power of contribution and collaboration leading to direct individual success. The success stories of open-source web companies initiated an array of new perspectives on collaboration, motivation, shared resources, and so on. At an unstoppable speed, a new economy was built on open-source ideology.

It wasn't long before open-source concepts began to manifest themselves in the material world. Open hardware communities and networks such as the Fablab network became the next big thing. Open and accessible machines and designs became the tools for empowering people. A shared set of values in the *Fab Charter* and *Maker Movement Manifesto* turned an ideology into the Maker Movement.

It was against this backdrop that Timelab was founded in 2010 as an experimental art organization looking at upcoming P2P communities as inspiring models for new ways to collaborate, work, and live together. We opened the first fablab in Belgium as a place for local makers and international artists to collaborate, producing locally and sharing globally.

MB – Lately, at the P2P Foundation we are moving into a new phase, focusing less on the productive community-entredonneurial coalition (our name for generative market entities that favour the commons and the commoners)-partner state relations, and more on the underlying dynamics for such a shift. In particular, we are now looking at how to develop contributory accounting and shared circular supply chains that can operate within the bio capacity limits of our planet, while at the same time addressing social conditions. In particular, we are interested in what we call 'commonfare', a new welfare system that covers subsistence and provides social protection for everyone, not just for salaried workers. Our aim is to arrive at a pre-distributive economy that produces in the right social and ecological way, rather than a redistributive economy, which extracts value from humans and nature in unsustainable ways and then merely tries to mitigate the resulting crises.

ES – This is such an interesting evolution, Michel; we are going beneath the surface, into the code and looking for real systemic transformation. I believe this is the result of repeatedly bumping up against the same obstacles and becoming aware of abstracts we had previously blindly accepted under the ruling ideology of capitalism. Market and state, supported by legislation, promote free-market values as part of our freedom as human beings, as part of our welfare and well-being, as part of our identity. The belief that we need individuals in competition for the market and welfare to flourish is a false assumption that has governed our society for 250 years. So many people still believe there is no alternative, but when exploring the underlying dynamics, many new options arise.

The shift from market-based to culture-based society is one of those new options with fundamental impact. Having operated in the art scene for nearly twenty years, I am a strong believer in the value of culture as the foundation of society, instead of the dominant market logic of today. I have seen how capitalism takes over and controls the life and production of an artist. As happened with culture, art has also become the result of free-market and neoliberal dynamics, which dampen the human propensity for creating beauty and being reflective. I also witnessed artists struggling with their position, their different roles and identity. They are troubled about how to relate to society, constantly dealing with questions of ownership and the form of the art piece, and, at the most fundamental level, the precarity of their livelihood. A number of assumptions dominate the modern-day art world:

> Art being art if placed in an art institution. Subversive art is only valuable in the 'safe' environment of the art institution. The artist as an outlaw.

To be poor is to be creative. True art is the product of the individual talented mind of the artist, all the others need to be subsidized to survive. The career of the artist is the result of individual achievements and claims of intellectual ownership. A smart artist is the one who knows how to sell or knows how to find a way to financial capital.

By introducing open-source hardware systems, shared knowledge, and peer production as part of an open, reliable and neutral cultural environment, an increasing number of artists are rejecting the artist-as-outlaw trope and taking on a collaborative role in a community.

The construct of our economy, our society, and our relationships that was built upon since the emergence of neoliberalism and capitalism, is being hacked by a new old belief that could be called: commonism. Current research shows the importance of collaboration, intrinsic motivation, appreciation, shared dreams, and belonging as driving the meaning of our existence. Commonism proves there is an alternative. That is what I learned from working with you, Michel. The process of commoning re-instils the value of unconditional contribution and proves that structural collaboration and intrinsic motivation are not only suiting the human condition and its balanced relationship with the environment but are also a legitimate fundament for a new economy as a side-product of a shared cultural environment.

MB – As part of this evolution, I have joined SMart, the original Belgian labour mutual, which is also an organizing force for the precariat. It was originally named 'United Passions', i.e. seeing creatives as passionate producers, just as peer production does. There is a direct link from artists as the first prefigurative precarious producers to how that precarity is increasingly becoming the general condition of production for all workers, and how the precariat, consisting of many nomadic project-based workers, are intrinsically connected to the networks and co-producing commons. In other words, I contend there is a natural affinity between the contemporary creative worker, the precariat as a kind of 'new class', and the commoners, as a subject-in-be-coming that is creating post-capitalist realities to overcome the crisis induced by the capital system.

ES – If I understand you correctly, you believe that the condition of the artist as an autonomous but financially poor being in neoliberal times foreshadows an upcoming class of commoners who, fed up with the capitalist system, will strive for a new and more collaborative reality, but will find themselves in the same precarious situation. How can we bypass this cycle?

Since we organized the series of talks about Urban Commons in Ghent, together, we have continued to reflect upon how artists are dealing with opportunities and changes created by the revival of the commons in the last couple of years. In the fall of 2017, Timelab came to the cautious con-clusion that we needed to reorganize the way that we, as an art organisation, support the artist. The first conclusion was to stress the importance of a residency programme, with the defined time and space artists need to have the freedom to just 'be'. Supported in their livelihood and personal growth and contributing to a community because of their autono-mous position, they will be free to hack things that we take for granted. They will create alternatives that will lead to systemic transformations without losing dignity, vulnera-bility, identity, or image. Secondly, we decided to replace the word 'artist' with 'being,' because being called an artist risks confining a person to a specific role. The third import-ant feedback we received from artists was that the focus of support is not on the production of the art piece, but on livelihood and personal growth through relationships. So, by taking time, being supported in basic livelihood, as an autonomous being, the artist will become resilient in soci-ety and give back the insights we need to become more resi-lient as people living and working together.

How will this process be initiated? We will learn and experiment with commons strategies and organiza-tional models of e.g. localization, peer production, and edu-cation. This will all happen in a shared space, which will have a maker lab, foodlab, an arena for political debate, a centre for wellbeing and quietness, and an open space for communal activities. The artist will be one of the players in the community, in reciprocity and with the ability to open up new perspectives. I can only imagine this could be a pilot for a larger scale residency programme for the commoners class.

I believe the role of the artist in commoning and commonism is not limited to hacking codes and opening new perspectives. I also believe the community of autonomous beings has the ability to initiate interesting pilots for commonfare, developing instruments and experiments of pre-distributive economic systems. As long as we don't cage the results in the institutionalized art market, I am convinced artists will play an important role in commonism. In order to do so, and still be able to support one's livelihood, we need strong cooperative structures. This is the point where artists and commoners can meet as peers.

MB – I am glad to hear this. As an outsider to the world of art, I have noticed a more communal spirit taking over in artist communities. I remember how, thirty years ago, I was shocked by the competition among individual artists, just as you can now see the toxic atmosphere in academia, where the competition for funding makes cooperation difficult. What I would like to see is more of what you are pioneering at Timelab, some kind of convergence between artistic activity, 'making' and community, whereby artists are not standing outside of society, but are part and parcel of the new commons-based making cultures. In this context, I have enjoyed reading about the resurgence of Proletkult founder Bogdanov, in McKenzie Wark's book *Molecular Red*, for example.

ES – What I understand from Bogdanov's writings is the affirmative aspect of ideology, how ideology can overcome resistance, and how we are all united when facing the same danger. In that sense, my experience tells me we have to look at the underlying structures instead of at differences. We have to look into the forms and systems we use to organize ourselves. The definition of the commons described by David Bolier, the one we have been using since our time working together in Ghent, includes exactly that idea of an underlying structure or ideology for collaboration that doesn't require agreement. This is why I find Keller Easterling's *Extrastatecraft* and McKenzie Wark's *Hacker Manifesto* so inspiring. This is also why, at Timelab, we focus on *how* to organize instead of *what* we organize. We call Timelab a city lab for new models, models for collaboration, for labour, for living together. The support we offer to residents is coaching on how to organize and collaborate, instead of productional support. This change in approach is based on recurrent feedback from the artists themselves.

MB – I don't know if you are familiar with the Indian caste system, which broadly represents four human types or societal functions: the intellectual/spiritual types, the warriors, the merchants and the workers. According to the negative cyclical theories of the Hindus—who believe we are in the degenerate Kali Yuga age—we saw a descent from Brahmin rule, to warrior rule to merchant rule and then to workers' rule, which is how some interpret the managerial dominance today.

Now notice what is happening in coworking, maker spaces, fablabs and artistic production centres such as Macao: doing and thinking are merging again, but the material work is all done because of intellectual and spiritual inspiration, a common object that the open-source communities gather around. I'll put it to you that this is an expression of the Bogdanovite dream: the producers (largely uneducated in his time, which is why the Proletkult pro-ject failed) is that we now have a unique breed of educated workers, who can both make and design things and be self-reflexive about it, individually and collectively. In other words, I am positing the hypothesis of a new cycle of history, centred on commons production, and led by this Brahmin-worker synthesis.

ES – What you state here is extremely important. Throughout the western liberalization process and the concomitant view on the nature of humankind there has been a loss of perspective. People operate as if the world does not exist beyond their own life or the life of their children, which is quite scary in light of the speed of degradation of our planet. If the merchants' era is breaking down into the workers' era, we will undoubtedly need new organizational models based on collective and trustful collaboration.

MB – It is in this light that I am troubled by the rapid increase in anarcho-capitalists and their extraordinary capacity to fund themselves. They are an expression of the creative class, especially developers and designers, who aim to wrest control of surplus value creation away from shareholders, so that each individual stands on his own. It is urgent to develop commons alternatives where these inequality-creating market dynamics can be subsumed to a larger common good, which is the reproduction of all commoners and contributors. What is needed is a convergence between solidarity and contribution.

ES – I am believer of the tolerant and warm nature of the human being—and I know you are too. At Timelab, we have promoted open and shared structures and knowledge for years. Timelab aims to be a safe environment for exploring those human values. Despite research in the field of neurology and psychology, proving human beings are soft-wired to be empathic, I can often hear people think,

> This is too obvious. We all know what happens when you take away the thrill of competition. It will undermine human identity. It will lead to corruption and the exploitation of our planet, also known as 'the tragedy of the commons'. It will bring us back to the dark ages. How naive it is to think empathy is the way out; this is against human nature.

Anarcho-capitalism is indeed a scary upcoming ideology that goes even further, aiming to shift public services to unaccountable private institutions, and assuming the nature of humanity is to strive for freedom by enslaving others. Still, isn't this the direct result of the degeneration of the commons? And isn't that the reason why the reconstruction of a new urban commons is so important? In the end, it all comes down to a different view on the nature of human beings.

This is my belief: As 'beings' we contribute to our shared culture through our relationships and the esteem we place on togetherness. Values such as trust, honesty, respect, empathy, collaboration, and the will to help each other, are fundamentally different from profit and economic competition that lead to envy, greediness, loss of dignity, and distrust.

MB – In my view, we have a struggle between three worldviews now: the vision of Leviathan, the state and corporate sovereigns that want to control us through data ownership and manipulation; the vision of Mammon, where everything becomes a market, up to the smallest micro level of human activity; and Gaia, the dream of working more communally again, in harmony with the planet and safeguarding social justice. The artists were the vanguard of the precarious class, which is now becoming the standard condition of workers, and so their problems are now the problems of the universal precariat. This is why the experimental findings of art collectives can contain lessons for all passionate producers.

What you say about reforming Timelab is in line with my work as a strategic consultant for the labour mutual SMart: we are also trying to move from 'income' to life. As you know, SMart's focus has been to create social protection and more income stability for a majority of artists. Now, however, we are exploring how SMart can become an agent of commonified, mutualized lifestyles, not just securing the income of the precarious worker, but making sure they can have the kind of life they want and reducing their costs by helping them affiliate with others. It is no coincidence that SMart first name was United Passions. I wish they had kept it!

ES – That is a very interesting evolution from a focus on product/income to livelihood/self-support, and at the same time, the idea raises many questions. I can't stop thinking about the importance of autonomy. The true artist is an autonomous thinker and actor. This is without a doubt the reason why you call the artists the vanguard of the precarious class. More and more commoners are becoming autonomous thinkers and actors, which makes them increasingly independent of market and state, but also very vulnerable. The negotiation between both parties is not clear, because it is shifted to a group. Logics of supply and demand are broken because individuals are contributing in ways that are not measured by the current market system. That is exactly why I believe we need to experiment on multiple levels.

I want to talk about one such experiment conducted by Timelab. Years ago, we started a co-op as an experiment to reward and acknowledge the role of the arts in our society. The artists created products from resources previously considered as problematic. A gin was made from the exotic invasive species Japanese Knotweed, and soon after a building material was fabricated from the same plant. To address the overpopulation of Canada Geese, a stew was created that incorporated the nuisance fowl in a useful manner (as opposed to pointless extermination). In a collaboration with business partners, these products, initially designed as an artistic expression and reaction to invasive species, entered the commercial market. A cooperative legal structure was set up to realize an indirect return for the artist. All artists in Timelab became shareholders and any possible production partner was requested to become shareholder too. All shareholders were asked to contribute an exclusive offer to the group of stakeholders. By the individual action of all stakeholders a shared stock of assets was being produced. This stock and network could then be used to support the livelihood of the artist. What we see here is a form of commoning. We built a set of shared assets together, based on contributive actions of artists and market. Through this experiment we gained many new insights about how we need to organize ourselves. But above all, we need to think about how to build a strong livelihood for artists. How do we build social rights? What about profits as the result of the work of the artist? If we cannot protect intellectual property, how do we define the value of the arts in society and how do we prevent the artist from precarity?

I do believe that is also the reason why you are involved in SMart. With all my heart, I do hope SMart or United Passions can be the platform to support a large group of creative workers and commoners. However, many people living in precarious situations today have neither the mental nor financial space to step into an unpredictable experiment. As such, we need to create safe zones first, and set up structures for unconditional financial support.

MB – I completely agree that experimentation is the way forward, and I think the best approach is indeed to mutualize governance and property. Finding the right combination of ethical markets, commons, and public common good institutions will be key and the right hybrids will depend on many specific contexts. However, if experimentation is the path, as you suggest, how do we avoid fragmentation, how do we learn from each other and form a knowledge pool for 'peer-to-peer' learning, especially concerning complex governance models?

ES – Firstly, we need a school. We need to exchange knowledge on an international level, in practice and not only digitally; we need to bring to life the knowledge developed in our network. We don't need to look for differences and check our competitive advantage; we need to look for common ground to build on. We need a partnership with the state that is based on unconditional support for creating space and time for experiments. We need to prioritize sharing our findings within this safe environment. We need more scientific methodology, better collaboration with academia, and a strategy for commoning the knowledge that is locked in institutions. We need transparent and honest exploration of logistical and manufacturing systems to recognize new opportunities for local manufacturing. We need education in politics, democracy and public domain. We need facilitators and coaches to guide new groups of commoners in their own governance structure and decision-making processes. We need decentralized auditing networks that evaluate business and governments in a peer-to-peer manner. And finally, but perhaps most importantly, we need a new vocabulary that can create a culture and identity based on true human values of contribution.

délicieux... ...pâté en croûte d'argent

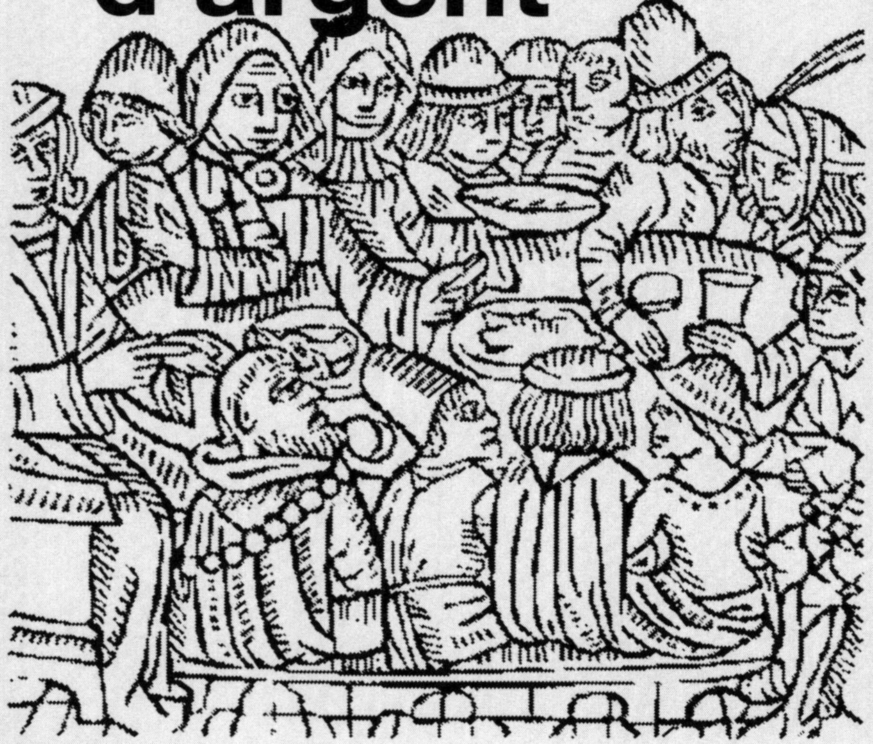

Délicieux…, *Nuke Magazine*, 2006

La aparente union del cielo y la tierra...

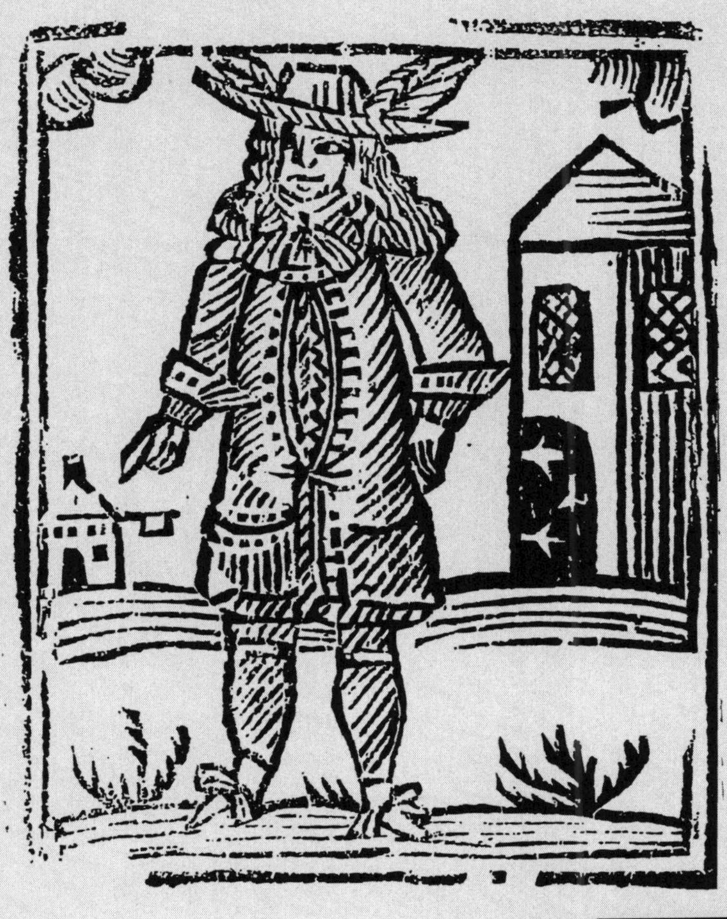

La aparente union del cielo y la tierra B, Locust Projects, 2010

No-Pressure Economies

Nico Dockx in Conversation with Rirkrit Tiravanija, Sedhapong Kirativongkamchon, Paphonsak La-or & Superflex about the *land* foundation

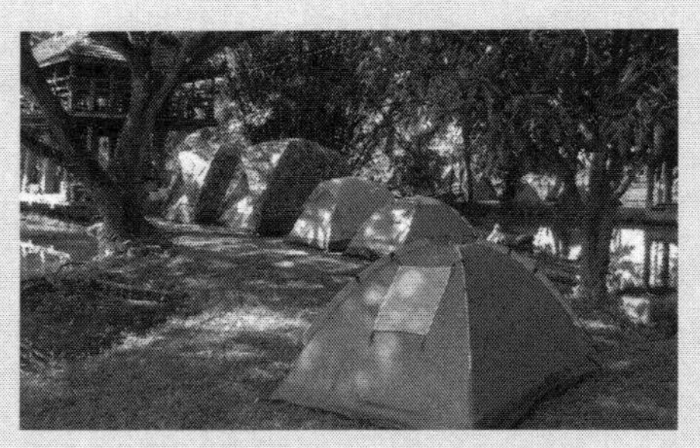

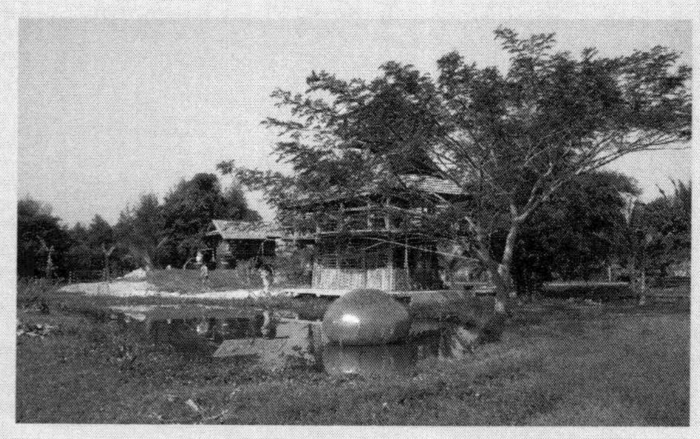

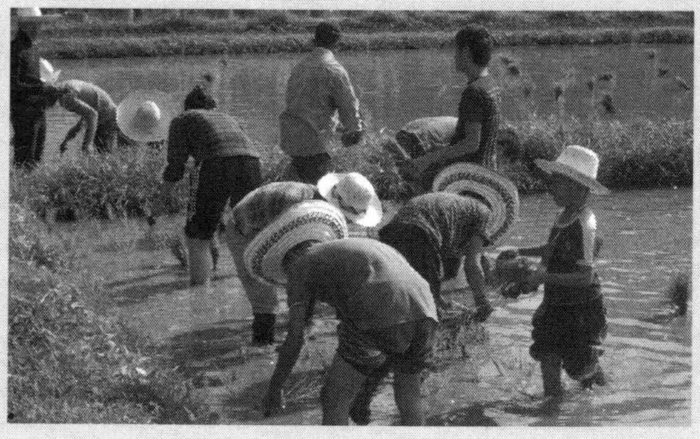

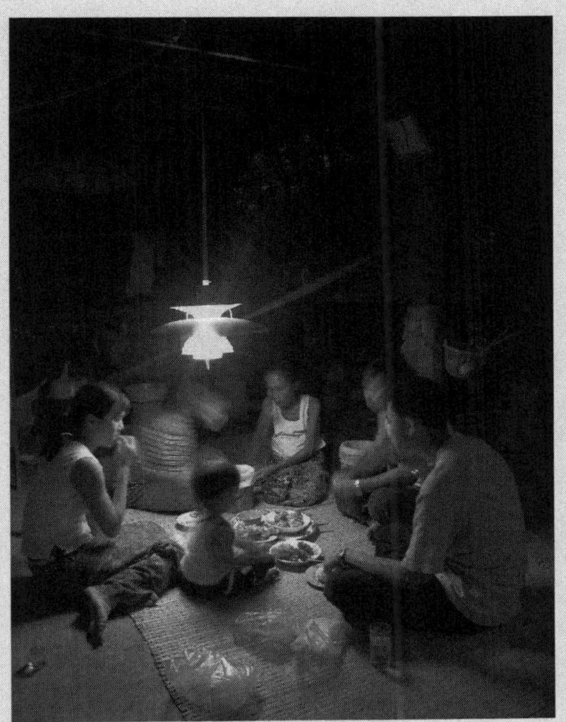

— © the *land* foundation archives
— the *land* foundation, installation photo,
Chiang Mai, Thailand, 2002,
© the *land* foundation
— © the *land* foundation archives
— Superflex, 2002,
metal, paint, gas container, glas,
cardboard box, 50 x 50 x 40 cm

History

The *land* foundation was founded on February 17th 2004 by a board of committee consisting of Rirkrit Tiravanija, Kamin Lertchaiprasert and Uthit Atimana. The foundation unites two projects: *land* and *Umong Silppadhamma*. The *land* project was founded in 1998 by a group of artists who aimed to open up this space for public purposes of self-sustainable natural farming and as a laboratory for experiments in the social aspects of living together. The *Umong Silppadhamma* was founded in 2002 by a group of artists who wanted to open up artistic and cultural space and time for young artists and activists with the intention of supporting self-knowledge through a variety of activities, such as *Vipassana* meditation, yoga exercises, and art.

Principles

1. Self-sustainability: The freedom to express one's thoughts is one of the most important things in life. And, this freedom will be complete only if fundamental needs such as food, clothing, shelter, and medical needs are fulfilled. In our present society, our lifestyle completely relies on consumerism and competition in order to advance our personal benefits. For example, agriculture today uses industrial products such as chemicals, genetically modified seeds, and so on, without taking into account their damaging effects on the environment and ecological systems we are part of. People only want to have more money and comfort. Therefore, the *land* foundation recognizes the significance of adequate living, and tries to be self-sustaining as much as possible. It also promotes natural farming practices to revive natural ways of living.

2. Self-control: Sometimes, when we have too much freedom to express ourselves, we start to neglect other people's freedom. A perfect society must involve sharing, helping each other and respecting personal rights. All this will not be achieved if in our society we don't understand real values within ourselves and others. Vipassana meditation techniques enable us to respect and understand values within ourselves, thereby bringing forward the acceptance of different opinions and thus respecting other people's values.

3. Dialogue: Creativity is at the heart of any social development. Creative communication originates from attentive listening,

exchanging information, and respecting different points of view. It empowers our learning processes. Art and culture are communication tools that make social development possible from the past to the present to the future.

Activities

Activities at the *land* foundation can be divided into three kinds of activities encouraging 1) natural farming, 2) self-knowledge (through *Vipassana* meditation techniques), and 3) art and culture.

The *land* foundation organizes rice paddy farming through a two-crop annual cycle (1st from August to November, 2nd from January to April).

All activities are open to people who are interested in learning together. The natural agricultural methods are influenced by the work of Masanobu Fukuoka and the agricultural layout of the *land* is inspired by the Buddhist farming concept of 'Uncle' Chalaoy Keawkong. Both farming concepts have a similar philosophy, which is actually to grow spiritual values. The energy used for cooking is obtained from a bio-gas system called 'Supergas' that was installed in 2001 by the artist group Superflex.

Nico Dockx – To go back to the very beginnings, how did the *land* foundation start? What were your first intentions, motivations, and were there any desires and expectations? Was there even a sort of (master) plan?

Rirkrit Tiravanija – I came to visit Chiang Mai on the invitation of Navin Rawanchaikul, for a conference, and then I met Kamin Lertchaiprasert, whom I had known before from living in New York, when he was going to the Artist League. So, when Kamin wanted to catch up with me, in our conversations he mentioned the idea of inviting some Thai artists/friends to come together and find a place for an 'artist retirement' (artist retreat), which seemed very interesting to me. Around that time, I had been working on developing an association and 'retreat home' together with some artists/friends in the West, including Philippe Parreno, Liam Gillick, Pierre Huyghe, and Dominique Gonzalez-Foerster. A place where we could retreat from exhibitions and the art world. But there were some complications as we were working with Le Consortium in Dijon where there were various bureaucratic hurdles which made the acquisition of a property very difficult.

So, I said to Kamin that we both had this very similar idea of a 'retreat home' and perhaps we could merge our ideas and energies. Kamin had already mentioned to me that some rice farmers near his studio wanted to move (because of some issues with water which they needed for cultivating their rice), and perhaps we could buy that property from them just to get started. We directly went to visit this property and pretty much bought it the next day, and that must have been way back in 1997, if I remember correctly.

As I just mentioned, we were sharing and merging our ideas. Kamin had a lot of ideas, particularly concerning the planning and organization of the *land* itself, as he had visited a local Thai farmer/philosopher, and he wanted to emulate as well as implement some of the ideas he had learned there. Kamin was also knowledgeable about and studying the writings of the Japanese farmer/philosopher Masanobu Fukuoka, and wanted to follow this organic, non-interventionist farming method. Fukuoka was a proponent of no-till, no-herbicide grain cultivation farming methods—traditional to many indigenous cultures—from which he created a particular method of farming, commonly referred to as 'natural farming' or 'do-nothing farming'. Personally, from my side, I was interested in introducing the idea of the *land* to some friends, and to talk together about the notion of 'retreat' and to use this place as a sort of think-tank possibility.

We knew from the beginning that we did not want this land to belong to any particular person (even though we both personally put in some money in order to purchase this plot of land). Actually, we did not want to have a property, we did not want to have a sculpture garden, we did not even want to have any plans or expectations. We just wanted an open space, a public space where people could come and go and use it. A piece of land that could be used in a multi-functional way, and which was based on our shared interests in art. The *land* became a platform for dialogue, a site of experimentation (like Fukuoka's farming ideas mentioned above). And we wanted it to be a living situation in which everyone could participate and exchange thoughts. An open invitation.

It was all based on the notion of being self-organized. To do whatever we can, with the will of the collective. For some time, Kamin had been teaching as an adjunct professor at the Chiang Mai University, and had many students following his classes. So he wanted to help them to further foster their ideas and to give them space and time to think and act and actually become artists. So, many of his students became members of the *land*.

We called it 'Te-na', which directly translates into 'rice field', and which we then translated (perhaps mistakenly) as 'the *land*'. And, we would emphasize, the *land*, all in lower caps... to not make one element higher or lower than the other. It should function as a sign that reflects the basic philosophical idea that we are all working together on equal levels, and that all our ideas and opinions are to be discussed at the same level. We (the older members of the *land*, as myself and Kamin) wanted to break with the traditional hierarchies between older and younger generations, and the overly oppressive level of respect that the elders had.

There was also no master plan in the sense that we did not want to be masterly, but perhaps rather like amateurs, with an open mind.

Superflex – For us, it all began in a bar in Bangkok in 1999 when we met Rirkrit Tiravanija for the first time. We were in Thailand for some business related to our tool 'Supergas', as it is explained in our book *Tools* published in 2003. In collaboration with CMS Engineering, we were exploring the use of biogas systems for waste-water treatment on small pig farms in Thailand. The *land* foundation became a laboratory for the development of our Supergas tool, used for biogas production. So, for us, the *land* foundation was an experimentation platform for the further development of this Supergas tool, a system utilizing biomass to produce gas for cooking and lighting. Therefore, the sole intention behind the project was to serve a specific function, to provide a service to the residents of the *land* foundation.

ND – And in addition to this first question: Is there a future plan for the *land* foundation?

N (Paphonsak La-or) – For the future plans of the *land* foundation, the operation will be the same as it has always been, which is to focus on additional developments related to the primary structures that would support the people's daily ways of living, during each single period of time. The *land* foundation will also continue to allocate time to experiment with all sorts of activities that relate to agriculture, creativity, community, and deep engagement with society in general. We may establish this experimental learning environment through a more intense curriculum but also with some degree of flexibility, which will be maintained to ensure consistency with very particular times and situations. Moreover, we have created other, different kinds of fundraising activities to support a wider spectrum of programmes and initiatives by the *land* foundation. This is very important in the further development of both big and small projects. These fundraising activities are no longer in the form of personal references as they will take on more characteristics of being the *land* foundation. Most of the fundraising and donation activities today come from the relational and potential structure that is closely related to individuals, especially to the founders of the *land* foundation themselves. If this point is not considered seriously, it may cause problems to the foundation's values in the long run. Nonetheless, this issue is part of the future plan and is seen as very important by the *land* foundation committees.

RT – We did not want to be labelled with the name of a foundation as such. But, at the same time, with the aim of becoming a public entity we looked into all legal structures to become an open zone as well as a non-property, and then we found out that under Thai laws the establishment of such a situation was best served by the idea of a foundation. There are always future plans for the *land* foundation, but when exactly these plans will be realized is another time and space continuum we live by. I think we have always been trying to improve the infrastructure, for example, to have a larger space for a larger group of people to stay over comfortably in all seasons, so that has been more of my personal goal. I am sure everyone else has their own ideas about what the *land* foundation could become in the future.

S – The *land* will continue to be a source of inspiration due to its intention of enabling experimentation of living on every level. It is a constant prospect in our practice for potential experimentation.

ND – Recently, I met with dear friends/artists Louwrien Wijers and Egon Hanfstingl at the 'Joseph Beuys: Greetings from the Eurasian' exhibition at the Museum of Contemporary Art in Antwerp. We talked about their little farm house and field in Hallum (Friesland, in the very north of the Netherlands, close to Scandinavia) where they have been living for over five years now. Living without electricity, gas heating, and water. It is a self-sustaining and self-organized life there. We spoke about how to bring people there. To bring friends/artists and their activities there, and actually work together on the land. I feel you have been trying to do the same at the *land* foundation in Chiang Mai. How do you organize the *land* now, bringing more dynamics there? Perhaps it is not only a sustainable farming in the literal sense of the word, meaning farming the land, but also a sustainable farming of both body and mind? A sort of retreating? How do you see the notion of farming there? It feels like a hybrid between meditation and work.

D (Sedhapong Kirativongkamchon) – Personally, I agree with this point of view. I have already learned and felt that sometimes meditation and work—in such a natural environment—can even be the same thing. There are moments in time, when you can connect meditation to something you have to do on a daily basis. For example, when you are sweeping the fallen leaves that lie on the ground. During these kinds of daily activities, you can try to create your own pattern of sweeping, a personal rhythm that matches with your own breathing rhythm. Hereby you can become aware of what is occurring in this very present moment of time. To stay present. However, it always takes me many years to learn every single lesson from nature when working at the *land* foundation.

N – Often, the work follows the principle of cohesion according to time as well as the conditions of a specific situation and it has, of course, flexible patterns. Actually, it is about working according to the potentials of each person involved in a given moment in their time. We do not create constraints because the structure of the *land* foundation has the quality of a so-called 'spiritual organization', and in this context, spiritual means 'inner force'. This spiritual organization allows us to see, recognize, and understand what generally happens in a system, as it is the work in which everybody can participate together at all times. It does not have any direct reward. If you look at it from a modern management perspective, this will be considered a risk, with even a high possibility of failure. However, this particular approach to management has always been in the interest of the *land* foundation because we consider all our work to be in the long term. This kind of organization will allow us to cover more dimensions and to understand and learn at the deepest level—spirituality as our inner force. We will also have the opportunity to acquire more knowledge about our human potentials in developing and changing things.

RT – Yes, I guess from the very beginning we have always had this dream of being a retreat, away from the regularity of our modern life. We are not rejecting anything, but when retreating one can take a pause, a moment, a breath... to take time and to contemplate, to meditate and to reflect on one's own existence. But then reality moves in, our world moves in, electricity moves in, all sorts of things move in... but perhaps we need to keep things balanced. To find a balance that still gives us that free breath of ideas, of thoughts, of philosophies of life. We are not always successful or correct, but we live with that possibility. We need to look at our lives holistically, and to take in all and everything that is there and make it balance.

ND – Is the *land* foundation a sort of retreating environment? Perhaps not in the sense of not doing anything but rather doing something different. To use a different energy within yourself? To reach another concentration? A coming together, a being together?

N – Exactly, but it doesn't mean not doing anything. It is about doing things depending on the relationships; they become the factors for making different things to happen under the conditions of that particular situation and time. However, this way of doing things requires a lot of experimentation on how to observe the various conditions of things. The interest of the *land* foundation does not lie solely in the ecosystem or agriculture. It also includes the community and social aspects. And this is the point where the *land* foundation has to be an open space for developing different points of view, which will help in building guidelines for understanding each period of time.

RT – I think that has been answered already? But my other description of the *land* foundation is that it is like a large table. Different people come and go, to and from that table. They can sit around the table and talk, have discussions, think about ideas, but they can also do things on the table, they can make things, things that can be used together or privately, things that are left behind for others to continue to interact with, and it changes. It can be dinner, food, it can be Supergas, it can be a tree... it is a living place and a laboratory for living... of course, all this is done while you are at this table, at the *land*... away from other things.

S – Yes, all of the above and much more. It certainly depends on who is using it at any given time, as it is the user who defines its purpose and relevance in each moment.

ND – The influence of Masanobu Fukuoka's book *One Straw Revolution* (1975) was very important for you when starting the *land* foundation and today is still an inspiring toolbox for letting both nature and art interventions run its own course at the *land*. Can you say something about it? And why there are no regulations, no desires, no judgements, no ideologies, no fixed ideas, no agendas in how to participate and intervene at *the land*. It is also a plot of land without fences. It is an open space, an open invitation!

D – Personally, I think it doesn't really matter as long as what is happening is in line with or goes along well with the objectives of the *land* foundation. Someone once said: 'There seems to be no standard appearances for the *land* foundation as it totally depends on the different inter-actions and interventions by the people involved and engaged.' And I totally agree with this.

N – Fukuoka's *One-Straw Revolution* provides some important principles for understanding the rules of co-dependent relationships in the ecosystem as well as in nature. These principles rely on many other additional elements, not only the understanding of these co-dependent relationships, but also a continuous observation. We have to accept the fact that we ourselves only constitute a very small part of the wider surroundings which cannot be directly controlled. The principles of co-dependent relationships are likewise the thinking/doing guide for the *land* foundation, which is not only used as a guide-line to understand the agricultural ecosystem. It is also applied to the idea of co-habitation such as community and society on a relational and dependent basis, even though it is much more complex than the agricultural ecosystem. At the very least, in certain aspects, such as change, community and society incur a much faster and more complex transformation than the ecosystem and nature. It is not easy to adapt this way of thinking to accompany the understanding of community and soci-ety. Nonetheless, *One-Straw Revolution* plays an import-ant role in many of our thinking/doing processes.

ND – The criticism of a 'disenchantment' of the world has been going on since modernity or even since the Enlightenment. As a result, and under pressure of extens-ive rational behaviour, any spiritual dimension becomes suppressed from our work and life. Maybe you can indicate and situate what a spiritual dimension means to you and especially how you develop and cherish it in your work with the *land*. Also, what is the role of that spiritual dimension in your daily life and work?

N – In terms of my own definition, the 'spirit' I mostly emphasize is the spirit of emancipation from living in such a society of contingency and confusion—the nature of society we all live in.

In other words, I emphasize practicing, exploring, and understanding by using my own inner force to attempt to appropriately make sense of the world around me. This is because I hope to discover an effective way and even gain enough energy for my life to move forward and cut through the said contingency and confusion. This is the meaning of the 'spirit' I have learned from Thasnai Sethasaree, an adviser for the *land* foundation.

ND – To me, personally, the *land* foundation feels like a space and time where people can meet and exchange thoughts with one another. A place without any pressure... and I really like this notion of 'no pressure'! It is slow. What and how are your experiences at the *land* foundation in this regard?

D – As for me, being at the *land* foundation on almost a daily basis and taking care of the land is the same thing as being closer or even going back to nature. Sometimes, nature is serious and sometimes it is comfortable, sometimes noisy and sometimes peaceful, sometimes green-and-wet and sometimes brown-and-dry, sometimes funny and sometimes sad. But all the time nature is always true. I have gradually and automatically learned from and been inspired very much by nature—which is the only one telling the real truth all the time. However, for me, the *land* foundation is not about true-false or right-wrong or agree-disagree. The freedom to express one's own thoughts is the point, and that is enough.

N – I felt the same way during those past few years of being involved in this land. The *land* foundation is a place where both people and environment can be connected. We have created a space for learning and digesting different things at the emotional as well as the thinking level. That doesn't mean that there is no pressure involved. The pressure in this area always seems to be present, which we will only realize once we have lived here long enough. Nevertheless, that pressure has become the meaning and opportunity to understand different things and ourselves more clearly. The significance of that pressure surfaces when we cannot fully control our existence in unfamiliar surroundings, be it the physical environment that appears to be open or the open architecture, but especially the time of the surroundings and the community-based way of living, which always relies on the environment as a crucial factor. In short, the whole physical environment of the *land* foundation is not static, it always changes, beyond control. Therefore, the area of the *land* foundation can have direct effects on us in terms of knowledge and understanding about different things. From what I hear, most people think that the *land* foundation encourages them to go back to primitive living but I have never thought that this is the intention or the idea. During the past two years of staying in the area continuously, the *land* foundation has faced relatively high pressures, but they encourage us to think about ourselves and things around us in order to build and maintain the equilibrium. If we think about what human nature is from our perspective and other people's perspectives, it would be difficult to live in that area because of the pressures. Under such circumstances we are required to understand things that can create equilibrium and that will help us to stay in the area. Therefore, the *land* foundation has decided to embrace the question of what human nature can become. Trust in this idea will develop the meaning and starting point in moving the overall capability forward, at least for us.

S – Until now, we have used it in a more pragmatic way, as a testing site.

ND – What is the role of the rice paddy within the practices of the *land* foundation? What I also find interesting is that, because of the rice paddy, the *land* is like a swamp balancing between land and water. How do you see this in-between state of being... between liquid and solid?

N – Regarding the physical state of the environment, it partly defines our living conditions. Different physical states create different life patterns and meanings. To elaborate beyond the relationship mentioned in the question, it is about the understanding of the relationship between things. This means that we should not only think about the physical relationship, but also that between other things both within themselves and the surroundings. For example, the possibilities of agricultural relationships in different forms have been experimented with while using the physical area of the *land* foundation. We also study the architectural relationship in this area, which is meaningful to internal living conditions and hereby create meanings in close dialogue with the environment. There are parallel projects in Norway, including Sørfinnset School, run by artists Søssa Jorgensen and Geir Tore Holm and curator Karolin Tempere. The founder was actually inspired by the *land* foundation. He expanded on these ideas and applied them to an area in Northern Norway, near a small village called Bodo, which no doubt has different physical conditions. In this project he tried to adapt the methods so that they suited this area. He mainly focused on art activities, ecological relationships, and communities. He also allowed people in the village and those living nearby to participate in setting directions for various activities that will take place in the area.

S – Accessibility to knowledge and exploring the commons is a constant in our work, as well as an important point of contact with the ideas behind the *land* foundation. In this context of exploring the limits between private property and the common, the tool Supercopy/Biogas PH5 Lamp was also developed at the *land* foundation. We modified an original PH5 pendant lamp into a biogas lamp, to be used by people living in areas without electricity. Originally designed in 1958 by Poul Henningsen, the PH5 lamp was meant for industrial production making it cheap to produce and hence accessible for a general population. The Biogas PH5 Lamp is a rethinking of the original concept adapted for a globalized world. It was developed for the *land* foundation with one of the families living there.

ND – It would be interesting to talk a bit about the notion of 'private property', which I think is a very old-fashioned idea and makes architecture very 'immobile', thereby producing very 'poor' social living conditions. You decided not to make it a 'private property' but a 'common ground'. Is the practice of the *land* foundation an exercise in exploring the 'commons'? It is owned by nobody but can be shared by many!

D – I think so. What I always say when I am asked by visitors (about what they should or should not perform during their stay) is that 'there is no ownership for this space'. The *land* foundation is owned by no one and also owned by everyone at the same time. You and I are equal now, and so I have no right to judge what you should or should not do. It is for you to think yourself what that actually means: (1) No Ownership and (2) Belongs to No One and also Everyone at the same time.'

N – It follows the idea of 'No Ownership'—which became the resolution since the organization was established as a foundation in 2004—to foster long-term flexibility in the structural change so that the management is suitable for each period. 'No Ownership' is implemented as the principal thinking structure of the *land* foundation from the idea of common understanding. The essence of which is to gather ideas from different groups and other types of activities in order to expand boundaries and possibilities of the *land* foundation itself in each moment of time.

ND – What is the duration of the *land* foundation? It is a living thing, so it needs time. What kind of time?

N – I may not be able to talk about the meaning of time directly because time is not uniform and in itself is not continuous. It is scattered and has different directions.

The question of time in this part, if asked in the context of the *land* foundation, reminds me very much of Kamin's and Rirkrit's ideas, which are co-related. The significant paradigm that connects to the practices in their daily lives can be extracted from the message often relayed by these two founders, 'The way things go' in the sense of learning, observing and acting within the circle of this meaning.

S – There is never any time limitation on the cultivation of the *land* foundation; it is there to be used and can be used by anyone who wants to engage themselves. For us, as artists, it is a potential site for continuously exploring new ideas for social development in our society.

ND – You once said that the *land* foundation functions more or less like a station, meaning that you come and go... perhaps return... and you leave traces for others to continue, to alter. So, it becomes a sort of laboratory of old and new knowledges that become crystalized over time and are shared with one another. Could the *land* foundation be considered an experimental university?

D – I agree with that. For me personally, it can be seen as an 'Experimental University of Sharing and Exchanging'. Although I have been involved with the *land* foundation for years now, I am still learning by doing and practicing every single day, especially when it comes to running natural agriculture and taking care of its natural environment. There seems to be no exact handbook for how to go about things here. Experimenting is the best.

N – Yes, this kind of meaning has always been in the interest of the *land* foundation, starting with the physical, natural area to the architectural buildings and then to the management of the foundation to the overall activities and the different bodies of knowledge accumulated over the years. This is combined with the understanding that conditions and necessities in each period will determine particular needs. The experiments will prove and expand former understandings inside the *land* foundation. Therefore, it can be said that the *land* foundation is one of the many areas that provide an opportunity to experiment and accept new, different possibilities.

RT – I guess my mentioning of the table is the same idea as the station. The table metaphor works quite well in terms as a lab idea, while the station is more about the transient nature of passers-by, visitors and even the participants and *land* members. I think what is important about the station is that it is a space for the public, a place to stop and rest, a place on the journey from one point to another. What I have also found useful is to realize that the *land* foundation is not a commune. I feel that a commune often falls victim to its own idealism, then it falls into the hands of the few who insist on staying. So, the table, the station... perhaps it is about scale, but it is good to be flexible even on that level. When we have a lot it becomes a lot, when we have less it can become less.

S – Yes, it is how we think it and use it.

ND – Architect Cedric Price talked often about this notion of 'wilderness', of being without any expectations. Perhaps you do not expect anything from the *land* foundation? Rirkrit, you once quoted Wittgenstein: 'Don't look for the meaning of things, look for their use.' Is the *land* foundation a good example of this?

D – Answering just for me: It is not really that we do not expect anything from the *land* foundation, but once something has started on some level, we perhaps let it develop its own movement by itself. How it would go further depends on any internal–external factors which may affect it as well. Results can be different from prior anticipations, or even might not be defined at all.

RT – I guess that the idea of scale is the answer. If a blade of grass or a patch of weeds is growing on the land, we have life, we have the 'wilderness'. When we have a group of people come together to plant rice and harvest rice, we have another scale. When we have the One Year programme, or the Seasonal Programme we have another scale... and

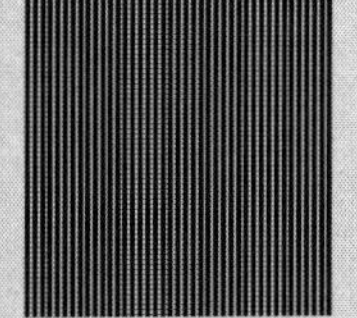

when we have artists building architectures at the *land* we
have yet another scale... all those interventions and interactions have a different scale.

The Value of Squatting a Nipple
Another Exchange Value

Nico Dockx
in Conversation with
Dennis Tyfus

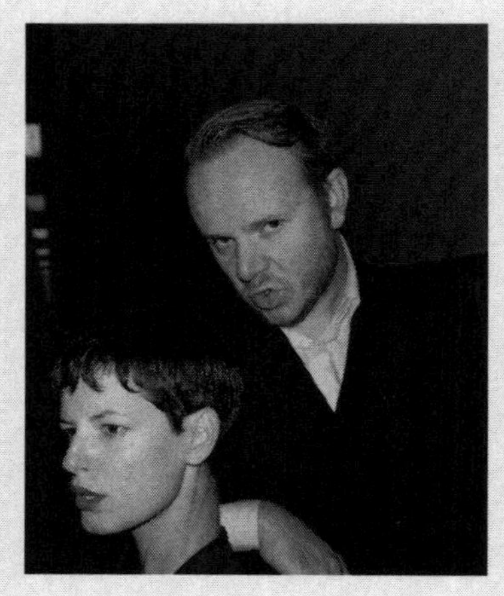

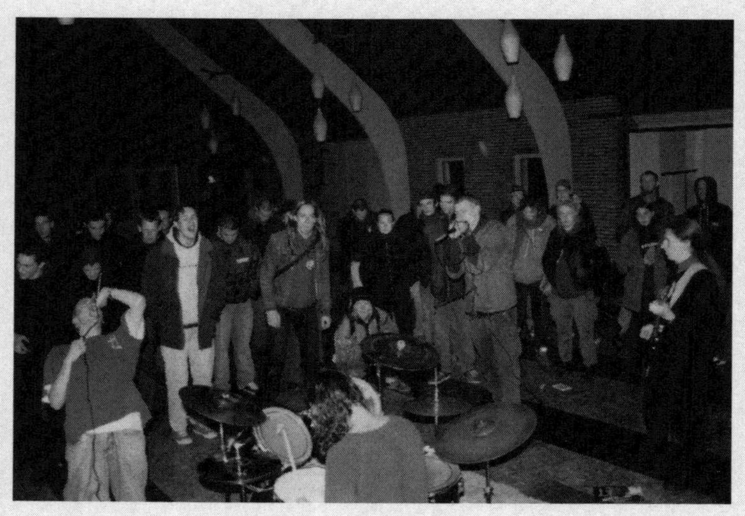

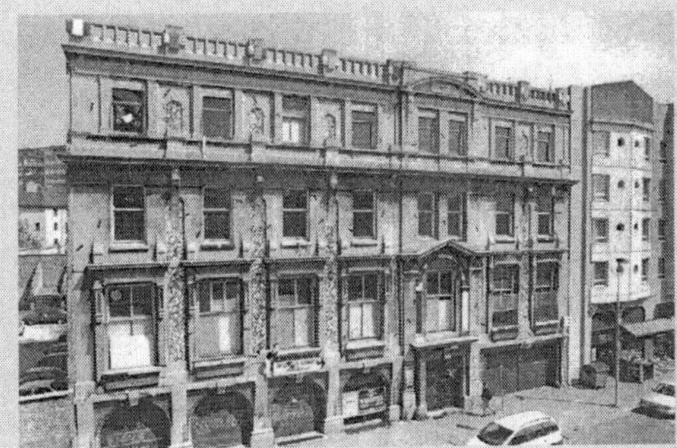

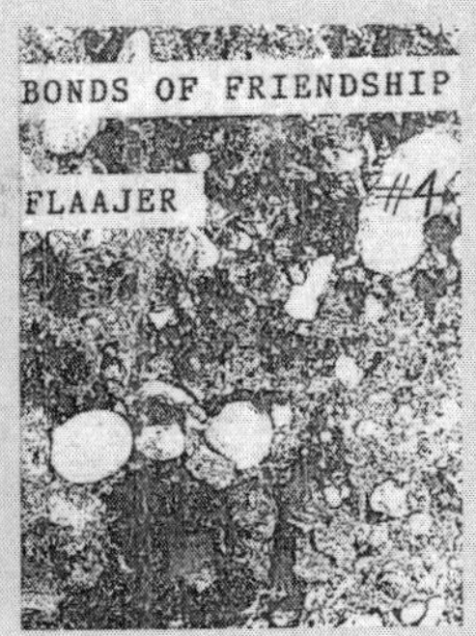

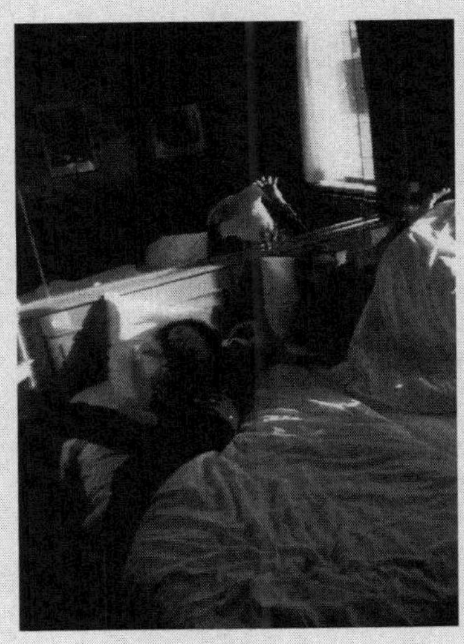

— Hanna Putz and Dennis Tyfus, 2017. Photo: Hanna Putz
— SYC at squatted church in Kapellen, 1997. Photographer unknown
— 'Vogelvrijstad' squat, 1996, newspaper clipping
— Bonds of Friendship cover, year unknown
— Neutral: s/t, 7", I Dischi Del Barone, 2017

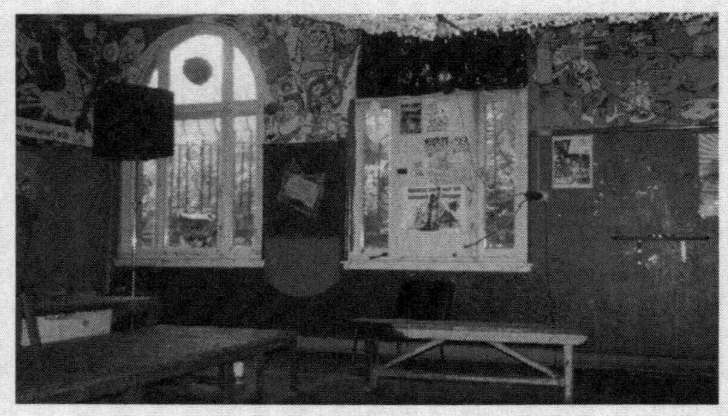

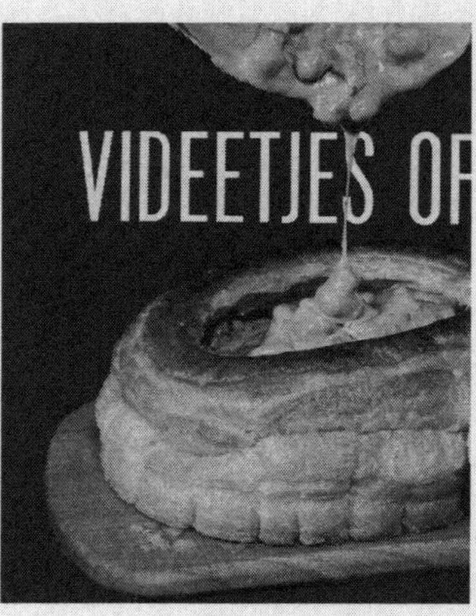

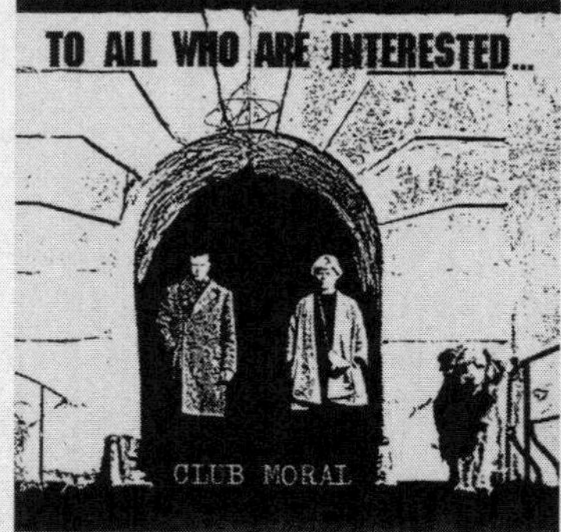

— 'Scheld'apen' concert
space, Antwerp, 1998.
Photographer unknown
— 'Vol Au Vent', found image
— Club Moral, *To All
Who Are Interested...*,
Cthulhu Records –CR 09,
Germany, 1989

In much, if not all, printed matter that the artist Tyfus produces on his own label Ultra Eczema (UE) he invites, engages, and collaborates with other artists, writers, musicians. His work is about many different things and one can perhaps even say that UE is a production platform rather than just a regular record label. It is also a communication tool that enriches and enlarges his personal network of friends and collaborations. His artists' books speak for themselves as they are simply things he really wants to publish, sometimes in conjunction with events, performances, or exhibitions, and sometimes just out of the necessity to share this work with friends. The great diversity of vinyl records that he releases on UE are mostly the product of collaborations in which the audio is created by musicians, artists, or performers he invites for a project. As part of his practice, Tyfus always designs and makes the artwork for these record sleeves. In most cases he tries to mix and collage both audio and visual materials. The personal relationship he has with other artists is the most important aspect in realizing all these collaborations. A lot of the music that UE releases is from Antwerp, as it totally makes sense—as a protest against forgetting—to document and record what is happening or what has happened in this small harbour city. Antwerp is pretty much known for its experimental music, fashion, and art, but there is still so much more to discover. UE wants to support, release, and communicate both his own practice as well as other people's practices and all of this happens because there is an immediate and mutual understanding of each other's work. It is all based on notions of friendship and *commoning*. Then again, collectivity brings its own difficulties. Sometimes, Tyfus has the feeling that collectivity is not feeding his energy but rather stopping it from taking place. He always has very clear ideas about the how and what of making a vinyl record, a book, an installation, a film, a performance, an architectural object. I guess this makes him a difficult, although very interesting and challenging character within any sort of group dynamics. A while ago—as part of our one-year long interview—Tyfus told me how he visited an exhibition of Assemble at the Architekturzentrum in Vienna. He told me that he was blown away by their work and their ideas as well as by their collective working attitude. And, to quote Tyfus: 'This (positive) power of many hands joined together.' Even though, in many cases, past experiences have indicated that collectivity is not where Tyfus functions at his best, there are a number of artists he has been working with for many years now and these collaborations are based on mutual understanding, humour, and especially a love of art. For example, the artist Vaast Colson, with whom he created many duo exhibitions and also ran two alternative art spaces (Gunther and Stadslimiet) for presenting and supporting a huge diversity of contemporary art forms. And at this very moment Tyfus, together with artists Peter Fengler and Vaast Colson and curator Helena Kritis, runs the project space Pinkie Bowtie. Besides all this, UE would not exist without the work of David Edren (website, sales, and so on) and Jef Cuypers (lay-out and computer mania). On the occasion of the 'Enfant Terrine' exhibition at project space 1646 in The Hague, Dennis Tyfus invited me, Nico Dockx, to interview him. On 12 July 2017, I started sending Tyfus one question every day and our conversation will continue until 12 July 2018. Tyfus will respond with both texts and relevant images from his archive. This interview of 365 questions and answers will be released as a monograph publication of Dennis Tyfus, in the fall of 2018.

20/07/2017, question 9

Nico Dockx – A few days ago, I found a very rare book on Dadaist Raoul Hausmann's anthropological and archaeological research of traditional peasant houses on the island of Ibiza, written between 1933 and 1936. Very interesting to see how one of the founders of Dada has spent a few years in retreat in Ibiza, investigating traditional architecture and related folklore elements such as dancing, singing, cooking, clothing, and so on. You have also often been working with architecture, perhaps not always in a very direct way but for instance with your intervention together with Vaast [Colson], breaking (through) a brick wall and thereby connecting two different gallery spaces in Antwerp (Stella Lohaus Gallery and Maes & Matthys Gallery). I also think of the artist-run spaces (Gunther and Stadslimiet) you have developed together with him in Antwerp. And, soon, in your forthcoming exhibition at 1646 where you will construct and programme a bar as part of your installation there, which later in 2018 will become part of your pavilion project at the open air sculpture park Middelheim Museum Antwerp. How important is architecture in (and to) your work? What kind of architecture inspires you? You already mentioned Assemble. I am curious who are your architect-heroes?

Dennis Tyfus – In essence, my interest in architecture grew out of the squatting movement/scene in the 1990s in Antwerp and Ghent. Around 1996, when I was still living with my parents in a small suburban village called Hoevenen, I was very eager to leave and go live in Antwerp by myself and get together with like-minded souls. In the summer of 1996, a huge, abandoned school building in the Meistraat was squatted and named Vogelvrijstad [Outlaw City]. Although we only remained there for two months (the police shut it down, violently!), it had a very big impact on me personally and also on the future of various cultural scenes in Antwerp; people from very different backgrounds met each other there. Really, there were no alternative spaces in Antwerp where such forms of self-organization and do-it-yourself practices could take place. I mean, there was a group of punks—usually hanging out at the Groenplaats [the main city square]—some young and older artists, also some political activists like Peter Terryn, Bart Peeters, and others; and there were people that set up gigs in youth clubs such as Lintfabriek in Kontich and Sorm in Deurne. There was a label called Conspiracy Records, and Radio Centraal used to report on everything that was happening there. For the first time, all these people worked together to transform this old school building into a sort of autonomous and unique centre for the arts and music. Although I was there only once, it made a big impression on me: not only this diverse group of people creating something together, but also the idea of re-using an architectural space that lay abandoned for many years. This idea of finding a new purpose for an abandoned building is something that later on became very important in my artistic practice.

Immediately following this squatting episode, a lot of political action emerged in Antwerp, coming from that same group of people. The most memorable (and funny) was Spaak & Tandrad, a bicycle guerrilla group, whose aim was to get rid of cars in the city centre (something that has, by now, almost entirely been achieved) and introduce free public transport (something that is still far from happening). A few people that joined forces at Vogelvrijstad started squatting abandoned spaces by the riverside, close to the river Scheldt. My first studio was at the lower floor of a squat across from Het Steen [a medieval fortress in the old city centre]. In the summer of 1998, Scheld'apen opened; a wonderful event. Formerly a canteen for train drivers, it was surrounded by a huge garden and situated between some abandoned rails and the river. It was perfectly hidden from any other living areas, yet still within the city's inner ring. On the opening day, I painted a huge fresco on the walls of a space that shortly after became the concert venue of this squat (it was the biggest drawing I had ever made). I also started organizing concerts there, and not long after I moved into Villa Delfia, an all-girls squat on the other side of the river, near where the museum MAS is now located. This squat had various artist's studios and was filled to the brim with creative people! Maskesmachine had their studio there as well—three, sometimes four or even five girls who came together to do performances, write songs, make clothes, produce a radio show, and so on. It was a very nice time, though it got a little cold inside this building in winter. It definitely shaped my awareness of the re-usage and transformation potential of existing structures and situations. Another thing I think of a lot, is 'looking up', though in a dense, small city such as Antwerp (and most other Belgian cities) you are bound to look ahead when walking or driving through all those narrow streets. However, when looking up a completely new world awaits you, rich with (often abandoned) architectural masterpieces. Much like my love of skateboarding, if I see an empty, ruined building, I often think of all its future possibilities, all the things that you could do with these abandoned places. Activating these architectures.

A little over ten years after the opening of Scheld'apen, Vaast and myself felt the need to share a space together, and so we came up with the idea of a shared studio where we could also organize public events, lectures, exhibitions, and concerts. The strange 'nothing works here' atmosphere of the mostly abandoned shopping centre next to Renaat Braem's Oudaan police tower seemed ideal for us. But, as with most found spaces, this empty building also had some negative elements. When the police finally found out what was happening there, and that it was not construction work, but hard-to-locate alternative music and sound performances, the fun was quickly over and so we had to leave and find another space.

We started Stadslimiet in front of the small bus stop across the street from Het Steen—basically next to where the artist Gordon Matta-Clark made his infamous (and sadly enough demolished) *Office Baroque* work. Once again, it was a space without heating or hot water, though very inspiring and in the summer pretty good for presenting work to small audiences. Somehow, I am always looking out for new, potential spaces to occupy; partly for pragmatic reasons and partly for the love of how they look (and might look) in the future. Another way in which architecture slipped into my practice is by working together with FVWW— a collective of young, local architects—who invited me to create an artwork for the façade of the Lessius University in Antwerp. It was a nice collaboration on many different levels. Aside from the commissioned artwork, they also asked me if I wanted to design the sportswear for their football team. Every year, they take part in this Archi Gold Cup—a soccer contest between various architectural studios. I agreed to do their shirts and shorts only if they changed their team name to UE164, and henceforth their team became an Ultra Eczema release as well. Those football games turned into mayhem evenings, as UE164 was the only team there with supporter hooligans.

23/07/2017, question 12

ND – I will return to the notion of fiction later, in a future question, as I first want to go back to the notion of alternative spaces. I was involved in the squatting of Meistraat in the mid-1990s and I was also there at the end of the two-month residency when the police arrived to violently remove the core group of squatters from the building. Being there, helping friends that were heavily attacked by the police, this event also strongly marked my practice as a person. I found a lot of inspiration in this very specific political, social, and cultural act in the Meistraat and it gave me much food for thought in the years that followed, when I started to organize concerts and exhibitions, and also support Conspiracy Records by silkscreen-printing record sleeves, and so on. I still remember helping out Joris De Buysser in the mid-1990s with the distribution of his *Bonds of Friendship* fanzines before he founded Conspiracy Records as a label in 1996. So, I would like to go back to this notion of self-organization in relation to moments of political, social, and cultural crisis and upheaval in a city like Antwerp. Of course, always strongly connected to events in other cities in Europe, the States and Asia, as these punk, hardcore, and hip hop scenes were in dialogue with one another on a global scale through mail art and fanzine mail. Most likely, there are still a lot of traces in your personal archives of magazines, books, records. Can you tell me more about the politics and poetics of the art and music scene in the mid- to late-1990s in Antwerp? Where and when you grew up as a curious, young artist? I feel there are a lot of interesting stories there that can give a good insight in how you work today and how you will continue to work tomorrow.

DT – Actually, I still have a clear image of Joris De Buysser being pushed away by the police, shown on the 7 o'clock news when Vogelvrijstad got evicted and all its inhabitants gathered at De Groenplaats. As Antwerp is a small city, though crammed with loud-mouths, artists, and characters of all sorts (like in any other city) there is somehow an inevitable blending among everyone who is interested in the (counter)cultural, which was supported by the activities of Radio Centraal, especially in those early, pre-internet times of the 1980s and '90s. It was a boiling pot of everything odd, artistic, musical and strange... also politically. Radio Centraal made it pretty clear from the very beginning that it was a leftist radio station, airing shows by minorities as well as not giving any voice to extreme right parties. Most importantly, I think that mixing different generations as well as creating things together through alternative broadcasting was special. My teenage mind was definitely and utterly confused by the absurd talk show *RTVS*, which included architect and ex-situationist Rudi Renson, whose studio at Ercola[1] I took over much later. I hardly understood what they were talking about, but it was all so absurd and different from anything I had ever heard before that it made me very curious. In between the Vogelvrijstad and Scheld'apen squats, which were only two years apart, a lot of events happened in this 'community'. A new space opened at Paardenmarkt, called Weik, where every Friday evening they served food and drinks accompanied by a lecture, usually in an anarchist/communist/activist type of atmosphere. A lot of protest groups were formed there too, including Spaak & Tandrad and Wordt Vervolgd [To be continued/persecuted]. Both collectives were basically turning the streets into some kind of playground. This is also where I met Benjamin Verdonck, who is probably the only artist I know from those movements who is still active today. I am breaking my head over where and when to start telling stories about this period as so many things happened, maybe these stories will just resurface when we talk more specifically about that time.

01/08/2017, question 21

ND – While visiting your archive yesterday afternoon, I noticed two very interesting things: your collection of zines, records, and other printed matter mainly seems to be based on an economy of exchange and not on this classical idea of buying and selling things. Can you say more about this notion of exchange that has not only inspired your archive but also your attitude of working as an artist? And, your archive also grows a network of friends, which is visualized in the ensemble of releases on your Ultra Eczema label—is that correct?

DT – Most of the time, though not always, it is true that a lot of the publications, records, and cassettes in my personal archives were traded with the artists and/or publishers that made them. Trading and sharing works was probably one of the main reasons why I started putting out records and books, which is obviously much cheaper than buying all that printed matter. But, at the same time, I do still spend most of the money that I earn straight away on buying records. When you put out an archival record, at best you get the chance to dig very deep into an artists' personal collection of things, and which is probably the closest you can ever look into someone's work. This person allows you inside their personal surroundings.

The same goes for trading, as this always happens out of a personal contact with another artist, and at best you become friends and the exchange continues for a lifetime, but often it just ends. I am not a collector who needs all and everything by a certain artist. My collection is not complete, but rather a pile of stuff that I came across while working as an artist. I will hardly ever throw anything away, as most of this stuff I received as presents from or trades with someone. So, it is connected to a moment in time or a specific friend. Of course, there is definitely a lot of stuff in my apartment and studio that I am wondering about where it all came from and what kind of relation I have with it. I feel that lots of the trading comes out of mutual interests, various excitements, and especially curiosity. And, there is still no better way to start the day than with a full mail box! This morning, a package of books by the Austrian artist Thomas Geiger as well as a package of Sofie Herner filled with records by her bands Neutral[2] and Enhet För Fri Musik[3] arrived, making it a great morning for me. Most of my communication with others, be it through handwritten letters, emails, phone calls and especially meetings in real time, generate new interests, contacts and collaborations. Somehow, the word 'network' got stained and polluted by 'careerism' in very dull ways. At best, a network is a (small) community of enthusiasts, spread all over the planet, sometimes eliminating the differences between audience and maker.

03/08, question 23b

ND – I want to expand on your reflections about the notion of 'network' as I also believe—as you already answered to a previous question of mine—that this word got seriously infected by 'careerism'. Networking has much more to do with self-organization, compassionate economy, friendship, and the idea of 'commons' and is something we learned through our experiences in the do-it-yourself attitude of the late 1980s and early '90s, when we were skateboarding in the streets, squatting abandoned buildings, and organizing concerts and exhibitions there...

DT – It goes back to just hanging out by yourself on the playground at school, or when being on holidays with your parents as a teenager and seeing that other boy or girl with a Tshirt of The Germs, sending a message of 'Please come to talk to me, I hate everyone else'. I guess, searching for a common ground and social contact. That incredible feeling of 'coming home'. I was never a good skater, though it was an excuse *not* to be home, a very good reason to be outside and discover a lot of words that were not used at home. It is funny that we talk about squatting so much, as today it has somehow totally disappeared in Antwerp. This idea of a group of different people coming together who were not even necessarily good friends but did have a common goal like squatting a huge, empty building and not being dependent on anything or anyone to organize something. In some way the general gentrification of this squatting movement made the younger folks extremely lazy. Nowadays, most of the young generation expect it all to happen for them, as a matter of course, like while growing up, for example, the city provided two or three gigantic skate parks. So, there is no reason at all for this young generation to do anything themselves.

08/09/2017, question 59

ND – It would be nice to talk more about the how and what of developing your own economy, not only financially, but the notion of economy on many, if not all, levels. Can you give me some insights into your personal economy of doing things? And what would you tell the younger generation when they ask you about where and when to start their work? How to build their own economy? Any inspiring suggestions? I strongly believe it is always important to give one another confidence and trust!

DT – I do not think that I ever developed an economy that was entirely my own. I always traded things with others, whether for food, drinks, records, books, as these are the few things that I really 'need', or would be sad not to have. For example, there have been times in my life that someone working in a restaurant liked my work and so I could go and eat there on a daily basis in exchange for some records and posters; and a few years ago, Restaurant De Lids purchased a work of mine for which they paid me with meals... Actually, I ate their great vol-au-vent every week for about eight months. At some point, I also had a running tab at café Witzli-Poetzli in trade for records and books. Recently, I tattooed a friend who will cook for me in trade for these tattoos. Graphic designer Janus (Prutpuss) Lemaire silk-screened record sleeves for Ultra Eczema in trade for a tattoo, and every time Gerard Herman prints something for me at the school where he works I also tattoo his leg, or do something with his third nipple, which I consider mine now. In one way or another, I squatted his nipple. I strongly doubt if many young people would ask me for some economical tips, though I could share with them what I do believe: 'It really starts by organizing things yourself, and not mirroring yourself to the success of famous artists—which is as rare as a terrorist attack.' Many of the artists that I know have other jobs besides their artistic practice. I never did that, but I definitely suffered financially at various moments in life. I consider this a personal choice, and I also know in advance that there will be most likely, now and then and for the rest of my days, times when it will be hard for me to survive, but then also other moments when everything will run smoothly. And I try very hard not to spend one single day doing things that I do not want to do, which I believe is quite economical. I have listened to Henning Christiansen's *Fluxid (Musik Essayistik)* LP on Borgen Records.

26/01/2018, question 199

ND – I'd like to get back to you to unravel together the word 'punk', as I feel we both have been partly inspired and formed by this historical movement through its visual, musical, and activist languages; but more importantly, I think by the energy of doing-it-yourself. It helped me in having the confidence in developing self-supporting structures within my practice as an artist but also as a citizen in my daily life. It would be nice to talk more with you about your personal 'philosophies', and small revolutions...

DT – I do not really know where to start this unravelling? The do-it-yourself spirit is of course much older than the punk movement and I was not even born when punk started to happen. According to my personal feeling it is a very organic process of (self-)organizing things that has been passed on generation after generation through different forms of counter-cultural 'scenes'. I am still reading that book about Crass[4] right now, until so far a very nice and interesting experience. I like reading about how people from what seems like total different environments had a link with each other. For example, free jazz percussionist Terry Day is showing up in this book pretty early on. Lots of Crass' ideas seem very interesting to me, though often I would not be able to take part in these things. The idea of an 'open house', for example, which was intended to be developed all over the UK and Scotland, and even further expanding to the rest of the world. Artists, music bands and so on could go from house to house and always have a place to stay. They could stay there in trade for a poem if you were a poet, or a song if you were a musician, or a meal if you were a cook. In theory, this all sounds wonderful but I think my past experiences of living together in squats and shared houses have proved to me that I live best just by myself. Nevertheless, these kind of 'open' places are interesting and challenging to participate in as an organizer of events. Scheld'apen was a good example of that. Early to bed today—long drive tomorrow! (listened to various Brainbombs records).

07/02/2018, question 212
ND – Bologna has historically always been a city to publicly carry out strong leftist politics. Today, I think, it has drastically changed because everywhere in Italy the right-wing party has become very powerful (as everywhere else in Europa and many parts of the world). Bologna was for decades and decades, especially in the late 1960s and '70s, a breeding ground for many anarchist movements, radical filmmakers, poets, student movements, and so on. Today, I

feel we have to leave this dialectic notion of 'left' and 'right' politics and create new models of politics. What would your answer be—as an artist and world citizen—towards our contemporary politics?

DT – I strongly believe that the way in which interesting artists organize themselves is a political statement as such. I am allergic to obvious political art as well as uninspiring protests. Of course, I am nevertheless for a resistance that is performative, that does not endlessly repeat the same old slogans. I think artists can play a role in all this! For example, by setting up happenings, speakers corners, producing public posters or doing interventions, and writing and barking poems that are smarter than 'Dump Trump'. My personal answer to contemporary politics is partly to neglect politics, as I feel that giving more attention to 'the enemy' is serving them well these days, especially through all the social media. I do understand that people are baffled and (re-)post articles on right-wing scum, though personally I do not want to share this verbal, visual and written diarrhoea. This might sound pretty naive, but I do believe in creating a positive social space apart from it. 'To All Who Are Interested' (to say it with a Club Moral[5] LP title). I am also for: strikes, pranking the enemy, food not bombs, peace, a different protest a day, a lot more public transportation, legal drugs, free beer for the punks, rage against the machine, painting 'Chernobyl Was No Accident' on the back of your leather jacket, squatting, sticking playing cards in your bicycle wheels, painting the dark-brown hall white, equal pay, open kitchens with free meals made from the mountains of daily left-overs of supermarkets, homeless shelters, spaces for clean needle exchange, free condoms, art and poetry instead of commercials on billboards, all commercials should only get printed on toilet paper, police uniforms designed by Leigh Bowery, street names made up by poets, writers or artists, etc... I have been listening to the first two LP's by Yello![6]

Notes

1. Ercola are an Antwerp artists collective, founded in 1968. They published the art journal Spruit and later designed sets for TV and theatre. Since the early 1970s, Ercola operates from a former hospice at Wolstraat 31.
2. Neutral are an experimental musical duo from Sweden.
3. Enhet För Fri Musik are an experimental improvisation collective from Sweden.
4. Crass were an English art collective and punk rock band formed in 1977 who promoted anarchism as a political ideology, a way of life and a resistance movement.
5. Club Moral was the name of the artistic duo Anne-Mie Van Kerckhoven and Danny Devos who made industrial music. It was also the name of a concert and exhibition venue that they ran in Borgerhout in the 1980s.
6. Yello is a Swiss electronic duo band formed in the late 1970s, consisting of Dieter Meier and Boris Blank.

Blockchain: Tragedy in Cyberspace? How the Commoner Could Benefit from the Free-Rider

Walter Van Andel
& Louis Volont

Contemporary debates on anything that is supposedly 'new' tend to centre around 'normality'. Take, for instance, debates on veganism, political preference, or gay marriage. People speculating on these issues often speak in terms of 'the normal' and 'the exception'. Some say that mankind has always eaten meat, and that therefore we should continue to do so 'because it has always been that way'. Gay marriage? 'Wrong! Let's keep our ancient traditions intact!' In the same vein, some say that capitalism constitutes humankind's default situation, whilst commoning constitutes the exception as a new, utopian, romantic discourse, deserving at best a heritage niche for those dreamers who still 'believe' in a world beyond market and state. In fact, discussions on the commons stem from parties who attempt to convince other parties about what is 'normal and realistic' and what is 'exceptional and unrealistic'. Opponents try to convince advocates of the commons by referring to a kind of universal, albeit hidden truth: 'We've always exchanged goods on markets' or 'mankind consists of self-interested individuals'. Interlocutors attempt to claim monopolies on supposed truths. Discussions on the commons, hence, evolve out of a clash of ideology and counter-ideology.

In an attempt to contribute to the discussion, we deem it a worthwhile endeavour to look more closely into arguments *contra* the commons and to see whether these arguments hold in the case of a recently and rapidly evolving instance of commoning in cyberspace: the blockchain. The blockchain is a technology that facilitates the online exchange of cryptocurrencies, such as the bitcoin, unmediated by either centralized market institutions nor by governmental regulations. The instance of the blockchain, we argue, is particularly well-suited to explore ideology and counter-ideology in the realm of the commons, for the blockchain constitutes a contested kind of commons: a market common, a monetary common, a kind of common that facilitates the accumulation of exchange value for, indeed, self-interested individuals. Firstly, we highlight the notion of the 'common-pool resource' (CPR) in order to further explore theory-based arguments *contra* commons. Secondly, we outline our central case. In the remainder of the text, finally, we evaluate the commons' counter-ideology through the lens of the blockchain. At this juncture, we can already hint at three alleged problems that supposedly put a strain on the commons: the problem of overuse, the problem of communication, and the problem of scale.

The Tragedy of the Commons: Overuse, Communication, Scale

In everyday parlance, it seems fairly easy to distinguish between private goods and public goods. The former relates to commercial products exchanged on a market (to buy a house), whereas the latter relates to facilities provided by a government (to use a road). Additionally, it seems fairly easy to distinguish between public goods and common goods. The former relates, for example, to information retrieved from a book we paid for, whereas the latter relates to information found on Wikipedia. Yet, the inherent specificities of the commons seem to demand clarification. What exactly differentiates the commons from other kinds of goods? In post-war neoclassical economics, the first key feature of a commons or common-pool resource (CPR) is *subtractability*, meaning that one person's use 'subtracts' or depletes value for others. The second key feature of the CPR is *non-excludability* (openness): theoretically, outsiders cannot be excluded from a CPR, a resource 'open to all' (Ostrom 1990, p. 30–33).

Later, the concept of the commons as a noteworthy scholarly subject entered the canon of the social sciences by way of Garrett Hardin's (1968) *Science* article entitled *The Tragedy of the Commons*. Hardin, a socio-biologist, held that the subtractible and open character of the commons would eventually result in overuse, depletion, and tragedy. In order to illustrate this tragedy, Hardin depicts a number of herdsmen who jointly feed their cattle on a shared pasture—a commons—that is 'open to all'. In order to survive, each herdsman will add more cattle, for each herdsman, as a rational being, aims to maximize benefit. This poses an inherent threat to the commons, since the costs of overgrazing are 'socialized' amongst all actors in the play, whereas the gain of adding one more animal befalls one participant only. In the absence of internal communication and coordination among the herdsmen, the commons will cease to exist and the tragedy is now complete. Hardin (1968, p. 1247), for whom 'the alternative of the commons is too horrifying to contemplate', concludes:

> Therein is the tragedy. Each man is locked into a system that compels him to increase his herd without limit—in a world that is limited. Ruin is the destination toward which all men rush, each pursuing his own best interest in a society that believes in the freedom of the commons.

Freedom in a commons brings ruin to all. (Hardin 1968, p. 1244)

Even though Hardin's parable has been interpreted mistakenly as an irrefutable argument for the superior efficiency of private property in a free, Smithian market, his solution sounds otherwise. Hardin (1968, p. 1244) explicitly argued *against* the 'dominant tendency of thought ..., namely, the tendency to assume that decisions reached individually will, in fact, be the best decisions for an entire society'. Hardin's thesis, hence, was an argument contra, not pro, a laissez-faire economy. Only through governmental regulation could humankind emancipate from the tragedy of the commons. Hardin's concern was related to the supposed tragedy of human procreation, yet the broader realm of his argument is crystal-clear: individuals locked into the logic of the commons will bring ruin to all. We mustn't forget, however, that Hardin's argument presupposes two hidden assumptions. One may rightfully ask whether the tragedy would occur if the herdsmen had known each other and if they had figured out a system of 'checks and balances' through internal collaboration. Ostrom, evidently, showed that those who share resources *can* effectively manage and sustain shared wealth under suitable conditions.

Back to commons' counter-ideology. In fact, many more theorizations may be added to Hardin's tragedy. From Hobbes' inevitable Leviathan to the mysteries of game theory: it seems as if the social sciences remain obsessed with the question of how individuals may or may not collaborate sustainably once the individual level transcends into the aggregate level. A transversal threat throughout these accounts is the presupposition that mankind constitutes an inherently gain-seeking creature. In that context, a final example *contra* commons is found in Olson's (1965) *The Logic of Collective Action*. Olson set out to counter the key presumption held in classical group theory, namely that individuals with common goals would decide voluntarily to collaborate and further their shared interests. Yet even though Olson's account is less pessimistic than Hardin's tragedy, he equally argued that the premise of collective action could only work in small-scale situations: 'Unless the number of individuals is quite small, or unless there is coercion or some other special device to make individuals act in their common interest, rational, self-interested individuals will not act to achieve their common or group interests.' (Olson 1965, p. 2)

Those who claim a monopoly on the 'tragic' and 'horrifying' character of the commons, we argue, presuppose that individuals who pursue interests through shared resources will eventually counter a threefold problem. The first issue is related to a commons' or CPR's aforementioned characteristic of subtractability. Because of the subtractible character of a shared resource, the use of one person will decrease the resource's initial value for others, eventually resulting in overuse or 'total ruin', as Hardin would have proposed. The second issue is related to a commons' or CPR's aforementioned characteristic of non-excludability (openness). Because outsiders can hardly be excluded, internal communication and monitoring among the resource users becomes increasingly complex. The third problem, finally, relates to scale: resource users may pursue common interests on a small, local scale, but the situation becomes increasingly difficult when the commons tend to transcend the community level. It ought to be clear that all three threats—overuse, communication, scale—are heavily interrelated. At the heart of each of these issues is the free-rider problem. Whenever a participant in a commoning process cannot be excluded from the benefits others provide, each participant is presumably seduced not to contribute to common interests, but to free-ride on the value created by others. After all, if many more resource users enter in a process of commoning, who will effectively communicate with, monitor, and sanction the free-rider?

In the following paragraphs, we aim to explore the recent and rapidly developing technology of the blockchain as a potential remedy for the problems of overuse, communication, and scale. We consider this exploration particularly valuable, for on the one hand the blockchain facilitates many new instances of commons, be they financial, peer-to-peer, or cultural; on the other hand, the blockchain serves both common and individual interests without any mechanism to exclude the free-rider and, most importantly, on a limitless scale. Aristotle once wrote: 'What is common to greatest number has the least care bestowed upon it.' The question is, however, whether this holds in cyberspace. We do not, as in the commons' counter-ideological discourse, want to claim a certain truth about mankind as being invariably self-interested, yet we *do* assert that the blockchain enhances that one thing that makes the world go around: to make money.

The Blockchain

As the popularity of online cryptocurrencies such as bitcoins continues to grow, growing attention is focused on its underlying technological infrastructure: the so-called blockchain. The seemingly simple technology of the blockchain was initially lauded within techno-savvy hackers' circles, but has recently attracted a large group of followers. Believers and users are found in both mainstream organizations as well as in individuals that dream of an alternative and sustainable economic future (Swartz 2017).

In its most simple form, the blockchain constitutes a continuously growing digital list of records, a ledger. As such, the blockchain can be used for bookkeeping in a similar way that ledgers have been used for centuries by many organizations and institutions. Banks, for instance, hold ledgers that contain information about your bank account, national governments hold ledgers that contain information about the degrees you have obtained. However, importantly, blockchains are different in certain key aspects, which derive from their digital, online nature. Firstly, they are distributed: the ledger does not function as a central database stored in one private location, but is shared among participants; secondly, they are public: every user has access, anytime and anywhere, to a historical chain of information; finally, they are write-only: new information can be written into it, but existing information that is already present cannot ever be deleted. Because of the blockchain's 'decentrality', publicness, and informational history, many consider the blockchain to be the technology that will change the world (Tapscott and Tapscott 2016). After all: it makes possible what until recently seemed unthinkable, namely to do without the public and private intermediaries (financial institutions, notaries, central banks, and even governments) that were up until now considered necessary to facilitate our economic reality.

In a blockchain system, all transactions that need to be registered on the ledger are grouped together every few minutes to form a new 'block'. Then, connected computers from all around the world verify the information in the block: they check whether the registrations are in agreement with the rules set forth in the protocol. For instance, when bitcoins are transferred from one person to another, the computers validate the transaction by looking through the historical blockchain to check if both bitcoin accounts are legitimate and if the transferring person has enough bitcoins in his/her balance. This distributed verification system is the unique feature of a blockchain. Anybody can participate in this verification process by making their computers available to jointly validate the information in a new block, a process that is called 'mining'. In return, miners can earn new bitcoins as a reward for their efforts, which makes it attractive for them to participate. Once all information in the new block is validated, a unique identifier key is generated, which contains a reference to its preceding block and an answer to a complex mathematical puzzle which serves to validate the transactions. By actively connecting a new block to its preceding block, a linear sequence of encrypted datasets is created, thus forming a 'chain'. As a general-purpose technology, the blockchain serves as a means of record, in a secure and verifiable manner, that reflects a particular state of affairs which has been agreed upon by the network (Wright and De Filippi 2015).

Bitcoin, the popular electronic currency, is the most widely recognized example of a technology built upon the blockchain. However, there are potentially many more applications of blockchains that all use the same general principle: a decentralized network of computers capable of verifying information that rewards behaviour deemed beneficial to the network. In order to recognize some of the potential of the blockchain technology, consider the example of Backfeed, a proposed blockchain-based application that aims to provide a social operating system for decentralized organizations and enables massive open-source collaboration without central coordination.[1] From the Backfeed website:

> Imagine. Facebook owned by its users, decentralized transportation networks independent of Uber, markets dominated by open-source communities where contributors are also shareholders, and where the value created is redistributed both fairly and transparently. Imagine the innovative potential of such organizations decoupled from the rigidities of hierarchical structures. For all of this and more... Backfeed provides the infrastructure for decentralized cooperation.

Still in the early stages of development, Backfeed is developing an open-source infrastructural protocol through which anyone can create a governance system that is based on Backfeed's central values: large-scale, free, meritocratic, and decentralized. Using the blockchain technology, Backfeed is able to combat some of the problems encountered by many open (online) communities in which people collaborate for the achievement of a common goal (consider Free and Open-Source Software, Wikipedia, OpenStreetMaps, CouchSurfing or WikiHouse) (Pazaitis, De Filippi, and Kostakis 2017).

> The majority of such communities operate on a very small scale, often on a local territory or in a niche area ... and usually comprise a small handful of highly motivated contributors, and a slightly larger number of people who contribute on an ad hoc basis. (Pazaitis, De Filippi, and Kostakis 2017)

Scaling up is usually only feasible through increased hierarchy, or through a market-oriented approach that accumulates necessary funds and rewards contributors with economic returns.

In Backfeed's meritocratic system, everyone is free to contribute to a particular community in the way they see most fit. Then, once the input is validated and appreciated by the members of the community, the contributors are rewarded with 'a reputation' that reflects their influence in the governance of the community and/or an economic compensation in the form of digital tokens. These tokens can be used to benefit from the services offered by the community, representing an actual (equity) share in the organization (Pazaitis, De Filippi, and Kostakis 2017). The Backfeed protocol therefore dynamically adjusts the influence of peers in a decentralized network, giving appreciation to valuable input, while mitigating potential centralization of the power through its consensus system, which is based on the pursuit of a common goal. In sum, the system supports any movement that would benefit from the decentralized, indirect coordination of large groups of individuals.

In a first experiment, the Backfeed protocol was tested in the organization of the 2016 OuiShare festival in Paris. OuiShare is an interdisciplinary festival that gathers creative leaders, entrepreneurs, movement builders, purpose-driven organizations, and communities from across sectors and countries who want to drive systemic and meaningful change. In this experiment, the festival organizers decided to use Backfeed to run their programme selection process in a decentralized manner, with the aim to improve the submission system by making contributions more visible and providing transparency by documenting them, enabling contributors to build a reputation (by participating in the evaluation process), and by finding 'consensus' by using the electronic system (Pick 2015). By utilizing the Backfeed system, the festival hoped to improve the sourcing of the best content from the community and make it easier for the members to contribute to the project and get recognized for the value they provide, all while organized in a non-hierarchical, decentral manner in which not one single voice can claim ownership.

Coda: Blockchain Dreams

The technology of the blockchain facilitates a plethora of sources to share. Urban commons (community gardens), cultural commons (OuiShare) and market commons (the bitcoin), among others, may emerge through the use of this 'extremely disruptive technology that would have the capacity for reconfiguring all aspects of society and its operations' (Swan 2015, ix). And although the further development of the blockchain's state-of-the-art remains to be seen, its advocates seem to agree that its only limitation is the imagination of the user community. By way of conclusion, we intend to expound on this view from a utopian and a dystopian perspective.

From a utopian point of view, the blockchain seems to annihilate the aforementioned threats that have long been considered to impede the commons: overuse, (absence of) communication, and scale. Firstly, we argue, the blockchain seems immune to the threat of overuse. In all: the larger the community, the more value it creates. The more use, the better. Therefore, commons created by the blockchain constitute what Kornberger and Borch (2015) have called a 'relational subject': contrary to Hardin's communal pasture, blockchain commons *increase* in value after use. The act of consumption, is equally an act of production. This makes Backfeed's system a powerful tool for bridging individual and collective motives in the aim of achieving common goals. Secondly, the blockchain facilitates internal communication among its users. The system offers full transparency to all users, since all contributions towards the common goal are subject to peer-to-peer evaluation, which further determines the perceived value of the network. All contributions are clearly visible to the entire community, making inputs that are detrimental to the common goal subject to dismissal. Even though anonymous and quasi-fictional, trust can be built within the user community. Hardin's hidden assumption, hence, regarding the absence of communication among those who share resources can be dismissed. Finally, the blockchain has the potential to reach scales far beyond the local level. Many commoning practices nowadays remain limited to low-scale and closed systems. The blockchain, by contrast, facilitates significant upscaling, for trust is instituted through the monitoring of behaviour. Also, the blockchain not only supports a larger scale, it actually benefits from it. A recent study proved that Metcalfe's Law, which states that the value of a network is proportional to the square of the number of its users, also applies to blockchain networks (Alabi 2017). Exit Olson's aforementioned thesis that pursuing shared interests cannot escape the curse of the low-scale. Exit Hardin's tragedy of the commons.

From a dystopian point of view, however, we conceive of the blockchain as a container of its own alterity. In this context, Swartz (2017) distinguishes between radical and incorporative 'blockchain dreams'. The former group relates to those who are rethinking society for the better, those for whom 'the tragedy of the commons is stamped out like polio by a collaborative network of trust ...' (Thorpe 2015). The latter group, by contrast, has no such ambitions. In recent years, efforts have been made to incorporate blockchain technology within the existing financial system. The Distributive Ledger project, for instance, is currently remaking banking infrastructure and receives the support of J.P. Morgan, Goldman Sachs, Deutsche Bank, just to name a few. These attempts, it ought to be clear, do not necessarily seek to alter the financial system from a social perspective. As Linebaugh (2008, p. 279) once wrote: 'Capitalists and the World Bank would like us to employ commoning as a means to socialize poverty and hence to privatize wealth.' Just as the sharing economy promised us decentralized commerce but quickly became an excuse for on-demand work, the blockchain's utopian visions might also shift from their original, decentralized impetus to economic exploitation. Also, not to forget, online communities based on the blockchain and centred around that other new cryptocurrency, Ethereum, still struggle to reach adequate communication and internal consensus regarding the further development of their underlying systems. 'At the heart of the blockchain dream', writes Swartz (2017, p. 91), 'there is a yearning for ever more direct communication.'

So, the blockchain's potential for ultimate 'disintermediation' helps us to imagine the future, evidently, but in what way? In our view, the answer will be found in how the blockchain will relate, in the years to come, to human labour. Virno (2004) once imagined how post-Fordism constitutes the 'communism of capital'. In the same vein, blockchain advocates are nowadays speculating how the technology might enhance what some call 'FALC': Fully Automated Luxury Communism. The blockchain enables capitalism to automate labour. Yet in recognition of that, only common ownership of that which is automated may prevent the blockchain from lapsing into corporate tragedy. The finale of the blockchain dream, we think, will depend on who eventually wins the battle between ideology and counter-ideology, or: who gets to claim a monopoly on 'what is normal' and 'what is exceptional'.

1   www.backfeed.cc.

References

— Alabi, Ken. 2017. 'Digital Blockchain Networks Appear to Be Following Metcalfe's Law.' *Electronic Commerce Research and Applications* 24 (July), pp. 23–29.

— Hardin, Garrett. 1968. 'The Tragedy of the Commons.' *Science* 162, pp. 1243–1248.

— Kornberger, Martin, and Christian Borch. 2015. 'Introduction: Urban Commons.' In *Urban Commons: Rethinking The City*. Edited by Christian Borch and Martin Kornberger, pp. 1–21. London: Routledge.

— Linebaugh, Peter. 2008. *The Magna Carta Manifesto: Liberties and Commons for All*. Berkeley, Los Angeles, and London: University of California Press.

— Olson, Mancur. 1965. *The Logic of Collective Action: Public Goods and the Theory of Groups*. Cambridge, MA: Harvard University Press.

— Ostrom, Elinor. 1990. *Governing the Commons: The Evolution of Institutions for Collective Action*. Cambridge, MA: Harvard University Press.

— Pazaitis, Alex, Primavera De Filippi, and Vasilis Kostakis. 2017. 'Blockchain and Value Systems in the Sharing Economy: The Illustrative Case of Backfeed.' *Technological Forecasting & Social Change* 125, pp. 105–115.

— Pick, Francesca. 2015. 'Decentralizing (Part of) OuiShare with Blockchain.' *OuiShare Magazine* (November), http://magazine.ouishare.net/2015/11/decentralizing-part-of-ouishare-with-blockchain-experiment-1/.

— Swan, Melanie. 2015. *Blockchain: Blueprint for a New Economy*. Sebastopol, CA: O'Reilly Media.

— Swartz, Lana. 2017. 'Blockchain Dreams: Imagining Techno-Economic Alternatives After Bitcoin.' In *Another Economy Is Possible*. Edited by Manuel Castells, pp. 82–105. Cambridge, MA: Polity Press.

— Tapscott, Don, and Alex Tapscott. 2016. *Blockchain Revolution: How the Technology Behind Bitcoin Is Changing Money, Business, and the World*. New York: Portfolio.

— Thorpe, Noah. 2015. 'How Society Will Be Transformed by Crypto-economics'. https://media.comakery.com/how-society-will-be-transformed-by-crypto-economics-b02b6765ca8c.

— Virno, Paolo. 2004. A *Grammar of the Multitude: For an Analysis of*

Contemporary Forms of Life. London: MIT Press.
— Wright, Aaron, and Primavera De Filippi. 2015. *Decentralized Blockchain Technology and the Rise of Lex Cryptographia*. New York. http://ssrn.com/abstract=2580664.

"Volvo!"

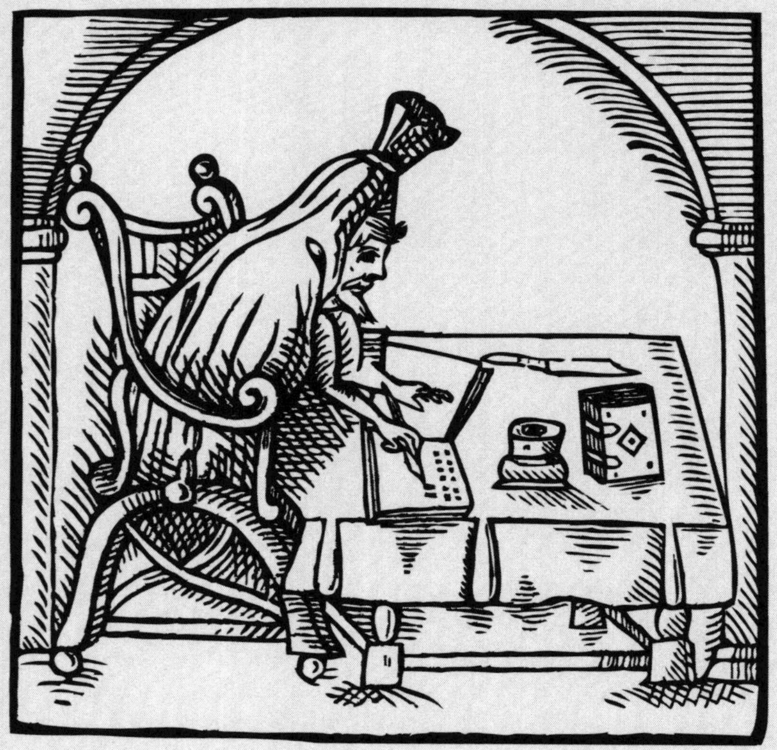

Volvo!, Soho House, 2010

plus de douleur!

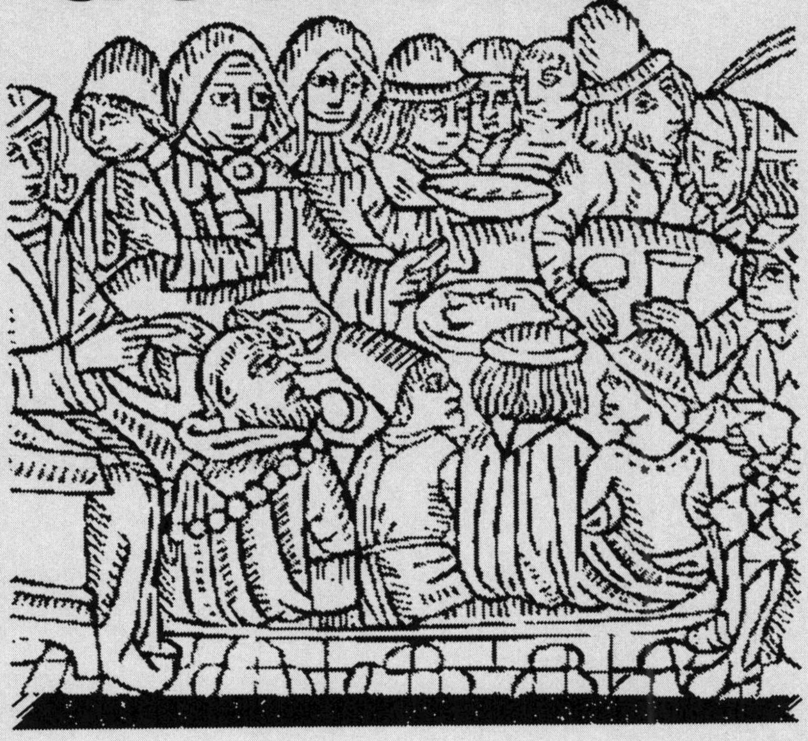

Plus de douleur, Modern Painters, 2008

Induced Legality and the Art of Building Common Infrastructures
An Interview with Santiago Cirugeda, Recetas Urbanas

Lara Garcia Diaz

Active since 1996, the Seville-based Recetas Urbanas (Urban Recipes), a design and advocacy collective of architects, lawyers and social workers explore the 'a-legal' common ground between market and government, between the private and the public sphere. With a complex fusion of activism, architecture, legal quibbles, social empathy, and an amazing human 'energy bomb', Recetas Urbanas generate a unique performative and effectual commoning practice. Founder Santiago Cirugeda is asked how he organizes and collectivizes his practice, and how he thinks commoning undertakings can survive in the long run.

Lara Garcia – How, when, and at what point did the need arise for Recetas Urbanas to rethink the notion of public space, setting out from an interpretation of the concept of common space?

Santiago Cirugeda – Actually, it materialized from an overtly personal concern. I was someone who started out working alone, until I realized that more people were needed if I wanted to exert real pressure and somehow change or uproot public policies. It was a way for me to approach the question of what is understood, institutionally, by good and bad, and at the same time consider that there are other ways of doing things collectively. It stemmed from a merely human concern with communication, including how one communicates with the public powers that legally and fiscally set a city in order. These public powers order and understand the city in one way, and I wondered whether I could do it in another; everything, as I said, with naivety, neither from activism nor a fixed political viewpoint. It was simply a matter of legitimacy. In other words, it was about how I live here and have rights. I guess it was about doing something. But, as you point out, I do distinguish between public space and common space. In my view, public space can be used without being familiar with it, without affection or involvement. A common space, however, is a space that the community decides to manage with its own means, driven by specific daily needs. Later, of course, the community that manages that common space may decide to open it up to the public sphere.

Self-management and Empowerment

LG – From your comments, I understand that active exercises to re-appropriate space are key to generating common space and the way it operates. Unfortunately, privatization processes have not only affected land and common spaces, but also social relations, practices, and images, which means that today we can see the fight for the commons revamped in, for instance, the fight for non-commercial education that can be directly managed by teachers, parents and students. Recetas Urbanas has collaborated on numerous occasions in the DIY construction of self-managed educational spaces. What role does education play in processes of making the commons?

SC – Various terms in your question concern me a little and, if you wouldn't mind, I'd like to focus on them for a minute. I refer to terms such as empowerment and re-appropriation because for me those ideas, ever-present these days, suggest the idea of total defeat; it's as though we've been defeated in a period in history or a time in which people only talked about the capacity of capital. What has happened, in my view, is that we have not accepted that we had a political responsibility as citizens, as part of a community in an urban settlement—in other words a city. For some time now, it has seemed as though we've finally realized that we can participate in how the public sphere, education, and teaching are shaped. Basically, in everything. To me the word re-appropriation is a clear example of the idea of recovering something you've lost. I go back to the fact that we have always had those established rights and we have always had that capacity, but we were distracted by other values. In all State Constitutions there is the right to participate, just as there is the right to vote, to choose who is going to govern, the right to put something forward, and so on, and that is a natural right in any settlement, whether it is an assembly, parliament, or republic. What has happened is that this right has been overshadowed by the market, which has occupied, and still occupies, worldwide decision-making structures that forget people and their well-being. The same thing happens with collectives, and economic structures of maintenance and livelihood; the link that makes productive exchange exclusively economic still largely affects us. Nevertheless, as you rightly mention, in that process in which we acquire the capacity for decision-making, for contributing, criticizing, and evaluating, education and culture play a role that is both essential and a priority. For example, we have a university system that resembles the citizen behaviour I described before: passive, and without grasping and understanding its rights as an education centre, without being a model of critical power. That's why I believe the university and the school have to work as spaces that debate the capacity a person must possess to be able to change content, propose projects, modify laws... At the moment that just isn't happening. I'm really motivated by more and more people taking the education experience and building self-managed schools in which 20 to 50 students independently set up their studies or their own projects and policies. Clearly these processes are the ones that help us to move forward. It's true that almost subconsciously Recetas Urbanas is linked to different education and mental health projects, but I also have to say that it's because they have called us, asking for help because maybe they've seen that, in that logic of creating situations of conflict with authorities to change legislation, there was a part set aside to change education issues.

LG – To what extent do your interventions question how resources and work are shared, and the idea of common good on a collective level? And if so, then how would you define this common good? Also, what role do practices such as yours, which at the moment are largely developed from the cultural sphere, play in that change of perspective?

SC – Well the answer to that question is very simple, but the way to develop it is highly complex. I mean, it's simple to answer because it's as basic as saying that anyone who is born, any human being, in any job, and with any family or education background, has the same rights. Everyone. Obviously, economic structures come into play here and hinder these rights being exercised equally, which is why Recetas Urbanas offers a set of tools to redress a little the balance in developing these natural rights, for instance the right to a proper education, a decent job, suitable shared tasks or responsibilities, and to the most human condition, which is collectivity and the freedom of choice. We are social creatures, which is why we live in cities. Therefore, I believe that political and citizen development that fosters creativity, freedom, and collectivity is the most reasonable form of development for humans. Moreover, it is no longer political; it is a matter of logic, and when people see that personally their collective capacity is limited, or their ability to get an education because they're working day and night just to get by, that's when people are being maimed by the system. In my view, that's not something reasonable.

My belief is that the better off the most disadvantaged are, the better off you are. We live in a collective that is ground down by certain political and administrative interests that disregard essential social, family, educational and cultural values. I honestly don't understand how any value can be maimed; I don't understand it but unfortunately it happens. Therefore, Recetas Urbanas has always set out to try to build small-scale tools, which may not always work, unfortunately. To try and redress the balance somehow. This is why we always say you have to be aware of laws and administrative mechanisms, for instance how to report to the authorities or communicate with various bodies. There is no need to wait for a public notice because you, as a citizen, male or female, have the right to go there first thing tomorrow and speak to your town council's urban planning department to expound the collective needs of your neighbourhood and demand solutions. This is exactly what Recetas Urbanas sets out to do. And although our projects have the capacity to find a solution to micro-social struggles, gradually, and starting from that point, they are more and more opening out into spaces of collective struggle.

The Aesthetic

LG – Through the reuse of material and research into different processes of construction and occupation, Recetas Urbanas appears to have consolidated its own unmistakeable aesthetic. I imagine that this style is the upshot of negotiations between the different actors in each intervention, but also, as far as I can see, of the availability of materials and the different economic, ecological, political, and social conditions in each case. Do you think that Recetas Urbanas' aesthetic can be defined as the aesthetic of the commons?

SC – I honestly don't think that Recetas Urbanas possesses an aesthetic that can be related to the commons. It's true that people always want to see, incessantly, exactly that; to define our aesthetic with those words. Obviously, there is some form of 'commons' strategy in our projects, but if you compare the projects we have done throughout our twenty years of work you will see that they are not related at all. It seems as if we have always been associated with an image that correlates more to a process of amassing ideas, and in many projects there is an accumulation of different elements because many people are involved in the process. Yet in others the design has been planned beforehand and clearly expounded in order to be voted for by the people who were going to use it. In this case, the capacity for decision-making is far more limited because sometimes the issue people want to resolve is based around having a canteen in the school, and they aren't bothered whether it's green, brown, blue, or purple. What they want is a canteen that meets regulations, and that's where we have to be efficient, with the little money they give you and with a non-professional workforce, in order meet those needs. In some ways, the aesthetic does have something to do with the process to be carried out in each case, but in Recetas Urbanas' projects it is not a continuous and perpetual process. That's why I have to say that in fifty percent of the projects we've done, the decisions made on the design have been ours, and not collective, regardless of whether the construction process is collective and the necessary modifications are done on-site and enable the base to be worked on from a specific design. I must stress again that, in the case of schools, the basic equipment must be approved by very specific regulations—even though you have bags of cork or wooden or metal girders, there are legal regulations you have to bear in mind. In the end this is also reflected in the aesthetic. If the question is whether we have forced the aesthetic of certain projects so as to make the commons, or common work, visible, then the answer is no, because we knew that it was somehow going to happen naturally.

A Common Infrastructure

LG – Many of Recetas Urbanas' projects lead to and raise the question, put forward by Paula V. Álvarez, of 'common infrastructure' (2009), an infrastructure, as you've mentioned on numerous occasions, that interweaves affective and social reality with a more material, economic, and legal reality. In approaching the reality of social relations in a 'common infrastructure', we could say that the Recetas Urbanas projects regard architecture not as a discipline moving towards a finite result, but as a never-ending collective process. In fact, some of your projects constantly remain under construction. But, how can the permanent investment of collective energy be sustained in the long term?

SC – To be honest, that's a highly complex question. Starting from activist knowledge or the knowledge of people who work in health care or ecology, it's not so much that maintaining a social structure, group, or network is complex, it's immensely difficult! Chiefly because the first thing we have to ask ourselves is exactly how long activism lasts in a person. On top of that, when we finish a project, and bow out by putting on a big farewell party, we leave with the conviction that this social-based maintenance is going to be developed specifically by the members of each structure. For us it's impossible to maintain all social structures in every open project we are working on. Obviously, we do try to follow social maintenance clauses in each case; for instance, proposing, and with the excuse of maintaining the building, a number of workshops that can work as encounters for us to meet. Activism, or energy, always seems to decline when the need for such a struggle is met, which is why keeping up that energy is so tough. But for me it's a key aim and clear as a bell. In that regard, I also think, just as a partner is perhaps not for life, many projects are not for life either. What I mean is, there's nothing wrong with a project ending; making something last cannot be a requisite, and you cannot ask people to fight for something, get what they're fighting for, and then continue fighting for another cause. However, maintenance can be understood on many levels, but maintaining information or technical aspects, or something affective, is difficult; political maintenance is virtually impossible to sustain because people become exhausted. So how do you pass synergies of struggles on to the next group? For example, in some cases I've forced parents at a school to collaborate in building another school that was not their own. For me, that's a methodological procedure. If you give something, or help someone, that person must return the help by giving something else or helping another person, which is how great experiences created in one place are transferred to another. Therefore, maintenance has many formulas. Social maintenance and involvement are difficult to sustain, but we can still offer tools for them to be strengthened. The word 'force' sounds bad but sometimes it's necessary and the results are great, emotionally speaking.

LG – Within that common infrastructure, or more specifically in reference to a more economic or legal reality, Recetas Urbanas seeks to create a new existing territory between the legal and illegal to uncover how the law is not able to span the versatility and richness of different present-day ways of life. On different occasions, you've used the term 'allegal' to refer to precisely those actions that take advantage of the existence of spheres where regulation is still confusing, or even absent. 'Allegality' moves ahead of the law instead of opposing it. On many occasions, what started out as an 'allegal' proposal in your projects has ended up influencing the legal landscape, transforming established laws— I think you call this process 'induced legality'. How do you relate the tactic of direct action to the process of 'induced legality' in your projects? In other words, do you fulfil short-term objectives through a method that takes in actions of continuity?

SC – In law there is a process called legal doctrine, which, roughly speaking, is a set of opinions that can make a law appear; meaning, practices that, according to lawyers and jurists, can become a law. A legal doctrine is a source of the right to uses and customs; therefore, many practices that often happen illegally are the result of slow administration processes—the reality is that the procedure is correct and legal, even though there is not yet authorization. The work of Recetas Urbanas has always been to consider situations, sometimes illegal or 'allegal', because they are yet-to-be-defined processes. We have, however, often searched for final legality to follow a set of democratic principles. But what does that mean? That many times people involved in occupying a space and finally attaining the right to use it are people with certain and specific qualities, either physical or personal. Yet I think we must bear in mind other types of people who, perhaps through shyness, or for personal, physical, or mental reasons, do not have the capacity to confront the occupation of space, but who, as I previously mentioned, should have the same right of use as anyone else who does so. Another of our clear objectives is the attempt for different practices, from the academic world to local authorities, to standardize our tools in order for us to have sources that validate our work, regardless of the opinion of any authority that says our technical construction criteria are not correct. That happens all the time, for instance, with the issue of self-builds, but, as I said, legality needs so much time that undoubtedly illegality will continue to be integral to our practices. In this case illegality, rather than being a political stance, is the result of the impossibility of things happening how they should happen. Once again, induced illegality comes through the democratization of the rights for which a specific group of people are fighting.

LG – On many occasions there is talk of common practices like those that move beyond the market and the State. How do you see this 'beyond' in terms of the tools Recetas Urbanas proposes?

SC – Another million-dollar question! As far as I can see, many structures coexist. On one side you have the State, on another the banks, and on yet another social structures, and so on. The way in which Recetas Urbanas is related to each one differs in each case, depending on how valid the structure we are working on is. In our case, for example, we have tried a number of times to negotiate with banking structures to see whether inside their real estate assets there is a space of action for immediate social solutions. But when you come up against these gargantuan structures you feel very small. The growing circle we are experiencing now, where the market seems to be on the rise again and financial institutions are only looking to make profits, means projects like ours struggle to find their place. What is also true is that local authorities have to grapple and fight to balance models because, if not, we'll be back in the same place we were in a few years ago, constantly going from cycle to cycle until it all blows up. Once again, however, moving between the market and the public sphere is really difficult. One reason, as we touched on before, is precisely the disparate temporalities between different structures. It's not easy balancing temporalities like our own—with weekly updates through daily requirements at a given time—with really sluggish administration times. Nowadays, there are temporalities that are impossible to balance out, and the sad thing is that often when administration times are adopted or models that fit within their temporalities, eventually nothing gets changed, just decorated a bit. That's why, in fact, the Arquitecturas Colectivas (Collective Architecture) network surfaced, because the network ostensibly has greater bargaining power. For instance, the power the network gives us because it's made up of different collectives has been useful in validating our proposals in Latin America, which was the case with the mobile library in Colombia. As I've mentioned, in the face of huge structures such as the banking structure or State power that has been democratically voted for, we need to create a network that is just as strong if we want to stand up and be taken seriously. Because I think there is definitely a gap between the market and the State. But support of local authorities is necessary; they need to believe in citizen participation and the possibility of another model. There are two scenarios here: One that fundamentally depends on the local authority through the issue of public land, and another, which is the local authority's regulations on private land and development. One is legislation and the other is believing in projects similar to those by Recetas Urbanas, projects which are ultimately more solid because they are based on effectiveness and affectivity, not on the guarantees of paying a mortgage. The problem now is: What tools do we have, or should we create, to talk to the State about controlling this whole landscape?

Territorial Struggles

LG – The survival of projects aimed explicitly at experimenting with new socio-economic structures that elude market logic is both difficult and complex. After so many years of experience, is it possible to remain outside this logic of capital and finances and survive in the long term? In an ideal setting, and from an economic and juridical perspective, as well as a personal and affective perspective, what would be required for Recetas Urbanas' practices and the like to keep on being creative, dynamic, and socially committed?

SC – Quite honestly, as things stand today, being on the outside is impossible. The Recetas Urbanas studio has lasted via conferences and education over many years, and a large part of the Recetas Urbanas team has come from overseas; we've tended to hire these people whenever possible. Many people who have come for work experience have been hired and then become part of the studio for years (Alice, Luca, Gergo, Pichuco, Alejandro, Tania, Harold, and so on). On other occasions, we have collaborated with people who have come for a few months and then took the experience back to their own country. And quite often the studio says no to projects because what clients are offering, money-wise, is not enough for us to survive. In these instances, I'm sure another team in a better position or with family money or another type of financial support would take it on. Perhaps the members of that team own a home and have many other guaranteed resources that ensure their survival and mean they can take on projects which, essentially, are interesting but are waiting to be developed and are financially very precarious. It's highly complex. The difference is, as opposed to complying processes of neighbourhood participation to clean up city areas, that of carrying out a process of empowerment in a small park—which is also okay, don't get me wrong—we should all be struggling against the discrepancies that exist in public contracting and work to collectively proceed with a technical lawsuit against the municipal committee if something seems suspicious. In fact, I've asked the local authorities if Recetas Urbanas could provide free counsel for the municipal committee that decides between tenders of contractors. The chosen project gets 20% of the budget to proceed with social mediation, not participation. And this mediation, believe me, barely happens. So, how, as citizens, can we control that this 20% is really, and usefully, *used?* Prior social mediation. What can't happen is that private companies take part in this type of public urban planning tenders, and then submit something that doesn't work, or doesn't provide what people need. In academia there is good power, in terms of the management of public money, and people are both cultured and clever, with many of them undertaking public and activist practices. We conduct our practices in any way we can, and I still have the same friendships I've always had. What I'm considering is how to put all the research done in academia into action, and how to find a way of working together. The question is, how do we reach an agreement between those of us in the practical field and those who are in the field of research so we can commit and work together? The problem with our practices is that we aren't taken seriously by local authorities, which is why support from the academic sphere would be a way to validate our work and gain trust. Nowadays the authorities use us for minor policies of consensus, and my belief is that the broader the means to connect, the more we all gain. What can't happen is that highly competent people full of energy and brilliant ideas who work in the field and create relevant processes of mediation and participation still work in a highly unstable situation. What can we do to avoid that? Because although we have the information and methodology, we do not have enough tools. We should ask ourselves why everyone who engages with possible alternatives, who proposes spaces of struggle for a better life for everyone, finally ends up working within a capital logic.

Part 3

Secrets & Commoning Politics

When Politics Becomes Unavoidable
From Community Art to Commoning Art

Pascal Gielen &
Hanka Otte

Government Art

Nowadays art subsidies can no longer be taken for granted. Governments are clearly finding it difficult to find the right legitimization for supporting a sector that certainly not everyone regards as a matter of public concern. For example, in the United States the arts rely heavily on the private sector and, since President Trump took office, the entire if modest contribution of the federal government to the National Endowment of the Arts (NEA) is under threat. For a short while, during the 1930s, the arts were considered so important for the cultural development of Americans that special cultural programmes were launched. The main reason for doing this was to combat the then huge unemployment, also among artists. With the Mexican Mural Movement as its model numerous artists were deployed to apply their painting talents to public buildings such as government buildings, schools, museums, libraries, orphanages, et cetera. The idea was that culture is not the exclusive domain of a separate, lofty art world, but that everyone can benefit from and has the right to cultural development. In the second phase of the New Deal, after 1935, the Federal One project was a comprehensive approach towards a federal cultural system consisting of five branches: visual art, music, theatre, writing, and historical archival research. The first four of these hired artists, theatre makers, musicians, and writers, respectively, to produce art nationwide that was then offered at very low rates or even for free. This is why Franklin Roosevelt's New Deal Cultural Programs are often regarded as the first wave of community art, although critics would later say that these cultural projects 'served as pacifiers, containing a potentially radical and threatening artists' movement by converting it to a form of government service' (Adams and Goldbard 1986, p. 7).

It was the American government itself who was frustrating the public function of art here, as the British government would also do much later, in the 1990s, according to Paolo Merli (2002), by embracing the community art movement of the 1960s and 1970s and turning it into a policy instrument.[1] Strongly influenced by the famous but meanwhile also notorious report 'Use or Ornament?' by François Matarasso (1997), the British government adopted his claim that art contributes to a stable, secure, and creative society. However, according to Merli, this is diametrically opposed to the aims of the community art of the 1960s and 1970s, which was also called 'countercultural art' for a reason.

While the [latter] was directed to the expression of conflicts, Matarasso's vision is directed to social stability
obtained by means of 'peaceful' popular consensus, the
underlying inspiration seemingly being that whereas the
rich are doing the 'right' things, the poor should be soothed
through 'therapeutic' artistic activities. While in the sev-
enties the aim was emancipation and liberation from any
form of social control, also (and above all) by means of
artistic creativity, in the revival of interest in participatory
arts advocated by Matarasso the aim is the restoration of
social control using the same tools, although otherwise
directed. (Merli 2002, p. 114)

In countries such as Canada, Australia, the Netherlands, and
Belgium the revival of this artistic practice since the 1990s was
very much related to an official cultural policy—such as Arts
Impact Fund (UK) and recently Kunst van Impact (NL)—that
provided subsidies for social-artistic projects or stimulated the private sector to support such projects in and with society through all
kinds of provisions. This has brought most community art into a
legally regulated or civic domain (Gielen and Dietachmair 2017).

A community art policy is the perfect legitimization of public support of the arts, especially in times of austerity. After all,
the artworks would directly and visibly benefit the population (the
taxpayers), especially those members of the population who would
normally not be confronted with art. A big difference between the
first and third wave of community art is that Roosevelt felt that art
participation as such was important to the cultural development of
all Americans, whereas governments who have been subsidizing
community arts since the 1990s mainly have high expectations of
its social effect on individuals and communities. As Merli already
suggested, these effects seem to be moving in only one direction
though. Makers of community art may be sincerely concerned
about social deprivation, social inequality, and other societal injus-
tices and it is for that very reason that they are asked to reinforce the
social fabric with their art. However, as widespread criticism has
it—rightly or not—this approach is sometimes hardly distinguish-
able any more from that of the social worker. Earlier reflections on
the phenomenon of community art stated that in the worst case it is
'guilty' of what Michel Foucault called 'pastoral power' (Foucault
1977-1978). Social workers can be deployed as helpers of the state

or even the police insofar as they detect, document, and try to correct behaviour that is not in line with prevailing values and norms in a society. They not only help the long-term unemployed, drug addicts, or rebellious teenagers with their daily social and mental problems, but they also try to bring them back to the straight and narrow by checking on them, for example by counting the number of toothbrushes and beds that were slept in in the homes of singles who receive benefits. In that sense social workers also contribute to the normalizing and disciplinary principles that are supposed to keep society running as it has always run. This is not an unimportant aspect, as in this respect social work affirms the existing social order without questioning it. So social work contributes mainly to socialization and integration within the existing hierarchy of culture and values, without disturbing it. Something similar occurs in the working process of community artists. For example when they hand out video cameras in a disadvantaged neighbourhood and try to strengthen social cohesion by having 'antisocial' figures and families interview and film each other or by producing a stage play together. The result of this 'process-like approach' is usually presented at a festive public screening or performance attended by local politicians and civil servants involved, and local press. This also means that the intimate details of private lives, including sometimes profound misery and impoverished living conditions are thrown out into the open. Whereas social workers still treat the individual clients' files with professional confidentiality, community artists organize them in public confessions.

Obviously, not all community artists participate in this machinery of social control. One cannot fail to notice, though, that their practices—either or not orchestrated, because subsidized by the government—manifest themselves in neighbourhoods and regions where in a more or less distant past local medical centre or a primary school provided social cohesion. Under the influence of public management and efficiency thinking such local social services have been closed, merged and centralized. Coincidence or not, a few years after such austerity operations, community artists show up in the same location, hired with some funding by local politicians or civil servants. These artists can then try to put together the broken pieces that are the result of the earlier policy of tearing down the local social fabric. The project-like mode of operation of the artist is at any rate cost-efficient, as it is only temporary and thus cheaper than maintaining a school building or a medical centre with a permanent staff. In addition, at the conclusion of their project the artists often produce a positive public story about the resilience of a neighbourhood or an unexpectedly creative and colourful community. Such a positive outlook is always a bonus in times of elections, but in fact the community artists help fill the holes that politics themselves created in the welfare state at an earlier stage.

Again, a growing number of artists and community artists are quite aware of the pitfalls accompanying these government commissions. Still, it is hard to adopt a critical attitude towards the hand that feeds you. Whether the commission comes from a government or private entity, neither of them looks favourably on artists who concern themselves with their politics. Just like Ai Weiwei was not sponsored by LEGO® because he is a 'political artist', likewise subsidies are frequently withdrawn as soon as the artist begins to show signs of political engagement.

Mono-cultural Imagination

Deploying community art then contributes mainly to social integration based on socialization within a dominant cultural order. Nowadays, more and more governments display a—sometimes nostalgic—longing for forms of internal social cohesion or a 'we'-feeling. This is a form of cohesion that is based on the recognition of and similarities among the individual who make up group or community, as was once the hallmark of thriving social life in many local communities. However due to globalization, digitalization, and migration, homogeneous communities are becoming increasingly scarce. Especially in large urban centres one often sees 'majority-minority' societies, in which the majority of the population belongs to a minority. But smaller towns and rural areas are becoming more diverse, which is not only caused by different cultural backgrounds, but al growing differences in status, social class, age, gender (LHBT), and income. This hyper-diversity is therefore often seen as the cause of violent outbursts and riots, such as in the *banlieues* of Paris or the London suburbs, but also in The Hague or the Brussels neighbourhood of Molenbeek. It seems as if the differences in beliefs and cultures cannot be bridged and are driving individuals and groups of people into a situation of deadlock in which resorting to violence seems to be the only recourse.

According to cultural scholar Christiaan De Beukelaer (2017) this deadlock is not so much caused by differences of opinion but rather by unbalanced power relations. Within a hyper-diverse society, the original homogeneous majority automatically becomes a minority itself among other minorities (Rosanvallon 2012). Still this (often white middle-class) minority goes on wielding power as if it is the majority. In doing so, it is holding on to an imagined mono-cultural nation, which expresses itself in a so-called methodological-nationalistic' cultural policy, according to De Beukelaer (2017). This is a policy that may not always explicitly hold a party-political or ideological nationalistic discourse, but certainly nurtures it in the core of and throughout its entire administrative organization. In a country such as the Netherlands, for example, this is evident from the important place reserved for the canon in art policy and the value that was suddenly attached to traditional popular culture a few years ago and, more recently, to the national anthem. The alleged cultural consensus that is thus imposed upon the population by such methodological nationalism will however only increase the risk of conflict. Not just because the alleged harmonious community of yesterday based on unity and a homogeneous majority no longer exists, but especially because policymakers hang onto it by means of more or less subtle instruments of power. However, clinging to a consensus model constantly wipes the diversity, dissensus, and tensions under the carpet holding up an artificial 'we'-feeling or, in more scientific jargon, a *binding* social cohesion. As said earlier, community art plays a rewarding role in this. It is in any case one of the reasons why this artistic revival is frequently embraced and supported by politicians.

The social reality of a minorities society requires a radically different politics, however. Such politics can still be aimed at social cohesion, albeit one that learns how to cope with fundamental differences. It is a social cohesion that is not based on consensus but, paradoxically, on shared dissensus. Not binding, but bridging differences then becomes the focus; not glossing over contradictions and tensions but learning to acknowledge the Other and learning to live with and next to the Other and that which is radically different. The methodological nationalism on which cultural policies are now based does not help to transcend huge contrasts between 'us' and 'them'. Therefore, De Beukelaer advocates a re-evaluation of the public debate about identity and meaning of public space. No longer should one specific identity be leading in this, but various notions of identity should be negotiable. such a 'methodological cosmopolitan' politics—for simplicity's sake we will call it 'cosmopolitics'—takes as its starting point our obligations with regard to our fellow men, regardless of their national identity (De Beukelaer 2017). Cultural policy and art that are in line with this can then no longer aim for socialization and binding cohesive behaviour but must find a way of dealing with fundamental differences. Social cohesion is then no longer aimed at the internal community or the homogenization of that community, but is consistently aimed at the outside world, which, paradoxically, has become more and more part of our 'inner world' or our 'own' community.

Art as a Public Affair

Earlier studies have established the relation between challenging art and external social cohesion by bridging (Otte 2015). Art as a game of imagination always refers to some reality or other, which is then interpreted in an idiosyncratic way by using our imagination. Art may simply reflect and confirm that reality, or it can challenge our experience of reality. In the first case, it confirms the measure of a culture (the prevailing values and norms or the dominant social order). In the second case it disrupts this measure and even sometimes attempts to install a new one (Gielen and Lijster 2015). Many cultural participation policies today are geared towards the first form, which we simply call 'confirmative' art. Community art and participatory projects, however, do not only go for this type of art because funding for it—either public or private—is easy to obtain, but also sometimes because of pragmatic considerations. Artists who wish to reach out to a difficult, not particularly artistically educated target group, for example, will then make use of cultural values and norms that this particular group is already familiar with. By staying within the framework of what people know and recognize, they will be much more likely to participate. The result, however, is the same: if social cohesion is enhanced at all, it is aimed at the internal homogenization and 'we'-feeling.

In most cases cultural policy does, still, allow challenging art, although it is mostly kept safely within the walls of a museum or theatre. In those places there is still room for experimentation, and transgression, dissensus, and controversy are even core values there. However, within the customary spaces of professional art the challenging play with cultural conventions concerns itself mainly with the already converted, a well-to-do (white) middle-class that loves to rave about its own openness and sense of adventure. In short, this class is confirmed in its own values and norms just as well by its weekly or monthly dose of imagination. Challenges are okay, even necessary, but preferably within the safe official walls of fiction, because as soon as these culture lovers leave the theatre or museum, the everyday order of things soon takes over again. And the artist or community artist who does dare venture outside of these walls with the wayward weapons of challenging contemporary art, often runs the risk of not being understood. The 'artistic' move does not find any connection whatsoever with a contingent public, as this public lacks awareness of all codes or conventions of contemporary art. Hence the dilemma of the community artist, but also that of policymakers, who think they can legitimize the public funding of art by offering it directly to the community, but at the same time do not acknowledge the intrinsic public and therefore also political value of art, by keeping it within the framework of the 'official art world'. Art historian and philosopher Steven ten Thije (2017) thinks this is because of a radical individualism that has become the norm in cultural policy. He concludes that, in the Netherlands anyway, discussions around cultural policy are often about the tension between the degree of government interference with art and safeguarding its autonomy, but are never about the public value of art. On one side of this debate we find the liberals who feel that the arts (like almost anything) will thrive best under market principles. This does not mean that art would have no value, but this value is limited to the private and personal sphere. On the other side of the debate is a socialdemocrat perspective in which it is evident that art does have a relation with society, but in this case via or 'through' the individual that makes the art or that views and contemplates it. Here the value of art lies in individual emancipation. In neither view we find a public value of art, namely that art can contribute directly to civil processes and therefore can be political. On both ideological sides policymakers have tried to legitimize public funding of the arts, but have done so on false grounds, concludes Ten Thije. Cultural institutions increasingly have to demonstrate their right to exist on the basis of visitor numbers. However, appreciation for art expressed as a large sum of individuals does not make a public affair of art.

Following Rancière, art contributes to public life, not because it is enjoyed by the many, but because it helps a community to come to terms with complicated conflicts and differences that exist within it. If the question of support for art continues to be waged as a debate on the popularity of art, then arts will remain trapped in ever different forms of exclusivity. (Ten Thije 2017, p. 84)

If a taste for art is seen as an individual matter or something of a specific group, it soon follows that that individual or group is then also responsible for the production of that art. The point is that nowadays both liberals and social-democrats within the methodological nationalistic government as outlined before, regard art as the individual and private affair of a white middle-class—a minority that still believes it is the majority. Both currents in fact defend a rather liberal, or perhaps neoliberal and Eurocentric view of man in which (Western) culture is a matter of individual taste and personal freedom to choose. Looking at how in the Netherlands or elsewhere in Europe cultural policy and policy tools have been developed—from subsidies, targeted competitive 'calls' and cultural programmes to evidence-based policy, monitoring, and systems of audits and accreditation—we can only conclude that this maintains the above paradigms and even cultivates it, in a top-down manner. Whether it is 'enforced themes' such as creative industry, cultural leadership and cultural entrepreneurship or participatory art and active citizenship, these are all imposed from the top by a minority that still thinks it is the majority; a minority that also believes that its culture is not just homogeneous, but is also simply the 'right' culture. It is little wonder then that cultural policy often comes across as patronizing.

Coming Up: Commoning Art

The prevailing cultural-political ideology and pressing top-down policy are making a growing number of artists and other cultural professionals, including community artists, feel more and more ill at ease. Everywhere in the world artistic initiatives are emerging that want to do things differently because they either do not fit within the current cultural political doxa, or because they simply have to do things differently due to austerity measures or lack of private interest. Artists who ignore the regulated and therefore civic frameworks and do engage with the realm of politics often find themselves in the liminal zone of the civil domain, a grey area between market and government, and sometimes also between creativity and illegality (Gielen and Dietachmair 2017). Artists who also express their political engagement outside of the museum and community artists who not only concern themselves with the social domain but also with policy, are soon deprived from sponsors, subsidies, or institutional support. Their twofold course on the social *and* the political level often makes it necessary for them to look for alternative working methods, including ways of funding. It is a search that drives cultural initiatives such as Culture to Commons (Zagreb), Recetas Urbanas (Sevilla) and l'Asilo (Naples), to name but a few, more and more towards the domain of the Commons, a social space where they may find free, albeit not unconditional, support for their work.

One of the most important entry conditions for the commons is perhaps 'reciprocity'. Those who make use of communally shared goods can only do so (and continue to do so) if they also contribute to these commons. In other words, commoners are continually obliged into commoning: generating and making freely available new material or immaterial goods and services themselves. This is why we had better call those community artists who, out of civil necessity, work in a field that belongs neither to the market nor to the public domain of the government 'commoning artists'. After all they not only make use of the commons in their practice, but they also continuously produce new commons in doing so. Commoning artists are therefore more autonomous than their fellow community artists, but also more autonomous than 'traditional' modern and contemporary artists who make a living from the market and/or government. The latter can only uphold their autonomy and idiosyncrasy in an artistic and discursive manner, as they are fed by the hand of capital or government. The former, however, can also position themselves as politically and economically autonomous through self-organization. This can only be done by taking part in the aforementioned social system of reciprocity. The art that is developed by the commoning artist is therefore radically different from that of his colleagues. The work is certainly singular and autonomous, but doesn't take an individual, inner world as its starting point, nor is it part of a conceptual or strategic move to profile themselves in the current art competition. And yet the commoning artist relates strongly to a context, but this is not the context of the professional art world. Their frame of reference is in the first place the social reality of the commons. Among other things, this means that their autonomous work or singular contribution consists of 'catching' and then channelling a shared creativity. This is how commoning artists use the commons. They are, as it were, living off the creative ideas, but also off the questions and needs of a specific community. There singular contribution is to materialize these creative ideas and offering idiosyncratic answers, which may often be unexpected and subversive to the collective itself. It's the only way to keep the commons open and keep its cultural biotope alive. Commoning artists also find it easier to relate to the aforementioned cosmopolitics, precisely because their creativity and chances of survival, just like those of the commons, only exist by the grace of diversification and therefore permanent openness and bridging to the Other.

What such a cosmopolitical-cultural policy would look like is beyond the scope of this essay. We do know, however, that a commons policy will be a bottom-up policy. Things will no longer be done by the hierarchic rules and principles that both social democracy and neoliberalism, and antique communism as well, designed for us. Cosmopolitics is commonist by its very nature, meaning that commoners, including commoning artists, make their own laws and can design their own logistic and financial structures. Work and daily life of commoners are inevitably always political in nature: they are constantly thinking about and moulding their own way of living together. Cosmopolitical governance would then be no more than checking whether such self-ruling and self-regulating bodies follow constitutional rules—for example, are they democratic, undiscriminating, do they protect freedom and privacy—and then confirming their legality. The rest is up to the commoners themselves and their basic-democratic administration through assemblies. Such a policy will probably be very complex, but it may be the only way to approach the complexity of growing minority societies.

Note

1 Others see the community art movement that emerged in the 1960s as the origin of the phenomenon (e.g. Adams and Goldbard 1986; Goldbard 2006; Merli 2002).

References

— Adams, Don, and Arlene Goldbard. 1995. *New Deal Cultural Programs: Experiments in Cultural Democracy.* www.wwcd.org/policy/US/newdeal. html (accessed January 2018).
— De Beukelaer, Christiaan. 2017. 'Ordinary Culture in a World of Strangers: Toward Cosmopolitan Cultural Policy.' *International Journal of Cultural Policy.* DOI:10.1080/10286632.2017.1389913.
— Foucault, Michel. 1977-1978 *Security, Territory, Population: Lectures at the Collège de France, 1977-1978.* Translated by Graham Burchell. New York and Basingstoke: Palgrave Macmillan, 2007.
— Gielen, Pascal. 2011. 'Mapping Community Art.' In *Community Art: The Politics of Trespassing.* Edited by Paul De Bruyne and Pascal Gielen. Amsterdam: Valiz.
—, and Philipp Dietachmair. 2017. 'Public, Civil and Civic Spaces.' In *The Art of Civil Action. Political Space and Cultural Dissent.* Edited by Philipp Dietachmair and Pascal Gielen, pp. 11-33. Amsterdam: Valiz.
—, and Thijs Lijster. 2015. 'Culture: The Substructure for a European Common.' In *No Culture No Europe: On the Foundation of Politics.* Edited by Pascal Gielen, pp. 19-66. Amsterdam: Valiz.
— Goldbard, Arlene. 2006. *New Creative Community: The Art of Cultural Development.* Oakland, CA: New Village Press.
— Matarasso, François. 1997. *Use or Ornament? The Social Impact of Participation in the Arts.* London: Commedia.
— Merli, Paola. 2002. 'Evaluating the Social Impact of Participation in Arts Activities.' *International Journal of Cultural Policy* 8, no. 1, pp. 107-118.
— Otte, Hanka. 2015. *Binden of Overbruggen? Over de relatie tussen kunst, cultuurbeleid en sociale cohesie.* Groningen: PhD thesis Rijksuniversiteit Groningen.
— Rosanvallon, Pierre. 2012. *Democratie en tegendemocratie.* Amsterdam: Boom.
— Thije, Steven ten. 2017. 'The Blind Spot: Art and Politics in the Netherlands.' In *Being Public: How Art Creates the Public.* Edited by Jeroen Boomgaard and René Brom Amsterdam: Valiz.

When Commons Becomes Official Politics

Exploring the Relationship between Commons, Politics, and Art in Naples

Giuliana Ciancio

... what is the point of doing theatre when you have a desert around you?

– Andrea (actor, producer and activist from l'Asilo, Naples)

The 'Fifth State' and the 'Suspension of Democracy'

In March 2012, a wonderful three-storey 16th-century building (about 4000 square meters) located in the pulsating historical city centre of Naples, known as the Ex Asilo Filangieri, was occupied by a group of cultural activists. The building had been recently renovated to host the Universal Forum of Culture in 2013 and was at the centre of a huge debate about the absence of transparency in the management of the event and indeed of the building itself.

The occupation started a new political 'adventure' in the city of Naples. Different political forces joined hands for the first time, together denouncing the diffused state of illegality and the misuse of public money in this period of crisis. Naples was (and still is) a city of fragmented bottom-up initiatives enacted by the civil society, political groups, activists, and artists. The city has often played a prominent role in the formation of national political movements such as general strikes, anti-war marches, and student protests. Since the 1990's the city has been the home of numerous 'occupied centres' that cannot be framed in one single ideological context (Dines 2012). They have represented different needs, political practices, and national affiliations, such as the area of Autonomia Operaia, Anarchism, or various local forms of bottom-up participation.

Most of these movements participated in the occupation of the Ex Asilo Filangieri but the 'leaders' were members of a new emerging 'creative precariat' composed of actors, theatre makers, researchers, and artists from different backgrounds and generations. This new 'emerging class' played a prominent role in the Occupy movement in Italy. It was also the protagonist of the occupation of the Teatro Valle, one of the historical theatres in Rome that was occupied in 2011 and the symbol of the 'Occupy' in Italy. Here they denounced the huge financial cuts to the cultural sector and the process of privatization by the Berlusconi government (leading a neoliberal right-wing coalition). This emerging class was indeed also the most active group (amidst a broader section of civil society and intellectuals) in promoting a debate around commons in Italy.

Between 2011 and 2013, the notion of *'quinto stato'* (fifth state) was adopted for describing this new creative category of activists who were generating a new cultural map of occupied spaces in different cities from Venice to Palermo, from Turin to Catania, Rome and Naples. In their books *Il Quinto Stato* (2013) and *La furia dei cervelli* (2011) Roberto Ciccarelli and Giuseppe Allegri described this movement and provided a picture of the life of the extended creative precariat: it was composed of self-employed, skilled, and mobile workers characterized by a permanent flexibility and deprived of fundamental social rights such as maternity leave or retirement benefits. These individuals are the 'fifth state', which refers to a mix of social classes and a typology of jobs that, although very different in nature, all carry the seeds of poverty. They represented a new labour force that was experimenting with forms of citizenship and economic resistance through forms of sharing economy, mutualism, and self-government.

> The Fifth State is the universal state of statelessness at home where at least eight million Italians live whose fundamental social rights are not acknowledged. The same condition affects at least five million foreign nationals who are also excluded from citizenship rights because of their extraterritoriality in a state. (Allegri and Ciccarelli 2013)

The occupation of Ex Asilo Filangieri (that from now was called l'Asilo) took place in Naples, after the election at regional level of the candidate supported by Berlusconi's party (Stefano Caldoro) in 2010. A significant implementation at municipal and regional level of the so-called 'spoils system' took place following these elections. In the cultural sector, the most important cultural institutions changed their boards and directors in favour of candidates linked to the new party in power. Accessibility to culture came under attack. The selection procedures for hiring new directors or collaborators in public institutions took place without any regulations or transparency. Even worst, the 'conflict of interests' that had characterized Berlusconi's government now took on concrete form in the city.

Public money devoted to the production of new events, the management of two of the biggest and publicly well-subsidized cultural Institutions, the re-instatement of an obsolete national theatre prize were concentrated in a few hands. The sector came under the control of a small group (playing simultaneously the role of financier, subsidizer and promoter) that started allocating space to artists or intellectuals who were open to accept an ancillary role capable of supporting their views. The ruling political class found in big cultural events and in managing cultural institutions a powerful opportunity (and this was no novelty) for making propaganda and for creating an arena of consensus (mainly thanks to obtaining political votes in exchange for job positions).[1]

Being based in Naples and involved in the cultural sector at the time when these events were taking place, I have personal experience of the spoils system that changed the cultural practices of the city. At the same time, I also witnessed the enthusiasm that accompanied the local municipal elections in 2011 when civil society was at the centre of political interest; and I also saw new bottom-up forces (like Occupy) grow stronger at national level.

I believe that the events that characterized the cultural sector in Naples during this period can be looked upon as a concrete example of 'suspension of democracy'. The only choices for the entire creative branch became either to accept the state of things, enter a form of exile, or to engage in protest. Andrea de Goyzeuta, (actor, producer, and activist of l'Asilo) describes the occupation in 2012 saying that:

> ... at the beginning, the leading group was constituted mostly of actors who were following the Teatro Valle experience. After one of the biggest manifestations in Rome, we felt the need to be together and to be back in Naples, bringing that experience and denouncing the difficult city context ... It was the moment at which the theatre activists came out from isolation. The debate around the commons was so strong in Italy that it had the capacity to be transversal to most of the social categories ... what is the point of doing theatre when you have a desert around you?

With this essay I mean to describe these events by giving attention to the practices of a new creative category in political activism and to the emerging notion of commons as political. Therefore, I will illustrate the process of conflict and collaboration between the top-down and the bottom-up forms of policy-making in creating a legitimized 'commonfare' in Naples as described by Michel Bauwens in this same publication.

Naples and the Commons

In 2011, new municipal elections took place. Emerging political forces appeared on the scene composed of civil movements and representing new political bottom-up forms of policy-making. One of the candidates for mayor was Luigi de Magistris (a judge, member of a larger movement of ex-judges). From the beginning of his political campaign, he foregrounded the notion of commons and the need for the city to re-start from the ground up (*dal basso*). In 2011, during his first mandate (2011–2016), the newly elected mayor nominated the first city-counsellor in Italy (and probably in the world) dedicated to the commons (he was in charge of facilitating the process of citizens' participation in the city). The mayor's administration changed the City Charter, introducing the legal category of the commons and the creation of an Observatory of Common Goods among the objectives and the core values of the City. His campaign and his government can be linked to two turning points.

Firstly, the national referendum for the recognition of water as a public and common good, which became a key moment in the debate on commons, democracy, and rights in Italy. About 27 million citizens voted and after a long process water was officially declared to be a public and a common good.[2] Secondly, the important juridical process that was enacted by the jurist Stefano Rodotà, the Teatro Valle, and the national community of the 'workers of immaterial labour', which gave birth to the 'Costituente dei beni comuni' (Constitution for the Commons) was aimed at a recognition in law of the commons in Italy and at finding a political answer to the important changes at cultural and political level. As Rodotà argued in 2012 in one of the main Italian newspaper, 'a new relationship between the world of people and the world of goods is taking place ... nowadays, the emphasis is no longer on ownership, but on the function that a common good has in society'.[3]

This new Constitution—which foregrounded the idea that commons have 'widespread ownership' and are an essential tool for citizenship rights and referred to Article 43 of the Italian Constitution—was focused on the possibility to entrust the 'user communities' (along with public bodies) with the management of essential services or energy resources. The theoretical shift was, from the notion of property to the 'management' of commons therefore implying a process of auto-determination of citizens and of participative democracy.

In this framework, the encounter (albeit a conflictual one) between the Municipality of Naples and the community of l'Asilo, has played a crucial role in the city, giving birth to a concrete experience of management of commons at city level, enacted thanks to a 'creative use' of juridical actions. The 'Declaration of the Urban and Civic and Collective Use' and the official Acts written in 2012, 2015, and 2016 are the results of a long journey of growth, conflict, and negotiation between the City and its (cultural) activists. Debates, protests, and occupations were all intrinsic parts of this debate. At the same time, jurists, policymakers, artists, intellectuals, and citizens from different generations and backgrounds from both parties built their legal assessment sharing (consciously or unconsciously) a common theoretical framework. Initially inspired by the 'Costituente dei Beni Comuni' and by the Italian debate around political commons, they have brought their local expertise and juridical perspectives in creating a new arena of debate.

The notion of 'civic use' is at the base of the new regulations that transform the relationship between the public administration and the citizens, a tangible example of a process of inter-legitimization of two arenas of practices (the formal and informal), which in the past it was impossible to imagine discussing at city level. In 2013, with the appointment of the new alderman for 'Urban Policies, Town Planning and Commons Goods', Carmine Piscopo, the juridical exploration of the notion of commons also became linked to the city's urban context and to the policies devoted to that. The difficulties the administration had in managing the extended architectural property in a context of near bankruptcy were made public. In order to give new life to part of the heritage, this heritage was conceived and defined as a good that belongs to the city. Almost a novelty for an Italian public administration.

Assemblies with citizens geared towards participative processes were enacted also thanks to the strong activism of movements such as 'Massa Critica', which in 2016 connected most of the political experiences of occupation in the city for creating a 'public agorà'. Together with the municipality, the city movements and the citizens opened up public debates about the concrete aspects of living in the city.

In a recent interview the city councillor Carmine Piscopo spoke to me extensively about the identity of urban places,

arguing that this identity cannot be defined by top-down urbanis-
tic definitions,

> ... this identity is sensitive, is immaterial, and is created
> by how the citizenry transforms it. If a good belongs to
> everybody, let's make it public ... Like a public garden,
> which is a shared property that belongs to the city, in the
> same way the properties that belong to the city adminis-
> tration have to be accessible every day at any moment by
> everybody in a non-exclusive relationship ... The materi-
> ality and immateriality of the common goods are deeply
> tied to architectural practices where a concrete form is
> linked to emotional ties and to the collective memory of
> the people who live there.

As mentioned by Giuseppe Micciarelli (theorist and
activist of l'Asilo) the notion of civic use is not only a terrain of
encounter, but also the arena of experimentation with the creation of a participative democracy where the institution gives
citizens the space to be active in forms of co-management of
the political and cultural process of the city. In this context, the
public administration changes its function. It does not intervene
in an authoritative sense, but creates the conditions, through
specific regulations of use, in favour of the development of a
civil environment, supporting the citizens in their process of
becoming a proper institution themselves.

The experience of l'Asilo, according to the official act of
2016, was extended to seven more occupied spaces, giving life to
a 'system' of 'freed spaces' in the city. These 'emerging commons'
have hence become a notion that coincides with a new way of
understanding institutions as something that starts from a collective basis and is characterized, to borrow from Hardt and Negri
(2009) and Virno (2004), by a multitude of singularities. The
emerging commons thus become public institutions that collaborate with citizens to produce well-being. All of this process is
happening through the creation of new regulations and aesthetics
providing a substantial shift from the notion of participation in
democratic life to an active creation of political forms moving
towards what the sociologist Pascal Gielen (2015) defines as the
'Common City'.

Art, Politics and Commons

In this context, the commons are a political practice, an ideological approach globally shared (as the movements raised between the 2008 and 2011) but firmly anchored in their local contexts. A system of a bottom-up welfare (or commonfare) is taking shape at city level thanks to the extended work of the (cultural) activists that are trying to come to terms with the crisis that the city is going through. Mayor De Magistris defined in 2017 what is happening in Naples as a political project that is based on a collaborative form of politics shared with other cities that are proposing alternative models of resistance to the central governments and to global forms of austerity and repressive neoliberal policies. Today, the so-called 'Rebel Cities' are representing a trans-national (or trans-local) network where forms of collaborative city-governance are practiced. This statement reminds us of what Held defined as a 'cosmopolitan model of democracy' where 'democracy has to become not just a national but a transnational affair if it is to be possible both within a restricted geographic territory and within the wider international community (Held 2006, p. 306).

The 'Declaration of Urban Civic and Collective Use' is, in this framework, a concrete instrument that regulates the entire life of l'Asilo and its interlocution with the City Council. L'Asilo is described as an independent 'cultural laboratory' based on the endowment and sharing of means of production in the field of arts, culture, and performing arts. The accessibility for the citizens, the definition of the status of the 'inhabitants' and their rights, duties, and responsibilities, the role of the 'Assembly' as the primary instrument of self-government, the working tables,[4] and the process of decision-making are all part of it. Therefore, the innovative aspect of l'Asilo is not only in the juridical process employed, but also in the creative and artistic practices represented within the arena where the experimentation takes place.

Gabriella Riccio (choreographer, activist, and researcher of l'Asilo) stressed, during my interviews with her, that what characterizes the art production and what is at the core of the 'model' of l'Asilo and regulates the relationships between the inhabitants and the extended citizens community is a notion of 'process'. At its core, l'Asilo has a theatre, a cinema, and laboratories of various types that are at the disposal of the citizens. A broader community of artists and citizens use these spaces thereby contributing to the life of l'Asilo with public presentations and/or cleaning and/

or exchanging goods. This process is fostering a reciprocal growth where art practices constitute the spaces for emotional experience that allow people to be connected and ideas and political interventions to be developed. Art is not ancillary to the political actions, but the zone where the political sphere can express itself.

As mentioned by the inhabitants of l'Asilo during my recent interviews, at the beginning the relationship with certain parts of the theatre community of the city—and especially with small- and medium- sized independent local theatres—was not easy. l'Asilo was perceived as a potential rival, facilitated by its 'illegal status' and, therefore, not obliged to pay royalties and regular costs. Promoting itself as a laboratory and not as a presentation venue, l'Asilo filled up a gap in the system, supporting the growth of independent and emerging artists. It made itself available as a space for rehearsals and reflection on developing new artistic processes. By doing so, it was accepted by the art community and also became a place of encounter for established artists and stakeholders, 'contributing' to the creation of the programming of small-sized independent theatres by guaranteeing the use of its rehearsal space for independent theatre companies.

Today, mainstream artists are also part of the broader artistic community. They are taking part in public talks or seminars and follow the experience at l'Asilo with interest. Also, events that include the participation of citizens or collaborative approaches among different creative forces of the city are strongly fostered.

The economic aspect of this process is still under observation from l'Asilo and from the City authorities. In light of the 'Declaration' and 'Communal act' of 2016, the Municipality takes care of the regular expenses (such as the cost of electricity), the watchman at the entrance of the building (for about eight hours a day), and extra work for the maintenance of the space. All the cultural activities such as courses, laboratories, the entire programme, the day-to-day organization, the implementation of technical equipment, the transformation of the spaces into venues accessible to the citizens fall under the responsibility of the occupants of l'Asilo. All these activities express the symbolical, social, and economic values that l'Asilo is bringing to the entire community.

All the activities are conducted on a voluntary basis. The revenues are exclusively used for the management of the activities or the production of specific collective events and may come from voluntary subscriptions on the occasion of events or thanks to crowdfunding campaigns (as was the case with the creation of the cinema). In September 2017, l'Asilo won a competition called 'Culturability' organized by Fondazione Unipolis. It was the first time that a bank foundation recognized the participation in a contest about social regeneration through art practices by giving the award to an 'informal community'.[5] Also, l'Asilo, as an 'informal community' represented a novelty in being part of a EU Network (as TransEuropeHall) participating in a European context with its practices and values in a reciprocal exchange at EU level.

In light of all these practices, questions about sustainability in times of crisis come to mind where artists and the creative precariat seem to play the role of economic problem-solver of social and political crises. On the other hand, this process could also be seen as an inevitable new path for creating a new form of governance and a new 'aesthetics of the real' as mentioned by Gielen in the introduction.

Andrea, Gabriella, Giuseppe and other theorists and activists from l'Asilo consider the recognition of the informal community in its variable and uncertain form by the public institutions, not as a way to accommodate or ease the conflict brought by new emerging forces, but, as Giuseppe underlines, as a way to 'to maintain a dialectical level in the debate in a new form of direct management that shifts the actual site of power from the political institution to the citizens'.

Where Are We Going?
The 'creative' juridical forms, the role of the art community, together with the innovative collaboration between two different political positions (the Institutions and the movements) and the affirmation of a new cultural precariat reminds us of what Gielen and Lijster called the 'social sequence' (Gielen and Lijster 2016). Starting from the expression of emotions—which often lies at the origin of civil actions (Castells 2015)—through 'rationalization', then 'communication', 'de-privatization' (going public) and finally 'self-organization' of this emotion, and through the exchange of values and practices a political reaction becomes a political form in the civil domain.

The Napoli experience can be read through this sequence as a concrete example of one of the possible ways to manage the notion of commons in a city context. As a concrete case, as I am writing this essay, a new political party is being born from the experience of the 'freed spaces' and the activism in the city.[6] Starting from the urban laboratories, nowadays an extended transversal group composed of the creative precariat, activists from the political unions, left-wing parties, and so on, has created a new political party 'Potere al Popolo' (Power to the People) which is stepping into the national political arena following the national elections, which took place on 4 March 2018.

Today, the city of Naples is under threat of bankruptcy and compulsory administration. A huge debate about the presence of baby-gangs crafted on the style of the TV-series *Gomorrah* (inspired by the award-winning book by Roberto Saviano) is on all the frontpages of the national newspapers, while the public health system and the public transport are on the verge of collapse. In a recent TV report presented by one of the best-watched national TV programmes (*Presa Diretta*), Naples is declared one of the worst cities to live in in the south of Italy.

At the same time, we are seeing an important presence of tourists in the city, B&Bs, new hotels that are built and with all this, new forms of deregulated gentrification are taking place. It is also a wonderful time for the cinema and the art scene, and forms of urban regeneration are pursued by private cultural organizations, while gallery owners and designers fight to overcome the risk of the control of the territory by a diffused micro-criminality. The 'Declaration of the Urban and Civic and Collective use' and the 'Communal Acts' are being presented in various arenas and are becoming a possible model for other cities in the Italian and European contexts. In 2017, the city council was honoured by the European programme Urbact for its innovative administrative action in fostering collective participation for the recovery of abandoned property.

Where are all these experiences leading us? Are the commons a new political path towards a 'cosmopolitan form of democracy', to borrow Held's words?

How this form may be sustainable in the long run for artists, citizens, and institutions is still a matter of debate and further analysis. These processes need to be observed under both local and global lenses and in a sustainable perspective. The role of the arts and of the extended creative precariat is introducing a new path, a form linked to a new way of being together, socializing values and economies in a world that is moving towards a post-global dimension and is under attack from new forms of localism and populism. A world that needs beauty to overcome the fear of otherness and of the private use of common sources.

As Hardt and Negri (2009) suggested, guaranteeing the commons is necessary to safeguard future cultural production. We may add that safeguarding the cultural production can bring us towards new aesthetics that are the result of civil processes that represent the multitude of singularities that our cities represent.

Notes

1   For more info see: Bianca De Fazio and Conchita Sannino, 'Sotto accusa De Fusco: Un contratto d'oro', *La Repubblica* (ed. Napoli), 15 July 2015; Bianca De Fazio, 'Assunzioni al Teatro Festival: La Miraglia sotto accusa', *La Repubblica* (ed. Napoli), 4 May 2011.
2   Nowadays, in Naples the agency who manages the water (ABC Acqua Bene Comune) is a common good.
3   In: Stefano Rodotà, 'Il valore dei beni comuni', *La Repubblica*, 5 January 2012.
4   These *tavoli di lavoro* are workgroups that focus on specific topics.
5   For more information: https://bando2017.culturability.org.

References

— Allegri, Giuseppe, and Roberto Ciccarelli. 2013. *Il Quinto Stato: Perchè il lavoro indipendente è il nostro future: Precari, autonomi, free lance per una nuova società*. Milan: Adriano Salani Editore s.u.r.l.

— Anheier, Helmut, and Raj Isar Yudhishthir. 2012. *Cities, Cultural Policy and Governance (Cultures and Globalization Series)*. London: Sage Publications.

— Castells, Manuel. 2015. *Networks of Outrage and Hope: Social Movements in the Internet Age*. 2nd ed., enl. and upd. Cambridge, MA: Polity Press.

— Ciccarelli, Roberto, and Giuseppe Allegri. 2011. *La furia dei cervelli*. Rome: Manifestolibri.

— De Magistris, Luigi. 2017. *La città ribelle*. Naples: Chiarelettere editore.

— Dines, Nick. 2012. *Tuff City: Urban Change and Contested Space in Central Naples*. New York and Oxford: Berghahn Books.

— Gielen, Pascal. 2015. 'Performing the Common City: On the Crossroads of Art, Politics and Public Life.' In *Interrupting the City: Artistic Constitutions of the Public Sphere*. Edited by Sander Bax, Pascal Gielen, and Bram Ieven, pp. 273-298. Amsterdam: Valiz.

—, and Thijs Lijster. 2016. *New Civil Roles and Organizational Models of Cultural Organizations: Reviewing the Potential of Contemporary Cultural Practices and Alternative Working Structures*. Unpublished research report. Amsterdam: European Cultural Foundation.

— Hardt, Michael, and Antonio Negri. 2009. *CommonWealth*. Cambridge, MA: Harvard University Press.

— Held, David. 2006. *Models of Democracy*. 3rd edition. Bloomington, IN: Stanford University Press.

— Landry, Charles. 2006. *The Art of City Making*. New York: Routledge.

— Micciarelli, Giuseppe. 2017. 'Introduzione all'uso civico e collettivo urbano: La gestione diretta dei beni comuni urbani.' *Munus* 1, pp. 135-162.

— Riccio, Gabriella. 2018. 'La pratica dell'uso civico come scelta estetica, etica e politica per il sensibile comune.' In *I beni comuni: L'inaspettata riscoperta degli usi collettivi*. Edited by Stefano Rodotà. Naples: La Scuola di Pitagora Editrice.

— Virno, Paolo. 2004. *A Grammar of the Multitude: For an Analysis of Contemporary Forms of Life*. New York: Semiotext(e).

Commons towards New Participatory Institutions

The Neapolitan Experience

Maria Francesca De Tullio

Introduction: Property and Democratic Participation

This work is a narration of the Neapolitan experience of commons, aimed at finding in that movement new possible patterns of participatory democracy (Allegretti 2010, p. 7; Chevallier 1999, p. 410).

Commons and participatory democracy follow, in principle, different logics. Nevertheless, they are getting more and more interlaced with each other due to two converging phenomena. The first one is the politicization of commons. Commons are becoming—in many parts of Europe—a way to rethink political subjectivation by imagining and practicing new forms of relation and institutional organization beyond the neoliberal imprint. In other words, political movements are generating 'emerging common goods' (Micciarelli 2014, pp. 67–69), i.e. commons defined not only by their nature and function, but also by their governing, shared between public sector and people. The second phenomenon comes from the opposite direction: the traditional institutions are actively seeking more responsive, accountable, and participatory forms of democracy, to face the distrust towards representatives and electoral mechanisms.

Therefore, there is an opportunity for commons to fill a void of political legitimacy of the institutions. A void which, presently, is also a battleground, for at least two reasons. The first one is that representatives are attempting to put in place weak procedures of participation, with the intention of gaining trust and consent from the citizens without giving away too much power. The second and perhaps more important one is that the weakening of elected organisms also leaves room to deregulation, privatization and, thus, inequalities.

Then, the main issue of this study is to use the Neapolitan case, and its challenges, to understand how the public sector can be 'thin' against grassroots participation, while being 'fat' against inequalities. This calls in question public property and spending, as material tools that help filling the gap between uneven socio-economic positions.

The Neapolitan Experience of 'Emerging Common Goods'

The path of urban commons in Naples started in 2012, with the occupation of the Ex Asilo Filangieri, a monumental building in the historical city centre, owned by the City of Naples. Occupants were mostly artists who intended to manifest against unemployment and precarious working conditions, as well as against national cultural policies they deemed inefficient and unequal (Gielen 2015, pp. 65–67). In fact, they attacked a symbol of these policies by grabbing a space that, at that time, had been given in concession to a Foundation in charge of organizing the UNESCO's Universal Forum of Cultures. The building was considered emblematic, because this kermesse, like many big events, was failing to stimulate all of the artistic texture of the territory. On the contrary, it produced a waste of money and concentration of funding in few hands.

However, soon the entire city was involved in the process of l'Asilo: cultural workers above all, but also other inhabitants and activists, who were experimenting with new ways to engage in politics. In a series of animated assemblies, they decided not to be 'occupants', but commoners. So, they transformed the public spaces in shared and freely accessible means of production, with lower costs and horizontal management, following collaborative rather than competitive logics. Consequently, a creative effort was made to pour that vision into a juridical construction. The aim was not to seek the protection of the law, but to 'hack' legality, i.e. to use the disruptive energy of the process to carve the rules and change institutions.

Eventually, they identified this new juridical instrument as 'urban civic uses', through an extensive interpretation of the 'civic use', a tool that—since ancient times—grants to a certain community collective rights over lands and pastures. But they also brought innovation to this juridical instrument, because they conceived the 'community' not in the traditional 'communitarian' meaning, but in an inclusive, heterogeneous, and ever-changing sense.

Thus they wrote collectively, in public and open assemblies, a Declaration of Urban Civic and Collective Use (*hereinafter* Declaration), formally recognized later, in 2015, by two Resolutions of the Giunta Comunale (City Government) (*Delibere* 400/2012, 893/2015). This Declaration 'rules the use of the spaces of l'Asilo and of the means of production that it contains, ensuring usability, inclusiveness, fairness, accessibility and self-government' (cf. Ostrom 1990, pp. 93–94). The Administration, on its part, by approving the Declaration recognized not only a mere access entitlement, but also 'the rights to the direct administration of the building itself'. The objective of the Giunta Comunale

(City Government) was not to express tolerance towards the occupation. Rather, it was accepting the challenge of transforming juridical science and practices.

Hence, the public domain is not used in an exclusive fashion, nor entrusted to a particular private subject, but opened up to the entire community. Indeed, the administration of the spaces, in consistence with their nature of common goods, is undertaken by Governing and Management Assemblies that are open to everyone (not only citizens and adults) and decide by consensus (Declaration, Art. 3). Moreover,

> the overriding principle in the programming of activities is the non-exclusive use of any part of the property, as turn-taking and the guarantee of use, access and usability of the space by the parties who benefit is the guiding principle of the whole urban civic use system. (Declaration, Art. 14).

In practice, the building was transformed in an 'interdependent' centre of artistic production, which has been crossed—in five years—by over 2,400 productive subjects, 7,800 public initiatives, and 260,000 beneficiaries. Anyone who wishes to employ the space to work, rehearse, or organize civil, political, and cultural initiatives only needs to propose the activity to the Management Assemblies. These do not exercise an artistic direction, but, as to the contents, only refuse fascist, sexist, and racist proposals. Yet, as requests grow in number, and spaces and energies remain limited, the community constantly engages in reasoning, to elaborate choosing criteria consistent with the destination of the building.

With this participatory establishment the Administration does not abandon its responsibilities. Indeed, by recognizing the Declaration, the Giunta Comunale (City Government) binds itself to very precise commitments:

> The City Administration ... provides, within the limits of the available resources, the management expenditures and what is necessary to ensure adequate accessibility to the property. It also provides what is necessary to ensure a safe environment for carrying out the activities and the protection of the property by preventing damages by vandalism. (Art. 20)

Not last, 'City Administration undertakes to intervene in any case ensuring access to and use of the spaces according to the scheduled activities' (Ibid.). These public expenses are justified through the recognition of the 'civic redditivity' of the experience, i.e. the ability of the commons to generate a social non-monetary value which is worth the expense of maintaining the building. That way, a piece of real estate became, through collective will, an 'emerging common good', getting to represent not only a platform of mutualism for workers in the field of arts, culture, and performance, but also an incubator for democratic participation.

Afterwards, the same path has been followed in favour of seven more spaces, which have been declared common goods in a new Resolution (*Delibere* 446/2016, 458/2017). Namely, these spaces are Villa Medusa and ex Lido Pola, in the suburban area of Bagnoli, together with ex Schipa, ex Opg (Psychiatric Criminal Hospital), Giardino Liberato (Freed Garden), Ex-conservatory of Santa Fede, and former juvenile prison Filangieri, now called Scugnizzo Liberato, in the area of the historical city centre. All of them have their own characteristics and vocation, but they share the same engagement to remain self-governed and accessible to everyone.

A Legal Frame for Commons and Participation:
Not a 'Small Government', but a More Open One

As shown in the brief description above, through commons the Neapolitan Administration has responded to regulatory dilemmas—such as art and culture policies, or urban planning and environment—by loosening its hierarchical power and giving up a proprietary interpretation of the public domain. In doing so, it adopted a new view of the administrators–administered relations.

Surely, there is a broader trend in the evolution of the Public Administration, seeking to shorten the distance between government and stakeholders by building nearly-horizontal structures and procedures of intersection and interrelation (O'Reilly 2010, pp. 12-13). The reasons for this movement are similar to the reasons that—we can assume—moved the Neapolitan Administration: involving civil society in rule-making ameliorates the reasonableness of the rules in light of the logics of the sector, increases the possibility to acquire knowledge, experience, and competence from the people, allows a quick update and entails a lower enforcement effort, because everyone is more likely to respect the rules that they have themselves created (De Minico 2005, pp. 130–131). However, such decisional powers usually are—except for few anomalies—a privilege of corporations, which have the strength to influence governmental mechanisms (Crouch 2004 [2009], p. 58).

Naples is one of these anomalies, because participation and public domain are progressively vindicated as a ground where government shall open itself to self-government and collective use. Hence, this path is different from the traditional participatory democracy, which does not really question the representatives' discretion (La Quadrature du Net et al. 2016, p. 3), but also from the neoliberal order, which in facts legitimates the prevailing of the strongest. Indeed, policy-making has not merely been opened up to everyone, regardless of who 'everyone' is. Instead, to gain a really broad inclusion, active and selective measures have been taken by the public sector to support the participation of poor, precarious, and marginalized subjects. Hence, this experiment is not a deregulation, because the Administration keeps intervening in the socio-economic field. The public sector does not withdraw but becomes an elastic net: the scope of its action is expanded, while its texture becomes wider and more porous to contributions by people. In concrete terms, the Giunta Comunale (City Government) does not provide pre-packaged social services or civic platforms but delivers to the have-nots the means for self-organization of production and democratic participation. Something that the haves can already access by virtue of private capitals.

These regulatory novelties move within the Constitution and implement it through political conflict. In particular, the goal is to concretize the core value of 'substantial equality', stated in Article 3.2 of the Constitution:

> It is the duty of the Republic to remove the economic and social obstacles that by limiting in fact the freedom and equality among citizens impede the full development of the human person and the effective participation of all workers in the political, economic, and social organization of the Country.

This rule is an obligation for the future, and means that formal legal equality is not enough, and the State is bound to enact a selective and positive support to overcome the uneven distribution of wealth and opportunities among workers. And precisely in that sense, commons are an implementation of the Constitution: not an undisputed interpretation, but a struggle to 'take equality seriously'. In this same way, the Italian Constitution fully admits and promotes self-government. Indeed, not only does it ensure collective rights, such as the freedom of assembly and association, but it goes even further. Article 49 states the right to 'concur in accordance with a democratic method to determine the national politics', not only in the elections. More importantly, Article 118.4 regulates the hypothesis in which civil initiatives go beyond the exercise of freedoms and overlap with public responsibilities, because they share the same commitment to general interest (Albanese 2002, pp. 66–72). Namely, the rule imposes that public entities 'favour the autonomous initiative of citizens, individual or associated, for the undertaking of activities of general interest, on the basis of the subsidiarity principle'.

Here, the struggle is to connect the verb 'to favour' with the already mentioned Article 3.2, interpreting it as an obligation of the Administration to not only avoid interferences with civil organizations, but also help—with funding, spaces, tools, or organizational support—the grassroots initiatives that mobilize themselves to pursue a general interest but cannot afford it.

So, when the government finds that the spontaneous initiatives are not able to fully cover a general need, the answer is not to direct power towards an authoritative level, but to first support the initiative (Cerulli Irelli 2004, pp. 14–16; for a different approach, see Antonini 2003, pp. 636–637). Otherwise, Article 118.4 would violate the basic principle of substantial equality, because it would empower only those who have enough resources to conduct an autonomous initiative (for example, run an artistic production centre on their own). In other words, the principle would be a key to legitimize the privatizations of social services, because enterprises are the only ones who can afford to deliver an efficient product. This is also a risk in many hypotheses related to the 'pacts of shared administration' originated by the *2014 Regulation* of Bologna *on the collaboration Between Citizens and Administration for the Care and Regeneration of Urban Commons*: if there is no clear assumption of responsibility by the Administration, the risk is to 'empower the already empowered' (Gurstein 2011).

Instead, through Neapolitan commons the City provides the people with means to exercise what has been defined as 'direct administration' (Micciarelli 2017, pp. 151-152). This expression was used because, as mentioned, activities of general interest overlap with the sphere of public power. To be sure, the Assemblies do not hold the same power as the Administrations, because the first ones cannot use coercion and force (to that aim, a law would be necessary); moreover, the public sector maintains the discretion to change the regime of the good. However, the community is entitled to rule the access to public property and social services, and this is still an important factor, because—as is explained below—supplying welfare is a form of power, even if a non-coercing power (Sunstein 2005, Ch. 8).

So, in this instance, what is normally an exclusive privilege of strong corporations is available to all, citizens and non-citizens, without subjective limits. This grants more legitimization to self-regulation, given that—as a general principle—the reason why legal rules stemming from civil society cannot be binding for all (*erga omnes*) is especially that not every affected person participates in their drafting (De Minico 2005, p. 151).

Lastly, the experimentation places itself in the framework of Article 42 of the Italian Constitution, which requires property to be consistent with its 'social function', i.e. to be regulated so as to give priority to collective personal rights, in confrontation with individual economic freedoms. However, the actual regime of property—and private property above all—is intrinsically hindering social function, because it leaves few alternatives to an absolute and exclusive ownership (Capone 2017, 121-122). Therefore, it makes it impossible, even for the 'things that express utilities functional to the exercise of fundamental rights, as well as the free development of the person', to 'ensure[d] their collective enjoyment' (Commissione Rodotà 2007). Also, in this case, the implementation of the Constitution has a controversial path, running between the universality of human rights, stated in Article 2, and the very narrow interpretation that the Italian Constitutional Court gives of Article 42, which is more in favour of property (Rodotà 1982, pp. 146-152).

In conclusion, the Neapolitan example has set a regulatory establishment, legitimized by the Constitution (especially Articles 2, 3, 118, 42, and 43), in which the Administration is not the citizen's 'agent' any more. Rather, public power helps the inhabitants while they become 'their own' agents (Arena 2005, pp. 194-196). This arrangement is still radically incompatible with neoliberal deregulation and privatization, at least for some basic elements, such as integral accessibility of self-government organisms, selective public provision of spaces, and funding to weak grass-root movements, and a constant questioning of property, which impedes any exclusive use or exclusive profit of a public good.

New Modalities of Political Participation and Welfare in the Age of the Crisis

All the characteristics highlighted before make it difficult to describe an ideology, or even a unitary idea behind the Neapolitan experience of commoning. Indeed, it is a still ongoing movement, based on a constant questioning of property and relations with State and market.

It is also a variegated reflection, combining many issues and ideological provenances. Indeed, no open community, despite undertaking a political action, constitutes a political collective or subject, or holds uniformity in views and actions. Rather, they share an agreement upon some basic visions and battles. The effect of entering a heterogeneous assembly and building consensus in it is that pre-existing opinions and ideologies have to be disarticulated and confronted with new questions and decisions, so that new political aggregations become possible (Merolla 2017, video interviews). This mechanism has been defined as a 'chain of equivalence', because it can create common actions among people and interests that usually intersect different planes (Micciarelli 2017, p. 143). However, the most important stake of the 'chain', here, is not to build a collective identity—seeking a representation of the unrepresentable, through a discursive operation (Laclau 2005 [2008], pp. 68-72)—but to engage in a long-term reflection about how to shape political actions, responding to the new features of capitalism and neoliberalism.

This is especially true for l'Asilo. Notwithstanding the fact that it is a highly politicized space, in the Declaration electoral campaigns are excluded from the activities allowed. This does not mean that there can be no discussions with parties. Actually, common goods have multiplied the spaces for democratic debate and have been incubators for different new political entities. However, the statement in the Declaration intends to avoid the space being occupied by a single political subject, thus losing its heterogeneity.

That given, someone would include such experimentation in a paradigm of deliberative democracy, because it transforms the initial preferences of the individuals, while avoiding negotiations and strategic behaviour. Still, there are some main differences, because the focus is not on an 'exchange of information and arguments, backed by reasons' (Bifulco 2011, § 1), where 'participants ... are committed to the values of rationality and impartiality' (Elster 1998, p. 8). By contrast, there is a strong dialectic of ideas in the commoning process, and the whole movement is an action of conflict against the current power relations and socio-economic *status quo*. So, the rational side is not the only relevant one, even for apparently technical choices. Indeed, consensus does not pursue reasonableness, but care of relations and extirpation of dynamics of racism, sexism, bullying, and violence.

In short, 'common goods' in Naples are a constant research of new ways to counter privatizations and boost self-government logics (Cozzolino 2017, pp. 1-2) by multiplying participatory institutions such as, for example, inhabitants' assemblies and civic observatories or audit processes. Thus, the effectiveness of this movement is measured by the change they are able to produce in the institutional structure and language.

In particular, one of the hardest undertakings is the creation of pathways to rethink welfare in times of crisis and austerity.

As mentioned, public spending is essential to equality and, consequently, democracy; nevertheless, budget constraints, at every level, are progressively inhibiting egalitarian and social policies. Hence, on the one hand, there is the struggle for the recognition of the 'civic redditivity' (*see supra*). Indeed, in many local realities budget limitations are a reason, or an excuse, to alienate and privatize public goods, instead of making them available for the common enjoyment. In that sense, a question arose about how to calculate the social and cultural value generated by an experience, to make this value emerge as something that can compensate, and sometimes exceed, the purely monetary loss. On the other hand, a broader reflection is taking place with regards to public debt. Recently, a document from Massa Critica—a joint platform for action and reflection within the movement of the common goods— advocated the abolition of the Fiscal Compact and the institution of a public audit commission on public debt, in charge of

> shed[ding] some light on the genesis of the debt, on the
> mechanisms that generate it at present and that strengthen
> it through the indefinite loop of the austerity policies, on

the technical parameters of the loans and active interest rates burdening the Comune di Napoli [Municipality of Naples], on the legitimacy of each and every part of it, with the aim of understanding which sections are hateful and illegitimate and therefore will not be paid. (Massa Critica 2017)

Moreover, an imaginative effort is needed to use commons to rethink welfare through mutualism. Indeed, public welfare as it is disciplines society, because it encourages certain choices and discourages others (Bazzicalupo and Clò 2006, p. 112; De Graaf and Maier 2017, pp. 48-49). In addition, it enhances the buying power, and therefore consumer spending, but does not solve the basic disparity given by the ownership of means of production. In that sense, commons are instead a way to gain both autonomy and access to shared means of production. Although, as mentioned, it would probably be utopian to imagine a total autonomy of these mutualistic forms, because they would be erased by more competitive market economies. So, the constant question mark of commoning experiences is how to imagine a systematic public intervention in economy that eliminates the roots of the inequality and supports mutualistic experiments without trapping them in a heteronomous order. Given that, perhaps it is no coincidence that the movement started in the field of art and culture.

Indeed, independent artistic expression, exactly like grassroots political debate, is an heterogeneous civic and cultural reality, intolerant of rigid rules, but at the same time precarious and vulnerable, in need of being protected from the competitive and normalizing logics of markets. In addition, in that sector, the contradictions of the proprietary model arise sharply, because intellectual property creates a conflict between, on the one hand, free accessibility of knowledge and, on the other hand, the workers' rights. This calls for a creative mix of public policies and mutualistic practices, able to foster and sustain the spontaneous emergence of cooperation mechanisms.

Conclusion

In synthesis, the Neapolitan experimentation with commons has contaminated the Administration with new languages and procedures, characterized by the complete accessibility of self-government organisms, the selective public provision of spaces and funding to weak grassroots movements, and a constant questioning of property and exclusive use.

A further question, then, from both a legal and political point of view, is to imagine how these tools can be useful in other realities and territories, where other commons are emerging. Here, the hardest challenges, besides the political ones, derive from the crisis of public debt, which increases the pressure towards privatization and clearance sale of public goods.

References

— Albanese, Alessandra. 2002. 'Il principio di sussidiarietà orizzontale: Autonomia sociale e compiti pubblici'. *Diritto Pubblico* 1.

— Allegretti, Umberto. 2010. 'Democrazia partecipativa: Un contributo alla democratizzazione della democrazia.' In *Democrazia partecipativa*. Edited by Umberto Allegretti. Florence: Firenze University Press.

— Antonini, Luca. 2003. 'Sulla giustiziabilità del principio di sussidiarietà orizzontale.' *Quaderni Costituzionali* 3.

— Arena, Gregorio. 2005. 'Il principio di sussidiarietà orizzontale nell'art. 118 u.c. della Costituzione.' In *Studi in onore di Giorgio Berti*, Naples: Jovene.

— Bazzicalupo, Laura, and Clarissa Clò. 2006. 'The Ambivalences of Biopolitics.' *Diacritics* 36, no. 2 (Summer).

— Bifulco, Raffaele. 2011. 'Democrazia deliberativa.' In *Enciclopedia del Diritto*, Annals IV, Milan: Giuffrè.

— Capone, Nicola, 2017. 'The Concrete Utopia of the Commons: The Right of "Civic and Collective Use" of Public (and Private) Goods.' *Philosophy Kitchen* #7.

— Cerulli Irelli, Vincenzo. 2004. 'Sussidiarietà (diritto amministrativo).' In *Enciclopedia Giuridica*. Roma: Treccani.

— Chevallier, Jacques. 1999. 'Synthèse.' In La *démocratie locale: Représentation, participation et espace public*. Paris: Presses Universitaires de France.

— Commissione Rodotà—per la modifica delle norme del codice civile in materia di beni pubblici [for the modification of the rules of the Civil Code regarding public goods]. Proposta di articolato 14 July 2007. *www.giustizia.it/giustizia/it/mg_1_12_1.page?contentId=SPS47624&previsiousPage=mg_1_12_1.*

— Cozzolino, Adriano. 2017. 'The Commons and the Civic and Collective Urban Use: From Theory to the Praxis of l'Asilo, Napoli.' Paper presented at the Conference 'Participatory governance in Culture: Exploring Practices, Theories and Policies. Do it Together.' 22-24 November, Rijeka (Croatia).

— Crouch, Colin. 2004 (2009). *Post-democracy*, Cambridge, MA: Polity Press. Translated in Bari and Roma: Laterza, 2009.

— De Minico, Giovanna. 2005. *Regole: Comando e consenso*, Turin: Giappichelli.

— Elster, Jon. 1998. 'Introduction.' In *Deliberative Democracy*. Edited by Jon Elster. Cambridge, MA: Cambridge University Press.

— Gielen, Pascal. 2016. 'A Caravan of Freedom.' In *Mobile Autonomy: Exercises in Artists' Self-Organization* (Antennae-Arts in Society). Edited by Nico Dockx and Pascal Gielen. Amsterdam: Valiz.

— Graaf, Willibrord de, and Robert Maier. 2017. 'The Welfare State and the Life Course: Examining the Interrelationship between Welfare Arrangements and Inequality Dynamics.' *Social Policy & Administration* 51, no. 1 (January).

— Gurstein, Michael. 2011. 'Open Data: Empowering the Empowered or Effective Data Use for Everyone?' *First Monday* 16, no. 2. http://journals.uic.edu/ojs/index.php/fm/article/viewArticle/3316/2764%20-%20author.

— La Quadrature du Net et al. 2016. 'Le "gouvernement ouvert" à la française: Un leurre?' *LaQuadrature.net*, December 5. www.laquadrature.net/files/20161205-article-pgo.pdf.

— Laclau, Ernesto. 2005 (2008). *On Populist Reason*. London: Verso. Translated in Bari and Roma: Laterza, 2008.

— Massa Critica. 2017. 'Se il debito è pubblico allora pubblicamente va discusso.' MassaCriticaNapoli.org, November 16. www.massacriticanapoli.org/2017/11/16/il-debito-pubblico-a-napoli/.

— Merolla, Sabrina. 2017. 'If Art Can Change the World...' https://readymag.com/u57649695/864292/.

— Micciarelli, Giuseppe. 2014. 'I beni comuni e la partecipazione democratica: Da un "altro modo di possedere" ad un "altro modo di governare".' *Jura Gentium* XI, no. 1, pp. 58-83.

—. 2017. 'Introduzione all'uso civico e collettivo urbano: La gestione diretta dei beni comuni urbani.' *Munus* 1.

— O'Reilly, Tim. 2010. 'Government as a Platform.' In *Open Government. Collaboration, Transparency and Participation in Practice*. Edited by Daniel Lathrop and Laurel Ruma. Sebastopol: O'Reilly.

— Ostrom, Elinor. 1990. *Governing the Commons: The Evolution of Institutions for Collective Action*. Cambridge, MA: Cambridge University Press.

— Rodotà, Stefano. 1982. 'Articolo 42.' In *Commentario alla Costituzione*. Edited by Giuseppe Branca and continued by Alessandro Pizzorusso. Bologna and Roma: Zanichelli/Foro Italiano.
— Sunstein, Cass. 2005. *Laws of Fear: Beyond the Precautionary Principle*, Cambridge, MA: Cambridge University Press.

Who Steals the Goose from off the Common? An Interview with Peter Linebaugh

Louis Volont

In recent years, the vocabulary of the commons and its derivatives has taken centre stage in debates on political and economic crises. If we are to believe Charlotte Hess (2008), Ostrom's lifelong commons companion, many 'new commons'—that is: 'new sources to share'—have seen the light of day: market commons may heal the wounds of austerity politics; the cultural commons may replace the archaic producer-consumer relationship in the arts; the knowledge commons may counter an increasingly closed circuit of scholarly insights; public space—Syntagma, Tahrir, Gezi—may lay the groundwork during struggles reclaiming public space for collective use. As the world observes with great interest how these alleged 'new forms of governance' reshape everyday life, the historical roots of the commons have too often been left untheorized.

The value of historian Peter Linebaugh's oeuvre is exactly to fill this gap. He teaches us rightfully that 'scarcely a society has existed on the face of the earth which has not had at its heart the commons' (Linebaugh 2014, p. 14). Linebaugh's *Magna Carta Manifesto* (2008) shows how the age of the commons preceded the age of the commodity; how the age of reproduction preceded the age of production; how the conviviality of the kitchen preceded the alienation of the factory; and how the age of subsistence existed long before the vocabulary of the (neo)liberals would begin to deride the commons by the ideological use of the words 'tragedy', 'impossible', or 'utopian'. Who was it that said that there is no alternative and no such thing as society?

Spatially, Linebaugh takes us back to 13th-century England, to a time when the commons were no 'alternative' but a means of subsistence. 500 years of European enclosure had yet to begin. Juridically, Linebaugh's work centres around two historical documents: Magna Carta (1215) and the Charter of the Forest (1217). The former related to the barons and gave us *habeas corpus* and *trial by jury*, the latter related to the common man and restored rights of access to the forests and hence to primary sources for survival. November 2017, the time of writing, marks the 800th birthday of the latter charter. Yet, one might ask, what remains of these documents in a time when the privatization of the Anthropocene is nearly complete? I meet with Peter in London, a few days after his keynote address in the State Rooms at the House of Commons, during which he argued:

The context requires us to remember that at that time in history there was no Hollywood to paint a happy picture or President Trump to tax and enclose us, but church and king instead. Those two sides of the ruling class battled the commons for land and soul.

No better occasion, then, to discuss the commons in a time wherein 'the commoners of the world can no longer retire to the forests or run to the hills' (Linebaugh 2014, p. 40), wherein common custom has become crime, and wherein the realm of commoning has transcended from the street to the state and from the peasant to the politician. I want to find out whether capital has nowadays discovered the commons, or if the commons can and must remain invisible in order to survive.

Louis Volont – The vocabulary of the commons has been around for centuries: in economics, law, land, and subsistence, in art and religion. Where does your interest in the commons come from?

Peter Linebaugh – My interest in the topic of the commons has many different layers. Some are political, some are linguistic, some are biographical. I would say that I am a child of 'empire'. I have grown up in the United States, in England, and in other parts of the world such as Pakistan and Germany. But my earliest notion of the commons comes from my childhood in England. There, the upper class referred to me as 'common'. As a little American boy in England I was considered 'common' or 'ordinary' in the upper-class schools I went to. But as a child, I never knew what a real commoner was. This I learned by encountering a true commoner of the Forest of Dean, who was like a godfather to me. That would become a first, biographical layer that sparked my interest. But there's also another, politico-linguistic layer. Namely, I grew up with debates about communism and social democracy. Also, not to forget, my father and mother suffered severe political repression during the McCarthy period in the US, in the early 1950s. But it wasn't until the fall of the Soviet Union and the beginning of the North American Free Trade Agreement (NAFTA) of 1994, and the emergence of the Zapatistas and the notion of the *ejido,* that I began to link these two subjects: the commons and communism. It's from that mixture of politics, biography, and history that my interest has grown.

LV – You emphasize the verb 'commoning':

> To speak of the commons as if it were a natural resource is misleading at best and dangerous at worst—the commons is an activity and, if anything, it expresses relationships in society that are inseparable from relations to nature.

Yet, would it be possible to organize commoning sustainably on a larger scale, in a time when gas has replaced wood, and the city has appropriated the fruits of the forest?

PL – In order to imagine this problem of scale, we would need to set up a thought experiment. Could you imagine oil workers from Saudi Arabia meeting fast driving Chinese motorists and assembly line workers from Stuttgart, along with Mexican electronics workers, all meeting together to organize the distribution of their labour and their common interests?

LV – That is difficult to imagine...

PL – Yes, but I am still doing the exercise. What is happening is a literal transformation of the scaling problem, a transformation that avoids the state. But still, we would need the cooperation of the sailors and the dock workers to bring it all together, and finally we would need people with land to arrange a meeting. And then, I would presuppose that all of these workers had effective power with their own means and modes of production. So, for me, this thought experiment should be taken further and further. And it will be, someday, somehow. Perhaps sooner than we think. Its value lies not in the elimination of the state, but in the presupposition of a classless society. So, I don't believe that the question of the commons can be effectively answered without discussing class divisions first.

LV – Do you consider the abolition of class as a precondition for commoning on a larger scale?

PL – Definitely. Commoning is the antithesis of capitalism. The opposite of the commons is the commodity. In the commodity, the social relations of creation and the social relations of subsistence are hidden. The commodity is about production. The commons, by contrast, are about reproduction, which is centred today in the neighbourhood, in schools, in libraries, in parks. In places that are peaceful, where you see parents, and especially mothers, with their children. Commoning is related to the kitchen, to the conviviality of the meal, to the family. In all these instances, social relations are not governed by the commodity. So again: the realm of reproduction, I believe, is key to commoning. Its principles are not those of the commodity, not those of accumulation, but those of subsistence and health. So how is that scaled up, finally? Well, even before we talk about scale, let's support *those* things first, before inventing new problems. Let's see how existing resources can be dispensed to encourage hospitals, neighbourhood cuisines, healthy water, and a place to live for those without a home.

LV – Arendt once wrote: 'Those who get together to constitute a new government are themselves unconstitutional ... The vicious circle in legislating is present not in ordinary law making, but in laying down the fundamental law.' In *The Magna Carta Manifesto*, you equally demonstrated a 'vicious circle' in relation to the commons, showing how processes of privatization have led to the criminalization of the commoner. Is commoning invariably situated between crime and creation?

PL – It's a beautiful question, and there are so many things to say about this. Let us focus on this continuum, between crime and creation. In the mid-1960s I came to England to study criminal records and to see if I could apply any statistical analysis to these criminal records. At the time, I studied Bonger, a Dutch sociologist who wrote *Criminality and Economic Conditions*, even though he was a positivist and did simple correlations. I also studied the work of Frankfurt scholars Rusche and Kirchheimer, *Punishment and the Social Structure*. But it was via Chevalier's *Classes laborieuses et classes dangereuses* that I recognized this inherent relationship between the commons, the working class, the state, and criminalization. State terror, it ought to be clear, relates very often to the expropriation of people, craftsmen or otherwise, from their means of production, from their materials of production, and from the products of their own labour. It happened in the past with the Waltham Blacks, and it happens today, for example in the Bolivian water wars. It reminds me of this ancient wisdom:

> The law locks up the man or woman
> Who steals the goose from off the common
> But lets the greater villain loose
> Who steals the common from off the goose

But even today, in urban and cultural and everyday settings, we can see how the state criminalizes those who rightfully use the fruits of their own commons. The issue that you raise: creativity, criminality and commoning, remains significant in different contexts. It's an important question, because commoners are not going to give away their knowledge to the intelligence officers from the powers of surveillance. That's the significance of the invisibility of the commons. I am not going to tell you where there's a secret spring of water if you're going to use that spring in order to transform our commons into commodities, into bottled water, and then make me pay for it. So yes, we have our secrets. And the state and the bourgeoisie are looking for those secrets. Let us not forget that the knowledge of the world is among the people who make the world. Final remark: How do we get out of enclosures? Again, the commons, in a way, have to be invisible, secret, clandestine. I feel that that story has not been written well by those who concentrate on the totalitarian power of the forces of surveillance. My early work *The London Hanged* (1991) was meant to be in dialogue with Michel Foucault who, I thought, overemphasized the story of incarceration in opposition to the story of 'excarceration', the story of escape. The fundamental story of human freedom is escaping from confinement, not 'being in' confinement.

LV – One of the merits of your work is that you showed how commoning constitutes humankind's 'default' situation, which existed long before neoliberal ideology would see the light of day. By contrast, today, others would like us to believe that commoning is something new, 'a novel form of governance', a hype. In this latter view, capitalism is seen as the default situation, whilst commoning is depicted as the aberration. Are we forgetting too much about the history of the commons?

PL – Take, for example, Rebecca Solnit's work *A Paradise Built in Hell*. She shows that in times of emergency, like with earthquakes, floods, or fires, people begin to practice mutual aid. People start to help one another. Yet a few days later, after the disaster, when federal emergency agencies or other parts of the state intervene to re-establish security, something else happens. What these agencies do is actually to destroy those networks of mutual aid. So here, the state no longer appears as a paternal figure but as a destructive force, a force that makes us forget that commoning is at the heart of human exchange. It's the state of emergency—today we see this in ongoing privatization and austerity—that brings people to commoning. Puerto Rico, the Houston flooding, the California fires: people start cooking, looking for water, dealing with waste, dealing with each other. But once these processes become co-opted by the state, as Solnit clearly showed, the commons tend to evaporate into this 'forgotten past', as if the commons were only temporary, as if the state is the only 'real' help. So, I would like to refer to this word: *agnotology*, which is the science of ignorance, the science of forgetting, the science of 'not knowing'.

LV – Which reminds me of this famous extract from a tobacco industry lobby document, stating: 'Doubt is our product.'

PL – Yes, creating doubt and 'not knowing' is to the benefit of these forces. Why are we ignorant of some things, and not of others? By processes of framing and governmental intervention, we tend to forget what lies at the heart of human reproduction. Through these processes, it's very easy to forget, or to confuse certain views on the commons. Are they real? Are they just an alternative? This has a history to it, and it's related, for those of us who are historians, to the issue of 'amnesia' or the science of forgetting. This is also highly selective, evidently. To get to the underlying logic here: When framing the commons, there's not just one ideology, but there are several ideologies in collision.

LV – When talking about the commons and ideology, one cannot avoid this other contested word: neoliberalism. With the notion of 'primitive accumulation', Marx described how enclosure constituted a precondition for capitalism to emerge. Today, by contrast, processes of expropriation are continuously present in modern-day capitalism. Could Magna Carta/The Charter of the Forest serve as a valuable source of resistance against neoliberal enclosure?

PL – First, I want to quote from the *Communist Manifesto*, where Marx says about the bourgeoisie: 'It has resolved personal worth into exchange value, and in place of the numberless indefeasible chartered freedoms, has set up that single, unconscionable freedom—Free Trade.' Here, we hear the old Marx talking against the old liberalism based on free trade. And he's saying that free trade, free contract, and private property replaced the numberless *indefeasible* chartered freedoms. So there, in my perception at least, is a direct reference to many charters, including of course the Magna Carta and the Charter of the Forest. But could these charters be a valuable source of resistance against neoliberalism? Well, the Shadow Chancellor of Great Britain, John McDonnell, thinks so at least. In other words, some politicians are beginning to answer this question, even though they don't have a direct answer. Still, I believe that Podemos in Spain, or people in Greece are giving a tentative 'yes' to this question. Korea for example, where *The Magna Carta Manifesto* has been translated, shows similarities. Contemporary commoning is in fact a direct critique against neoliberalism, against the tremendous violence that accompanies it, against the tremendous poverty and pollution that come with it. Let's not forget that the destruction of water, the destruction of health, the homelessness around the world and the crisis of the refugees all are direct results of this neoliberal regime.

LV – You once wrote: 'The Supreme Court adapted Magna Carta to the dominant institutions and social forces of the US, private property, commerce, capitalism, slavery.' Where lies the thin line between the inside and the outside of the commons? Where lies the thin line between commons and property?

PL – Let us turn to the Latin word *comunis*. We have the 'co', which means 'together', but the 'munis' means 'under obligation'. Commoning is not only about sharing, but also about the mutual obligations we have to one another. You can join us, but you have these obligations of reciprocity. Imagine we have this lake. As a fellow-commoner, you are not to dump your sewage into it, because that prevents us from swimming and the other species living in it will die. That's why I'd say that the kitchen and the meal, theoretically private assets, constitute the primary locus of commoning. You can have the soup from the kitchen, you can sit down at the meal, but will you help with the washing up when you are able? It doesn't have to be an exchange, but you have to pitch in somehow, you have to help out. I would call this 'indirect reciprocity'. Commoning has to do with a redefinition of work and labour as a human mutuality, rather than as an exploitation and exchange. Lexically, this is what I derive from the Latin *comunis*: 'what we own together', and 'what we owe each other'. Not as a matter of ownership, but as a matter of mutual subsistence. I think there's a very important distinction here. To add another important point: there is no commons without an exterior. Every commons presupposes those who are not common to it.

LV – The proletariat, the precariat, the multitude... Who are, in your perception, the subjects of commoning?

PL – I have used the term 'working class' over the years. I did this in a very open way, to include all those who are active in reproduction. But it leads to a certain misunderstanding very frequently, for I would like to denote with it a much broader realm of commoning actors. When you look at the Sixth Declaration from the Lacandon Jungle of the Zapatistas, you see clearly how they include many more: transgendered people, queer people, people like myself who are senior citizens, people with disabilities, 'those from below', they wrote. Many of those are on the margins, and for those, the message of the Zapatistas is crystal-clear: We appeal to the humble and simple people of the world. Then of course, there's the 99%, or Guy Standing's precariat ... Each of these terms has its history and its political position. But whatever term we use, we can be sure that there will be spin-doctors of the ruling class that are going to turn it upside down. (long silence) Isn't it terrible what they have done to our language over the years?! Isn't it terrible how language can be abused for the interests of the ruling class?! You know, the old Greeks used the notion of *ecclesia* to denote an assembly of people without any hierarchy of domination. I am sympathetic to that. Or we can just praise the Buddhists and the Quakers who take a vow of silence and let their actions speak.

LV – The 13th-century English commoners were homogeneous commoners, at least geographically and socio-economically. By contrast, recent theorizations explore how commons may be created throughout heterogeneous communities and singularities: the 'multitude' in Hardt and Negri or the 'threshold community' in Stavrides, just to name a few. What lessons can be learnt from the rights in the Charters, if we want to organize the commons heterogeneously today?

PL – Firstly, the Magna Carta and the Charter of the Forest never speak of 'rights'. They speak of 'powers' or 'liberties'. 'Rights', if I may say, is a discourse of the Enlightenment, several centuries later. The significance of this, is that rights 'appeared' to be granted from the state as a part of the discourse of law. But, at the time of King John for example, when we speak of the 'powers' and the 'liberties' of common people, we presuppose that the common man *has* these powers, whilst the notion of 'rights' does not presuppose that. But of course, every victory of the common man will always be interpreted as a gift from the ruling class after they have been defeated. So, we should be careful with this vocabulary 'granting rights'. Secondly, these charters of the past arose at a time when diverse ecclesiastical authorities within the ruling class were struggling for power. The Charter of the Forest was sealed by somebody representing the Pope of Rome and the Christian Church, and the Magna Carta was sealed by King John. These were powerful systems of domination over soil, at a time of struggle for the soul of human beings. However, we should not look at it from the ruling class' point of view, but from the commoner's point of view. And there, in the English common village, you will have travellers, and you will have squatters, there will be a place on the sedentary commons to accommodate the needs of vagabonds. Does this count as heterogeneity? I doubt it. But let's not forget that for example the Zapatistas in Mexico built their *ejido's* with communists who had fled Mexico City and with liberation theologians who were working with the peasantry. So, to me the question is still open.

LV – Some argue that the (welfare) state can and should take over issues of commoning. In *The Magna Carta Manifesto*, you wrote:

> During the New Deal the federal government responded to demands of the mass worker both for increasing the value of the working class and for taking a hand in its reproduction. The experience led many to think that the government could replace many of the functions that commoning had historically fulfilled.

What role should be expected from the state if we want to organize commoning sustainably?

PL – We expect help from the state, to stay out of our business. When I say 'stay out of our business', I mean: please do not send the army and the police into those people at Standing Rock, Dakota, who are trying to protect their water. That's number one. Number two: Don't throw people's books into the water at Occupy. These books can be used! And number three: give us some help. Food and water, a government can supply that. Give us some aid and stay out of our way when we are meeting our mutual needs. The government has tons of money, and we want that money back. Also, this is the number one principle from the Charter of the Forest: The Charter said that the king must *disaforest* what he has taken. Not to forget: to *disaforest* means to remove the forests from royal jurisdiction, to make them available again as a source of subsistence for the commoner. We want reparations for the harm that has been done. We want to decapitalize capitalism. What capital is now, was to *discommon* back then. That's a real word from the 18th century, *discommoning*, which we would call 'privatizing' today. People all over the world are searching for new political entities. Here in Britain, this explains the Scottish independence movement, and perhaps it even explains the Brexit or the Catalonian issue. For sure, I do not see these events in terms of nationalism or fascism only, that's just a possibility. Perhaps I am being utopian, but there might be other possibilities. Also, look at Rojava in Syria, the Zapatistas in Mexico... It all comes down to honouring the labour of those who preceded us—'dead labour', as Marx teaches us in *Das Kapital*—and saving the labour of future generations. But are we even trying to do that? Of course not! Capital and the state are only temporary. The commons, on the other hand, belong to our struggle against war, against domination, against exploitation. Viva Zapata!

References

— Hess, Charlotte. 2008. *Mapping the New Commons*. Presented at the 12th Biennial Conference of the International Association for the Study of the Commons, Cheltenham, UK.

— Linebaugh, Peter. 1991. *The London Hanged: Crime and Civil Society in the Eighteenth Century*. London: Verso.

—. 2008. *The Magna Carta Manifesto: Liberties and Commons for All*. Berkeley, Los Angeles, and London: University of California Press.

—. 2014. *Stop, Thief! The Commons, Enclosures, and Resistance*. Oakland, CA: PM Press.

Part 4

Affects &
Commoning
Space-Time

Uncommon Common
Spatial Denial in Urban Settings of Los Angeles

Harry Gamboa Jr.

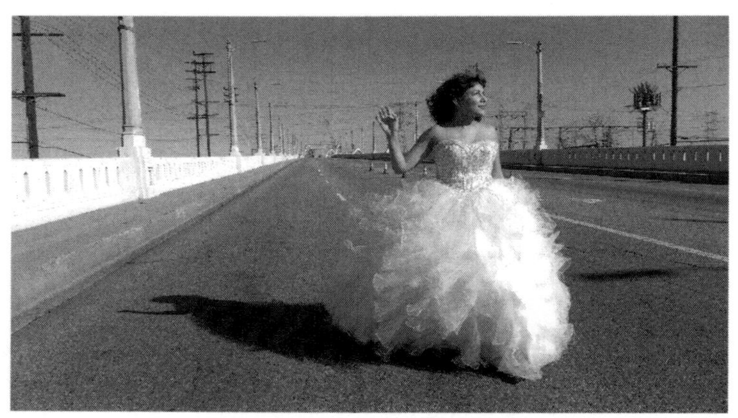

The Sixth Expanse, 2015,
©2015 Harry Gamboa Jr.,
chromogenic print,
16 x 20 inches, Edition of 10
Performer: Ana Garcia

I recently led a group of local and international students who enrolled in my *L.A. Urbanscape* course at the California Institute of the Arts (Valencia, CA) through a maze of concrete, asphalt, and waves of automobile traffic as we walked across terrain that is often relegated to those who may have lost their direction in the urban area or are particularly dedicated to preserving order, obedience, and conformity. The back streets of the downtown area of Los Angeles are subject to sudden earthquakes, a subtle shifting of tectonic plates, and the declaration that all must be quiet on the temporary on-location Hollywood movie set. The collective action of walking in Los Angeles is usually met with official suspicion because the city has been completely designed for movement via private automobile. The City of Los Angeles is located within the broader boundaries of Los Angeles County, which consists of an area of 4,751 square miles and is home to more than 10.17 million people. It is all tied together with massive concrete ribbons of freeways and major thoroughfares. Los Angeles has an extensive history of mythical glamour complicated by major battles of social strife and famous riots. If you are walking rather than driving, then you are exhibiting autonomous behaviour that might not be easily regulated or readily fit into the parameters of the ever-present digital data collection panopticon.

The surface area of the Civic Center, L.A. Arts District, Little Tokyo, and Financial District areas within downtown Los Angeles is completely covered with manufactured materials that eliminate direct contact with the topsoil. Each slab of cement, brick, or expanse of low-grade asphalt is mismatched and not levelled for smooth transport. All public service roads, freeway ramps, exterior sets of stairs, sidewalks, bridges, buildings, parks, and other useful objects and institutions were originally built based on taxpayer contributions and the general assumption was that it would all be available for common use by the people in perpetuity. The notion that any public space could or would be restricted on behalf of private concerns was once considered to be repugnant and an insult to the American people. The possibility that anyone could be prosecuted or subject to use of force by police agents for entering, walking on, or passing through surface areas that were constructed for free public activity was also anathema to citizens and visitors alike. The current era, when 1% of the world's population is rewarded with 82% of the global wealth has spurious roots that touch down where we could easily become entangled to trip and fall onto an area that has been newly gentrified or recategorized as being privatized via joint public-private ventures. I pointed to various chunks of concrete on the ground and warned my students to watch their step and to avoid crossing invisible boundaries that might result in authoritative punitive action in the form of fines, fees, and possible court appearances.

The students are adept at perceiving the subtleties of grand theft and the overt oppressiveness of the unseen all-seeing eyes of multiple surveillance cameras posted on high poles and on the sides of commercial buildings. We moved forward under a brilliant blue sky and were fanned by temperate winds while walking for three hours until we were back at our starting point: the historic Union Station where all train services and many commuter bus services converge. It was built in the 1930s using taxpayer funds and has gone through various eras of flagging use but most recently has been highly populated by commuters who utilize heavy rail, light rail, underground rail, and various bus and shuttle lines that provide round trip service to suburban areas from the epicentre of the urban experience. The ethnic and economic diversity of the people in the crowded station serves as barometer of tolerance for officials who often make their presence known by wearing military-style combat-ready uniforms while bearing sophisticated militarized weapons. They represent a wide range of enforcement agencies to battle crime, hunt undocumented immigrants, and prevent any form of indiscriminate violence that could represent terrorism. Formerly common areas are now cordoned off and only those with properly enhanced identity papers and valid tickets are allowed to sit on benches or seats. Although Los Angeles has the largest population of homeless in the United States, such individuals are not allowed to remain in the space for more than a few moments, and everyone on site is subject to random searches of body and personal property. At times, the overall scene is reminiscent of dramatized dystopian films and actual nefarious points in history. To improve the transportation system in Los Angeles, it has recently received tremendous tax payer financial support but ridership has fallen in part due to a milieu that promotes a particular demeanour by uniformed officials that might suggest to many that driving a car would be the best option in the face of the multiple systems of surveillance and police presence that could result in undue physical intervention and unexpected fines of up to $1,000.00 per minor infraction.

The weekly class session came to an end and the students dispersed in all directions. I descended to the lower level where I would board the Metro Red Line subway train. The stark cavity of space is lined in monotonous grey concrete and occasionally reveals a work of public art, commissioned by a committee with veto power that considers many aspects of what will be shown before the work can be fabricated and put into place. All Metro train stations are designed for occupation only during the periods between individual train arrival and departure. The stations themselves are lifeless and disallow eating, drinking, loud talking, running, playing of music, and, most importantly, insist that each individual utilize a TAP smart card that captures electronic payment but also provides data thus registering the user with whatever systems are observing the transaction. Most often, while waiting on the platform for the train to arrive, the sensation of being very much alone can outweigh the enjoyment of sharing a common space. I often compare the experience of subway stations in Los Angeles with those to be found in Mexico and Europe, where there is a daily overriding excitement that everyone can engage in normal human behaviour while utilizing various services that provide food and drink, while listening to a variety of musicians or discussing issues with other people talking and laughing during the waiting period on the station platform. The Metro Red Line train took only a few minutes to appear and the exchange of people moving in and out of the train cars was quickly concluded as the doors closed and I soon found myself sitting among a diverse crowd of riders. Everyone remained silent as the train moved quickly from one station to the next. I disembarked at Wilshire/Vermont Station and rode the escalators up to the exit where imposingly armed officers insisted on placing an electronic reader over each individual's TAP card to ensure that payment had been made at the start of the journey. Several riders were detained and were about to receive citations for fines. Fortunately, I was able to pass through quickly to get out onto the streets.

In 1972, I co-founded Asco, an East L.A.-based art group that would create various street performances that I would photograph using cinematic film stock to produce several works that continue to reverberate in contemporary circles of art, scholarship, and mass media. During that period, Chicanos were targeted by

Nixonian efforts to eradicate creative, intellectual, and political actions by anyone of Mexican heritage. The Vietnam War ensured that a disproportionate large number of Chicano young men would die in combat while the remaining Chicana/o population would be subjected to various levels of discrimination, unemployment, poor educational services, and tremendous police violence involving numerous injuries. And there was the assassination of Ruben Salazar, an acclaimed journalist for the English-language Los Angeles Times and for the Spanish-language KMEX television station, during the massive anti-war protest demonstration known as the Chicano Moratorium of 1970. The complex environment of East L.A. was not the most likely place for producing a cadre of conceptual artists that would challenge the tenets of American Art and mass media, all while conjuring up positive alternatives to the negative stereotypes that were being fabricated in corporate and governmental offices at the highest levels. In the period of 1970 through 1974, East L.A. was subjected to something akin to Martial Law that disallowed the gathering of small groups of young people at any time of day. My experience of defiance in making certain that I would gather young people to perform and pose for photographs under such conditions instilled in me a clear sense of rejecting of denial of public access to public space.

I founded Virtual Vérité (2005–2017), a performance troupe that would be composed of more than one hundred local and international performers, mostly based in Los Angeles (several performers reside in Antwerpen, Mexico City, Paris, Copenhagen, and Berlin). The troupe was often employed to engage with various places in Los Angeles that could arguably be considered to be suitable for public use such as bridges, streets, entryways to skyscrapers, parking lots, aboard public transit buses and trains, universities, and other sites that often allow for some form of foot traffic. The performers (one to fifty, per event) would often pose in various stages of dance and/or social acrobatics to imply a severe sense of imbalance and counterbalance to result in a visual, precarious balance of a social setting against a realm of spatial restraint. Sometimes they would be directed to scream, yell, laugh, walk slowly, crawl on hands and knees, or simply stand as a defiant target, and also to push against the immovable mass of structures that define the impermanence of all things in Los Angeles. The various performances were photographed for use online or to create print media *fotonovelas* (for example *Aztlángst*) that would accentuate existentialist commentary while supplying clues to the spiralling decay of democracy, the collapse of an equitable economy, and the repeal and reduction of *commonism* in the daily lives of people within the United States of America.

During 2015–2016, I photographed the many performers of the troupe for *The Sixth Expanse*[1] project while they encountered the two-year long demolition/destruction of the historically significant 6th Street Bridge. Each performance/photography event was set against a rapidly receding length of bridge and support pillars. The ephemeral actions involved various forms of fun and social friction that would counter the obvious assault of gentrification against the predominantly Chicano district of Boyle Heights. The one-mile long asymmetrical bridge that spanned the concrete Los Angeles River had been built in the early 20th century with public funds. Its designated Historical Landmark status was repealed and then it was ruthlessly smashed by the hyper-capitalist wrecking ball. Destroying bridges is not always a successful civic action nor is it a meaningful diplomatic metaphor.

In 2017–2018, the pace of spatial denial in urban settings of Los Angeles has increased by turning both interior and exterior areas into potential no man's land for a wide spectrum of people who are either economically disenfranchised or who fit specific biometric profiles. All this with particular attention to undocumented Mexican immigrants who are profoundly denounced by the highest elected officials despite the fact that their indigenous North American lineage can be traced back to nearly 15,000 years of continuous occupancy. The recent introduction of a new federal law requiring people to carry what is essentially an internal passport will dramatically curtail what areas may be used for daily activities such as walking, commuting, attending school, or going to work. Also, the imposition of massive data collection of automobile license plates will affect who will be allowed to drive on public roads. The various draconian measures that are already in place will be enhanced to make it difficult for anyone who might have the slightest misgivings regarding their social status from being visible or having their voices heard. The efforts to eradicate certain groups is already affecting large numbers of people from being able to use any public services, including medical assistance, police protection, educational opportunities, and properly remunerated work, for themselves and for their children with citizenship, who might actually qualify to receive such benefits.

The harsh conditions of privatized immigration detainment facilities bring the risk of a dangerously opaque abuse of human rights. Although Los Angeles and California have adopted sanctuary statutes, various other national enforcement agencies are being directed to pursue intensified efforts to make it difficult for anyone who carries visible ethnic traits to conduct normal activities in public spaces.

It is important for all people to recognize our innate humanness and to realize the shared value of free common space. The privatization of public space is an artificial construct that violates societal trust and undermines the integrity of agencies that are supposed to defend the rights of the people. In the United States, corporations have been granted legal rights equal to humans thereby upsetting the balance of what would be plausible for a secure and beneficial society. The militarization of domestic agencies has complicated the relationship with the people, who could easily become targeted as if they were enemies in a war setting. The allowance and promotion of hate speech via mainstream media and the complete absence of Chicano representation in mass media allows for ongoing image distortion, which creates a virulent social environment. Although most people are free to come and go while they traverse the streets of Los Angeles, it would be comforting if everyone could gather to appreciate the common good.

Note

1   Harry Gamboa Jr., *The Sixth Expanse* (2018), self-published, 104 pages, ISBN-10: 152324495X/ISBN-13 978-1523244959.

Fiat Strada!

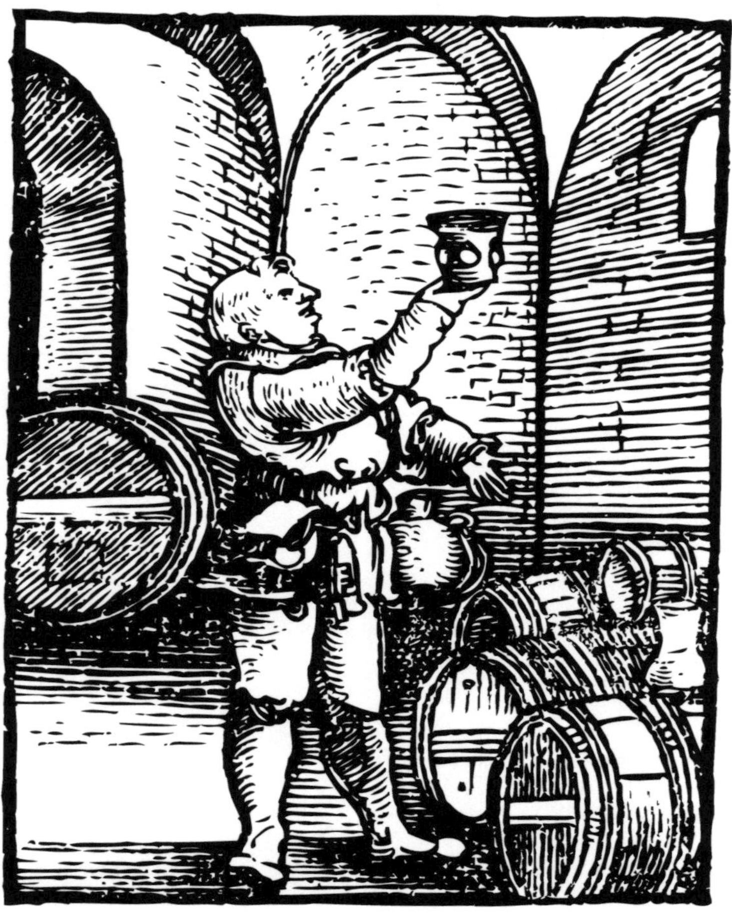

Fiat Strada! Eva Presenhuber, 2011

Cabriolet...

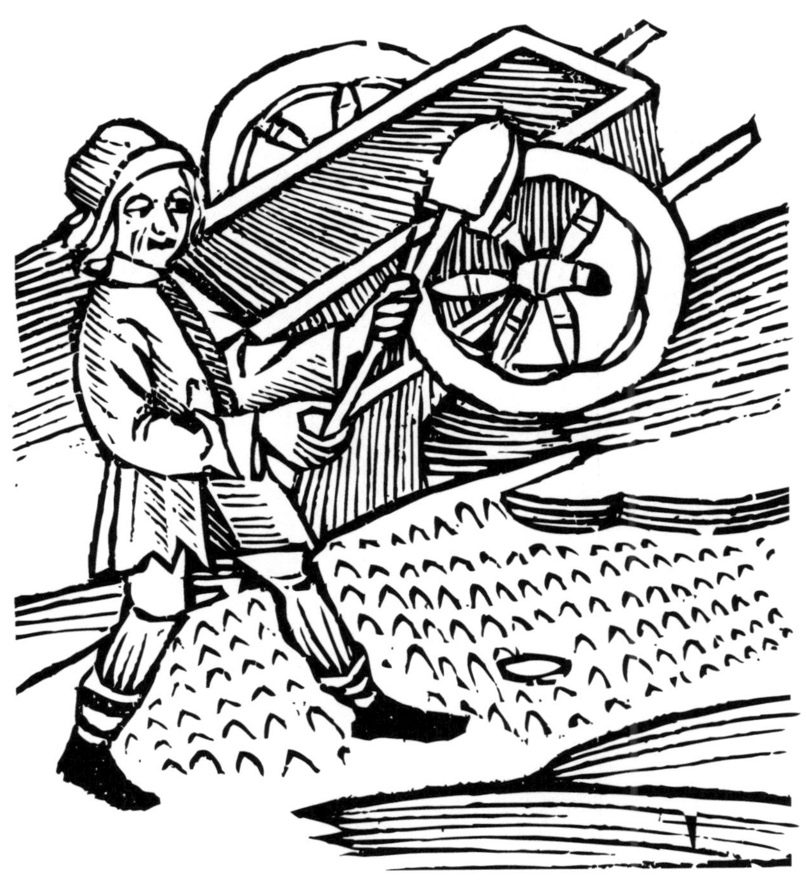

Cabriolet, Casey Kaplan, 2013

The Potentials of Space Commoning
The Capacity to Act and Think through Space

Stavros Stavrides

Concrete social realities have their spaces. They unfold in and through space. It is by interacting with spatial attributes and characteristics that the experience of individuals and groups unfolds. If every society reproduces itself by reproducing the habits and structural relations of its members, then the regulating of shared experiences is among the most powerful means to pursue this goal. Spatial arrangements, however, are more than containers of social life and shared experiences. Spatial arrangements interact with social experiences both by giving them concrete context and by supporting representations of those experiences, which actually make them sharable.

By being an active co-producer of social life and of the experiences that characterize it, space becomes a powerful means to control the distribution of the sensible. Let us remember Jacques Rancière's definition: 'I call the distribution of the sensible the system of self-evident facts of sense perception that simultaneously discloses the existence of something in common and the delimitations that define the respective parts and positions within it.'[1] This process actually channels sense perception to socially imposed patterns that are connected with meaningful representations of the social world. The perception of spatial forms and characteristics is part of this kind of social ordering. The normalization process, which lies at the foundations of social ordering, tries to ensure that future experiences will be shaped according to deeply embedded 'dispositions', a term Bourdieu uses to describe the results of socially inculcated tacit knowledge.[2]

However, what makes space a means to control both the shared experiences and their representations, gives space the power to shape *possible experiences*. A way of exploring this power is by thinking-in-images.[3] In this case, the power to construct representations of social life through spatial qualities is used to project elements of possible social worlds through thought-images of possible spaces of social life. We know, of course, that the history of utopias is a history of utopian sites, utopian worlds, utopian cities and utopian spaces, in many cases envisaged, depicted or narrated in the greatest of detail. What distinguishes thinking-in-images from this history of utopian spatial projections is the fact that thought-images can be hybrid combinations of thoughts about a possible future and of spatial relations related to this future (conceived diagrammatically rather than in full imagistic detail). The term, which originated in the writing of the Frankfurt School theorists (Benjamin, Adorno, Bloch, and Kracauer), 'self-consciously exposes the inescapable contamination of the theoretical by the figurative'.[4] Thought-images, thus, do not offer (or seek to construct) depictions of a possible future but rather shape arguments about the future developed through the processing of images. Here lies the emancipatory potential of this process: A possible emancipatory future is connected to both the concreteness of available shared experiences and to their shared representations, as well as to that abstract generalizing reasoning that learns from such experiences and representations (and does not use them merely as examples or illustrations).

If emancipation has to do with the envisioning and testing of specific forms of social organization, possible spaces (understood as imagined arrangements or as specific possible sites) may become the means of both envisioning and testing those forms. Space, concrete and relational, abstract and specific is truly connected to a crucial human capacity: to understand experience and imagine the world through arrangements of objects and subjects. Through space and spatial attributes (for instance, distance) humans make their experiences meaningful but they also long to reach beyond what they face as reality.

A comparison with the capacity of language may be instructive. This capacity is considered to be innate: Humans may produce language as part of their species-specific armature for survival.[5] Language, thus, may take different forms in different historical periods but also different levels of this capacity are being reached by different individuals in different language communities. In all cases, however, language is an area of potential. To use Paolo Virno's suggestion, linguistic potentiality is never exhausted in the specific utterance or 'speech act' that is actualized in different contingencies. Potential becomes the measure of what actually exists (in the case of language of what is uttered) but it is also the very precondition of going beyond it.[6]

What seems to be common to P. Virno and Giorgio Agamben is an effort to rescue human capacities from their direct exploitation by current capitalism, which they consider not merely as a distinct production system but also as a form of government based on biopolitics. They both focus on language as the most important human capacity, which connects and even directs all the other capacities. And it is language, according to both, that is completely instrumentalized in contemporary work relations and production relations as a generic ability that all humans can employ. Actually, it is language, instrumentalized in the form of an all- pervasive communicability, which subordinates human communication to productive work (through information and tele-communication technologies) and to the shaping of consumption habits (especially through the mass media as well as the social media). Thus, according to Agamben,

> [I]n the society of the spectacle, it is this very communicativity [the communicative essence of human beings], this generic essence itself (that is language as *Gattungswesen*), that is being separated in an autonomous sphere. What prevents communication is communicability itself.[7]

For Agamben, to reclaim human capacities from direct capitalist exploitation, to restore communication as the ground of human community means to restore the potentiality inherent to those capacities. Drawing heavily from Aristotle's problematization of potentiality (*dynamis*), Agamben suggests that potentiality is not and should not be reduced to its actualizations. For the 'coming community'[8] to be different from existing forms of social organization, which are based on 'belonging' and on identity categorizations and hierarchies, we need to restore potentiality as the basis of the common. 'We need to secure a pure potentiality that does not pass over into actuality.'[9] 'We need to think man ... as a being of pure potentiality (*potenza*) that no identity and no work could exhaust.'[10]

Pure potentiality becomes the power of means, the power of mediality, once it is released from its necessary connection to specific social ends, or, more specifically, once it is released from actuality as potentiality's necessary outcome. Politics, thus, becomes for Agamben 'the sphere of pure means',[11] 'the sphere of a pure mediality without end intended as the field of human action and of human thought'.[12]

It is in such a prospect that potentiality will become the common denominator of shared life in a 'coming community'. Singularities will be shaped in 'forms-of-life', in ways of living in which 'mediality' (form considered as means without end) is to become the only distinguishing factor.

What is at stake then, is a life in which the single ways, acts and processes of living are never simply facts [therefore imprints for governance and rule making] but always and above all possibilities of life, always and above all potentiality (*potenza*).[13]

The capacity to produce spaces and to think through spaces is indeed a human capacity which, as language, is never reducible to concrete social realities. This capacity corresponds to a potentiality that transcends any actual social reality. Virno believes that what he names as 'potentials' 'attest to human beings' poverty of instinct, undefined nature, and characteristic constant disorientation'.[14] Stressing the importance of human disorientation as the condition of human life he insists: 'Potential is intimately connected to disorientation',[15] which results from the 'lack of a pre-given environment in which we can take an innately secure place once and for all time'.[16] Following a different reasoning, Agamben comes to a conclusion that can be considered as similar. For him, man 'appears as the living being that has no work, that is, the living being that has no specific nature and vocation'.[17]

However, the capacity to think and act by employing spatial attributes and spatial denominators (such as, for example distance, height, and so on) cannot be rescued from its instrumentalization in capitalist society the way Agamben seems to suggest in referring to language and life (life as form). Pure potentiality in terms of space will mean an absolute emphasis on the mediality of space completely cut off from any of its concretizations in lived human environments. Reduced to a means without end, space will be closer to the abstract space of capitalist production, which is so severely condemned as alienating by H. Lefebvre.[18]

True, we can compare this abstract 'spaceness' of space to the pure communicability that destroys communication, which Agamben links to the conditions of capitalist exploitation of human capacities. And we may assume that Agamben's 'sphere of pure means' is not a sphere separated from the rest of social life (the way communicability is in capitalism, resulting in the emptying of its human potentiality) but indeed the centre of a coming community life.

However, space as capacity is developed through experiences of actual spatial arrangements. The power to think beyond those actual arrangements and their material existence is developed from within those experiences. Thus, we may retain the effort to keep open the potentialities related to this capacity only if we continuously open possibilities to experience different actual spaces. The actualization of spatial potentialities further opens the field of potentialization.

Spaces, concrete lived spaces, are works (the result of labour), but also the means to shape possible future worlds. If we connect this perspective with Lefebvre's idea that the city is the collective 'oeuvre' of its habitants,[19] then the potentialization of space is always the result of commoning, of sharing aspirations but also of working together, of working in common. Lived spaces are shaped through human interactions that develop shared worlds. To potentialize those shared worlds, which means to challenge their meaning and their power to present the distribution of the sensible as an indisputable order of life, people have to activate the potentials of commoning. And this essentially amounts to the liberation of commoning from capitalist command.

Agamben thinks that in the feast 'what is done—which in itself is not unlike one does every day—becomes undone, is rendered inoperative liberated and suspended from its "economy"',[20] Similarly, dance is the 'liberation of the body from its utilitarian movements' and the poem is rendering language inoperative, 'in deactivating its communicative and informative function in order to open it to a new possible use'.[21] In all those cases, it seems, potentiality is really experienced as the expansion of the field of the possible because there exist human movements that are not dance and because there is a variety of human discourses (human interactions through language) that are not poetic. 'Inoperativity' in this context defines a describable externality, although the boundaries between the poetic and the non-poetic (as well as those between dance and everyday gestures) are socially marked. The potentialization of everyday gestures, everyday language or everyday acts of survival does not happen, however, because we become able to render them inoperative but, rather, because the externality of dance, poetry, and feast, respectively, is only relative in terms of history: It is by contaminating everyday normality that art or collective joy may transform it. Potentialization is a dynamic, contingent process that transforms habits and not the restoration of an unpolluted, ontologically different beyond.

Possible Spaces

Thus, to think about space as potentiality is to connect experiences of space to possibilities of expanding them and transcending them. To explore the potentials of space is to explore the potentials of spatial relations and the ways those relations may happen. Materiality is not merely an aspect of the actualization of spatial potentialities in a specific context but an essential constituent of the potentiality of space.

Space becomes potential when it is performed. And performance is not only a process of repetition, of normalization based on spatially acquired dispositions. Performing space, performing through space, is always open to discovering space through performance, much like a dancer discovers possible movements by dancing and an actor possible gestures by acting or by rehearsing. By performing space we may transform actually existing spaces. Performing space actually means performing social relations, it means experiencing them as concrete unfolding realities, rather than as abstract definitions of social identities. And this is a way to live potentiality by creating it.

Maybe 'what is at issue in Agamben's thinking of potentiality is simply and intensely creation – creation in its most radical form, a form that, to truly create, must make the complete of the dictated incomplete, must grasp decreation'.[22] Creation, however, may become the substratum of a multiple process of displacements and experiments that unfold in a myriad of ways in everyday practices as well as in moments of rupture. Creation, thus, is both mundane and heroic, as is the process of potentializing space. Rendering space inoperative is no way of discovering possible spaces. Destroying the instrumentalization of space imposed by capitalist governance may possibly become the motor of the potentialization of space. But this is something that is necessarily exposed to the messy contradictions of lived reality.

One can even go further in challenging the emancipating promise of pure potentiality: Potentiality should never be reduced to the actual only because the actual always feeds potentiality. To go beyond what exists we need to use the experiences and thoughts that are born in what exists and struggle to transcend it.

Spatial capacity, the faculty to perceive through spatial attributes and to think through spatial attributes, can be said to be part of the ability of humans to create their own history, to be members of societies unfolding in history. This capacity shapes specific spaces but also may support the projection into future possible spaces of experiences that unfold in the present. In Virno's theory the process through which potentials shape the present is not equated to actualization. For him potential is pre-historical and non-chronological.[23] It 'is the unrealized past against which the living measures itself while it lives'.[24] Potential, thus, cannot be connected to a certain moment in the past but it can be evoked by memory as that which measures the present. Potential always remains 'unrealized' but for this reason we can say that it gives meaning and attributes value to actual experiences.

It is interesting to observe how Virno treats Benjamin's approach to the past. Benjamin's theory on history is based on the idea that historical time is full of discontinuities and ruptures and, therefore, a narrative reconstruction of the past is only illusionary and mythologizing,[25] Moreover, such a narrative approach is essentially part of the mythology of continuous progress, which, transposed to politics, legitimizes a social-democratic view of social change as gradual and linear.[26] Ruptures indicate, for Benjamin, moments that reveal potentialities. Unrealized potentialities in the past can provide us with a knowledge that is crucial for the present: How to pursue a different future, an emancipatory future, by taking advantage of potentialities that were not followed in the past. By trying to win where others have lost.[27]

This approach to potentiality, to the potential, according to Virno, needs to be supplemented by an interpretation of the present's relation to potential. It is because the 'present moment itself entails the past-in-general – potential – as one of its intrinsic component',[28] that the present can be connected to a specific past and thus become meaningful in the prospect of social change. Potential makes the historical past a dynamic challenge for the future. Potential keeps the past as an unresolved pendency in the present.

There is something very useful here for a possible theory of the potentialities of space (or for space as part of the potential): If past and present experiences, shared (and thus socialized) through representations, actually provide people with the means to construct possible visions of a different future, then it is important to see the past not as a finished and fully describable reality but as a propelling force for the discovery of potentialities in the present. Re-activating the past, thus, might mean using, among other ways, images of the past, spatial configurations of past experiences, in order to discover in them potential spaces and potential spatialities. In the process of printing the images of the past with the powerful developing solutions of the present (an image that allures to a technology of image printing made obsolete by contemporary xerography), spatial characteristics acquire new meanings, appear in a new light, and are being transformed or possibly distorted (but, of course, an initial 'authentic' form of space is just as imaginary as any of its projections). To put it in different words: To see spaces of the past as opportunities to rethink what may change or what should change, necessarily entails the capacity to think through space, to construct possible spatialities.

Considering space then, as a capacity to experience and to think of different forms of social organization, links space to the project of social emancipation. This does not amount to reiterating that new societies need new spaces. Emancipated societies, societies in which human emancipation unfolds, produce and need new spatialities, new ways, that is, to understand and employ space as a crucial factor of shaping human relations. Spatial potentialities support creative explorations of possible human relations.

Space and Prefigurative Politics

By focusing on space as potentiality and by acknowledging the capacity to think and act through space as a crucial human capacity we can reformulate the problem of prefiguration and prefigurative politics. The simple and historically most enduring way to conceive of prefigurative politics is as those practices in which means reflect (mirror, look like) the ends. In prefigurative politics, visions of a different society are supposed to shape struggles to establish such a society according to the same values that support these visions.[29] There is of course an important problem that makes the comparison between means and ends highly precarious. We experience acts as they unfold in time. And we can connect them to scopes either judging by ourselves or by taking into account words or other forms of expression that are used by the subjects of those acts to explain what they aim at. There is, however, an unbridgeable gap between words and deeds, scopes and acts, discourses and practices. Actually, what we try to compare cannot really be compared.

We can observe and judge acts (including the performance status of enunciations) but scopes we have to infer. And words that declare scopes merely do that: declare. Shouldn't we then say that acts reveal (according of course to an interpretative stance) scopes rather than pre-figure them? Shouldn't we realize that acts (including enunciating acts) may indeed be considered as means to accomplish something but that ends can only be inferred? And, surely, results of actions do not necessarily establish (let alone 'prove') the scopes of those actions.

J. Holloway, in his subtle definition of prefigurative struggles, suggests an interesting way out of this conceptual impasse. A 'consciously prefigurative' struggle 'aims, in its form, not to reproduce the structures and practices of that which is struggled against, but rather to create the sort of social relations which are desired'.[30] By talking about the 'form' of struggle, Holloway may try to show that means can be considered as forms rather than as concrete realities, the way the realities of acts are. Focusing on the formal aspect of acts may establish a common ground between acts and scopes. What need to be compared are, thus, not acts and scopes but the forms of acts and the form of scopes. Values in both acts and scopes can, therefore, be connected to their forms through which they are embedded in social relations. And what seems to differentiate those forms is power. It is because power relations take different forms that we can distinguish between different forms of relations between people. A certain society's members enter into differentiated social relations because of an overall arrangement of power distribution that characterizes this specific society.

Direct democracy and horizontality are forms of relations that construct modes of social organization based on the values of equality. Specific ways of distributing and controlling power are developed in the spatio-historical context of groups or societies that establish such relations. And, of course, those ways are being developed in time: Forms characterize relations but in a way that is open to the historicity of struggles—forms are open to transformation. Prefiguration is actually being performed and prefigurative practices do not prefigure a future condition but actually prefigure a future process by unfolding as a process.

Commenting on the prefigurative politics of alter-globalization movement, M. Maeckelbergh seems to suggest exactly this. Namely, that this movement was not creating 'a prefiguration of an ideal society or type of community or abstract political ideology ... [but] ... a prefiguration of a process, a prefiguration of a horizontal decentralized democracy, which is at once a goal and current practice of the movement'.[31]

Returning to space as capacity: Spaces can be pre-figurative because they can show possible arrangements of social relations by way of analogy: Spaces do not simply illustrate or represent social relations that may inhabit them, spaces contribute in the shaping of those social relations. It is because space is both a medium (analogically able to show possible new ways on inhabiting) and also part of the projected future, that space can prefigure and materialize, at the same time, a different social condition.

This gives the shared capacity to use space the power to contribute to prefigurative politics by destroying the considered as indisputable polarity between means and ends. In actual spaces. people can experience the future and the means to reach it. Space, when it becomes enmeshed in prefigurative politics, is both experienced and potential, an actual materiality of arrangements and a dynamic construction of possible human relations that unfold in the present. Space as potential is more like a testing ground for the future: through real-time experiments parts of the future are brought to the present.

Space acquires its relational power, its power therefore to become a medium but also an aspect of social relations, through the shaping of its form: Space-as-form is connected in three ways in social life. Thus, space-as-form connects to social organization (form-as-organization), to the expression of social values and meaning (form-as-expression), and to the processes of labour and technology (form-as-materialization).[32]

It is because space is shaped as form through social practices that space may be potentialized in prefigurative politics. Space is part of social life and not a way to establish a pure externality to life as it unfolds in a certain society. This is why space may be experienced and thought as both an external and an internal reality when it is part of prefigurative politics. 'Pre-' does not exactly describe its status in terms of time: (pre)figurative spaces unfold on multiple levels of temporality—they may connect actual and remembered experiences with aspirations and dreams. And this multivalence of practices may happen during the process in which space is actually produced in action.

An activist fighting for indigenous rights in Mexican Chiapas is actually juxtaposing different temporalities in spaces that are potentialized through collective actions of resistance:

A remembered space of community, a sought-for space for indigenous autonomy, and an experienced space of everyday struggle are co-present in *territorio Zapatista* (Zapatista territory). 'Alternative social rationalities'[33] emerge in Zapatista communities as new forms of social organization and government are being tried out. This is a process that sustains dissident ways of practicing politics aimed at emancipatory changes, which are developed against dominant neoliberal policies of discrimination and 'expulsion'.[34] 'We might best characterize the Zapatista strategy, then, as the construction of another structure of relation between a newly produced collective subject and space – a new "territoriality..."'.[35] Zapatista territory, thus, does not exist outside the capitalist Mexican state and the global flows that shape it. Zapatista territory emerges as an unfolding potentialization of dominant spatial relations in an effort to create expansive networks of commoning and self-governance. This is the meaning of Zapatista autonomy, which is clearly distinguished from the declared autonomy of whatever state.

Prefigurative power is a propelling force for spatial figuration, which happens in the re-configuration of space. In search for possible spaces and practices of emancipation, we need to potentialize existing spaces and to potentialize existing practices, which amounts to an inventive re-appropriation of the power of commoning.

This text is going to be included in the author's forthcoming book *Common Spaces of Urban Emancipation* (provisional title) to be published by Manchester University Press.

Notes

1   Rancière 2006, p. 12. See also
    Rancière 2010, p. 36.
2   Bourdieu 1977 and Bourdieu 2000.
3   Stavrides 2016a, pp. 209-227.
4   Richter 2007, p. 25.
5   Virno 2009, pp. 98-99.
6   Virno 2015, pp. 23-26.
7   Agamben 2000, p. 84.
8   Agamben 1993.
9   Braun 2013, p. 174.
10 Agamben 2014, p. 69.
11 Agamben 2000, p. 60.
12 Ibid., p. 117.
13 Agamben 2014, p. 73.
14 Virno 2015, p. 87.
15 Ibid., p. 88.
16 Ibid, author's italics.
17 Agamben 2007, p. 2.
18 See Lefebvre's discussion on 'abstract
    space' in Lefebvre 1991, pp. 50-53.
19 Lefebvre 1996, pp. 173-174.
20 Agamben 2014, p. 69.
21 Ibid., p. 70.
22 Deladurantaye 2000, p. 22.
23 Virno 2015, p. 186-187.
24 Ibid., p. 120.
25 Benjamin 1992, p. 255.
26 Ibid., p. 252.
27 Ibid., p. 247.
28 Virno 2015, p. 144 note.
29 See Breines 1982, a work in which the
    term prefigurative politics was
    introduced, and Van de Sande 2017.
30 Holloway 2002, p. 153-154.
31 Quoted in Van de Sande 2013, p. 232.
32 Stavrides 2016, p. 82.
33 Porto-Gonçalves and Leff 2015, p. 86.
34 Sassen 2014.
35 Reyes 2015, p. 421.

Literature

— Agamben, Giorgio. 1993. *The Coming Community*. Minneapolis, MI: University of Minnesota.
—. 2000. *Means without End: Theory Out of Bound*. Minneapolis, MI: University of Minnesota.
—. 2007. 'The Work of Man.' In *Giorgio Agamben: Sovereignty and Life*. Edited by Matthew Calarco and Steven DeCaroli, pp. 1-10. Stanford, CA: Stanford University Press.
—. 2014. 'What is Destituent Power?' *Environment and Planning D: Society and Space* no. 32, pp. 65-74.

— Benjamin, Walter. 1992. 'Theses on the Philosophy of History.' In *Illuminations*. London: Pimlico.

— Bourdieu, Pierre. 1977. *Outline of a Theory of Practice*. Cambridge, MA: Cambridge University Press.
—. *Pascalian Meditations*. Stanford, CA: Stanford University Press 2000.

— Braun, Nahum. 2013. 'The Modality of Sovereignty: Agamben and the Aporia of Primacy in Aristotle's Metaphysics Theta.' *Mosaic* 46, no. 1 (March), pp. 169-182.

— Breines, Wini. 1982. *The Great Refusal: Community and Organization in the New Left: 1962-1968*. New York: Praeger.

— Deladurantaye, Leland. 2000. 'Agamben's Potential.' *Diacritics* 30, no. 2 (Summer), pp. 3-24.

— Holloway, John. 2002. *Change the World Without Taking Power: The Meaning of Revolution Today*. London: Pluto Press.

— Lefebvre, Henri. 1991. *The Production of Space*. Oxford: Wiley-Blackwell.
—. 1996. *Writings on Cities*. Oxford: Wiley-Blackwell.

— Porto-Gonçalves, Carlos Walter, and Enrique Leff. 2015. 'Political Ecology in Latin America: The Social Re-Appropriation of Nature, the Reinvention of Territories and the Construction of an Environmental Rationality.' *Desenvolvimento e Meio Ambiente* vol. 35, pp. 65-88.

— Rancière, Jacques. 2006. *The Politics of Aesthetics*. London: Continuum.
—. 2010. *Dissensus: On Politics and Aesthetics*. London: Bloomsbury Academic.

— Reyes, Alvaro. 2015. 'Zapatismo: Other Geographies circa "The End of the World".' *Environment and Planning D: Society and Space* vol. 33, pp. 408-424.

— Richter, Gerard. 2007. *Thought-Images: Frankfurt School Writers' Reflections from Damaged Life*. Stanford, CA: Stanford University Press.

— Sande, Mathijs van de. 2013. 'The Prefigurative Politics of Tahrir Square: An Alternative Perspective on the 2011 Revolutions.' *Res Publica* no. 19, pp. 223-239.
—. 2017. 'The Prefigurative Power of the Common(s).' In *Perspectives on Commoning: Autonomist Principles and Practices*. Edited by Guido Ruivenkamp and Andy Hilton. London: Zed Books.

— Sassen, Saskia. 2014. *Expulsion: Brutality and Complexity in the Global Economy*. Cambridge MA, 2014.

— Stavrides, Stavros. 2016a. *Common Space: The City as Commons*. London: Zed Books.
—. 2016b. 'Toward an Architecture of Commoning.' *ASAP Journal* 1, no. 1 (January), pp. 77-94.

— Virno, Paolo. 2009. 'Anthropology and Theory of Institutions.' In *Art and Contemporary Critical Practice. Reinventing Institutional Critique*. Edited by Gerald Raunig and Gene Ray, pp. 95-112. London: MayFlyBooks.
—. 2015. *Déjà Vu and the End of History*. London: Verso.

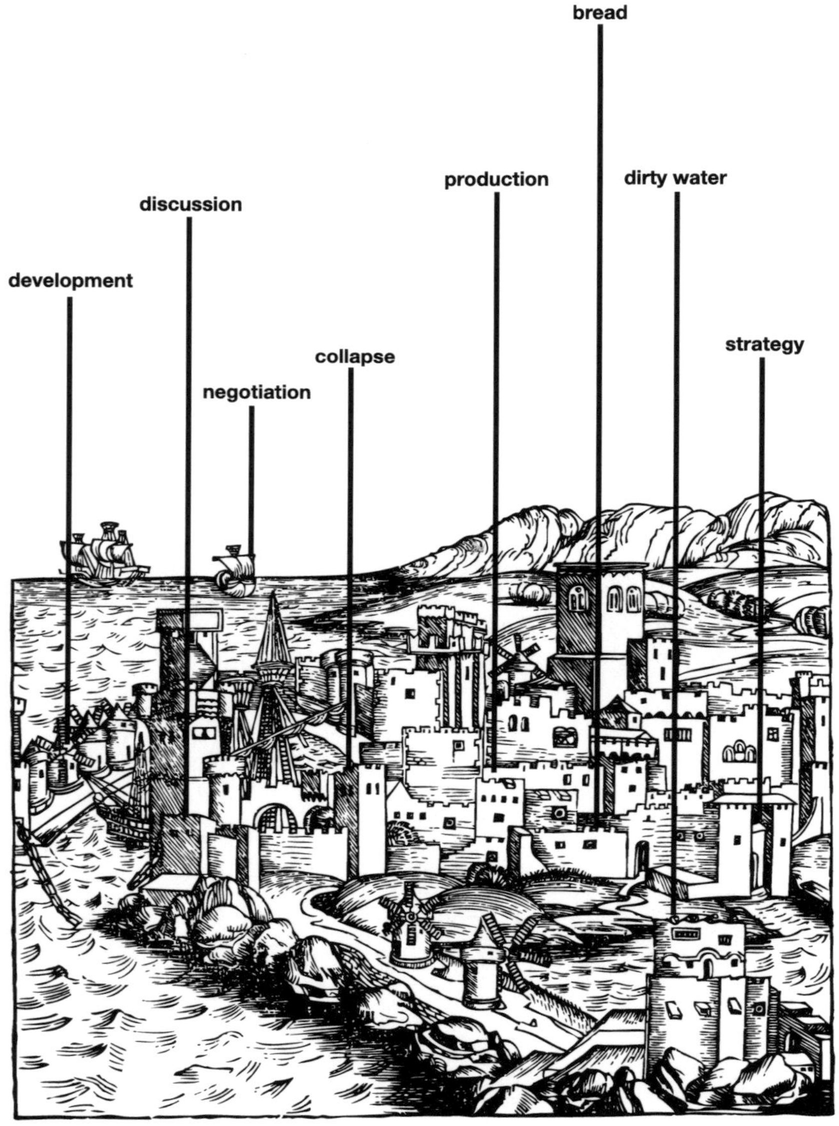

Development Discussion Negotiation Collapse, Thames & Hudson, 2012

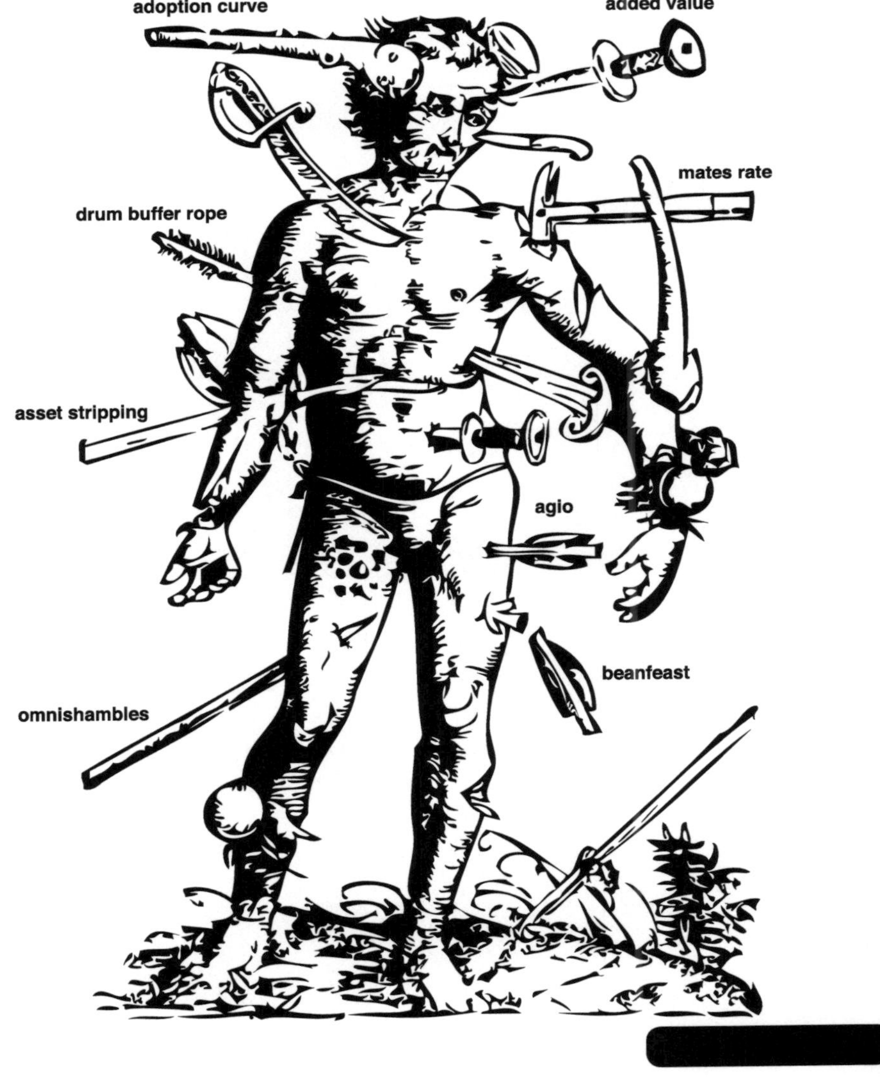

Man stabbed by rhetoric, Locust Projects, 2013

Building Bridges
Art as a Space for Rehearsal

Jörn Schafaff

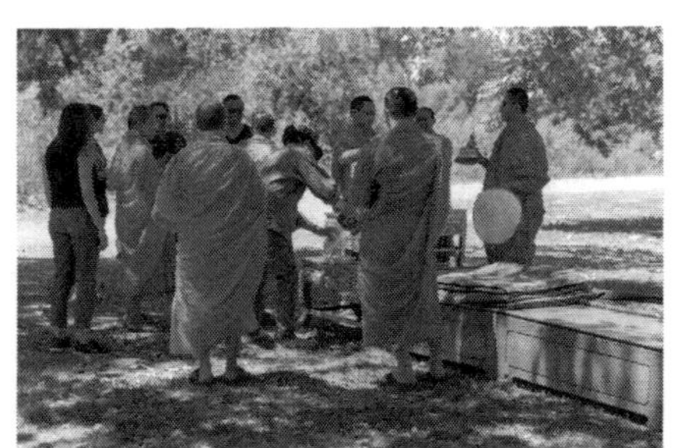

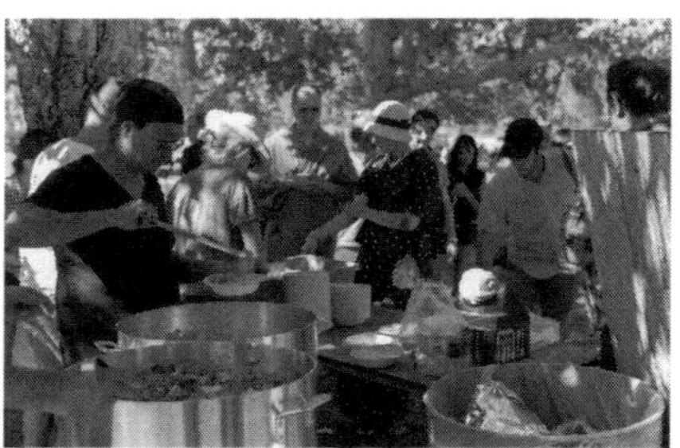

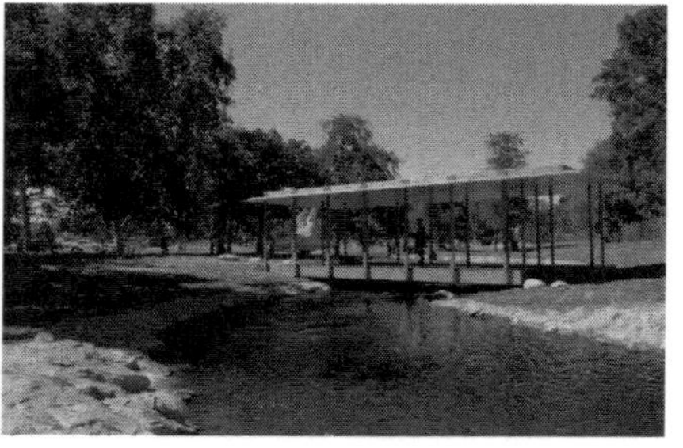

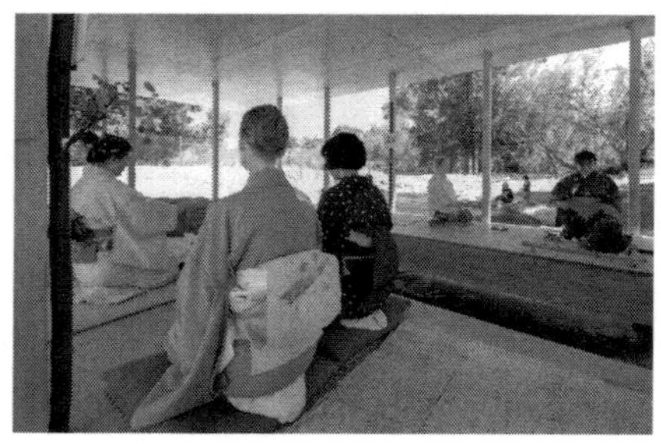

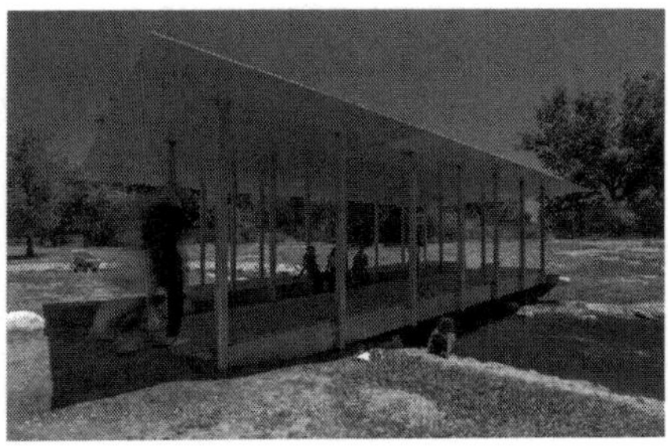

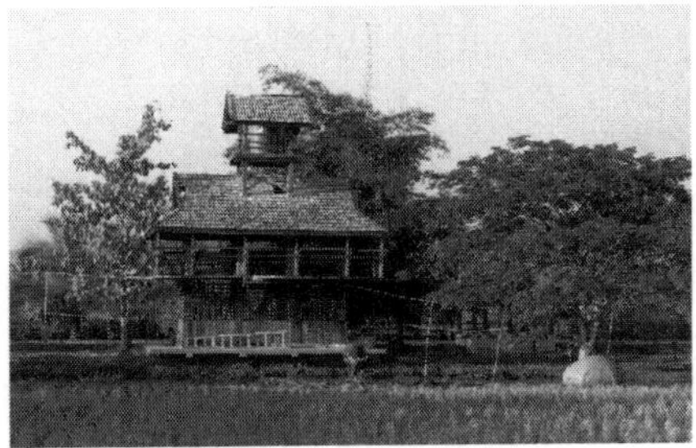

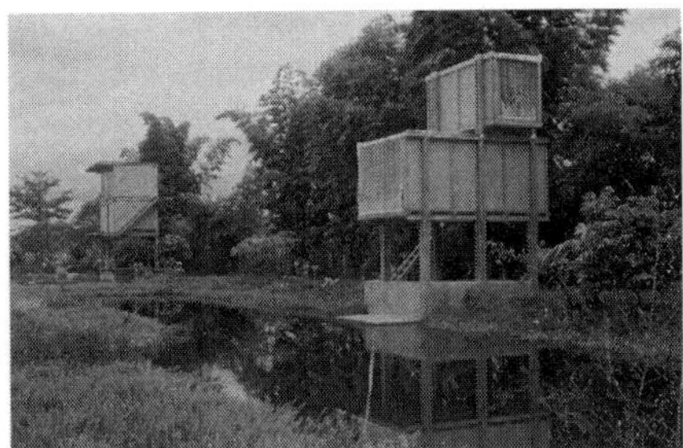

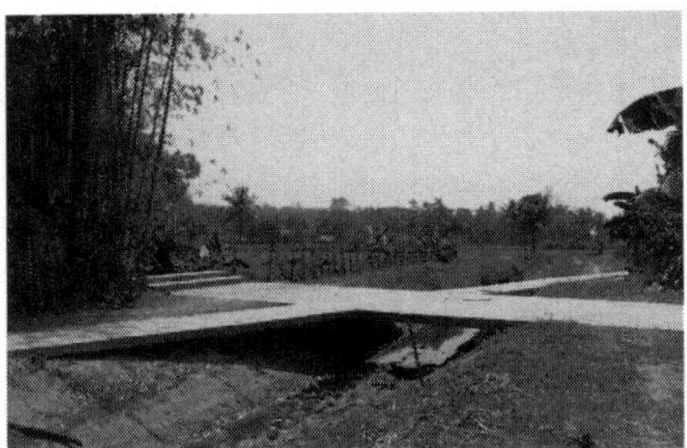

— Rirkrit Tiravanija, *untitled 2016 (LA water, water pavilion)*, 2016, Khuan Ban Mai blessing ceremony.
— Rirkrit Tiravanija, *untitled 2016 (LA water, water pavilion)*, 2016, Communal event.
— Rirkrit Tiravanija, *untitled 2016 (LA water, water pavilion)*.
— Rirkrit Tiravanija, *untitled 2016 (LA water, water pavilion)*, 2016, Tea Ceremony.
— Rirkrit Tiravanija, *untitled 2016 (LA water, water pavilion)*.
— *the land*, building by Kamin Lertchaiprasert and Superflex biogas system (photo taken in 2004).
— *the land*, buildings by Tobias Rehberger and Rirkrit Tiravanija (photo taken in 2004).
— Nico Dockx, *A 3rd land for the land*, 2017.

On July 17, 2016, a group of nine Buddhist monks appeared in the Sepulveda Basin Recreation Area in Northern Los Angeles. They proceeded to a particularly beautiful spot where the stream running through the park goes down a little waterfall before flowing into the LA River. There, they reached their destination, a curious architectural structure reaching from one bank of the stream to the other. Made from timber, the wooden structure appeared to be serving both as a bridge and as a resting place. Its reduced, minimalist design resembled both Western Modernism and traditional East Asian—or more specifically: Japanese—architecture. In other words, the structure was a hybrid of more than one kind. It was a bridge, it was a pavilion, it was mixing features from different cultures. Besides that, it was also a work of art: Rirkrit Tiravanija's *untitled 2016 (LA water, water pavilion)*.

Artistic practices that aim for direct participation in processes of commoning often operate on the boundary between art and activism, using aesthetic strategies to attain their goals and allocating themselves to the field of art mainly for tactical reasons—as a cultural framework that provides a freedom of action not necessarily granted elsewhere in society. What I would like to suggest, however, is that with respect to the topic of this book one potential of art lies exactly in its remoteness from the elements, circumstances, and actions that form reality. While at first sight the distance that exists between life and art may appear to work counter to what is at stake in commoning—representing a bourgeois idea of culture and thus of a society defined by separation rather than by 'commonism'—it may nonetheless be fertile to consider the reflexive power that this distance may generate. By taking Tiravanija's *untitled 2016 (LA water, water pavilion)* as an example, and by relating it to the *land*, another project the Thai artist has been involved in since the late 1990s, I shall argue in the following for art's potential to provide a space for rehearsal—a space (and a time) to imagine, develop, test and train, but also to question and reject issues of social concern. The bridge/pavilion in Los Angeles was not intended as a contribution to any particular project of commoning, nor was it planned as a model for how processes of commoning should or could be carried out. Yet, it still worked to draw attention to some of the elementary features that are at play when 'the myriad, situated relations and practices of (re)production that exist between people and the manifold resources they rely on'[1] are being shaped into that 'continuous making and remaking of the commons through shared practices.'[2]

Tiravanija is known for works that encourage activities such as eating, drinking, and conversing, but also making music, reading, watching films, contemplating, or resting. These activities usually take place within sets designed by the artist in order to provide scenarios of true-to-life, everyday situations. While on the one hand the activities carried out by the visitors are perfectly real—actually taking place—on the other hand they are framed, not only by the sets, but also by the framework of the exhibitions they are usually situated in. To a large extent, Tiravanija's works rely on the distancing effect provided by the presentational format of exhibition: something is taken out of its context and transferred to another place where it is made accessible in order to be considered in its particularity. In the case of Tiravanija it is not just objects that are exhibited, it is the visitors *making use* of objects. In these *exhibited situations*, use becomes a way of understanding via experiential encounter—an offer and opportunity to rehearse and reflect some of our ways of being in the world—of how we use things in order to relate to who we are and what and who is around us.[3]

What qualifies these exhibited situations as spaces for rehearsal is their theatrical structure. When we think of people handling things and interacting with each other in an institutional framework made for observation, we usually do not think of 'exhibition', but rather of theatre. In art discourse, theatricality has long been identified with a lack of autonomy, with artificiality and manipulation. Theatre was considered the sphere of the spectacle, of that which is not real, therefore irrelevant, and ultimately false.[4] From the perspective of current theatre or drama studies, however, theatricality is seen in a more positive light: Firstly, as an anthropological constant, a cultural practice that can be found in any society. And secondly, as a means to play through and reflect certain aspects of life relevant to a culture beyond the level of the individual. In the broader sense, theatricality is a means to adapt to situations that include other social actors. As Matthias Warstat writes: 'Every actor—be he a professional performer or simply someone acting in the everyday—who wants to adapt to a person opposite, will model or stage his behaviour in a certain way.'[5] In the stricter sense of 'theatre', the 'as if' mode of a theatrical performance allows for a situation to unfold, but without the consequences it would have in reality outside the theatre.[6]

It is from these two aspects of theatricality that the aesthetic and reflexive potential of Tiravanija's work emerges.

In the case of *untitled 2016 (LA water, water pavilion)*, the work was framed by the exhibition 'CURRENT: LA Water', a public art biennial presented by the City of Los Angeles Department of Cultural Affairs Public Art Division. Those who knew about it approached the bridge/pavilion as an exhibit of the biennial and thus knew about its symbolic dimension. To come back to the theatre reference I suggested, they could identify the architectural structure as a set that served as a marker to integrate and thus highlight the environment it was placed in. What happened within this scenery was taking place for real, but in addition gained a theatrical or symbolic dimension. The monks performed a rite for good fortune and prosperity, as part of a Thai housewarming ceremony called 'Khuan Ban Mai' (fig. 1).[7] In Thai culture, the blessing of a new house or building traditionally brings together friends and family. As an equivalent to this, the blessing of the bridge/pavilion was followed by a 'Communal Cooking Event' (fig. 2) for which Tiravanija cooked a Thai curry using water from the stream that had been purified by a solar-powered water purification wagon contributed by *Water One World Solutions*, a 'non-profit committed to providing ... solutions for safe drinking water'.[8] Whoever wanted to help prepare the food was invited to do so, the dishes were given out for free. This means that on the day of the opening of *untitled 2016 (LA water, water pavilion)* two elements that frequently appear in discourses of commoning were performed: the culture of sharing and the enhancement of communal infrastructure that is not guided by profit interest. They were actually happening, while at the same time the framework they were taking place in rendered them the object of the visitors' observation, inviting them to reflect upon their features, means, and meaning.

However, it is quite possible that on that day in July 2016, there were people in the park witnessing the gathering by the bridge/pavilion without knowing that they were looking at something that was part of an exhibition. These people first and foremost experienced something that was unusual to happen in a public park in Northern Los Angeles. Of course, if a random passer-by had joined the ceremony and event they soon would have found out about the artwork character of the situation. What is important, however, is that the distancing effect worked even though there was no obvious indication for either of the framings mentioned above. Far from being dramatic or spectacular, what was going on nonetheless stood out from what is usually expected to happen when visiting a recreational area. In a similar way, the architectural structure crossing the stream differed from the conventional mindset of what a bridge or pavilion is (fig. 3). It was close enough to normal that it was identifiable as either of the two, but at the same time different enough to cause some irritation. For example, it was strange that there was no path leading towards it. In fact, there had been no bridge there before. On one side of the structure, field rocks were placed in such a way that they either invited to sit down on them or to balance on them as one approached the planks. This balancing would eventually initiate a heightened awareness of one's own movements, an awareness that could also be triggered by the little step one had to climb if one ascended the pavilion/bridge. But how was it supposed to be used in the first place? Pavilions are usually made to linger and spend some time in, rather than walk through them. Bridges are made for walking over. How were the users to coordinate these options, not to mention the other usages that were suggested by the biennial organizers in the weeks following the inaugural event? Announced in the biennial programme, a tea ceremony (fig. 4) workshops in mediation and watercolour painting were held, or rather performed. At other times, people would just sit underneath the roof, using the two pathways as benches, finding shelter from the sun and enjoying the flow of the water running underneath (fig. 5).

To sum up, for the second group of people encountering the water pavilion it was the aesthetic and functional difference that potentially caused the distancing effect otherwise provided by the exhibition framework—the difference between *this* pavilion/bridge and the conventional forms and usages of bridges and pavilions that exist in the culture. It was this difference that caused the situation for the visitors; it drew them into an experience that required some orientation with regard to the elements they encountered: Is it a bridge, is it a pavilion? Why does it look like it does?[9] Is it okay to sit down or should I leave room for people who want to cross? If I walk over the planks, won't this make them dirty? How do I coordinate my own interests with those of the others? Things were unclear, not yet resolved, causing those involved to make decisions about how to deal with what they had found. Then again, this also meant there was still room for manoeuvre. In the small space framed and marked by the architectural structure, not everything was determined by the predominant cultural and social order. Situated in a public park, *untitled 2016 (LA water, water pavilion)* therefore also demonstrated an understanding of the public domain as a space that is not closed, that relies on given codes of meaning, use, and behaviour but remains open to change.

In its subtle, basic way, *untitled 2016 (LA water, water pavilion)* or the artistic strategy it exemplified to some extent served as a model not for, but *of* commoning. As John Miller writes, in art discourse 'model' stands for

> an example to be emulated, an ideal, a simplified representation, a particular version of a product. ... All these meanings serve to inflect the specificity of model as a contemporary art form. What activates the word model in art and criticism is its implied intervention in the social order. The model is not an intervention in and of itself. Rather it is the preparation for an intervention.[10]

The situations evoked by the pavilion/bridge certainly did not serve as an ideal in the sense that they represented a perfect way of commoning, an example to be followed. Rather, they were simplified representations of some of the basic processes that are at work when the public domain is being performed in the sense of commoning, namely the coming to terms with the relationship between one's own interests with those of others. Public space, as I understand it, is a cultural and social relationship rather than a given place or site. A zone of encounter and of exchange between social actors, with rules and codes that are performatively reconfirmed—or put into question. The pavilion/bridge practically set the frame for such a zone of encounter. It served as a gathering point where social actors met and by doing so were practically required to negotiate its meaning and use. And while this was taking place for real, the design of the architectural structure, the way the structure was situated, and the programmed activities that took place served to generate what Gregor Stemmrich calls 'Reflexionsdistanz':[11] a distance that lays the ground for a position from which to consciously look at and reflect upon that which one encounters.

A model is the preparation for an intervention—let's take this definition as a point of departure for the second example that I announced in the beginning of this article, the *land*. The first time I visited the *land* was in March 2005. At the time a so called One Year Project was going on, a residency of sorts that involved a group of young artists, most of them from Thailand. The idea of the residency was to test the possibility of actually living on the land while continuing to follow one's own artistic practice.[12] After conversations with the participants I wrote a short text to summarize my impressions:

> Take a sheet of paper.
> Write 'real' on one side.
> Write 'symbolic' on the other side.
> Think of 'real' as of something that actually happens.
> Think of 'symbolic' as of something that happens all the same, but in a staged manner. Don't think too long. Then:
> Write 'art' on one side.
> Write 'social experiment' on the other side.
> Write 'observation' on one side.
> Write 'meditation' on the other side.
> Write 'architecture' on one side.
> Write 'agriculture' on the other side.
> Write 'action' on one side.
> Write 'reflection' on the other side.
> Write 'community' on one side.
> Write 'institution' on the other side.
> Write 'openness' on one side.
> Write 'restriction' on the other side.
> Write 'me' on one side.
> Write 'the other' on the other side.
> Write 'life' on one side.
> Write 'lab rats' on the other side.
> Write 'success' on one side.
> Write 'failure' on the other side.
> Write 'inside' on one side.
> Write 'outside' on the other side.
> Write 'sculpture' on one side.
> Write 'house' on the other side.
> Write 'sustainability' on one side.
> Write 'entropy' on the other side.

Write 'image' on one side.
Write 'process' on the other side.
Fill up the list.
For each term, choose whichever side you like.
Don't write utopia.
Don't forget to look at the thin edge of the sheet of paper.
Now, think of the LAND.[13]

The *land* is an initiative founded by Tiravanija together with his friend Kamin Lertchaiprasert in 1998. The two artists acquired a lot of farmland situated near the village Sanpatong, a few kilometres south of Chiang Mai, Thailand. Stretching over 9600 square metres, the site had been abandoned by the local farmers for its lack of productivity. For Lertchaiprasert and Tiravanija, it was a fertile ground to foster their ideas and visions, as well as those of others who would feel motivated to contribute to the development of the *land* in the years to come. At first, their imagination had been about a desirable form of living together with a group of good friends as they would grow old, one of them being Uthit Atimana, an artist and art instructor at Chiang Mai University who was closely involved in the early development of the project. But then—and maybe as a consequence of the initial considerations—those involved had moved on to conceive the *land* in a less directed way, as a zone of encounter of different interests and practices: 'The land was to be cultivated as an open space, though with certain intentions towards community, towards discussions and towards experimentation in other fields of thoughts.'[14] In order to keep its independence and as a measure to prevent land development, most probably followed by an increase in value of the premises in the area, the founders refused the offer to connect the *land* to the local water, drainage, and power infrastructure.

As one of the first initiatives, two ponds and several smaller pools were laid out according to the ideas of Chaloui Kaewkong, a Thai farmer/agriculturalist who had combined agricultural techniques with Buddhist thought.[15] The *land* became a site for exercising alternative farming methods, mostly carried out by members of the local art community. Another focus was on architecture, starting with the house that Lertchaiprasert designed for the caretaker of the *land*, a peasant farmer from the nearby village who became the only person to live on the lot permanently. In

2000, another house by Lertchaiprasert was erected, a kitchen house conceived as a central gathering place (fig. 6). A biogas system was installed by Danish artists group Superflex. In the same year, the first two 'living units' were contributed by Tiravanija and fellow artist Tobias Rehberger (fig. 7). Associated with traditional Thai architecture in their design, these houses provided basic facilities for an extended stay, i.e. more or less closed rooms for retreating and sleeping.[16] Further units of differing design and function followed, most of them conceived by local and international artists and architects.[17] The latest of these projects is a new residency building designed by German architects Nikolaus Hirsch and Michael Müller. The building is supposed to be the first structure to be erected on an extension of the original lot that was donated by artist Pierre Huyghe. Conceived as a means to provide a new infrastructure for long-term stays at the *land*, the building is planned in a way that new facilities can be added successively, depending on needs and funding.

Even though the *land* is not a project initiated by Tiravanija alone, it nonetheless shares with his artistic approach some of the features that I have sketched above, first and foremost its reflexive structure. This structure relies on two things: a) the difference between what is happening on the *land* and the cultural (and social) conventions it is embedded in; b) its own hybridity. In the beginning, the people in the nearby village were quite alienated by the new activities going on in their vicinity. People from town came rushing in, foreigners visited the site for reasons that were outside the mindset of the villagers' daily life. There was farming going on, but with different methods and not for profit. Instead, the harvested rice was partly divided between the people who took part in the harvesting, partly given to people in need. The houses that were built, but not all, resembled traditional Thai housing architecture and even those differed quite a lot from the normal houses and huts one finds in the region. It was through the caretaker that step by step some sort of understanding could be achieved.

For visitors from outside, it is mainly the hybrid status of the buildings that triggers reflections about what the *land* might actually be or be about. The architectural structures are functional, but only to a certain extent. The fact that most of the structures were contributed by local and international artists emphasizes their sculptural quality, potentially qualifying them

373

as works of art. And whoever you speak with in the Chiang Mai art community will most probably give you a different idea about the *land*'s meaning and use.[18] No matter from which perspective one approaches the *land*, it defies unification under one label. Not least, this also holds for the question whether it would best be perceived as an intervention or a preparation for an intervention in the social order—as a model, or even a model for commoning. Just as the bridge/pavilion of *untitled 2016 (LA water, water pavilion)* it was neither conceived as an intervention nor as a model for commoning in total. But in a similar way, there are certain aspects that resonate with both attributions.

Some of the ideas and activities on the *land* point to its model qualities and some of them bear close relationships to the realm of commoning: the communal aspects of the housing/ working trajectory, for example, the structure and appearance of most of the houses themselves, the experimental character of the farming, and the collective efforts to cultivate the terrain without profit.[19] Separated from their environment, they are not meant to intervene in the predominant cultural, social, economic, or political order directly. From the perspective of the villagers, however, the inauguration of the *land* certainly was most probably experienced as an intervention in the normalcy of their social life, despite—or because of—the fact that they hardly ever got directly affected by what was going on there. Then again, it was not an intervention in the public domain, simply because it was confined to private property.

In fact, the property issue may well be one of the most revealing aspects of the *land* with respect to the issue of commoning. Initially, the founders had conceived it to be an entity without ownership, meaning that there was no-one claiming authorship and no institutional body that served as an identifiable legal subject. In practice, all financial transactions were executed via Lertchaiprasert's private account. In 2003, however, the tax-related and other legal difficulties deriving from this approach led to the establishment of the *land foundation*.[20] Basically an institution without capital, the foundation has since then taken on the role of legal and organizational representative and public 'face' of the *land*. In terms of financing and development, though, the initial regulations are still the same. Anyone can make suggestions for the *land,* but for a project to be realized one has to take on full responsibility regarding financing, production, and maintenance.

For other requirements, the foundation is dependent on individual donations and incidental fund raising.

One example: After Pierre Huyghe had bought the roughly 4900 square metre lot of land next to the original site in 2006, he donated it to the foundation and thereby provided a new blank space in which the idea of the *land* could be extended, but also re-thought and started over again. In reaction to this, Nico Dockx, the co-editor of this volume, started to plan *A 3rd land for the land*—a bridge over the small stream that separates the old and the new lot and is flanked by two field paths used by the farmers of the surrounding rice fields (fig. 8).[21] This project marked a novelty as it was the first artistic/architectural project that was not located on the premises of the foundation, but rather on public ground. Therefore, Dockx decided to systematically involve the local community in the design process, an undertaking without precedent in the history of the *land*. Via the caretaker he managed to get in contact with children from other local farmers in Sanpatong and— together with artist Helena Sidiropoulos—organized workshops for them that dealt with their ideas and imaginations regarding the bridge. This then brought him into contact with the farmers who owned and worked on the farmland around where the bridge was to be located. As it turned out, they welcomed the bridge as a means to facilitate access to their fields. This in turn met with one of the central preconditions that Dockx had had in mind from the outset: that the structure would have a practical use not only for the *land* but also for the local community. Ultimately, he designed the bridge as a hybrid of a path to get from one side of the stream to the other and a place for gathering—herein similar to Tiravanija's bridge/pavilion in Los Angeles. Financed via friends from his personal network, it was built by people from the village who had been hired by a local contractor.[22] Even before its official inauguration, which was supposed to take place around Spring 2018, the process of appropriating the bridge for all kinds of purposes unconsidered in the design process has started to unfold as local farmers are planning to use the bridge as a platform to dry their freshly harvested rice. Dockx himself is working on the idea to organize film screenings there in close collaboration with Thai filmmaker Apichatpong Weerasethakul.

Arguably, *A 3rd land for the land* is the one project realized in relation to the *land* that is closest to what is usually meant by the notion of 'commoning'. Situated in the public domain, involving communal dialogue in its development process, and at least partly intended to permanently improve the local infrastructure, it is an example of how aesthetic strategies can be helpful in organizing processes of common interest. Unlike *untitled 2016 (LA water, water pavilion)* it provides a model not only in the sense of 'a simplified representation' *of* commoning processes, but also in the sense of 'an example to be emulated'—especially the process of the realization of the bridge can be recognized as a model *for* commoning. However, its model character differs from the definition suggested by Miller. Both the bridge and its creation were direct interventions in the local reality, not just preparations. This, in turn, takes us back to the beginning of this article, namely to the distinction between art using aesthetic strategies for activist goals and art as a space for rehearsal. Miller's definition of the term 'model' implies exactly that distance that I introduced as a precondition for art's reflexive potential. Consequently, it could be argued that the way that it is woven into reality makes *A 3rd land for the land* a powerful example of artistic activism, but not so much a powerful instrument for aesthetic reflection. On the other hand, with its form resembling a distorted cross the bridge shows a sculptural quality that goes way beyond mere utility. Even if Tiravanija's bridge was, literally, more outstanding in this respect (it stood out visually from its environment), the design by Dockx introduces a difference that might potentially trigger reflections about the conditions and meaning of the bridge and its uses. Just like the water pavilion in Los Angeles, the hybridity of the linking structure in between the old and the new premises of the *land* creates an openness that requires those using it to consider the consequences of their actions in relation to the interests of others. By way of conclusion I would hence like to suggest that, despite of their obvious differences in appearance and orientation, both *A 3rd land for the land* and *untitled 2016 (LA water, water pavilion)* are remarkable examples of what I intended to bring into the discussion of art and commoning: examples of art providing a space of rehearsal.

Notes

1   Patrick Bresnihan, 'The More-Than-Human-Commons: From Commons to Commoning', in *Space, Power,* and the *Commons: The Struggle for Alternative Futures*, eds. Samuel Kirwan, Leila Dawney, and Julian Brigstocke (Abingdon and New York: Routledge, 2016), pp. 93–112, p. 95.

2   Ibid., p. 96.

3   There exist numerous catalogues and articles about Tiravanija's work. For a recent detailed study of the situational aspects of his work see Jörn Schafaff, *Rirkrit Tiravanija: Set, Szenario, Situation, Werke 1987–2005 (Set Scenario Situation. Works 1987–2005)* (Cologne: Walther König, 2018).

4   The most influential text in this respect still is Michael Fried, 'Art and Objecthood', *Artforum* June 1967, reprinted in Gregory Battock, ed., *Minimal Art: A Critical Anthology* (New York: Dutton, 1968), pp. 116–147.

5   Matthias Warstat, 'Von der Pflicht, Schauspieler zu sein—Darstellung und gesellschaftliche Disziplinierung', in *Schauspielen heute: Die Bildung des Menschen in den performativen Künsten*, eds. Jens Roselt and Christel Weiler (Bielefeld: transcript, 2011), p. 205.

6   Josette Féral, 'Theatricality: The Specificity of Theatrical Language', *SubStance* Issue 98/99 (Vol. 31, no. 2-3), 2002, pp. 94–108.

7   For this event and the further programme taking place as part of *untitled 2016 (LA water, water pavilion)* see www.currentla.org/artists/rirkrit-tiravanija/ (accessed 17 November 2017). The monks came from Wat Thai, a nearby Buddhist temple. With their presence, they represented some of the diversity of the neighbourhood in which the park is located. Site-related elements that en passant heighten the awareness for the broader context the visitors find themselves in are common features of Tiravanija's art.

8   www.currentla.org/water-purification-wagon-demonstrations/ (accessed 17 November 2017). See also the website of the organization http://wateroneworldsolutions.org/.

9   According to Tiravanija, the architectural structure was modelled after a pavilion that Tiravanija had seen in the Okayama Korakuen Park in Okayama, Japan. Cf. Neil Logan, 'Rirkrit Tiravanija', *Dizzy* Spring 2017, 35ff. Apart from the difference in size, the main difference between the original pavilion and the structure in Los Angeles was that the former does not serve as a bridge. Called *'Ryuten Rest House'*, it was designed for resting only. The seating areas on the ground floor are located on each side of the stream running through the middle of the building.

10   John Miller, 'Modell/Model', in *Kunst Begriffe der Gegenwart*, eds. Jörn Schafaff, Nina Schallenberg, and Tobias Vogt (Cologne: Walter König, 2013), pp. 193–197, p. 193.

11   Gregor Stemmrich, 'Liam Gillick: Eine Debatte über das Debattieren', *Parkett* May 2001, pp. 64–76, p. 64.

12   The programme also included meditation courses and discussions, which took place at Umong Art Center, located within the city limits of Chiang Mai. Consisting of a building for exhibitions and seminars and a meditation pavilion, it had been established by Lertchaiprasert in 2001. Umong Art Center also hosted the office of the Land Foundation after it had been established in 2003. The office was later moved to other premises in the city.

13   Originally, the text was intended as a contribution to the art project of one of the participants. He had decided to ask each external visitor to the land to send him a commentary. In 2015, it was published in Rirkrit Tiravanija et al., eds., *Do We Dream Under the Same Sky* (Berlin: Sternberg Press, 2015), pp. 60–61.

14   www.thelandfoundation.org/about (accessed 21 November 2017).

15   On the website of the Land Foundation it says that the 'ideas around the cultivation of the topography which is 1/4 earth (mass) and 3/4 water (liquid), is based on the composition of the human body'. Ibid. The farming methods were partly derived from Masanobu Fukuoka, *The One-Straw Revolution: An Introduction to Natural Farming* (Emmaus: Rodale Press, 1978) (jap. 1975). Cf. Nikolaus Hirsch and Rirkrit Tiravanija, 'The Land', in *Do We Dream Under the Same Sky*, eds. Rirkrit Tiravanija, et al. (Berlin: Sternberg Press, 2015), pp. 16–21, p. 17.

16   Especially in Northern Thailand down to the Bangkok area, houses

would traditionally be built on
pedestals, assuring protection from
the regular floods and providing
shade for the inhabitants in the
outside area underneath the structure
in which much of social life takes
place.

17   Angkrit Ajchariyasophon, Mit-Jai
Inn, Philippe Parreno and François
Roche, Carl Michael von Hausswolff,
Tobias Rehberger, Somyot Hananun-
tasuk and Thaivijt
Poengkasemsomboon, Markus
Heinsdorff and Suwan Laimanee.

18   Cf. Claire Bishop's report about her
conversations with Kamin Lertchaip-
rasert, Rirkrit Tiravanija and Uthit
Atimana in Jennifer Roche, 'Socially
Engaged Art, Critics, and
Discontents: An Interview with Claire
Bishop', in *Artistic Bedfellows:
Histories, Theories, and Conversations
in Collaborative Art Practices*, ed. Holly
Crawford (Lanham, MD: University
Press of America, 2008), pp. 202–209,
p. 208ff.

19   As Paphonsak La-or reported during
the 'Making Public Domain' summer
school in Antwerp in September 2017,
there are frequent visits from
university classes in art, architecture,
and agriculture who take the land as a
case study, most of them coming from
universities in Thailand.

20   As in most other countries, it is
impossible in Thailand for a piece of
Land not to be owned by some legal
subject. The foundation was an
attempt to keep ownership away from
individual actors, and still meet the
legal requirements of the administration.

21   Thank you Nico Dockx for
information about the project and its
process.

22   In order to raise the money, Dockx
divided a steel model of the bridge
into 60 parts which were sold for
€ 900 (excluding VAT) each. Buyers
opting in received the unique object
and a certificate signed by Dockx,
delivered in a specially designed
packaging. Furthermore, they
received a copy of a limited book
edition documenting the building
process after completion. *A 3rd land
for the land foundation*, dossier for
crowd-funding written and designed
by Nico Dockx, 7 pp.

Organizational Aesthetics and Emotional Infrastructure

Nomeda &
Gediminas Urbonas

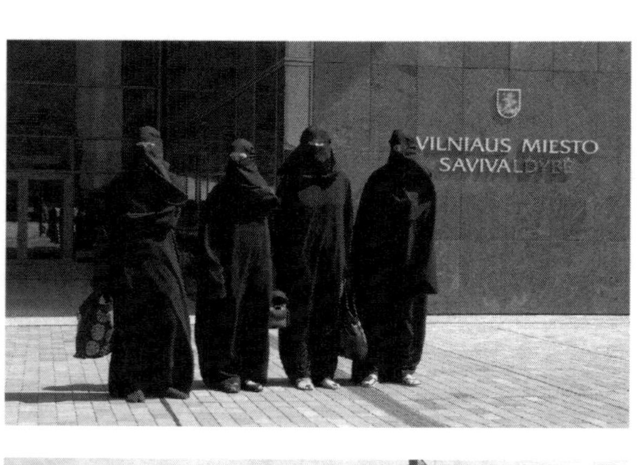
VILNIAUS MIESTO
SAVIVALDYBĖ

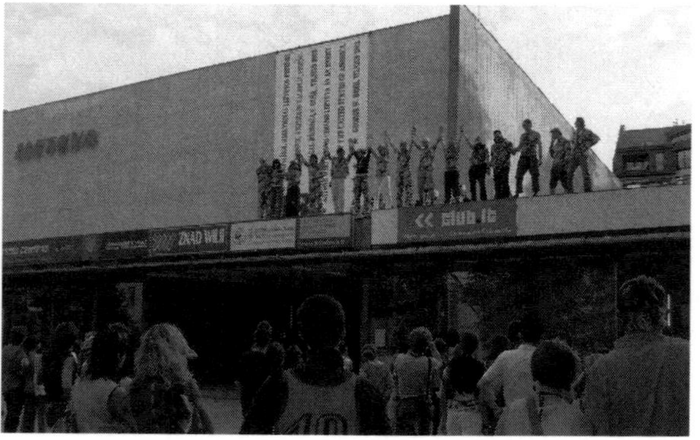
ZNAD WILII
club 16

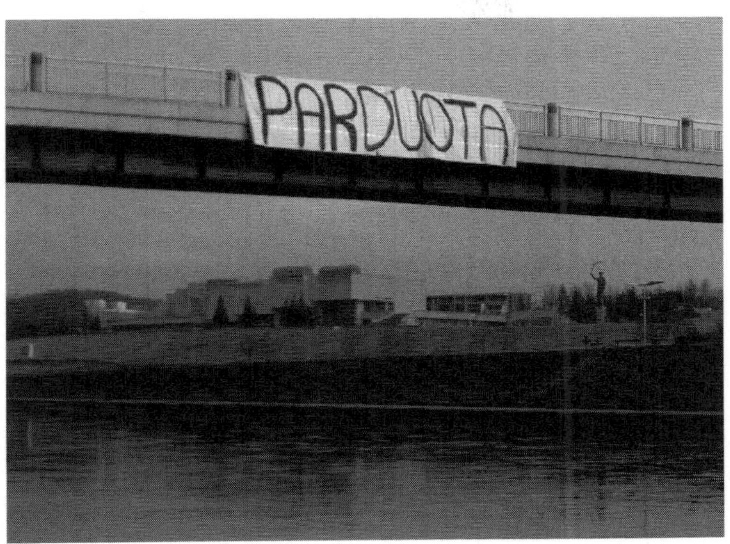

— Pro-test Lab actions, against
  privatization, property development
  and demolition, Vilnius LT
— Pro-test Lab action in front of the
  cinema Lietuva, organized by ASK,
  Vilnius LT, 2005
— Pro-test Lab action, Sold out, poster
  action in public spaces, Vilnius LT, 2005

This essay focuses on a case study: The Pro-test Lab, a project that started as a call to reclaim public space in Lithuania and, in particular, to bring art, fiction, and speculation as devices to question destruction of cultural and public monuments, in this case the largest cinema in Vilnius from being demolished. With overlapping artistic and social components, this art experiment was developed into a multi-layered and multi-year organizational structure, addressing memory, trauma and emotion attached to public space. It combined public discussions, exhibitions, media channels, performances, an educational programme, a series of petitions, and even several lawsuits aimed at challenging existing policies, culminating in laws in territorial planning being rewritten and in questioning a collective definition of public space. By investigating artistic form and methodology, this essay investigates the forces constituting organizational aesthetics without which *commoning*[1] and cohabitation of space would not be possible.

Structures of Feeling
The Pro-test Lab was set in motion in 2005, with the initial statement that protest is impossible. Already in the sixties, urban theorist Jane Jacobs and later, in the eighties, sociologist Sharon Zukin both observed unjust developments in cities, critically addressing privatization, gentrification, and corporatization of public space as trends that dehumanize and abstract urban space. Regardless of the symptoms of civic crisis provoked by the processes of globalization—such as Occupy Gezi in Istanbul (May 2013), the Husby riots in Stockholm (May 2013), and the Occupy movement and Zuccotti Park (2011–2012)—the 'contemporary left tends towards a folk politics that is incapable of turning the tide against global capitalism' (Srnicek and Williams 2015, p. 85). In their book *Inventing the Future: Postcapitalism and a World Without Work* (2015) Nick Srnicek and Alex Williams question the lack of a utopian dimension in protests:

> The numerous protests and marches and occupations typically operate without any sense of strategy, simply acting as dispersed and independent blips of resistance. There is far too little thought given to how to combine these various actions, and how they might function together to collectively build a better world. Instead we are left with actions that sometimes succeed but which rarely have an

overarching eye to how this contributes to medium and long-term goals. (Srnicek and Williams 2015, p. 49)

If these claims would have been brought up twelve years earlier during the Pro-test Lab, they could have polemicized our invented artistic, experimental, and performative forms of protest, laying the grounds for a new subjectivity and politics. This is especially true given the particular context of a post-Soviet condition where social and political bonds had been dismantled and where new forms of speculation on an alternative political imagination became possible.

Therefore the question of self-organization was crucial in this new situation where the common goods seemed to be reduced to individual and private interests as they transitioned to becoming privately owned and managed individually. What is the role of art in this time of transition, what are the new forms of organization that aesthetics may set in motion? Does art have a role in these new forms, and can artists conceive of organizational forms that reflect on the *form of life* (*Lebensform*)[2] in such a time of uncertainty? Could an organizational aesthetics emerge as an attempt to understand the form of life and commonalities beyond a shared language?

Organizational aesthetics is an aesthetic practice that engages the structuring of the public sphere by questioning and challenging the relative autonomy of art and simultaneously interrogating representations of reality. Lauren Berlant (2011) argues for aesthetic interventions to structure a public sphere dominated by emotions and affects, sentiments, and feelings of hope and fear rather than colloquial reasoning. To borrow from her, organizational aesthetics could be related to public spheres that 'are always affect worlds, worlds to which people are bound ... by affective projections of a constantly negotiated common interestedness.'

Alluding to *Lebensform* may help to articulate organizational aesthetics as a hybrid, non-representational network of complex relationships that unfolds in time, between tangible and intangible objects, spheres and contexts. To understand the form of such relations, we suggest a hypothetical model of 'emotional infrastructure'. Here the concept of 'structures of feeling' could be useful as a device to understand the inner dynamic of an emergent narrative formation 'that could be only sensed as a trajectory'. As Raymond Williams argued, it is not a language, but an intervention—perhaps an artistic one—on an articulation in becoming:

> As thought is described, in the same habitual past tense, it is so different, in its explicit and finished forms, from much or even anything that we can presently recognize as thinking, that we can set against more active, more flexible, less singular terms—consciousness, experience, feeling—and then watch even these drawn towards fixed, finite, receding forms... It is also that the making of art is never itself in a past tense. It is always a formative process within a specific present. (Williams 1977)

Unlike energy, transportation, telecommunication, water supply, sewerage and other fixed and conventional types of infrastructure, emotional infrastructure would draw on elusive patterns, suggesting hybridity, an assemblage of living elements that are in search for alternatives to the brutal rationale of economy; it could model cultural and critical forms of civic engagement, build on the senses, on memory, human rights, dignity, safety, and certainty. There is an urgency for utopian claims in these dystopian times, as Srnicek and Williams suggest. Thus, such a hypothetical infrastructure would carry with it implications of play (disinterested play, or play without the promise of a reward, as Richard Sennett (2008) has described), exercise, and experimentation. Furthermore, these practices would come with and through artistic forms of non-violent social, cultural, and disruptive engagement as complex systems that are alternatives to formal planning and city development.

Reassembling Civic Infrastructure
Where is that utopia of 'grand civic space', that transitional object, providing an experience of security and of social ideals, whether in the West or in the East? One may consider its embodiment in architecture of the public brutalist buildings that themselves are witnesses to a paradox of public space. On the one hand they protest against conventions of hegemony of traditional society bringing social and collective concerns to the fore, and on the other they impose a hegemony of a global techno-cultural modernism. As the demolition of the Pruitt-Igoe social housing projects marked the start of a decline of social attitudes in 1970s

America, the dismantling of the social in the East Bloc countries was launched with the fall of the Berlin wall, followed by the privatization of cultural and recreational buildings and sites of civic culture. Once factories for the production of affect and collective memory, the cultural halls and art house cinemas, were turned into sites for real estate speculation. Planes of culture were subverted into entertainment industries, casinos, shops, or supermarkets. An overriding interest in the economy and consumerism rendered a new type of homogenized buildings, places, and activities that radically denied *differential* space (Lefebvre 1992), and through a process of abstraction, replaced forms of culture and civic engagement. This leads to a change of values—to a type of citizenship and belonging in the neoliberal era.

Stripping down the modernist facades and interiors as carriers of past promises of progressive life and erasing once evocative titles alluding to a radical inhabitation of space, such as Cosmos, Planet, Star, Victory, or Pioneer, the privatizers of post-Soviet Lithuania not only took over the tangible or measurable—blocks of concrete and square footage—but also something that is intangible: emotions and attachment. The last and the most symbolic one, cinema Lietuva in Vilnius, survived until 2002 when it was privatized upon the condition that its function would be kept for three more years. Built in 1965 as the most modern film screening facility of its time, it was named after the country and without a Soviet overtone. Privatized by the VP Market group, a notorious holding company in the Baltics that owns the Lithuanian supermarket chain Maxima, the cinema became the breaking point in the battlefield of privatization. The new imaginary that Maxima evokes with their most expressive constructions such as the Maxima Pyramid, the Acropolis, and the Hermitage refer to the symbols of past imperial infrastructures built on slavery, creating a paradigmatic shift in existing urban landscapes. The titles that allude to supposedly exotic destinations not only eject the 'grey Soviet monsters of the past', or the very promise of the future, but also the collective experience of time and place, and thus of collective commonality. If the inhabitation of the universe was a collective promise, it is clear that exclusive destinations are accommodating only a wealthy few.

This spatial contrast accelerated with an architecture of disaster. In 2013, one of the Maxima supermarkets in Riga collapsed, killing 54 civilians.[3] The reasons were mundane: these pyramid shopping worlds are developed within dynamics of the 'systemic edge' where privatization and deregulation push people out, even to death. To paraphrase Saskia Sassen (2014), extraction and expulsion bring diverse systems to bear on daily life: economic, social, and in terms of biosphere. Spaces of expulsion call for the importance of 'making visible' their enabling processes—deregulation and financialization—which are allowed to thrive, thanks in great part to their impenetrably complex 'subterranean' nature. The 'systemic edge' as a new value system is assembling to overwrite a past framed as 'backward-looking' and totalitarian.

Under the Soviet totalitarian regime film was considered a superior art. Leaders saw the power of cinema to shape minds and opinions. Cinema theatres without doubt had the function of distributing ideology. However, regimes of governmentality are not necessarily completely in control. Spaces (of affect) can slip out of control, and this slippage is the space of carnivalesque opening possibilities for shifts to happen. A reinterpretation of the cinema and its role in culture was as important for the Pro-test Lab as an attempt to introject a notion of 'differential space' and thus produce a space of possibility and imagination. (Lefebvre 1992)

In Spring 2005, once Maxima's intentions of closing the cinema became apparent, there was not a single person asking why, let alone a voice of protest. Provoked by the absence of dissent and protest voicing, a few artists and activists met in the cinema. From there the initiative of the artistic project was launched, to intervene in the annual film festival and to ask the audience if they were aware of the fact the cinema would be closed and, if so, why were they silent.

Producing (Pro-test) Space

In his invocation for the 'production of space', philosopher Henri Lefebvre (1992) criticizes the abstraction of space that (through the 'representation of space') homogenizes buildings, places, and activities and denies 'differential' space that celebrates bodily and experiential place, as well as a non-negotiable 'right to difference'.

The Pro-test Lab engaged several groups of cinema lovers, heritage activists, militant journalists, and other autonomous movements[4] asking them a bold question: What could a protest scenario possibly be? Launched in a pre-Facebook era, where social media was yet in the 'proto' stage, it had to be run through an email list reaching out to 400 members discussing how to organize. The Pro-test Lab negotiated access to the ticket office by making an agreement with the management of the privatized cinema. This first meeting founded the citizens' movement For Lietuva without Quotation Marks.[5] This movement assembled an eclectic group driven by the urgency of radical alternatives where heritage protection martyrs were challenging a pseudo-historical vision of the planners, while anarchists and vegans insisted on ruins and composting. In this case, the Soviet brutalist building that epitomizes ideology became the centre of the battle to sustain memory.

The cinema Lietuva, located on the edge of the old town, is in an area under UNESCO heritage protection that safeguards the visual links between the old baroque city and its surrounding hills covered in pine trees. The developer's plans to demolish the cinema and build a higher building would obstruct the 'viewshed', interfere with the vistas between environment and architecture, and would be seen as a violation of UNESCO heritage.

Besides those concerned with heritage protection, there was a variety of interest groups and individuals in search of their own space, identity, and forms of organizing: students from architecture, film and theatre schools, new-left activists and neighbours concerned with new development. The cinema, then, was no longer only a site of projection, but also a site of production of protest, similar to the Lumière brothers' first camera, which had the capacity to both film and project. The Pro-test Lab articulated the cinema building as an apparatus that could record and project its own protest.

In 2005, just twelve years after being liberated from a totalitarian regime, people in Lithuania had difficulty protesting. On the one hand, protest was seen as a slippery territory that some would not like to be associated with—mass media perpetuated a demonized image of rebellions in their broadcasts showing cars being burned and windows being smashed in various places of the world. On the other hand, recent memories of a totalitarian past of compulsory participation in the state organized celebrations, demonstrations, and parades still haunted personal experience. Discussing how rules of language choreograph the personal and the collective, and how punctuation conditions politics of memory, members of the movement came with the proposal of double agency: to insert a hyphen between 'pro' and 'test'. The hyphen is a mark of punctuation, as a use of spacing and a typographical device, and as an aid to understanding and correct reading—both silently and aloud. It became a proposition for the 'pro-test'—that is not to be against someone or somebody, but instead to be pro-active, it is an agent, it is 'for'. This double agency carries with it an invitation to a space, a laboratory to test the possibility of protest, to test the forms of protest, and ultimately to prototype protest.

The regulation of space during this time was proliferating. How could we develop so-called 'devices for action' that could create room between the manifold rules and regulations that safeguard access to public space and define the allowable presence of bodies and their assemblies? One has to work within the economy of bureaucracy and administration, accelerating it and making its precarity even more apparent by engaging it, exposing it, and working with it. To get permission for a protest was almost impossible. But to get permission for a film, a performance of protest, was viable. Slipping into a territory less defined by the law, finding cracks in legislation, and using the double agency of art is a way to carve a path, a trajectory towards the space of potentiality.

The Pro-test Lab was programmed as a media space, developing several zones that would each render their protest scenarios and contribute to a broadcasting of events, accepting artists in the role of editors of encounters, or as facilitators and curators of others. The group of young architecture students (ASK) developed a Monopoly-like game for the street where participants could buy and sell any public site of Vilnius, including the cinema Lietuva, and debate the privatization of the city. Vegans would create spaces of togetherness by testing alternative recipes without a big interest in privatization issues or the cinema per se, as they were just in search for a space where they could imagine alternative eating habits in the city. Musicians and sound artists joining the Pro-test Lab contributed to the radical extremes including the production of a 'festival of the worst bands in the country'. Everyone was welcome to come and perform 'for Lietuva'—a play of meanings, as Lietuva means not only the cinema but also the name of the entire country. Some of the groups were so bad that one had to think twice about having them perform there. Was there an agreement by reasoning? Perhaps not. It was lived experience of accepting contradictions, of adapting to something like 'agonistic space', as Chantal Mouffe (2007) has coined. The contradictions accelerated towards conflict as anarchists using the space would leave a mess while designers confronted them by insisting on responsibilities. Ad hoc calls for events and announcements for public gatherings disgusted the designers as they saw a lack of protest identity or spirit of revolution. The radical left, formed in the clandestine movements of the Free University, might address such a situation in despair: 'Look, these designers are impossible, they're demanding to frame our spaces, to design and package our feelings, while we are trying to build the spirit of rebellion and dissent.' In its radical form, the Pro-test Lab had to embrace the condition of living with contradictions and allow for protesting against the protesters and itself.

A model of collectively produced system as in Peter Watkins' making of *La Commune* (2000) was discussed at the time as the Pro-test Lab was looking at how the various parts could yet cohabitate in the space. They saw that they could deploy the tools of media production, where they could perform themselves and their contradictions. Watkins had involved the cast in the preparation for the film, and then during the filming the cast became a community—some even continued the process after the filming was complete, forming a non-hierarchical association called Le Rebond pour la Commune.

By appropriating and hacking into mainstream media production formats, such as the talk show or the 'TV bridge', the Pro-test Lab produced its own 'TV channel'. Exercising creative disruptions, it oscillated between a library of references and a pedagogical space, including a pirate screening programme and a free school[6] in becoming. The thinking of scenarios and choreography of forces that could evoke the need for public space raised several questions: How is space occupied, inhabited and cohabitated? Who are the participants? How are the images of affect, feeling, and public interface created that could hack and infiltrate regimes of governmentality? How do we challenge the circulation of discourse beyond self-affirming echo chambers?

Whether notions, messages, and images are broadcasted through mass media, public debates, administrative offices, court houses, or art exhibitions, these spaces—this 'vast network of pipes' (Brecht 1932)[7]—are not apparatuses of distribution but of communication. Thus, the relationship that is both on-site and off-site produced a topology for the Pro-test Lab to address this two-way movement of media circulation. While the actions are performed locally by a variety of clandestine groups and individuals, the archive renders and collects images in a more curated and edited form and creates access to the Pro-test Lab from remote locations. Whether it is installed at the Gwangju, Moscow or Venice biennials, viewers can enter a space of commonality, while the protesters themselves participate in a dialectical tension between the lived reality of the actions they conceive and the imagined real of their performance. This tension between the exhibition as a site where protest and dissent are interrogated with their diverse variables of design production (including fashion, architecture, and other) and the political experience of the protest site triggered contradictions and even conflicts with some of the Pro-test Lab members who were solely focused on the real politics yet were dismissing the double agency of art, the dialectics of artistic form and intervention.

Fashion, for example, could be used as an undercover agent and as a tactic for intervention, conveying secret messages to a wider public. The unisex 'Collection for Work and Rebellion' received media attention and deceiving military camouflage patterns composed from rue plants (a typical pattern on female workers' headscarves in Soviet factories) and printed on linen was used to make a collection of overalls and jumpsuits to dress the army of protesters, using the roof of the cinema as a catwalk.[8] To cover this new fashion label, an internet kiosk (through which the collection was distributed) was created that surreptitiously leaked a statement on privatization, ironically, on privatized cinema. These ideas would have been impossible to present independently of the fashion label, as discussion around privatization was silenced.

Starting from the cinema as site of pro-test production, actions spread to other sites of the city. The 'Citizens of Vilnius', as they called themselves, would collectively draw a huge banner saying 'Sold Out'. Early mornings on Sundays, the group would carry the banner to the city and hang it on the bridges and monuments of Vilnius. Even though one could hardly imagine these sites to ever be privatized, the banners would be there as a form of prophecy or accelerated desire—and they would stay up until noticed by the police. Images taken by passers-by or by the police themselves documenting the crime were leaking into the public domain and inspired other kinds of alternative imagination.

Every pro-test action was challenged by questions of endurance and of public time. A swimming pool action called to form a human chain of swimming enthusiasts embracing the site of a swimming pool that had been demolished in half a day. The group that came was too small for an ambitious action, thus a choreographic technique performing a time lapse was deployed: a small circle of swimming enthusiasts ran around a camera that slowly moved around the lot. After five minutes of this choreography, all were wet, but from sweat rather than pool water.

Expanding towards the city, the Pro-test Lab charted an invisible map of the vanished cinemas of Vilnius riding the open top bus. A group of discussants led by film critics, historians and philosophers unearthed the sites of privatized, demolished, or converted cinema theatres, reactivating and reconstituting the personal and collective memories. The repetition of the tour would probe an emotional infrastructure that was uprooted and dismantled but could now be reconstituted.

In an attempt to experiment with imagination beyond the human and embracing the radical proposition that protest cannot be exclusively considered from the human perspective, the Pro-test Lab approached dogs (and their owners) to perform a sound event where official noise levels were measured on the cinema site. It was an assembly of parrhesiastes where dogs encouraged humans to speak truth to power.

Tinkering with Amateur Citizenship

Instead of the intended one-week intervention, the Pro-test Lab as space continued for more than six months. Artistic actions generated publicity for the citizens' movement, and various public debates kept the Pro-test Lab activists busy. The movement gained public recognition on a national scale: it was even granted the Civil Society Building Award. Maxima, the owner of the cinema, was annoyed and closed the cinema in 2005, with the plan to demolish it to develop a multi-functional residential-commercial centre designed in a pseudo-historical style. The Pro-test Lab space of production of artistic interventions transformed itself into a platform for legal activities (including the petition) and investigations in the sphere of the law. Conceived by a work-group of citizens, the petition 'For the Cinema Lietuva and the Cultural Policy Related to It' aimed at 'the preservation and development of the tradition of public cultural space established by the cinema Lietuva... thus further on this (tradition) to be modelled in respect to the public interest and under the principles of democracy'.[9] The petition was calling to formulate and to articulate the notion of public space in the legislation. This was a provocative attempt, as if the fixed and final definition of public space would even be possible.

Since the 1990s, when Lithuania regained independence, it was the third such citizen-initiated petition that was recognized and accepted by parliament. The government had to gather all of the ministries in a committee to discuss the definition of public space in two areas: territorial planning and the cultural domain. As the mayor's office was refusing to use the term 'public space' in official documents, the challenge was to transition from something that technically did not exist to inscribing it into legislation.

The petition triggered the launch of a Kafkaesque process. Four lawsuits started in 2007: two administrative and two civic cases. In the administrative cases, members of the citizens' movement were questioning Vilnius' approval of the developer's plans. The court ruled that the investors were attempting to make profit from sites that have public importance. On that basis, development of the cinema Lietuva was suspended. As a consequence, the developer took four members of the citizens' movement to civil court, accusing them of causing damage to their investment on the site, harassing the activists with financial responsibility. The claim started at 100,000 euros, and within several years it increased to seven million euros. Since then, almost every month the developer would harass the protesters, calling for a court session and threatening them with confiscation of their properties. While the civil court was contingent on the administrative one, the final statement was conceptually helpful in articulating artistic practice, as the court ruled out that artists were 'accountable for the amateur experiments in the sphere of the public interest'. The court explained that artists cannot represent the public interest as they are amateurs—only the attorney general could legally do it. But can amateurs have rights? The only thing you have, they said, is emotional attachment. Indeed, it was exactly what artists had!

Writer Shumon Basar describes the symbiotic model of two parts where the professional and amateur cohabitate:

> The Professional' part directs its capacity to become specialist and particularist *towards* 'The Amateur' part whose fundaments concern dwelling precariously on the margins of knowledge, competence and credibility... being outside the mainstream knowledge space the professional

'Amateur' consolidates their outsider context and believes it to be another species of 'inside' that happens to be 'outside' of the normative 'inside'. (Basar 2006, p. 34)

Inhabiting space of indeterminacy produced by the miscommunication between the professional and the amateur (often called 'the idiot'), draws in matters of positioning and affects that which one considers 'thinking with'.

The third civic case was initiated by a media monitoring group hired by the developer to find a slip in the language, looking for anything that could be used as a proof that the reputation of the developer was impinged upon. One of the members of the citizens' movement, an expert in cultural heritage, was called to the court for damaging the developer's reputation. The developer hired an expert from the Institute of the Lithuanian Language and presented the court with the recorded evidence that had to be transcribed. As punctuation marks are vital to disambiguate the meaning, they had to be indicated on the base of listening to the pauses in the recording. The transcript indicated marks in such a way that it could prove that damage had been done. The Pro-test Lab brought an expert from the A. J. Greimas Centre of Semiotics and Literary Theory to interpret the pauses and all other inaudible evidence in the speech, resulting in the conclusion that the transcript provided by the monitoring company was false. The latter was proven in court, and the civil case was won.

Through these legal proceedings, the Pro-test Lab became convinced that the fight for cinema Lietuva and public space is not against the developers or institutions, but instead situated within a larger apparatus of a 'heterogeneous ensemble consisting of discourses, institutions, architectural forms, regulatory decisions, laws, administrative measures...' (Foucault 1977). The reflection that there is no central separation between these parts, 'no clear locus of control', suggests the space of public practice as a grey zone, often beyond the law, that was yet to be defined, full of possibilities and opportunity. The making of language—like a seed bomb—that feeds into new legislation, producing it and maintaining it, practicing it and self-organizing it, is a way of actively contributing to and shaping the commons.

Indeed, one of the reasons the court decided that the members of the movement could not represent the public interest was a misinterpretation of the language in the Aarhus convention.[10]

This law establishes a number of rights of the public with regard to their environment and guarantees people's participation and decision-making in territorial planning. Lithuania ratified the convention, but instead of granting the access and right for the public to participate, an incorrect translation instead deprived them of this right. To win the court was to engage with the language, to tweak it, to tune it, and to question and clarify the actual meaning of it. The only chance for citizens to finally win in court was to correct the convention's translation. The exchange between the citizens and parliament took several years, until the corrections were approved. It was a breakthrough not only for the citizens movement For Lithuania Without Quotation Marks and the cinema Lietuva case, but also for the other, future stories of the city.

From artistic performances to rally support for the Lietuva cinema theatre to a broader political action demanding changes in legislation and gathering thousands of signatures, and then participating in lawsuits that eventually followed, we were on a public-private cusp. To paraphrase Jodi Dean (2017), the artistic project was the way to generate an opening for a movement, and we had to step through that opening in order to make it a political and even juridical project. The Pro-test Lab was initiated as artistic form, consequently the artistic aspect literally changed the political and cultural terrain so we ourselves could act politically.

What are the assemblages and forms of choreography from the artistic perspective and how do they enhance the circulation of the humanities from the dog's voice to the legal language and to the new social formation? The work of art is inherently programmed with the organizing principles that are scripted and coded in its materials and action of making. The script that is embedded in language with which the work is made and operates, performs the concepts and ideas through gestures creating micro-choreographies, associations, and images that engage public. The affect of image unfolds through the props, exhibits, devices, tools, and techniques. The work of art becomes organizational principle where aesthetics is contingent on a constant questioning of the conditions of its own making. Aesthetics as such should not be understood as a project of autonomy. Sven Lütticken (2017) argues that 'aesthetic is the constant questioning of art and ... of claims for art's autonomy, counteracting its reduction from persistent problem to ideological given'. He continues: 'If the aesthetic problematizes the relationship of autonomy and heterotonomy, then this means that an act or, beyond that, a praxis can be termed aesthetic insofar as it *lets autonomy appear sensibly as a problem* in a world where subjectivities and objectifications are profoundly entangled, where different agencies coexist and collide...'

The emotional infrastructure is a hybrid one. It is simultaneously an affect, a space and a network and, like a hyperobject, is too elusive to be defined as a whole. One can only capture its fragments, fixtures, and relations, which are performed and encountered between the tangible and intangible signifiers. Publics experiencing the images, projections, attachments, evocations, or sounds, remembering, envisioning and discussing relations contribute to the construction and constitution of this infrastructure. Thus 'making together', cohabiting the space and the continuous labour of care enables its existence.

1   Papadopoulos 2018 articulates the commoning as actively shared worlds between those who participate in their maintenance; as the space of co-action; as practices that are self-organized; as care for specific worlds; as entering the field of processual, more-than-human worlds.
2   Even though Wittgenstein does not give a precise definition of what 'Lebensform' is, he notes that 'form of life' is not an agreement in opinions expressed in language, defining what is false or true, but in a form of life.
3   Available from: https://en.wikipedia.org/wiki/Zolitūde_shopping_centre_roof_collapse (accessed 1 January 2018).
4   ASK (a self-organized Architecture Students Club from VGTU) Gediminas Technology University of Vilnius; Erdvės Mieste (Spaces in the city), a discussion platform organized by the activist Evelina Taunyte; Green Movement the first post-Soviet environmental NGO established in Lithuania; Hardcore.LT—a leading platform for alternative culture in Lithuania.
5   For Lithuania Without Quotation Marks (Už Lietuvą be kabučių)—was the first larger citizens' initiative founded at the Pro-test Lab, an initiator of series of petitions and public actions against the privatization of public space, erasure of cultural memory, and destruction of cultural heritage.
6   Pirate Cinema was developed with the help of Geert Lovink from the Institute of Network Cultures in Amsterdam.
7   Bertolt Brecht suggested a change of the radio as apparatus of distribution to one of communication to become 'the finest possible communication apparatus in public life, a vast network of pipes'.
8   'Collection for Work and Rebellion' was a collaboration with the Lithuanian fashion designer Sandra Straukaite.
9   Conceived under the auspices of For Lithuania Without Quotation Marks, the petition underlined 'that the public was excluded when the administration of the Vilnius Municipality has taken decisive resolutions in relation to the land use and privatization of the cinema Lietuva'. Addressing the President of the Republic of Lithuania, the National Government, Parliament, the Ministry of Culture, the Vilnius City Municipality and Vilnius County, it was signed by more than eight thousand people and accepted by the national government.
10 The UNECE Convention on Access to Information, Public Participation in Decision-making and Access to Justice in Environmental Matters, known as the Aarhus Convention, grants the public rights regarding access to information, public participation, and access to justice, in governmental decision-making processes on matters concerning the local, national and transboundary environment. It focuses on interactions between the public and public authorities. http://ec.europa.eu/environment/aarhus/ (accessed 13 January 2018).
11 Brian Massumi argues 'in affect we never alone... affects are basically ways of connecting, to others and to other situations, of affecting and being affected. They are our angle of participation in processes larger than ourselves.' (Massumi 2017, p. 110)

Literature

— Basar, Shumon. 2006. 'The Professional Amateur.' In *Did Someone Say Participate? An Atlas of Spatial Practice*. Edited by Markus Miessen and Shumon Basar. Cambridge and London: MIT Press.

— Berlant, Lauren. 2011. *Cruel Optimism*. Durham, NC: Duke University Press Books.

— Brecht, Bertolt. 1932. *The Radio as an Apparatus of Communication*. Trans. Stuart Hood. *Screen* 20, no. 3/4 (Winter 1979/80), pp. 24–28.

— Dean, Jodi. 2017. 'Reflexivity and Resistance in Communicative Capitalism: Jodi Dean with Gediminas Urbonas.' In *Public Space? Lost & Found*. Edited by Gedeminas Urbonas, Anna Lui, and Lucas Freeman, pp. 298–299. Cambridge, MA: MIT Press.

— Foucault, Michel. 1977 (1980). 'The Confession of the Flesh.' In *Power/Knowledge Selected Interviews and Other Writings, 1972–1977*. Edited by Colin Gordon, pp. 194–228. New York: Pantheon Books.

— Latour, Bruno. 1991. *We Have Never Been Modern*. Cambridge, MA: Harvard University Press.

— Lefebvre, Henri. 1992. *The Production of Space*. Oxford and Malden: Wiley-Blackwell.

— Lutticken, Sven. 2017. *Cultural Revolution: Aesthetic Practice after Autonomy*. Berlin: Sternberg Press.

— Massumi, Brian. 2015. *Power at the End of the Economy*. Durham, NC: Duke University Press.

— Mouffe, Chantal. 2007. 'Artistic Activism and Agonistic Politics.' In *Atlas of Transformation*, tranzit.cz.

— Papadopoulos, Dimitris. 2018. *Experimental Practice: Technoscience, Alterontologies, And More-Than-Social Movements*. Durham, NC: Duke University Press.

— Sassen, Saskia. 2014. *Expulsions: Brutality and Complexity in the Global Economy*. Cambridge, MA: Harvard/Belknap Press.

— Sennett, Richard. 2008. *The Craftsman*. New Haven, CT: Yale University Press.

— Srnicek, Nick, and Alex Williams. 2015. *Inventing the Future: Postcapitalism and a World Without Work*. London: Verso.

— Watkins, Peter. 2014. *The Media Crisis: Foreword*. Available from: http://pwatkins.mnsi.net/Intro_MedCr.htm (accessed: 1 February 2018).

— Williams, Raymond. 1977. *Marxism and Literature*. Oxford and New York: Oxford University Press.

— Zukin, Sharon. 2010. *Naked City: The Death and Life of Authentic Urban Places*. Oxford and New York: Oxford University Press.

The Commons as a Deliberative Counter-Ideology

Eric Kluitenberg

Long ago, Paul Virilio observed that we have entered the era of the real-time, or to use a slightly different but closely related term: the era of immediacy. This shift to the real-time, to immediacy, is primarily brought about by the introduction of evolving generations of real-time (communication) media on an increasingly global scale: global radio signals, global telephone networks, global satellite communications, and media relays, and of course the proliferation of internet access, high capacity broadband networks, and wireless data exchange standards (gprs, umts, lte—or 2g, 3g, 4g, and beyond). The exponential increase in the density of communication and data networks precipitates this shift towards immediacy. Increasingly, the entire world is available to us mediated in real-time by these overlapping technologies and networks, producing a pressing and unceasing flow of real-time impressions, a dictatorship of an eternal now.

This omnipresent and unceasing eternal now, produced by the real-time technologies, has important political consequences. When asked about the real-time coverage of the first Gulf War[1] in 1991, Paul Virilio lamented the dominance of the real-time. For him it was clear that the immediacy of the real-time media destroys the possibility of a democratic politics, which is based on time and reflection. A politics of the real-time, instead, can only be authoritarian: an event has taken place and is present from a distance in real-time and there has to be an immediate reaction. Without time to share—data, impressions, observations—and reflect, the decision-making process becomes inherently authoritarian. The only thing remaining to be shared are the feelings (in real-time—an ever-pressing flow overwhelming conscious deliberation). Virilio's prophetic final observation in the interview remains persistently acute:

> The immediacy, the omnipresence and the complete visibility are the elements of the politics of tomorrow. Momentarily nobody controls the 'real-time'. Nobody is asking the questions of the induced effects. All distances have been reduced to zero. This worldwide reduction will have fatal consequences for the individual, for our customs. It is time to develop a media-ecology.[2]

This conversation took place in 1991, before the massive adoption of the internet by an audience of billions on a near-global scale, before the introduction of the world wide web, before the rise of 'social media', before online live-streaming, before 'smart phones' and a plethora of other media forms. The media ecology that Virilio called for has since not been established. Yet, its urgency has only been increased by the evolving generations of real-time media and their potentially disastrous effects.

The question explored in this short essay is twofold: How can the dominance of immediacy/the real-time be transcended? And, what role can commons-based approaches perform to develop a media ecology that is able to transcend the dominance of the real-time, in search for a desperately needed deliberative space for (political) reflection?

All human activity is ultimately organized in space and time. In space, bodies assemble, lives are led, and institutions manifest themselves, whereas time is the measure of deployment of these activities. While the present analysis will not ignore or forget about the spatial, and in part draws on theories of space, the emphasis here lies on the temporal dimension of human activity. In practice the spatial and the temporal are of course tightly intertwined. However, the emphasis on the temporal is necessary to create an entry point from where the current reign of immediacy can be analyzed, critiqued and challenged. In this sense this exploration can be seen as a complement to previous investigations into new and emergent 'orders' of the spatial (Kluitenberg 2015, 2017). What can draw the spatial and temporal analysis of the 'reign of immediacy' together is a shift towards aesthetic and arts practices. These can help foster a deeper sensitivity for the forces of coercion that result from the real-time systems, and they might indicate ways out.

Such a project cannot position itself as a merely 'disinterested' analysis or reflection (if such a thing is possible at all). It presupposes an ideological gesture: It is here that the commons enter as a deliberate ideology of deliberation that opposes the rule of the real-time. To suggest and follow such a gesture is a political act, and therefore this text is not a disinterested academic exercise.

Virilio's discourse of the real-time has played a pivotal role in understanding the fatal strategies implicit within real-time systems. However, his discourse, if only because of the adoption of what is in essence an engineering term, remains somewhat stuck in technicity. To indicate that we are confronted here with an ideological and political construct, not a fatal consequence of a technological genre (assumed to be beyond ideology and politics), I want to replace the phrase 'the rule of real-time systems' by the 'reign of immediacy'.

There is a somewhat paradoxical 'double' at work within the reign of immediacy. At first sight it seems to consist of two rather unrelated, to some extent even seemingly antithetical elements: the immediacy of the real-time economy[3] and the immediacy of affective or affect-driven relationships. Whereas the first suggests the final completion of the Taylorist project of the complete rationalization of production, the second seems to refer to the unmediated impressions on the biological body (affect) that constitute its vitality and its potential for interaction, but importantly, in an entirely precognitive and semiotically unstructured field. What binds these two together is their temporal logic. Increasingly we should come to recognize both as much more tightly interlocked than they may appear to be at first sight. Together they point at larger problems implied by the reign of immediacy. It is useful, however, to first discuss them separately, and then to develop their specific relationship within the context of current networked cultures and economies.

The Immediacy of the Real-Time Economy

The core idea of the real-time economy is the aim, and indeed the ideology, to take all lag out of business processes. This objective/ ideology is pursued by deploying information processing technologies, automated sensory and tracking systems, and high-capacity data network technologies (wired and wireless) throughout all stages of the production and distribution process: from the collection of base materials right up to the delivery of finished products and/or services to the end user/consumer. The aim of the real-time economy is not only to make sure the production process never stalls, but more importantly, to ensure that the optimum volume of resources (materials, energy, human and knowledge capacities) is allocated to each successive stage of the production process, i.e. neither too much nor too little.

To achieve this ambitious aim a continuous feedback process needs to be set up where all parts operate interconnected in real-time. Any change in any part of the process or its environment affects the organization/allocation of all other parts of the process. The production system of the real-time economy is thus reconfiguring continuously in response to changing internal and external conditions. Such a system needs to take into account external influences such as weather conditions, climatic disruptions, accidents, social and political turmoil, or any other type of event that may affect the production process directly or indirectly. Furthermore, information on these changing conditions must be available in real-time to the controllers of the process, but equally to the end users, the consumers/customers to achieve optimal levels of resource allocation at any stage of production and distribution.

In the process of establishing such monitoring and feedback capacities a control system is constructed that aims to neutralize any risk posed to the lag-free operation of the system as a whole. To enable such a system that can counteract any potentially disruptive influence from the larger environment, a new type of networked control society is brought into existence that dwarves the control systems of the disciplinary societies so effectively critiqued by Foucault. The new system of real-time control operates with an unprecedented level of detail. The control mechanism becomes ubiquitous and infinitely malleable, literally programmed in the software and hardware of current networked socio-technical assemblages.[4] The strategic imperatives for economic and political actors (hyper efficiency and maximization of control) to engage in the construction of this control system are clear. The political implications of the implementation of the real-time logic across the economy and social relations are however not compatible with open or democratic forms of governance.

Another critical factor for real-time systems and, by extension, the real-time economy, is the speed of analysis required to optimize real-time processes. Inevitably, as the technological systems accelerate largely automated logistic processes, the human factor in the chain increasingly becomes a liability. Under these conditions the speed of technological processes will eventually pass the threshold of human perception and cognition: Processes will then operate at a speed beyond the human perceptual and cognitive apparatus because the minimum time for processing an event, even the most minute ones, is no longer available. At this point the system will either stall (wait for the human operator to 'catch up') or require the removal of the human element from the chain.

While such processes of automation have a long history in the replacement of human physical labour, they now venture further and further into the domain of cognitive labour. As these automated tasks are sped up even more by evolving lineages of cognitive technologies, the processes themselves start to operate in a new time form that was first suggested by Paul Virilio in his book *The Vision Machine* (1988). Virilio contrasts two forms of time here: The Extensive Time of human perception and cognition where past, present, and possible futures are still available for analysis and reflection, and the Intensive Time, which is a technologically constructed time form where processes operate at a speed inaccessible to human perception and cognition. Events manifest in ultra-short duration too short to be consciously registered. The (automated) processes that operate in the Intensive Time can only be imagined—human consciousness no longer has direct access to them.

The Immediacy of Affect(-driven) Relationships
In the essay '(Re-)Designing Affect Space' (2017), I have argued that the ever-increasing densities of contemporary hybrid spaces, where physical and electronically mediated processes overlap and form ever tighter networks of association, precipitate a shift towards the primacy of affect-driven relations. Particularly so in urban public spaces. This shift dramatically changes the functional characteristics of these spaces and the forms of association that manifest within them.

The strategic drive of the real-time logic for increasing connective capabilities trickles down into the quotidian streets and squares, into people's pockets and bags, pushing the density of potential linkage and forms of association across the 'affective threshold': Information overload, viral visual, auditory, and textual messages, continuous demands for responses, haptic feedback mechanisms (buzzing phones, thumbing wearables) induce the shift from deliberation to the play of affective registers. (Kluitenberg 2017, 'The Affective Threshold').

The affect level of intensity registered by the body before cognitive processing has taken place, shares the Intensive Time form with the accelerated technological processes, operating beyond the human perceptual and cognitive threshold. (Kluitenberg 2017, 'Intensive Temporality'). Following Canadian philosopher Brian Massumi I understand affect as a non-conscious intensity, impinging on and registered by the body, that precedes cognition (Massumi 2002). In what Massumi has so famously identified as the 'missing half second' between the beginning of an event and its completion in a consciously directed outward response, a space of potential is constituted, as yet undirected, a-signified, semantically and semiotically unstructured.

Laboratory experiments conducted by neurophysiologists and cognitive psychologists have repeatedly shown that the time required for cognitive processing of these 'impingements' on the body averages at 0.5 seconds but can take up to 0.8 seconds to complete. While bodily responses (including changes in galvanic skin resistance) can be observed between 0.2 and 0.3 seconds. Averaged at 0.25 seconds it suggests that affect (bodily registered intensity) moves at twice the speed of human cognition.

Similar then to the technological processes operating in the Intensive Time, the affect level of intensity operates in the Intensive Time of ultra-short duration, where human consciousness principally has no access. According to Massumi, will and consciousness are subtractive—limitative, derived functions that reduce complexity too rich to be functionally expressed (Massumi 2002, p. 29). Similar to the technological processes of the Intensive Time we can only imagine the operations of processes at the affect level of intensity. Consciousness is principally locked out from affect.

The political problem in this is that while we have no direct access to such affect-driven processes, they are nonetheless highly prone to manipulation. And indeed mechanisms of soft coercion are inbuilt in the software applications that drive the largest 'social' media platforms, particularly in mobile applications. These mechanisms are increasingly the object of public debate and critique as their operations lie largely outside of public and democratic scrutiny. It may even be arguable whether the corporate actors who unleash these connection machines on the public, are truly in control of their own inventions and their induced effects.

A Deliberately Deliberative Intervention

Despite the obvious economic rationale of the real-time technologies and the biological matter-of-factness of the affect level of intensity and its mechanisms of immediacy, and despite a disconcerting international trend at a renewed predominance of authoritarian forms of political governance, there is no reason to accept the reign of immediacy as a given. We can understand this new 'regime' in all its dimensions—technological, economic, biological, political—but analysis, critique, and understanding are only a first step. What is needed to transcend the logic of the real-time and the reign of immediacy is an ideological move. Such an ideological move implies first of all a deliberate insistence on the primacy of the political over the utilitarian logics of immediacy. The ideological gesture required here is to acknowledge the economic rationale of the real-time in order to then deny it and give precedence to a political process and enable it to unfold. The ideology here is to wilfully disrupt the real-time economics to allow any kind of political process to enter.

This shift towards the ideological becomes less problematic to conceive of when the 'matter-of-factness' of the real-time logic and the reign of immediacy is challenged, and the regime itself is understood as an ideology that serves specific utilitarian objectives defined by those actors who benefit most from this particular form of social organization. Once the reign of immediacy is accepted as an ideology (geared towards the optimization of value extraction of the productive process through the deployment of real-time technologies that operate principally outside of human scrutiny), it becomes possible to understand deliberate interventions that disrupt the real-time processes as a counter-ideology, aimed at opening up spaces for reflection and (collective) deliberation.

Such a counter-ideology can take many different forms. What is crucial in each of these is that the counter-ideology rests on a clear and conscious choice against the suggested inevitability of the reign of immediacy. One such form of counter-ideology, and one that I hold might be extremely productive, is that of the commons.

The Commons as a Rule-based System (or: Why the Free-Rider Problem Does Not Apply)

Following commons researchers Elinor Ostrom (Ostrom 1990, 2009, and Hess and Ostrom, 2007) and David Bollier (Bollier 2014 and Bollier and Helfrich 2012, 2015), I regard the commons first of all as pools of shared resources. Crucially these resources do not generally reside in the public domain,[5] where they would be subject to appropriation by anyone and not owned by anyone in particular. Instead the commons retain some form of ownership, usually by a community, which can have a more or less formalized structure.

The first important thing to notice here is that there are clear boundaries to a commons and that there is some form of 'ownership', collective, deferred (in the sense of some person or agency making a resource available), or otherwise (state guaranteed, municipality owned, and other arrangements). This 'ownership' implies an actor who assumes a responsibility for the resource to be made available, and often also for its maintenance, governance, or at least its subsistence. A further implication is that such commons pool resources, which can be open to appropriation by anyone, but they need not be, and in practice they often are not entirely open to such unrestricted appropriation.

This already hints at an eternal debate linked to the discussion of the commons: the deplorable 'tragedy of the commons', where overexploitation and terminal exhaustion seem to be the inevitable fate of any commons that is freely accessible, as outlined by biologist Garrett Hardin in his infamous paper 'The Tragedy of the Commons' of 1968. Repeated research by economists and commons scholars has found that Hardin's view is mistaken in four important respects: (1) Hardin discusses open access rather than managed commons, (2) he assumes little or no communication between those who share (in) the commons resource, (3) he assumes that people act only in their immediate self-interest (rather than taking some extent of joint interest into account), and (4) he only offers two possible solutions for over-exploitation: privatization or government intervention (Hess and Ostrom 2007, p. 11), thus excluding the possibility that local communities can (and in fact do so overwhelmingly) introduce forms of collective self-governance that produce effective and locally specific solutions for sustainable exploitation of shared resources (Ostrom 2009).

Important in this rebuttal of the Hardin critique of the commons by Hess and Ostrom is the implication that there is always a set of rules, explicit or implicit, governing the commons. These rules have been articulated by someone or some agency. They indicate how the commons are supposed to be used and maintained, what uses are acceptable and which not. They also suggest that there is an implicit mechanism how to deal with misuses of the commons, most notably over-exploitation. These rules can in some cases be guaranteed by the prevailing legal order in any given territory—for instance the rules governing the use of common land in the United Kingdom, protecting these lands through common law since the late 16th century. In other cases, the rules governing a specific commons resource can be defined and implemented by a community relying on a variety of formal and informal methods of conflict resolution.

From this it then also becomes evident that the commons are inherently a deliberative system, both in terms of their design (how a shared resource is set up) as well as in terms of how this resource is sustained. Within the framework of the real-time economy a commons cannot exist. Deliberation requires time and reflection, but time is exactly what is not provided by the real-time logic. Quite the contrary, the ideology of immediacy considers 'idle' time as 'lag', which needs to be eliminated at all cost. What remains in the ultra-short 'response-time' of immediacy is affect, a-signified, non-conscious, precognitive and semantically unstructured. The commons need to transcend this real-time operational logic and has no choice but to challenge the reign of immediacy as a dominant form of social organization. The commons do not constitute a denial or negation of the market or the state—its protagonists refer to it as 'a world beyond market and state' (Bollier and Helfrich 2012) suggesting complementarity rather than opposition. However, the commons do stand in opposition to the real-time logic of the reign of immediacy.

If we accept the reign of immediacy as an ideological construct, then we can regard the deliberative process of the commons, and by extension any other open and/or democratic process of political deliberation as a counter-ideology to the rule of immediacy. The commons require a deliberately deliberative intervention that disrupts the real-time logic of immediacy and allows the political to enter—regardless what the specific politics in question might be. Without this disruption a deliberative political process is strictly impossible.

This leads to the final question, which is how to conceive of such a possible disruption and what its relation to the 'commoning' process may be?

Leaving aside the most obvious candidates for such a disruption—sabotage, physical blockage, Distributed Denial Of Service attacks, viral contamination, insurgencies, terrorist attacks, strikes, occupations, squatting, or power cuts—which all carry their own undesirable side-effects, we may be well advised to devote some attention to the domain of aesthetics and the role that interventionist and participatory art practices might perform in opening up spaces for deliberation, commoning, and 'real'[6] democratic processes.

Temporal Aesthetics of the Real-Time

First the aesthetics of the real-time: in their purest form, following Paul Virilio's thesis of the Intensive Time, the real-time images disappear from sight, as they are too fast for human beings to register. They become invisible. The disappearance of these images does not suggest that they no longer exist, or that they no longer matter. Quite the contrary: they might be more important than ever; do not forget that Virilio developed his ideas in response to pertinent, emerging trends in contemporary warfare and the system of nuclear deterrence in particular. Furthermore, what has at times been described as Virilio's 'theory-fictions' have since by and large been confirmed by actualized trends in military conduct and acknowledged by military experts.

The absence of the image therefore 'communicates' something of crucial importance to us: the potential event. And Virilio would hold that its absence is ominous, a prefiguration of a fatal accident that is surely to come. The operations of these 'vision machines' (Virilio 1988) meanwhile remain invisible to us. They only enter the Extensive Time of human consciousness again when there is a (fatal) accident, at which moment it is too late for deliberation.

The public form of the aesthetics of the real-time is marked by a different aesthetics, one of constant mobility. These are the images of continuous streams of financial data, the impact images of 'smart bombs' transmitted in real-time from the cameras mounted in the nose of the explosive device right up to the moment of impact, satellite imagery in military briefings, recordings from the head-mounted displays of fighter-jet pilots, drone imagery of counter-terrorist strikes on a global scale—what theorist McKenzie Wark would call 'vectoral images' (Wark 2006).

Distinctive of the aesthetics of the real-time is its insistence on a technologized imagery that instils a sense of accuracy, efficiency, of mastery and control, an image that remains 'clean' even in the act of destruction. This public real-time image is the seductive image of power. It is inherently violent, both in its military and its civic incarnation.

An Aesthetics of the Unspectacular of the Commons

The aesthetics of the commons could hardly stand in greater contrast to this hyper-violent aesthetics of the real-time. The aesthetics of the commons is first of all unassuming. The image of the commons is a quotidian image—it is the image of the everyday, the expression of the common denominator. In its radical un-particularity the quotidian image of the commons is not a critique of spectacle in any form, it is not a counter-spectacle. Instead, precluding any form of sensationalism, it is the denial of spectacle altogether. It is in this sense that we must recognize the aesthetics of the commons as part of the aesthetics of the unspectacular.

The unspectacular image is hard to recognize at first. In its quotidian averageness it almost disappears from our awareness, but other than the invisible visuality of the Intensive Time, the unspectacular image always remains in plain sight. It is simply so self-evident, so mundane, that it becomes 'vernacular'. We see this image, in fact we see it all the time, but we do not immediately register and recognize it, at least not consciously at first. It takes an effort to unearth this image from beneath the crust of the vernacular to judge and appreciate it in its own right. The unspectacular image, and by extension the unspectacular act, does not communicate anything at first. It simply exists, it marks existence, it marks presence. It does not demand attention, least of all from the masses. The image and the act become 'phatic', which is to say that rather than communicating a message or transferring information, they serve social and emotional purposes. They are tiny acts that open up micro-conduits of possible communication, while they do not communicate anything specific in themselves, just this desire or need for communication itself.

The crucial shift required for their proper appreciation is to no longer ask what these unspectacular images and acts tell us, but to see them as quotidian markings of presence. The presence of these quotidian markings does not tell anything, it does not espouse a specific politics, but it does something quite crucial nonetheless; it suggest the possibility of a new politics, which can only emerge in some form of collective deliberation.

Artistic Practices for the Commons

Participatory art practices constitute one of the most pertinent domains in which to look for strategies that are able to intensify the aesthetics of the unspectacular, and strengthen commons-based practices to open up spaces for collective deliberation. I do not want to argue that participatory art is the exclusive domain for commons-based approaches to aesthetic and artistic practice. Neither am I blind to a variety of critical perspectives on participatory art and media. There is an extensive vital and important debate on these questions elsewhere (Elliott, Silverman, and Bowman 2016; Bianchini and Verhagen 2016). Instead, I want to conclude with a brief consideration of two types of participatory art practices that can contribute to heightening our sensitivity for the aesthetics of the unspectacular of the commons and opening up spaces of collective deliberation.

The first is exemplified by the communal staging of Bertolt Brecht's *Days of the Commune* by artist and filmmaker Zoe Beloff during Occupy Wall Street in Lower Manhattan in early 2012.[7] In Brecht's infamous play on the Paris Commune of 1871, citizens take control of their neighbourhoods into their own hands and exercise a form of direct democratic governance. By staging it in Manhattan's financial district in public space, the project created a form of communal disruption of the operational logic of this deeply contested strategic economic space. This common(s) play was thereby directly pitted against the flow of the real-time (financialized) economy, disrupting it at the pedestrian level.

A second type of artistic practice to consider is the extensive body of participatory art projects developed by Dutch artist Jeanne van Heeswijk, 'radicalizing the local'.[8] In these projects she becomes deeply embedded in a specific local context, to the extent that she becomes invisible as an artist in the final outcome of the process. What is created then is a collective outcome, where, rather than a mere facilitator, the role of the artist is that of a catalyst, an 'intensifier' of whatever local energies might be slumbering just below the surface of official reality. Tacit assumptions about the environment, both from within the community itself as well as perceptions of it by outside agencies are made explicit and are put up for scrutiny and debate, with the explicit aim of activating local communities to change their own environment according to their own most urgent needs. Quotidian realities, buried in vernacular, hidden by their unassuming aesthetics of the unspectacular, are transformed into active markers that generate agency to change the local environment. The 'radicalization' of the local lies in this deliberate intensification.

The other notable aspect here is duration: As opposed to the real-time logic of immediacy, these communal processes unfold over long stretches of time, incrementally and haphazardly, not always equally successful. There is no absolute measure of duration that determines the success or failure of a project, as each will require its own duration, while the outcome remains uncertain. Such participatory art practices resist the authoritarian temporality that the reign of immediacy and its real-time logic attempt to impose on all social processes. They cannot but create an extended space for deliberation, otherwise they are a priori destined to fail. Indeed, this space of deliberation can extend for years if not decades, thereby constituting a particularly relevant model to resist the authoritarian temporal regime of immediacy.

Notes

1 From an interview with Paul Virilio republished in *Kunstforum international* Bd 114, 'Imitation und Mimesis', July/August 1991, pp. 270–271.
2 Ibid.
3 A useful introduction can be found in the special report on the real-time economy, published January 31, 2002 by *The Economist*, www.economist.com/node/949071.
4 Particularly the data-monitoring capacities of social media applications, predominantly accessed via mobile devices, creating a continuous feedback mechanism tailored to each singular end user.
5 For a detailed discussion of the concept of the public domain and its distinctiveness from the commons see Boyle 2008.
6 'Democracia Real Ya!', manifesto archived at: www.tacticalmediafiles.net/articles/3492.
7 http://daysofthecommune.com.
8 www.jeanneworks.net/.

References

— Bianchini, Samuel, and Erik Verhagen, eds. 2016. Practicable: *From Participation to Interaction in Contemporary Art*. Cambridge, MA: MIT Press.
— Bollier, David. 2014. *Think Like a Commoner: A Short Introduction to the Life of the Commons*. http://thinklikeacommoner.com.
—, and Silke Helfrich, eds. 2012. *The Wealth of the Commons: A World Beyond Market & State*. Amherst, MA: Levellers Press.
—, eds. 2015. *Patterns of Commoning*. Amherst, MA, etc.: The Commons Strategies Group.
— Boyle, James. 2008. *The Public Domain: Enclosing the Commons of the Mind*. New Haven and London: Yale University Press.
— Elliott, David J., Marissa Silverman, and Wayne D. Bowman. 2016. *Artistic Citizenship: Artistry, Social Responsibility and Ethical Praxis*. New York: Oxford University Press.
— Hess, Charlotte, and Elinor Ostrom. 2007. *Understanding Knowledge as a Commons*. Cambridge, MA: MIT Press.
— Kluitenberg, Eric. 2015. 'Affect Space: Witnessing the "Movement(s) of the Squares".' *Open! Online Platform for Art, Culture, and the Public Domain* 10 March. www.onlineopen.org/affect-space
—. 2017. '(Re-)Designing Affect Space.' *Open! Online Platform for Art, Culture, and the Public Domain* 19 September. www.onlineopen.org/re-designing-affect-space
— Massumi, Brian. 2002. *Parables for the Virtual: Movement, Affect, Sensation*. Durham, NC: Duke University Press. In particular: 'The Autonomy of Affect', pp. 23–45.
— Ostrom, Elinor. 1990. *Governing the Commons: The Evolution of Institutions for Collective Action*. Cambridge, MA: Cambridge University Press.
—. 2009. Nobel Prize acceptance lecture delivered by Elinor Ostrom on December 8, 2009: Beyond Markets and States: Polycentric Governance of Complex Economic Systems. www.nobelprize.org/nobel_prizes/economic-sciences/laureates/2009/ostrom-lecture.html
— Virilio, Paul. 1988 (1994). *The Vision Machine*. Bloomington, IN: Indiana University Press/British Film Institute.
— Wark, McKenzie. 2006. 'To the Vector the Spoils.' *Cabinet*, Issue 23 Fruits (Fall). www.cabinetmagazine.org/issues/23/wark.php.

Contributors

Michel Bauwens (1958) is the founder and director of the P2P Foundation and works in collaboration with a global group of researchers in the exploration of peer production, governance, and property. Michel is also research director of CommonsTransition.org, a platform for policy development aimed towards a society of the commons and a founding member of the Commons Strategies Group, with Silke Helfrich and David Bollier, organizers of major global conferences on the commons and economics. He has (co-)published various books and reports in English, Dutch and French, such as (with Vasilis Kostakis), 'Network Society and Future Scenarios for a Collaborative Economy'. Michel currently lives in Chiang Mai, Thailand, and in 2017 has crafted a Commons Transition Plan for the city of Ghent in Belgium, after a similar project for Ecuador in 2014. For the next three years he is also adviser to SMart, a fast-growing European labour mutual for autonomous workers, seeking welfare reform (commonfare), while looking into biocapacity-based, contributive accounting mechanisms.

Giuliana Ciancio (1973) is a cultural manager and lecturer in cultural management. Author and curator of a variety of transnational cultural projects, she is presently the co-curator and project manager of Be SpectACTive!, a large-scale EU-funded project focused on active spectatorship in the performing arts. Since October 2016 she is researcher at the CCQO (Culture Commons Quest Office) at the Antwerp Research Institute for the Arts, University of Antwerp. Her research focuses on the relation between top-down policies and bottom-up movements in four EU cities in the context of performing arts and cultural policies. Giuliana lives and works between Belgium and Italy.

Santiago Cirugeda (1971) is the founder of Recetas Urbanas. He has developed subversive projects with distinct ambitions in urban realities, from the systematic occupation of public spaces in containers to the construction of prostheses in façades, patios, roofs, and lots. He negotiates legal and illegal zones, as a reminder of the pervasive control to which we are all subjected. He is now working together with local governments to implement new housing models for the socially disadvantaged. He has also written many articles and taken part in all manner of educational and cultural events, giving workshops, lectures, seminars, conferences in schools and universities, and has participated in solo and group exhibitions worldwide.

Maria Francesca De Tullio (1991) is PhD candidate at the University of Naples Federico II, with a thesis on Constitutional Law, concerning online and offline participatory democracy. She graduated from the same university and was an intern at both the Bank of Italy and the Court of Naples, division Copyright and Patents Law, Corporation Law and Public Contracts Law. Recent publications include: 'La *privacy* e i *big data* verso una dimensione costituzionale collettiva' (Privacy and Big Data towards a Collective Constitutional Dimension) (2016); 'Trade Agreements and Internet Governance: Data Flow and Politics in the TiSA's Governmental Rationality' (co-authored with G. Micciarelli), *forthcoming*. De Tullio lives and works in Naples (Italy).

Nico Dockx (Ekeren, 1974) works as a visual artist, curator, publisher, and researcher with a fundamental interest in archives. His interventions, publications, texts, soundscapes, images, installations, performances, and conversations—which are usually the result of collaborations with other artists—embody the relationship between perception and memory, which he interprets differently each time. His work has won him a DAAD grant in Berlin (2005), and various prizes such as De Grootste Belg (2005), Cera Award (2005), Ars Viva Sound (2007), and Young Belgian Art Prize-Emile & Stephy Langui Prize (2009, together with Helena Sidiropoulos). Since 1998, he has exhibited his work at home and abroad and has published more than forty artist's publications with his independent imprint Curious. He is co-founder of interdisciplinary projects such as Building Transmissions (2001–2013), Interfaculty (2007–2012), Extra Academy (2010–..., together with Steve van den Bosch), A Dog Republic (2012–...), and La Galerie Imaginaire (2015–..., together with Sébastien Delire). Together with Louwrien Wijers, Egon Hanfstingl and many other collaborators, he has been working on his PhD research project The New Conversations at the Royal Academy of Fine Arts Antwerp and he obtained his degree in 2014 at CAC

Brétigny upon invitation of curator Pierre Bal-Blanc. He also co-organized, with Pascal Gielen, the summer schools *Mobile Autonomy* (2015) and *Making Public Domain* (2017).

Futurefarmers (Amy Franceschini, 1970, San Francisco, USA; Lode Vranken, 1962, Ghent, BE; Marthe Van Dessel, 1975, Antwerp, BE) is an international constellation of artists, architects and farmers with a common interest in creating frameworks for exchange that catalyze moments of 'not knowing'. They have published *A Variation on Powers of Ten* (Berlin, Sternberg Press, 2012); *For Want of a Nail* (NoPlace Press, 2018). Their work has been exhibited at Yerba Buena Center for the Arts in San Francisco, 2018, at the Solomon R. Guggenheim, 2010, New York Museum of Modern Art 2008 and ZKM, Karlsruhe, 1999, and many other places.

Harry Gamboa Jr. (1951), is an artist, writer, and educator. He is a faculty member of the Photo/Media Program at California Institute of the Arts. He is the founder and director of Virtual Vérité (2005–2017), the international performance troupe. He is a co-founder of Asco (1972–1985), the Los Angeles-based performance group. His most recent performance/fotonovela project: *See What You Mean – Fotonovelas* (Getty Artists Program 2017, The J. Paul Getty Museum). His work has been exhibited nationally/internationally at Whitney Museum of American Art, New York; Centre d'Arts Plastiques Contemporain Bordeaux, France; De Appel, Amsterdam; Lentos Kunstmuseum Linz, Austria; Nottingham Contemporary, England; Smithsonian American Art Museum, Washington D.C.; Le Musée d'Art Contemporain, Marseille; Tate Liverpool; Musée de l'Élysée, Lausanne; Centre Pompidou, Paris; Museo del Palacio de Bellas Artes, Mexico City.

Lara Garcia Diaz is a PhD researcher at the Antwerp Research Institute for the Arts (Antwerp University) and the Culture Commons Quest Office (CCQO). Her research focuses on collectives and organizations in the artistic field that experiment with forms of collective self-organization and decentralized structures based on processes of 'commoning' to eliminate components that feed processes of precarization or self-exploitation. She has

contributed to books such
as *What's the Use* (2016) and
the journals *Cultural Policies:
Agendas of Impact* (2016) and
Precarious Work Precarious Life
(2017).

Pascal Gielen is Full Professor
of Sociology of Art and Politics
at the Antwerp Research
Institute for the Arts (Antwerp
University), where he leads
the Culture Commons Quest
Office (CCQO). Gielen is
Editor-in-Chief of the international book series Arts in
Society. In 2016, he became
laureate of the Odysseus grant
for excellent international scientific research of the Fund for
Scientific Research Flanders
in Belgium. His research
focuses on creative labour, the
institutional context of the arts
and cultural politics. Gielen
has published many books,
which have been translated
in English, Korean, Polish,
Portuguese, Russian, Spanish,
and Turkish.

Liam Gillick (Aylesbury,
1964) deploys multiple forms
to expose the new ideological
control systems that emerged
from the beginning of the
1990s. Recent exhibitions
include: 'Extended Soundtrack
for a Lost Production
Line: Ton und Film', Eva
Presenhuber, Zurich, April
2017. New Order and Liam
Gillick, Σ(No,12k,Lg,17Mif)
So it goes... Manchester
International Festival (2017);
'Were People This Dumb
Before TV? Grafische Arbeit
1990–2016', Esther Schipper,
Berlin (2017); 'The Lights are
No Brighter at the Centre',
CAC Vilnius (2017). Recent
publications include: *Industry
and Intelligence: Contemporary
Art Since 1820* (2016).

The **Karrabing Film Collective**
is a grassroots Indigenous-
based arts and film group
working in the Belyuen
Community in the Northern
Territory of Australia. They
use aesthetic practices as a
means of maintaining their
modes of belonging to each
other and their lands and
intervening in global images
of Indigeneity. Their films and
installations have appeared
in numerous film festivals,
biennales, and galleries, including the Berlinale, Melbourne
International Film Festival,
Contour Biennale; Jakarta
Biennale, Tate Modern,
London, Centre Pompidou,
Paris, documenta-Athens,
the Gertrude Contemporary,
Melbourne, Institute of
Modern Art, Brisbane, and the
IFA Berlin.

Eric Kluitenberg (1965) is a theorist and curator based in Amsterdam, currently teaching at the ArtScience Interfaculty in The Hague. His work deals with intersections of (media) technology, politics, art, and culture. He is the editor in chief of the Tactical Media Files online documentation resource. Important publications include: *(Re-)Designing Affect Space* (2017); *Legacies of Tactical Media* (2012); *Delusive Spaces* (2008); *Book of Imaginary Media* (2006). Recent projects include: *Tactical Media Connections* (2014–2017); *Technology/Affect/ Space* (2016–2017); *Economies of the Commons* (2008–2012)

Rudi Laermans (1957) is professor of Social Theory at the Faculty of Social Sciences at the University of Leuven. He has been a guest lecturer at many art schools and has published numerous essays and several books, in Belgium as well as internationally, on social and cultural theory, cultural policy, contemporary dance, and visual arts. He often deploys a sociological perspective, but just as often advances a wider view inspired by contemporary philosophy and political theory. Among his most recent books are *Moving Together. Theorizing and Making Contemporary Dance* (2015) and *Max Weber* (2017; in Dutch, together with Dick Houtman).

The land **foundation** was legally founded on 17 February, 2004 by Rirkrit Tiravanija, Kamin Lertchaiprasert, and Uthit Atimana. The *land* foundation unites two projects; 'the land' and 'Umong Silppadhamma'. 'The land' project was founded in 1998, aimed to open the space for public purposes for self-sustainable natural farming and as a laboratory for an experiment in the social aspects of living together regularly and naturally. 'Umong Silppadhamma' was founded in 2002 by a group of artists who wanted to open an artistic and cultural space for young cultural activists with the intention of supporting self-knowledge through Vipassana meditation, yoga, and art. The *land* foundation aims to promote and support artistic and cultural activities, natural farming, and self-knowledge by Vipassana techniques. As a not-for-profit foundation, 'the land' aims to create a nexus between socio-ecological sustainability and contemporary international arts practice, and to foster interaction between emerging and established artists. 'The land' has been extensively represented in Europe as a platform for experimental and conceptual integration of eastern and western ideals. 'The land' is widely recognized in its sustainability art, in exploring the potential for land use and lifestyle to be an artistic medium. 'The land' encourages artists participating in projects to produce art on a reclaimed rice farm near Chiang Mai, to attempt to explore the potential of the land itself using as much as possible renewable resources, power, and sustainable work practices as both subject and materials of their art.

Sonja Lavaert (1958) is a philosopher based at the Free University of Brussels VUB. She published on early modern political philosophy, radical contemporary philosophy, critical theory, philosophy of art, and translation studies. She is the author of *Het perspectief van de multitude. Agamben, Machiavelli, Negri, Spinoza, Virno* (2011), and co-editor of *The Dutch Legacy: Radical Thinkers of the 17th Century and the Enlightenment* (2017) and of *Aufklärungs-Kritik und Aufklärungs-Mythen. Horkheimer und Adorno in philosophiehistorischer Perspektive* (2018). Her research looks into the genealogy of political concepts in the interdisciplinary area of philosophy, literature, and translation from the present, the late 17th century and Renaissance.

Peter Linebaugh, historian and student of E.P. Thompson, is emeritus professor at the University of Toledo, Ohio (US). He is the author of the acclaimed social history of crime and the death penalty in eighteenth-century England, *The London Hanged* (London Verso, 1991), co-author (with Marcus Rediker) of *The Many-Headed Hydra: Sailors, Slaves, Commoners and the Hidden History of the Revolutionary Atlantic* (London: Verso, 2000), *The Magna Carta Manifesto: Liberties and Commons for All* (Oakland: University of California Press, 2008), and *Stop, Thief! The Commons, Enclosures and Resistance* (Spectre/Hodder & Stoughton: London, 2014). He was a member of the Midnight Notes Collective and writes for the online magazine *CounterPunch*.

Pat McCarthy (1987) is an artist working primarily in sculpture, zine-making, and short film. He apprenticed for the artists Tom Sachs and JJ Peet. He approaches sculpture as a public practice, most notably spending the past seven years raising pigeons atop his Brooklyn studio as a framework for exploring ritualized craft, living systems, architecture, and poetry in fugitive gesture. Recent solo exhibitions include: 'Pat's Pigeon Brunch' at Boo-Hooray, Montauk NY, 2017; 'Brick by Brick' at the Fonds Régional d'Art Contemporain Provence-Alpes-Cóte-d'Azur, Marseille, 2016; 'Shelters' at Ever Gold [Projects], San Francisco, 2015; and 'Slabs' at agnès b. galerie, New York, 2015. Recent projects include traveling on transatlantic sea freighter alongside his sculpture; converting a NYC gallery into a functionally pigeon supply shop; and working in the social housing districts north of Marseille to create a mobile gas-powered zine-making studio for teaching the craft to school children. McCarthy lives and works in Brooklyn, NY.

Antonio Negri (Padua, 1933) is a political philosopher, independent researcher, and writer. He taught State Theory at the University of Padua and in France he taught at the University of Paris VIII and the Collège international de philosophie. He is the author of more than thirty books, including the well-known *Empire* (2000), *Multitude* (2004), *Commonwealth* (2009) and *Assembly* (2017), all with Michael Hardt; *Insurgencies: Constituent Power and the Modern State* (1999), *The Savage Anomaly* (2000), *In Praise of the Common*, with Cesare Casarino (2008), and *Marx and Foucault* (2017).

Hanka Otte (1974) is a cultural policy researcher and holds a postdoc position at the University of Antwerp, where she partakes in the Cultural Commons Quest Office. Her research focuses on the question what conditions are needed for a balanced artistic biotope and what (policy) efforts can be made to generate creative commons. Her PhD research (2015) was about the relationship between arts participation and social cohesion. For a period of ten years she has been working as a policy advisor for arts and culture for regional and local governments. Otte works in Antwerp and lives in Groningen.

Elizabeth A. Povinelli is an anthropologist and filmmaker. She is Franz Boas Professor of Anthropology at Columbia University, New York and one of the founding members of the Karrabing Film Collective.

Povinelli's writing has focused on developing a critical theory of late liberalism that would support an anthropology of the otherwise. This potential theory has unfolded primarily from within a sustained relationship with Indigenous colleagues in north Australia and across five books, numerous essays, and four films with the Karrabing Film Collective.

Jörn Schafaff (1970) is an art historian researching, writing, and teaching about art of the 20th and 21st century, with a special interest in the inter-relations between art and other artistic disciplines. Recent publications include *Rirkrit Tiravanija: Set, Szenario, Situation: Werke 1987–2005* (2018), *Sowohl als auch dazwischen* (*As well as in between*) (co-edited with Benjamin Wihstutz) (2015), and *Timing – On the Temporal Dimension of Exhibiting* (co-edited with Beatrice von Bismarck, Rike Frank, Benjamin Meyer-Krahmer and Thomas Weski) (2014). Schafaff lives and works in Berlin.

Stavros Stavrides (1957), architect, is Professor at the School of Architecture, National Technical University of Athens, Greece, where he teaches graduate courses on housing design (including social housing), as well as a postgraduate course on the meaning of metropolitan experience. His research is currently focused on forms of emancipating spatial practices and urban commoning. His recent publications include Common Space: The City as Commons (2016, also forthcoming in Greek and Turkish), Towards the City of Thresholds (2010), Suspended Spaces of Alterity (2010) and From the City-as-Screen to the City-as-Stage (2002, National Book Award) as well as numerous articles on spatial theory and the role of arts in a commoning culture. He has lectured in European and Latin American Universities on urban struggles and practices of urban commoning. Stavrides lives and works in Athens. http://courses.arch.ntua.gr/stavrides.html.

Evi Swinnen (1977) is a practitioner of commons strategies operating within the field of the arts and activism. Swinnen studied at the Henry van de Velde institute, University of Ghent and University of Antwerp, and is the founder and coordinator of the city lab Timelab and president of the P2P Foundation. As a pacesetter experimenting with and implementing transition ideas, she operates between private and public domains and builds on community- and value-driven dynamics. She is a coach in conceptualization and role definition in open community groups and professional teams.

Dennis Tyfus (Antwerp, 1979) is known for an oeuvre that is difficult to categorize. It grows out of the things he finds important and results in a practice that is unceasing. Ranging from drawings, paintings, installations, and videos to magazines and books (published & distributed under his own label Ultra Eczema) to music, vinyl record productions, and radio shows on air at Radio Centraal, or concerts & performances organized in artist-run spaces such as Gunther, Stadslimiet, Pinkie Bowtie and soon 'De Nor'. Upcoming exhibitions include a solo exhibition at Middelheim Museum, Antwerp. Recent exhibitions at Pinkie Bowtie in Antwerp, Gelateria Sogni Di Ghiaccio in Bologna, NICC in Brussels.

Nomeda (Kaunes, 1958) **& Gediminas** (Vilnius, 1966) **Urbonas** are artists, educators, and co-founders of the Urbonas Studio, an interdisciplinary research practice that facilitates exchange among diverse nodes of knowledge production and artistic practice in pursuit of projects that transform civic spaces and collective imaginaries. The Urbonas' work has been exhibited at the São Paulo, Berlin, Moscow, Lyon, and Gwangju biennales, and Folkestone Triennial; at the Manifesta and documenta exhibitions; and in solo shows at the Venice Biennale and the MACBA in Barcelona, and many others. Urbonas co-edited *Public Space? Lost and Found* (2017) an examination of the complex interrelations between the creation and uses of public space and the roles that art plays therein. Urbonas are curating the upcoming 'Swamp Pavilion'—a future learning environment at the 16th Venice Architecture Biennale 2018. Gediminas Urbonas is Associate Professor at the MIT Program in Art, Culture and Technology (MIT). Nomeda Urbonas is PhD researcher at the Norwegian University for Science and Technology (NTNU) and MIT research affiliate.

Walter Van Andel (1981) is a PhD researcher at the Culture Commons Quest Office of the University of Antwerp and holds a Master degree in Economics at the Erasmus University Rotterdam, and a MBA from Western Illinois University. His research focuses on sustainable business models, innovation, and organizational tensions at creative organizations. Van Andel lives and works in Antwerp, Belgium.

Visible is a contemporary art research project devoted to producing and sustaining socially engaged art practices in a global context, co-directed by Matteo Lucchetti and Judith Wielander. Operating since 2010, it has taken a global and interdisciplinary approach to researching the physical and theoretical spaces in which these practices affect society. In 2011, Visible initiated the biennial Visible Award, the first European award for socially engaged artistic practices, in collaboration with leading museums and other art institutions (such as Van Abbemuseum, Eindhoven; Tate Liverpool; and Queens Museum, New York), establishing discursive platforms in the form of public juries as temporary parliaments. Visible is initiated by Cittadellarte–Pistoletto Foundation in partnership with Fondazione Zegna.

Louis Volont is a PhD researcher at the University of Antwerp. Working within cultural and urban sociology, he looks at how urban commons are produced through artistic practice. Previously, as a research fellow at SMart Belgium, he has worked and published on topics such as career paths of artists/creative professionals, sustainable creativity, and 'third places'.

Antennae-
Arts in Society
Book Series

Index

Colophon

Colophon

Commonism
A New Aesthetics of the Real

Editors
Nico Dockx & Pascal Gielen

Contributors
Michel Bauwens
Giuliana Ciancio
Santiago Cirugeda
Maria Francesca De Tullio
Nico Dockx
Futurefarmers
Harry Gamboa Jr.
Lara Garcia Diaz
Pascal Gielen
Liam Gillick
Eric Kluitenberg
Rudi Laermans
the *land* foundation
Sonja Lavaert
Peter Linebaugh
Matteo Lucchetti
Pat McCarthy
Antonio Negri
Hanka Otte
Elizabeth A. Povinelli
Jörn Schafaff
Stavros Stavrides
Evi Swinnen
Dennis Tyfus
Nomeda & Gediminas Urbonas
Walter van Andel
Louis Volont
Judith Wielander

Antennae-Arts *in* Society Series n°25
by Valiz, Amsterdam

Translation
Leo Reijnen

Copy Editing
Leo Reijnen, Els Brinkman

Proofreading
Els Brinkman

Index
Elke Stevens

Design
Metahaven

Paper Inside
Munken Print 100 gr 1.5

Paper Cover
Bioset 240 gr

Printing and Binding
Bariet Ten Brink, Meppel

Publisher
Valiz, Amsterdam, 2018
www.valiz.nl

ISBN 978-94-92095-47-3

This publication is based on a research project by Nico Dockx and Pascal Gielen which also resulted in the summer school event 'Making Public Domain' (11–15.09.2017) organized by the Royal Academy of Fine Arts Antwerp in close collaboration with Middelheim Museum Antwerp, Antwerp Research Institute for the Arts (ARIA), Culture Commons Quest Office—University Antwerp, Extra City kunsthal Antwerp, Flanders Arts Institute, Kunstcel Vlaamse Bouwmeester—Department of Culture, Youth, and Media.

This publication was made possible through the generous support of

Royal Academy
of Fine Arts Antwerp
AP | ARTESIS PLANTIJN HOGESCHOOL ANTWERPEN

ap-arts.be

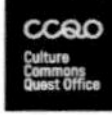

ARIA
Antwerp Research Institute for the Arts
University of Antwerp

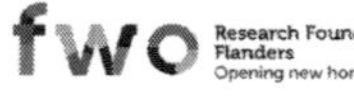

CCQO
Culture Commons Quest Office

ccqo.eu

fwo Research Foundation Flanders
Opening new horizons

fwo.be

The authors and the publisher have made every effort to secure permission to reproduce the listed material, illustrations and photographs. We apologise for any inadvert errors or omissions. Parties who nevertheless believe they can claim specific legal rights are invited to contact the publisher.

Distribution:
USA/Canada/Latin America: D.A.P., www.artbook.com
GB/IE: Anagram Books, www.anagrambooks.com
NL/BE/LU: Centraal Boekhuis, www.cb.nl
Europe/Asia: Idea Books, www.ideabooks.nl
Australia: Perimeter Books, www.perimeterdistribution.com

ISBN 978-94-92095-47-3

Printed and bound in the Netherlands

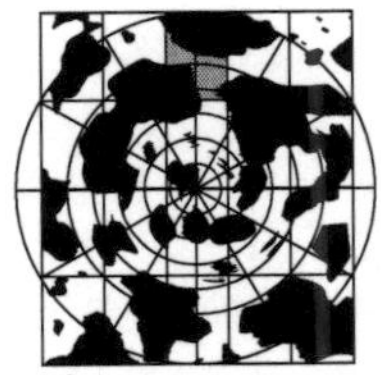

Antennae

Antennae Series

Antennae N° 1
The Fall of the Studio
Artists at Work
edited by Wouter Davidts & Kim Paice
Amsterdam: Valiz, 2009 (2nd ed.: 2010),
ISBN 978-90-78088-29-5

Antennae N° 2
Take Place
*Photography and Place
from Multiple Perspectives*
edited by Helen Westgeest
Amsterdam: Valiz, 2009,
ISBN 978-90-78088-35-6

Antennae N° 3
**The Murmuring of the
Artistic Multitude**
Global Art, Memory and Post-Fordism
Pascal Gielen (author)
Arts *in* Society
Amsterdam: Valiz, 2009 (2nd ed.: 2011),
ISBN 978-90-78088-34-9

Antennae N° 4
Locating the Producers
Durational Approaches to Public Art
edited by Paul O'Neill & Claire Doherty
Amsterdam: Valiz, 2011, ISBN 978-90-78088-51-6

Antennae N° 5
Community Art
The Politics of Trespassing
edited by Paul De Bruyne & Pascal Gielen
Arts *in* Society
Amsterdam: Valiz, 2011 (2nd ed.: 2013),
ISBN 978-90-78088-50-9

Antennae N° 6
See it Again, Say it Again
The Artist as Researcher
edited by Janneke Wesseling
Amsterdam: Valiz, 2011, ISBN 978-90-78088-53-0

Antennae N° 7
**Teaching Art in the
Neoliberal Realm**
Realism versus Cynicism
edited by Pascal Gielen & Paul De Bruyne
Arts *in* Society
Amsterdam: Valiz, 2012 (2nd ed.: 2013),
ISBN 978-90-78088-57-8

Antennae N° 8
Institutional Attitudes
Instituting Art in a Flat World
edited by Pascal Gielen
Arts *in* Society
Amsterdam: Valiz, 2013, ISBN 978-90-78088-68-4

Antennae N° 9
Dread
The Dizziness of Freedom
edited by Juha van 't Zelfde
Amsterdam: Valiz, 2013, ISBN 978-90-78088-81-3

Antennae N° 10
Participation Is Risky
Approaches to Joint Creative Processes
edited by Liesbeth Huybrechts
Amsterdam: Valiz, 2014, ISBN 978-90-78088-77-6

Antennae N° 11
The Ethics of Art
Ecological Turns in the Performing Arts
edited by Guy Cools & Pascal Gielen
Arts *in* Society
Amsterdam: Valiz, 2014, ISBN 978-90-78088-87-5

Antennae N° 12
Alternative Mainstream
Making Choices in Pop Music
Gert Keunen (author)
Arts *in* Society
Amsterdam: Valiz, 2014,
ISBN 978-90-78088-95-0

Antennae N° 13
The Murmuring of the Artistic
Global Art, Politics and Post-Fordism
Pascal Gielen (author)
Completely revised and enlarged
edition of Antennae N° 3
Arts *in* Society
Amsterdam: Valiz, 2015,
ISBN 978-94-92095-04-6

Antennae N° 14
Aesthetic Justice
Intersecting Artistic and Moral Perspectives
edited by Pascal Gielen &
Niels Van Tomme
Arts *in* Society
Amsterdam: Valiz, 2015,
ISBN 978-90-78088-86-8

Antennae N° 15
No Culture, No Europe
On the Foundation of Politics
edited by Pascal Gielen
Arts *in* Society
Amsterdam: Valiz, 2015,
ISBN 978-94-92095-03-9

Antennae N° 16
Arts Education Beyond Art
Teaching Art in Times of Change
edited by Barend van Heusden &
Pascal Gielen
Arts *in* Society
Amsterdam: Valiz, 2015,
ISBN 978-90-78088-85-1

Antennae N° 17
Mobile Autonomy
Exercises in Artists' Self-Organization
edited by Nico Dockx & Pascal
Gielen
Arts *in* Society
Amsterdam: Valiz, 2015,
ISBN 978-94-92095-10-7

Antennae N° 18
Moving Together
*Theorizing and Making
Contemporary Dance*
Rudi Laermans (author)
Arts *in* Society
Amsterdam: Valiz, 2015,
ISBN 978-90-78088-52-3

Antennae N° 19
Spaces for Criticism
Shifts in Contemporary Art Discourses
edited by Thijs Lijster, Suzana
Milevska, Pascal Gielen,
Ruth Sonderegger
Arts *in* Society
Amsterdam: Valiz, 2015,
ISBN 978-90-78088-75-2

Antennae N° 20
Interrupting the City
Artistic Constitutions of the Public Sphere
edited by Sander Bax, Pascal Gielen
& Bram Ieven
Arts *in* Society
Amsterdam: Valiz, 2015,
ISBN 978-94-92095-02-2

Antennae N° 21
In-between Dance Cultures
*On the Migratory Artistic Identity of
Sidi Larbi Cherkaoui and Akram Khan*
Guy Cools (author)
Arts *in* Society
Amsterdam: Valiz, 2015,
ISBN 978-94-92095-11-4

Antennae N° 22
Imaginative Bodies
Dialogues in Performance Practices
Guy Cools (author)
Arts *in* Society
Amsterdam: Valiz, 2016,
ISBN 978-94-92095-20-6

Antennae N° 23
The Practice of Dramaturgy
Working on Actions in Performance
edited by Konstantina Georgelou,
Efrosini Protopapa,
Danae Theodoridou
Arts *in* Society
Amsterdam: Valiz, 2017,
ISBN: 978-94-92095-18-3

Antennae N° 24
The Art of Civil Action
Political Space and Cultural Dissent
edited by Philip Dietachmaier, Pascal
Gielen
Arts *in* Society
Amsterdam: Valiz, 2017,
ISBN: 978-94-92095-39-8

Colophon